MAJOR & M
DEFINITIVE BATTLEFIELD GUIDE TO THE

SOMME

TONIE & VALMAI HOLT

"The central feature of this book – the golden thread that
runs through it – is the focus that the Holts give to the stories
of individuals."

Sir Martin Gilbert

Pen & Sword
MILITARY

At the going down of the sun...

MAJOR & MRS HOLT'S
DEFINITIVE BATTLEFIELD GUIDE TO THE

SOMME

TONIE & VALMAI HOLT

WITH FOREWORD BY
FRANÇOIS BERGEZ, SOMME TOURISM DIRECTOR

Pen & Sword
MILITARY

By the same authors:

Picture Postcards of the Golden Age: A Collector's Guide
Till the Boys Come Home: WW1 Through its Picture Postcards. 2014
The Best of Fragments from France by Capt Bruce Bairnsfather
The Biography of Capt Bruce Bairnsfather: In Search of the Better 'Ole. 2014
Picture Postcard Artists: Landscapes, Animals and Characters
Stanley Gibbons Postcard Catalogue: 1980, 1981, 1982, 1984, 1985, 1987
Germany Awake! The Rise of National Socialism illustrated by Contemporary Postcards
I'll be Seeing You: the Picture Postcards of World War II
Holts' Battlefield Guidebooks: Normandy-Overlord/Market-Garden/Somme/Ypres
Visitor's Guide to the Normandy Landing Beaches
Battlefields of the First World War: A Traveller's Guide
Major & Mrs Holt's Concise Guide to the Ypres Salient
Major & Mrs Holt's Battle Maps: Normandy/Somme/Ypres/Gallipoli/MARKET-GARDEN
Major & Mrs Holt's Battlefield Guide to the Ypres Salient + Battle Map
Major & Mrs Holt's Battlefield Guide to Gallipoli + Battle Map
Major & Mrs Holt's Battlefield Guide to MARKET-GARDEN (Arnhem) + Battle Map
Major & Mrs Holt's Definitive Battlefield Guide to the Somme + Battle Map
Major & Mrs Holt's Definitive Battlefield Guide to the Normandy D-Day Landing Beaches
Violets From Oversea: Reprinted 1999 as Poets of the Great War
My Boy Jack: The Search for Kipling's Only Son. Revised limpback 2014
Major & Mrs Holt's Guide to the Western Front – North
Major & Mrs Holt's Guide to the Western Front – South
Major & Mrs Holt's Pocket Battlefield Guide to Ypres & Passchendaele
Major & Mrs Holt's Pocket Battlefield Guide to the Somme 1916/1918
Major & Mrs Holt's Pocket Battlefield Guide to D-Day. Normandy Landing Beaches

This book first published in 1996, Second Edition 1998, Reprinted 1999,
Third Edition 2000. Fourth Revised Edition 2003. Fifth Revised Edition 2007. Sixth Revised,
expanded Edition 2008. This Revised, much-expanded Edition 2016 by

Pen & Sword MILITARY

an imprint of
Pen & Sword Books Limited
47 Church Street, Barnsley, South Yorkshire, S70 2AS

ISBN 978 1 47386 6 720

Text copyright © Tonie and Valmai Holt, 2016
Except where otherwise credited, all illustrations remain the copyright of
Tonie and Valmai Holt.

Typeset in Palatino by Pen & Sword Books Limited
Printed by Imago, in China
For a complete list of Pen & Sword titles please contact

CONTENTS

LIST OF MAPS

Foreword

by François Bergez, Director of Somme Tourism

The Somme was deeply marked by the battles of the First World War: the August invasion and the race to the sea in September 1914, the battle of the Somme from July to November 1916, the German spring offensive in March 1918 and the consequent Allied counter-offensives in Picardy from August to September 1918. In 1916, in contrast to the Franco-German dual at Verdun, the Somme became a world arena: a meeting point for more than 20 nationalities and where three million soldiers fought on the 45-kilometre front line.

Nowadays the Somme is amazingly quiet and peaceful, hard to imagine the human tragedy which took place 100 years ago. Every year some 300,000 visitors from the United Kingdom , France, Canada, Australia, South Africa and many other countries come to the battlefields for remembrance and to pay respect to the men who fought and gave their lives during the Great War but also to have a better understanding of this terrible page of our history. By walking in the footsteps of these men and visiting the numerous cemeteries, memorials and traces of the battlefields, visitors can nearly imagine the scale of the disaster.

You now have in hand the most helpful, practical and detailed battlefield guide to make the best of your visit in the Somme. This battlefield guide, written and regularly updated by Major and Mrs. Holt, will be needed to prepare and organise your journey whether you are a first time visitor or a frequent visitor to the area. You will be able to choose between three approach routes and six recommended itineraries depending on your interest and time availability. Because Major and Mrs Holt have been touring, travelling and exploring the Somme for well over 35 years they are able to talk like locals (or even better!) and share with us through this guidebook their own moving experience of the battlefields. Knowing each country road, trail, cemetery, memorial and site perfectly, they have chosen not to write another academic history book on the

Somme but have developed their own and efficient way to help you visit and experience the battlefields by revealing, not only the battles and action, but also by giving human, historical and literary information which depict an essential dimension of the Great War.

When reading and using this great guide book you will come across personal, family or regimental stories, it will take you from the largest and most well-known memorials to the smallest and well-hidden ones in the country side. Major and Mrs Holt have kept the secret of making it very informative and yet pleasant reading.

Interest in remembrance and history will undoubtedly increase during the centenary. Media

François Bergez, Director
Somme Tourism

coverage, new books, movies, conferences and ceremonies will definitely help to bring a better understanding of each aspect of the Great War, including its causes and consequences. However, information and knowledge of this world war would be insufficient if not completed by a trip to see landscapes, remains of the battlefields, British and Commonwealth, French and German cemeteries, memorials and museums.

When I was a child, I had always wondered when seeing French WWI veterans at the Monument aux Morts on November 11th, what they had lived through, seen and endured during the Great War. I was just a kid and never had the mind to question them and still regret it.

Years later, I moved to the Somme region and one of my British friends gave me a tour on the battlefields. We visited many WWI sites and cemeteries such as Serre N°1 and N°2 Cemeteries, the small Railway Hollow cemetery located further up the hill and close to the Accrington Pals memorial. As I was looking at the graves, I stopped a bit longer in front of the grave stone of Private A. Goodlad from the York and Lancaster Regiment. The engraved message read "The French are a grand nation worth fighting for". He was 23 and died on July 1st 1916. I felt very moved by his message and since then my desire that the sacrifice of these men never be forgotten has grown stronger each day.

No veterans of the Great War will be with us to share the Centenary, so we must make this period an opportunity to pass on the message of remembrance to the younger generations who will be the link so that this worldwide tragedy will never be forgotten.

For many years Major and Mrs. Holt have highly contributed to promoting and showing the true value of the battlefields of the Somme through their guidebook but also as tour operators on the battlefields. They have always been dedicated to keeping *l'esprit des lieux* and the flame of remembrance alight. Their aim is to provide accurate information about the battles and battlefield sites to help visitors understand what occurred in the Somme 100 years ago. I should say that I have learned and understood so much about the Somme thanks to this battlefield guide which is not only about military facts or battles but also depicts the courage, the fear, the hardships, the brotherly love as well as the art and literature that the war inspired in men in both sides who took part in the war

With this new and updated edition of their guide, I would like, as a friend, to take this opportunity to thank Tonie and Valmai Holt for the incredible quality of their work which mixes a unique approach with an original outlook on the many different facets of the Great War in the Somme.

They have truly provided a wealth of information for the thousands of visitors who will come to the Somme and use their guidebook to follow the marks left by the Great War and experience the emotions of the battlefields. Finally, I would also like to thank them for their perfect knowledge and understanding of our region, its history, its memories and the local people all of which have enabled them to recount this moment in history as a part of our common heritage.

François Bergez
Director of Somme Tourism

ABOUT THE AUTHORS

Respected military authors Tonie and Valmai Holt are generally acknowledged as the founders of the modern battlefield tour and have established a sound reputation for the depth of their research. Their *Major & Mrs Holt's Battlefield Guides* is without doubt the leading series describing the most visited battlefields of the First and Second World Wars.

They have a unique combination of male and female viewpoints and can draw upon approaching 40 years of military and travel knowledge and experience gained in personally conducting thousands of people around the areas they have written about.

Valmai Holt took a BA(Hons) in French and Spanish and taught history. Tonie Holt took a BSc(Eng) and is a graduate of the Royal Military Academy Sandhurst and of the Army Staff College at Camberley. They are both Fellows of the Royal Society of Arts and Science and have made frequent appearances on the lecture circuit, on radio and television.

In January 2014 they received the *Médaille Centenaire* of the *Conseil Général de la Somme* for their work in promoting knowledge of the Great War and tourism in the *Département*.

The authors receiving their WW1 Centenary Medals from the President of the Somme Conseil Général.

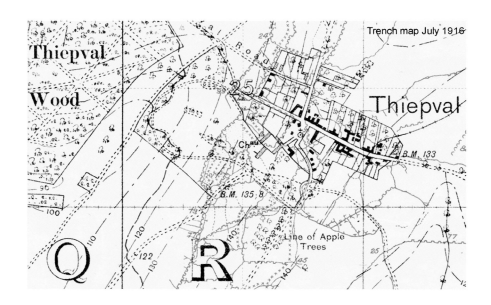

INTRODUCTION

*'The general conduct of the war has been entrusted to incompetent men —
there the trouble lies.'*
War Diary of King Albert of the Belgians, 5 December 1916

Few campaigns of recent history provoke such emotive opinions as those frequently expressed in a discussion of *'The Battle of the Somme'* in 1916. There are two main camps: those who believe the British Commander-in-Chief, Sir Douglas Haig, to have been an incompetent butcher who covered up his mistakes (e.g. Denis Winter in his 1991 book, *Haig's Command - A Reassessment*) and those who, for whatever reason, profess admiration for his moral and leadership qualities (e.g. Duff Cooper's *'Haig'*).

Apart from the growing awareness among the general public of the human cost of the two World Wars, the inclusion of these wars in the history syllabuses of British schools, and perhaps most significantly, the Centenary of the Somme 1916 and 1918 battles, there is the visible evidence of war memorials and cemeteries scattered beside the trans-Europe holiday routes to serve as a lasting reminder and to prompt enquiring minds.

Over the past approaching 40 years we have travelled the battlefield of the Somme alone or in the company of hundreds of such enquiring minds, aged from 9 to over 100, each striving to come to terms with the grim statistics of World War One, and in particular with the casualties suffered by the British on 1 July 1916, the first day of the battle, one of the worst single days in the history of the British Army.

Some modern historians, like Professor Peter Simkins, formerly of the Imperial War Museum, the late John Terraine and Lt Colonel Phillip Robinson of the Durand Group (qv), in their careful analysis of the casualty figures for the whole war, are anxious to dispel what they consider to be the emotional myth of a whole generation of Britain's youth being wiped out. But there is no disputing the horror of that single, black day, and its effects in the home towns and villages of the Pals Battalions of the Midlands, the West and the North. Almost 60,000 men were killed, wounded or missing. In a single column, spaced at arm's length, they would stretch 30 miles. Their nominal role would take two weeks to read.

Many of the professional soldiers of the British Expeditionary Force, the 'Contemptible Little Army' of Mons, le Cateau, Neuve Chapelle and Loos were already dead or had 'Blighty ones'. It was, therefore, on the whole, a brave new army that climbed over the top on that hot summer's morning. It was a citizen army, Kitchener's Army, volunteers all, most new to battle, most young and most to become casualties. One-third of the latter still lie under the battlefield.

In March 1918 the German Army launched 'Operation Michael', a final, all-out attempt to win the war. It nearly succeeded. German forces were stopped just 10 miles from Amiens by British and Australian tenacity and the blame for the near disaster was laid upon General Gough and his Fifth Army. Foch became Supreme Commander, tank fought tank for the first time, the fresh and enthusiastic Americans joined the battle and a final Allied drive to Victory began.

In addition to the host of wartime memoirs, some of which appeared as factual accounts, others disguised as novels, the tradition of guidebooks about the battlefields of the Somme is a long one. As early as 1917 John Masefield published *The Old Front Line*. From 1919 the Michelin series of *Guides to the Battlefields* were published - with two volumes on *'The Somme'* and a separate volume on *'Amiens'*. In 1928 H. A. Taylor, Capt (retired) Royal Fusiliers and General Staff, wrote *Good-bye to the Battlefields* and in 1935 Lt Col Graham Seton Hutchison DSO, MC, wrote *Pilgrimage*. Seton-Hutchison, who at the age of 27 commanded a Machine Gun Corps battalion on the Western Front, had

also served in Egypt, the Sudan, South Africa and Rhodesia. A friend of Maj Gen Sir Ernest Swinton, originator of the tank, he became a member of the Army Society for Historical Research and fellow World War I soldier, Field Marshal Sir Bernard Montgomery, wrote a glowingly complimentary foreword to Seton-Hutchison's 1945 book *The British Army*.

Since the end of World War II there has been a resurgence of such books. This particular guidebook conducts the reader to those memorials and sites of both the 1916 and 1918 battles, and the actions of 1917, that have been most requested over the years by our travellers.

International Circle of Death, Basilique behind, Notre-Dame de Lorette

The brief commentaries at each stop are designed to summarise events and to orientate the reader so that he or she knows broadly who was where, and what happened. A continuous description of the various parts of the Somme battles are given in the Historical Summaries below.

It is also our aim to prompt more questions than we answer: it must not be sufficient merely to tour the Somme battlefield and to say, 'So this is where it happened'. We must ask, 'Why?', and then each seek an answer.

Certainly the number of new Museums, Information Centres, accommodation and refreshment facilities that have sprung up on the Somme would indicate that the flame of interest and remembrance is burning even more brightly than ever. This interest has been accelerated by the Centenary of the 1916 and 1918 Somme Battles, in preparation for which a proliferation of new Interpretation Centres, road-widening, parking projects and memorials has sprung up. They include the important Information Centre at Villers Bretonneux, the new Museum at Bullecourt, the new Interpretation Centre/Museum at Thiepval, the redesigning of the *Historial* at Péronne, the impressive Circle of Death and the WW1 Interpretation Centre at Notre-Dame de Lorette.

New projects are still being planned and executed, others are modified by the constraints of budget or changes in policy/personnel as a consequence of national, departmental and local elections. It is therefore advisable to check these informative websites before embarking on a tour: www.somme-tourisme.fr www.somme-battlefields.com/about-centenary www.ww1westernfront.gov.au www.anzac-france.com www.cwgc.org

Also therefore consult the websites of Museums & Interpretative Centres in the Itineraries for recent changes.

Incorporating these new developments plus covering some aspects of the adjoining 1917 Battles for Arras and Bullecourt, The Kaiser's Offensive of March 18918, the 1918 American, Canadian and French sectors and adding some suggested walking tours, has vastly expanded the scope and range of this book to make it a veritable encyclopaedia of the Somme and surrounding WW1 Battles. There are well over 100,000 individual stories on one side alone, of valour, of loyalty and of endurance that could be told to bring alive this historical battlefield. By highlighting some of them we hope to perpetuate the battlefield and the memory of the men who fought, and often died, here.

The Commonwealth War Graves Commission's Charter states that the British and Commonwealth memorials and cemeteries should be maintained 'in perpetuity'. Just how long is 'perpetuity'? It is up to those who seized John McCrae's torch to make sure that it means 'forever'.

Tonie & Valmai Holt
Woodnesborough,
Spring 2016

ABBREVIATIONS

Abbreviations used for military units and acronyms are listed below. Many of these are printed in full at intervals throughout the text to aid clarity. Others are explained where they occur.

ABT Australian Battlefield Tour
ADS Advanced Dressing Station
AIF Australian Imperial Force
Att/d Attached
Aust Australian
BEF British Expeditionary Force
Bn Battalion
BWI British West Indies
Cam Cameron
CCS Casualty Clearing Station
Cem Cemetery
CGS/H *Conseil Général de la Somme/Historial*
CIGS Chief of the Imperial General Staff
C-in-C Commander in Chief
CO Commanding Officer
Coy Company
CRP *Conseil Régional de Picardie*
CWGC Commonwealth War
Graves Commission
DLI Durham Light Infantry
DSO Distinguished Service Order
E of I Empress of India's
FA Field Artillery
GOC General Officer Commanding
HE High Explosive
HLI Highland Light Infantry
KOSB King's Own Scottish Borderers
KOYLI King's Own Yorkshire Light Infantry
KRRC King's Royal Rifle Corps
L/Lce Lance
LNL Loyal North Lancs Regiment

MC Military Cross
Mem Memorial
MGC Machine Gun Corps
MM Military Medal
Mon Monument
NSR North Staffs Regiment
NSW New South Wales
OP Observation Point
RB Ross Bastiaan Commemorative Plaques
RE Royal Engineers
RF Royal Fusiliers
RFC Royal Flying Corps
RHA Royal Horse Artillery
RI/R d'I (French) Infantry Regiment
RIF Royal Irish Fusiliers
RIR Royal Irish Rifles
RIR (German) Infantry Reserve Regiment
RIT (French) Territorial Infantry Regiment
RN Royal Navy
RND Royal Naval Division
RWF Royal Welsh Fusiliers
SAF South African Forces
SLI Somerset Light Infantry
SOA Site of Action
Sqn Squadron
SWB South Wales Borderers
VAD Voluntary Aid Detachment
V-B Villers Bretonneux
VC Victoria Cross
WFA Western Front Association

MILITARY UNITS & RANKS
Army Formations and Ranks and Their Relative Strengths/Seniority

The relative sizes of military units and ranks can be confusing to those who do not have direct experience of them. The tables below are approximations intended only to provide guidance rather than absolute accuracy, because although the names of military formations (e.g. Company) remain the same, their compositions can vary (e.g. sometimes three and sometimes four Platoons to a Company).

Military ranks however remain constant in their relativity to each other BUT not necessarily in the formations to which they are attached. This is particularly so in wartime as casualties mount and lower ranks assume command of higher formations whose commanders have been killed (e.g. a full Colonel may take the place of a Brigadier General in commanding a Brigade, a Captain may replace a Major in commanding a Company and so on).

The tables show infantry formations/ranks in descending order of size/seniority.

Formations		Commanding Ranks
Army	(can be two or more Corps)	Field Marshal
Corps	(can be two or more Divisions)	Lieutenant General
Division	(up to four Brigades)	Major General
Brigade	(generally two to four Battalions)	Brigadier General*
Battalion*	(generally two to four Companies)	Lieutenant Colonel
Company	(generally two to four Platoons)	Major or Captain
Platoon	(three or four Sections)	Lieutenant/Second Lieutenant
Section	(nine or ten men)	NCO (Non Commissioned Officer)

*Battalions are formations of around 1,000 men (14 –18) and Regiments very often had more than one battalion. Thus 'Regiment' is a collective noun for formations that in theory have some common identity e.g. all the men were recruited from a particular county – hence a 'County' regiment such as the Royal West Kents which at one time had 18 battalions.

*The ranks here are those associated with the Infantry i.e. the fighting soldiers. But there are others such as 'Staff' (what might be called 'Management'), Engineers, Artillery etc. where the rank of 'Colonel' is found and whose number swell the final strengths of formations.

HOW TO USE THIS GUIDE

T his book is designed to guide the visitor around the salient features, memorials, museums and cemeteries of the Somme battlefield, and to provide sufficient information about those places to allow an elemental understanding of what happened where.

PRIOR TO YOUR VISIT

Before setting out read this Section thoroughly and mark the two recommended maps with the routes you intend to follow. Make sure you take with you any essentials such as medication, emergency telephone numbers, waterproof footwear and binoculars etc...

CHOOSING YOUR ROUTES

The content and sequence of the itineraries are based upon our long experience of visiting the area with interested people. Itinerary One, therefore, contains those features that have been the most requested, and Itinerary Two those next in popularity, especially for British visitors… and so on. Thus, if you are a first-time visitor, you will probably wish to start with Itinerary One and follow the sequence. This is also the itinerary that you may well choose if you only have one day. ANZAC, North American, S. African and French visitors will probably first wish to see the sectors where their countrymen fought.

You should also decide upon your base for the tour and read the various Approach Routes offered before you set out – see below.

IF YOU WISH TO VISIT A PARTICULAR SPOT

Use the Index to locate what you wish to visit. If it is a particular grave, find the location from the Commonwealth War Graves Commission Debt of Honour website before you set out (see below). Using your GPS you can go directly to your chosen destination.

THE ITINERARIES

There are six Itineraries. The first three are long – each approximately 8 hours of touring if followed in full – while the fourth, which is short, can be done on a return journey to the Channel Ports. **Itinerary One** contains what are probably the main features of remembrance for the British for the fighting of 1 July 1916 – north of the Albert-Bapaume Road, the Ancre and up to Serre. **Itinerary Two** focuses south of the road on the action at 'the Woods' (Mametz, Bernafay, Trônes, Delville and High) and **Itinerary Three** covers the action of the Australians in the 1918 Defence of Amiens, the Allied successes of August 1918, together with some lesser-known and French 1916 sectors in the Somme Valley. **Itinerary Four** covers British, French and Australian actions around Péronne and St Quentin to Bapaume (and extends to Bullecourt) of 1914, 1916, 1917 and 1918. This is followed by **Itinerary Five** which covers some of the American, Canadian and French 1918 sectors. **Itinerary Six** covers the Kaiser's March 1918 Offensive. Details of the itinerary routes are given at the beginning of each so that you can mark them on your maps. Finally there are 4 suggested **Circular Walking Tours** of varying length.

These Itineraries and Approaches are copiously illustrated and, in order to fit them all in, some pictures are quite small. By using a magnifying glass on these pictures you will be able to see far more detail.

EXTRA VISITS/[N.B.]S

In addition extra visits are described to sites of particular interest which lie near to the route of the main Itineraries. These are boxed and highlighted in gray so that they clearly stand out from the main route. Estimates of the round-trip mileage and duration are given.

Boxed sections headed [**N.B.**] point out further sites of interest which you may wish to stop at as you pass or make a small deviation from the route to visit.

MILES COVERED/DURATION/OP/RWC

A start point for each itinerary is given, from which a running total of miles is indicated. Extra Visits and [**N.B.**] s are not counted in that running total. Each recommended stop is indicated by a clear heading with the running mileage total, the probable time you will wish to spend there, the Map Reference and GPS Location. The letters OP in the heading indicate a view point, from which salient points of the battlefield are described. RWC indicates refreshment and toilet facilities. Travel directions are written in italics and indented to make them stand out clearly. An end point is suggested, with a total distance and timing – without deviations or refreshment stops.

It is absolutely essential to set your mileometer to zero before starting and to make constant reference to it. These can vary from car to car, so your total mileage may differ slightly from that given in this book. What is important, however, is the distance between stops. Distances in the headings are given in miles because the trip meters on many British cars still operate in miles. Distances within the text are sometimes given in kilometres and metres, as local signposts use these measures.

LENGTH OF STAY

Some fortunate visitors to the Somme Battlefield may have the luxury of two weeks in the area – in which time a leisurely and thorough coverage of the battlefield would be achieved and all the itineraries and extra visits could easily be made. Most people, in our experience, have between one and three days.

The itineraries are designed so that sections of them can be followed at the individual's convenience – you may not be interested in visiting every item that is described on an itinerary. All cemeteries that are on or very close to an itinerary are, at least, mentioned. Reading the descriptions in advance will help you decide whether you wish to stop or to embark on a diversion or not.

APPROACHES

On the assumption that most visitors reach the Somme from one of the Channel Ports, the Tunnel Terminus, or Paris, several interesting approaches are suggested. The **Eastern Approach** takes the short and direct route to Péronne via the A26/A1 and takes the visitor into the eastern edge of the battlefield thereby starting the tour by visiting the important museum, the *Historial* at Péronne,. It offers a longer alternative Extra Visit en route. The **Central Approach** peels off from the Eastern on the A1 Autoroute to go straight through to Albert – the very heart of the British Sector. The **Western Approach** goes directly to Amiens on the A16 and offers alternative Extra Visits en route.

If visiting the Somme from Paris one would probably arrive by train or via the motorway to P[e with an acute accent]ronne, or from Normandy via Abbeville to Amiens.

Note that most of the Autoroutes are Toll roads (*Péages*).

MAPS

The guide book has been designed to be used with *Major & Mrs Holt's Battle Map of the Somme*, packaged with this book, and the words 'Map –' in the heading indicate the map reference for that location. Frequent use of this map will also assist you in orientating, give a clear indication of the distances involved in possible walks and show points of interest which are not included in the itineraries or extra visits.

Also recommended is the *Michelin No 301: Pas de Calais-Somme. 1cm= 1.5km.* A warning, however – French road numbers change with alarming frequency. Be philosophical if the road numbers given either in this guide or the map have changed when you reach them.

GPS LOCATIONS/TRENCH MAPS

In view of the increasing use of 'sat navs' for navigation and for the convenience of readers who wish to go directly to specific locations, we have added GPS references to all stops in this guidebook. We have used the digital form of GPS as this is the simplest. It can be typed directly into most modern sat nav devices and into Google Maps. The references apply to the nearest parking place to the site. Though a satellite navigation system can be of great help, we do not recommend that you rely exclusively upon it as it may direct you away from a route that is integral to the understanding of the 'shape' of the battle.

Great War Digital has released a searchable DVD set containing 750 British Trench Maps for France and Belgium called **LinesMan**. This innovative software permits navigation on screen between modern IGN French maps and trench maps, and when used with a GPS receiver the user's real-time position is shown over a moving map display. The software has to be registered by internet or phone to obtain full functionality and some patience and application are needed to become familiar with the system, but for the enthusiast this facility will become a must. Details can be found at www.greatwardigital.com

HISTORY OF THE BATTLE

The historical notes given at each recommended stop can in no way be continuous and sequential. It is therefore recommended that the visitor precedes his/her tour by reading the Historical Summaries starting on pages 16

ENJOYING THE SOMME

The *Département* of the Somme is a particularly beautiful region of France and there are some excellent restaurants and hotels in the area. Some handily-placed hostelries are mentioned as they appear in the itineraries (indicated in a **distinctive typeface**) For more information, read **the Somme Past and Present** (page 339) and **Tourist Information** (page 339) sections. Make sure that you keep your tank well topped up with fuel as petrol stations are few and far between in remote parts of the battlefield away from the Autoroutes and main towns. Also, if you wish to take a picnic, stock up at the nearest supermarket or local shops before you set off in the morning as the rare village shops may well be closed for lunch.

A WARNING

It is most unwise to pick up any 'souvenirs' in the form of bullets, shells, grenades, barbed wire etc that may be found on the battlefield. To this day, builders making foundations and farmers on the Somme when ploughing – especially fields which have been used as pasture for many years – turn up the sad remains of World War I soldiers, bits of

equipment and ammunition. The latter are then piled up at a corner of the field to await collection by the French Army bomb disposal unit. During the making of the TGV railway line, 140 tonnes of WWI 'hardware' were collected, and an average year yields 90 tonnes. It is known as the 'iron harvest', and it is extremely dangerous to handle – accidents still often occur. Indeed, in the summer of 1985 several deaths occurred on the Somme from WWI ammunition, much of which is extremely volatile. Leaking gas shells are particularly unpleasant. The authors once saw one smoking in a field next to the CWGC Cemetery at Delville Wood. Cuts from sharp, rusting objects can cause blood poisoning or tetanus. It also seems more fitting for such items to be left where they are, as many of them find their way into local museums, where they can be seen by generations of future visitors. Safe souvenirs can be bought at various museums and hostelries on the itineraries.

Iron harvest displayed in the Ulster Tower

HISTORICAL SUMMARIES

1916

'The news about 8a.m. was not altogether good.'

Sir Douglas Haig, 1 July

The Battle Plan – in Brief

The 1916 Battle of the Somme lasted from 1 July to 17 November. It was opened by a mainly volunteer British Army, over half of which was new to battle and had, barely 18 months earlier, answered Kitchener's call to arms.

The Commander of the British Expeditionary Force (BEF) was also new. General French had been replaced by his critic, General Haig, and now the latter had to prove his worth.

At the end of 1915, the French and British planned for a 1916 joint offensive on the Somme, with the French playing the major role. Masterminded by Joffre, the plan was (as far as Joffre was concerned) to kill more Germans than their pool of manpower could afford. But when the German assault at Verdun drew French forces away from the Somme, the British found themselves with the major role, providing sixteen divisions on the first day to the French five.

The British plan was based upon a steady 14-mile wide infantry assault from Serre in the north to Maricourt in the south. On the first day 100,000 soldiers were to go over the top at the end of a savage artillery

General Sir Douglas Haig.

bombardment. Behind the infantry – men of the Fourth Army, commanded by General Rawlinson – waited two

When the early assaults failed to penetrate the German lines, the British Staff set about denying that they had ever intended to do such a thing. To many, their protestations appeared to be attempts to cover up the failure of Haig's plan, and, as the C-in-C continued with his costly and unimaginative attacks, other voices demanded his removal. But he kept his job. He was, after all, a confidant of the King and a pillar of the Establishment.

By the time that the battle ended, British casualties exceeded 400,000. The British secret weapon, the tank, had been used against expert advice in a 'penny packet' operation in September at Flers-Courcelette. Could it have been a desperate attempt by Haig to gain some sort of victory that would offset his earlier failures?

In October and November, piecemeal attacks continued when the heavy rains allowed, and, in a break in the weather on 13 November, the British took Beaumont Hamel. What had been achieved since July? On the ground very little: a maximum advance of 8 miles. Haig said that the battle had been a success and had achieved the aim that he had placed first on his list of aims – 'To relieve the pressure on Verdun'.

Certainly the German offensive at Verdun had been stopped, but how could the C-in-C maintain that it had been the prime objective of the Somme offensive when the decision to attack the Somme was made by him and Joffre a week before the Verdun battle began? There is the smell of a smokescreen in the air. There can be no denying, however, that the administrative preparations for the coming battle were very thorough.

Administrative Preparations for the 1916 Somme Battle

In 1915 at Loos, the orders for the attack were contained on some two pages. In February 1916, GHQ issued a fifty-seven-page memorandum setting out the preparations that should be undertaken before large-scale operations. Things had changed.

To prepare for the battle, a mini-city had to be built and supplied. The planning requirement looked for '7 weeks' lodging for 400,000 men and 100,000 horses'. Extra accommodation was set up for 15,000 men per division in wooden framed tarpaulin-walled huts – but only with lying down space of 6ft x 2ft per man. New trenches, roads and railways were constructed. It was estimated that the Fourth Army alone would need thirty-one trains per day to sustain it. Not only was it necessary to prepare roads and railways prior to a battle, but they had to be extended forward to maintain supplies of immediate needs, such as infantry stores, guns and ammunition essential to sustain an advance. Specialist RE units, together with labour and/or pioneer battalions did the work.

Following the successful September 1916 attack on 'the Woods', 7th Field Company RE was tasked to build 'tramways' forward, and used 60m Decauville prefabricated track. By the end of October, 8 miles of track had been laid in two lines. One was from Contalmaison to beyond Martinpuich and the other from Mametz Wood to High Wood. The second in command of the company was a Lt Glubb, later to be known as **Lt Gen Sir John Glubb KCB, CMG, DSO, OBE, MC – 'Glubb Pasha'**, Commander of the Arab Legion, with whom the authors communicated.

Water supply was a particular problem and more than a hundred pumping plants were set up and over 120 miles of piping laid. The range of facilities to be provided for was legion – food, ammunition, medical reinforcements, workshops and postal facilities – all involving movement. A telling measure of the scale of the challenge is given in the *Official History* (1916, p 283). One of the critical tasks on a battlefield is traffic control and a 24-hour traffic census taken at Fricourt three weeks after the battle began lists the following, almost unbelievable, administrative activities:

'Troops 26,536, Light Motor Cars 568, Motor cycles 617, Motor lorries 813, 6-horse wagons 1,458, 4-horse wagons 568, 2-horse wagons 1,215, 1-horse carts 515, Riding horses 5,404, Motor ambulances 333, Cycles 1,043',

and this is not a complete list.

The Commander-in-Chief

As pointed out in the Introduction, those who study World War I tend to fall into two main camps: those who are anti-Haig and those who are pro-Haig. But there are those who veer from one opinion to the other, according to the quality of the debate. Was the C-in-C a dependable rock, whose calm confidence inspired all around him, whose far-seeing eye led us to final victory, and who deserved the honours later heaped upon him? **John Masefield**, asked by Haig to write an account of the Somme battle, visited him at GHQ in October 1916. Masefield was extremely impressed by this 'wonderful'

Apprehensive faces two days before the battle. Picture dated 29 June 1916

man. 'No enemy could stand against such a man', he enthused. 'He took away my breath.' He described Haig's 'fine delicate gentleness and generosity … pervading power … and a height of resolve …. I don't think anyone could have been nicer.'

Was this the real Haig, or was he an unimaginative, insensitive product of the social caste system that knew no better: a weak man pretending to be strong, who should have been sacked? **Dennis Wheatley**, in his war-time memoirs, *Officer and Temporary Gentleman* opines, 'He was a pleasant, tactful, competent, peacetime soldier devoted to his duty, but he had a rooted dislike of the French and was not even a second-rate General. Many of the high-ups were well aware of that, but the question had always been, with whom could they replace him?'

Many more pages than are available here are needed to pursue those questions fairly and to examine the Battle of the Somme in any detail. But some pointers can be set by a skeleton examination of the battle that, with Passchendaele in 1917, led soldiers, rightly or wrongly, to describe their C-in-C as 'Butcher' Haig.

The Different Parts of the Battle

The Battle is divided into 5 parts:

Part 1. The First Day: 1 July
Part 2. The Next Few Days: 2 July +
Part 3. The Night Attack/ The Woods: 14 July +
Part 4. The Tank Attack: 15 September
Part 5. The last Attack: 13 November.

Part 1. The First Day: 1 July

At 0728, seventeen mines were blown under the German front line. Two minutes later, 60,000 British soldiers, laden down with packs, gas masks, rifle and bayonet, 200 rounds of ammunition, grenades, empty sandbags, spade, mess tin and water bottle, iron rations, mackintosh sheet, warmed by the issue of rum, 'to each a double spoonful, fed baby-fashion by the sergeant' [Williamson], clambered out of their trenches from Serre to Maricourt and formed into lines 14 miles long. As the lines moved forward in waves, so the artillery barrage lifted off the enemy front line and rolled forward.

Now it was a life or death race, but the Tommies did not know it. They had not been entered. Their instructions were to move forward, side by side, at a steady walk across No Man's Land. 'Strict silence will be maintained during the advance through the smoke', they were instructed, 'and no whistles will be blown'. It would be safe, they were told, because the artillery barrage would have destroyed all enemy opposition.

It started on 24 June. Over 3,000,000 shells had been stockpiled but these proved to be insufficient. There were still many duds, despite the outcry of the 'Scandal' about duds after the Battle of Loos. Most of them were due to shoddy and defective workmanship – substandard steel casings cracked and burst prematurely; copper driving bands were faulty; the hot summer weather caused the explosives to exude; unburnt fuses remained in the bore and many other lethal inadequacies caused some gun crews to christen themselves 'the Suicide Club'. Despite borrowing guns from the French, the Artillery were short of heavy weapons.

The original date for the assault, ('The Big Push'), was 29 June. On 28 June the offensive was postponed to 1 July because of bad weather and there was insufficient ammunition to maintain the same level of bombardment intensity for an extra two days. Because of these factors and the doubtful efficacy of artillery against wire, the Germans were not destroyed, as had glibly been promised. They and their machine guns had sheltered in deep dugouts, and when the barrage lifted, they climbed out, dragging their weapons with them.

The Germans easily won the race. They set up their guns before the Tommies could get to the trenches to stop them and cut down the ripe corn of British youth in their thousands (as is the somewhat cliched habitual description), many on the uncut wire that they had been assured would be totally destroyed. As the day grew into hot summer, another 40,000 men were sent in, in successive waves, stepping over the bodies of their wounded companions ('All ranks are forbidden to divert attention from enemy in order to attend wounded officers or men'), adding only more names to the casualty lists. Battalions disappeared in the bloody chaos of battle, bodies lay in their hundreds around the muddy shell holes that pocked the battlefield.

And to what end this leeching of the nation's best blood? North of the Albert-Bapaume road, on a front of almost 9 miles, there were no realistic gains at nightfall. VIII, X and III Corps had failed. Between la Boisselle and Fricourt there was a small penetration of about half a mile on one flank and the capture of Mametz village on the other by XV Corps.

But there was some success. XIII Corps attacking beside the French took all its main objectives, from Pommiers Redoubt east of Mametz, to just short of Dublin Redoubt north of Maricourt. Overall some thirteen fortified villages were targeted to be taken on the first day, but only two – Mametz and Montauban – were actually captured. The French, south of the Somme, did extremely well. Attacking at 0930, they easily took all their objectives. 'They had more guns than we did', cried the British Generals, or 'The opposition wasn't as tough', or 'The Germans didn't expect to be attacked by the French', or 'They had easier terrain'.

But whatever the reasons for the poor British performance in the north, they had had some success – on the right flank beside the French.

Therefore, if the attack was to continue the next day, would it not make sense to follow-up quickly on the right where things were going well?

Part 2. The Next Few Days: 2 July +

Other than the negative one of not calling off the attack, no General Command decisions were made concerning the overall conduct of the second day's battle. It was as if all the planning had been concerned with 1 July and that the staffs were surprised by the appearance of 2 July. Aggressive actions were mostly initiated at Corps level while Haig and Rawlinson figured out what policy they ought to follow. Eventually they decided to attack on the right flank, but by then the Germans had had two weeks to recover.

Part 3. The Night Attack/The Woods: 14 July +

On the XIII Corps front, like fat goalposts, lay the woods of Bazentin le Petit on the left and Delville on the right. Behind and between them, hunched on the skyline, was the dark goalkeeper of High Wood. Rawlinson planned to go straight for the goal. Perhaps the infantry general's memory had been jogged by finding one of his old junior officer's notebooks in which the word 'surprise' had been written as a principle of attack, because, uncharacteristically, he set out to surprise the Germans and not in one way, but in two.

First, despite Haig's opposition, he moved his assault forces up to their start line in Caterpillar Valley at night. Second, after a mere minute's dawn barrage, he launched his attack. At 0325 on 14 July, twenty thousand men moved forward. On the left were 7th and 21st Divisions of XV Corps and on the right 3rd and 9th Divisions of XIII Corps. The effect was dramatic. Five miles of the German second line were over-run. On the left Bazentin-le-Petit Wood was taken. On the right began the horrendous six day struggle for Delville Wood. Today the South African Memorial and Museum in the wood commemorate the bitter fighting. But in the centre, 7th Division punched through to High Wood and with it were two squadrons of cavalry. Perhaps here was an opportunity for a major break-through at last. Not since 1914 had mounted cavalry charged on the Westen Front, but, when they did, the Dragoons and the Deccan Horse were alone. The main force of the cavalry divisions, gathered south of Albert, knew nothing about the attack. The charge was a costly failure, the moment passed, the Germans recovered, counter-attacked and regained the wood. Then followed two months of local fighting under the prompting of Joffre, but, without significant success to offer, the C-in-C began to attract increasing criticism. Something had to be done to preserve his image, to win a victory – or both. It was done, and with a secret weapon.

Part 4. The Tank Attack: 15 September

Through the prompting of Col Ernest Swinton and Winston Churchill, the War Office sponsored the construction, by William Foster & Co in Lincoln, of a machine that could cross trenches and was both armed and armoured. By August 1916 the machine, code-named the 'tank' because of its resemblance to a water tank (later christened variously by journalists as 'Diplodocus Galumphang', 'Polychromatic Toad' and 'Flat-footed Monster'), was, following highly successful trials, beginning production. Both Swinton and Churchill considered it essential that no use should be made of the secret weapon until it was available in large numbers. But Haig insisted that he needed them and, late in August, forty-nine were shipped to France. Still very new and liable to break down, only thirty-two tanks assembled near Trônes Wood on the night of 14 September for dispersal along the front, and the following morning at 0620, following a three-day bombardment, eighteen took part in the battle with XV Corps. Their effect was sensational. The Germans, on seeing the monsters, were stunned and then terrified. Nine tanks moved forward with the leading infantry, nine 'mopped up' behind. Barely over 3 hours later, the left hand division of XV Corps followed a solitary tank up the main street of Flers and through the German third line. Then Courcelette, too, fell to an infantry/tank advance.

The day's gains were the greatest since the battle began and much jubilation was felt on the Home Front, whipped up by the press. But there were too few tanks and, after the intitial shock success, the fighting once again degenerated into a bull-headed contest. The opportunity that had existed to use the tank to obtain a major strategic result had been lost. Many felt that it had been squandered. Yet the tank had allowed Fourth Army to advance and the dominating fortress of Thiépval finally fell on 26 September, helped, it was said, 'by the appearance of 3 tanks'. At last the British were on the crest of the Thiépval-Pozières-High Wood ridge. But Beaumont Hamel in the north still held out.

Part 5. The Last Attack: 13 November

At the northern end of the battlefield, seven Divisions of the Reserve (Fifth) Army assaulted at 0545 on 13 November. Bad weather had caused seven postponements since the original date of 24 October. V Corps was north of the River Ancre and II Corps was south. The preparatory bombardment had been carefully monitored to see that the enemy wire had been cut, but this eminent practicality was offset by the stationing of cavalry behind the line to exploit success. Past battle experience should have made such an idea absurd, the weather's effect on the ground alone should have rendered it unthinkable. The generals were as firmly stuck for ideas as any Tommy, up to his knees in Somme mud, was stuck for movement.

But this time the mines were fired at the right time. On 1 July the Hawthorn mine above Beaumont Hamel had been blown 10 minutes early. The Sappers now tunnelled back under the old crater, which had been turned into a fortification by the Germans and placed 30,000 lbs of explosives beneath it. It was blown at 0545 and covered the German trenches with debris. The attack went in with a shield of early morning dark and fog, the troops moving tactically from cover to cover. Beaumont Hamel and the infamous Y Ravine were taken by the 51st Highland Division and their kilted Highlander Memorial stands there today in memory of that achievement. Immediately to the south of the 51st, the Royal Naval Division took Beaucourt early on the morning of the 14th and their memorial stands in the village. Fighting continued for several more days and 7,000 prisoners were taken – though Serre did not fall. But, at last, enough was enough. The attack was halted. The 1916 Battle of the Somme was over.

Casualties (killed, wounded and missing)

'Lies, damned lies and statistics' (*attributed to Mark Twain*)

Casualty figures and statistics generally are weapons which can be, and often are, falsified to discourage the enemy, encourage one's own forces or alter a view of events to particular advantage. The Somme figures are given here alongside those for Verdun, because only by comparison can the Somme casualties be seen in a meaningful light. We do not claim any absolute numeric accuracy for our figures, which have been deduced from a number of sources, including official histories, which often have a nationalistic bias.

The Battle of Verdun is often presented as the most horrific conflict on the Western Front in terms of human casualties. Yet even allowing for inaccuracies, the comparative figures below show:

a. that the British had at least equal, if not greater, losses on the Somme than the French at Verdun;

b. that the Germans had greater losses on the Somme than they did at Verdun.

Joffre, therefore, had succeeded in his aim of joining the British and Germans in a battle of attrition. By the letting of so much young blood the British were now firmly in the conflict, Joffre had dispelled the French idea that the British were 'not pulling their weight', and the process of wearing down the Germans had speeded up.

Nation	Somme		Verdun
	1 July	Total	Total
Britain	58,000	420,000	—
France	4,000*	195,000	370,000
Germany	8,000	650,000**	330,000

*No accurate figures are available but it can confidently be assumed to be less than half the German total.

**The Germans did not issue figures. This is the official British figure, but many historians consider this to be British wishful thinking, and that the German casualties totaled much the same as the British and Dominion.

The Fourth Army ORBAT on 1 July (Rawlinson)

VIII CORPS (Hunter-Weston)
Hébuterne to Beaucourt
48th (SM) Div (Fanshawe)
31st Div (O'Gowan)
4th Div (Lambton)
29th Div (de Lisle)

III CORPS (Pulteney)
Ovillers to la Boisselle
8th Div (Hudson)
19th (W) Div (Bridges)
34th Div (Ingouville-Williams)

XIII CORPS (Congreve, VC)
Carney to Maricourt
18th (E) Div (Maxse)
30th Div (Shea)
9th (S) Div (Reserve)

X CORPS (Morland)
Hamel to Authuille
36th Div (Nugent)
49th (WR) Div (Perceval)
32nd Div (Rycroft)

XV CORPS (Horne)
Bécourt to Mametz
21st Div (Campbell)
17th (N) Div (Pilcher)
7th Div (Watts)

SM = South Midlands; WR = West Riding; N = Northern; E = Eastern; S = Scottish
Formations are shown north to south, with inclusive responsibilities.

1917

'I have of course, as a Prussian officer, no doubt whatever. War means the destruction of the enemy without scruple and by any means. War is the harshest of all trades, and the masters of it can only entertain humane feelings so long as they do no harm...

Ernst Junger, 73rd Hanoverian Fus Regt, commenting on the moral justification of the utter destruction during the German's withdrawal to the Hindenburg Line

Although the emphasis when studying the battles of the Somme is upon the preceding and following years, fighting did not, of course, cease in this general area in 1917! It was the year which saw the Germans' strategic retreat to the newly formed defensive **Hindenburg Line** (known to them as the **Siegfried Line**), in which they undertook the systematic and brutal destruction of every town and village they passed through, poisoning wells and setting mines and booby traps (shades of General Sherman's 'March to the Sea').

Notable also was the Battle of Arras, within which was the Canadian action at Vimy and the Australian assault at Bullecourt. As these sites of 1917 actions in the Somme proper are passed, they are described in the main Itineraries of this book. But, just as 'The Big Push' was concentrated in the *Départment* of the Somme in 1916, in 1917 actions in this part of France moved northwards to the *Départment* of the Pas de Calais and the Battle of Arras. Some aspects of this are covered in Eastern Approach (**Vimy** and the surrounding sectors, see page 41) and in Itinerary Four (**Bullecourt**, see page 284) but the battle of **Cambrai** is covered in *Holts' Western Front-South* book and **Passchendaele** in both *'Western Front – North'* and *'Ypres'*.

1918
THE KAISER'S OFFENSIVE.
MARCH-AUGUST

'There is no other course open to us but to fight it out! ... With our backs to the wall and believing in the justice of our cause, each one must fight onto the end'.

GOC Order of the Day 11 April 1918

The Battle is divided into 2 parts:
Part 1. The Main Thrust from St Quentin to Amiens (see Itinerary 6)
Part 2. The American, Canadian and French Sectors (see Itinerary 5)

Part 1. The Main Thrust from St Quentin to Amiens
After the failure at Cambrai in 1917 the BEF went into a defensive mode and began to construct positions in depth similar to the Germans. A forward, lightly-held zone was meant to delay the attacker, while behind it was a main battle zone held in strength and depth. In both zones small redoubts (defended positions) and machine-gun posts were to be scattered like cherries in a Dundee cake. The battle zone was generally to be separated from the forward zone by a gap of two to three miles and was to be 2,000 to 3,000 yards deep. Four miles further back still was a rear zone, effectively a second position to which the defence could retire if need be. All of these positions had to be prepared and, as it attracted the lowest priority, the rear zone in many places was hardly

more than a belt of wire known as the Green Line.

The British C-in-C., Haig, reasoned that the most critical part of his line was in the north, shielding the Channel Ports, and he put forty-six divisions to cover what amounted to two-thirds of his front. The remaining third, on the right, was covered by Gough's Fifth Army which mustered fourteen divisions. Already thinly spread compared to the north, the Fifth Army was given a further twenty-five miles to cover which were taken over from the French early in 1918. Foch also wanted Haig to contribute nine divisions to a central Allied reserve to be controlled by Foch. Haig refused. Instead he made a 'gentleman's agreement' that each would come to the other's aid with six divisions after five days' notice if the need arose.

On 29 November 1917 hostilities ceased on the Russian Front. A week later Rumania stopped fighting. The Germans now had spare forces which they could move to the Western Front. In the period up to the opening of the Kaiser's Offensive their strength rose by 30%. British strength, compared with the summer of 1917, fell by 25%.

Ludendorff held a conference, ironically in Mons on 11 November 1917, at which the plans for the *Kaiserschlacht* were discussed. He decided to strike first in the area of Arras and St Quentin where the ground would be firmer than in Flanders. He also chose to attack the British whose forces, he believed, had been weakened by Passchendaele and whose Generals, he felt, were more inept and less flexible than the French. In addition he introduced a wholly new tactical philosophy. Ludendorff adopted an attack concept, originated by Capt Geyer, of a light tactical assault unit, the infantry group, made up from a few riflemen, mortar teams, engineers and light machine guns. These groups of 'storm troopers' incorporated in a thin screen would move forward to probe and penetrate enemy defences, bypassing any centres of opposition according to circumstances and not limited by a rigid timetable. The main attack force, following behind and reinforced with its own under-command field artillery would overcome any resistance remaining. In addition, artillery tactics were also revised. Von Hutier had introduced the idea of silent registration on the Eastern Front and it had been used with great effect at Caporetto. His chief gunner was Oberst Georg Bruchmüller and he now became the great conductor for the battle and orchestrated a score for the March artillery programme that was to confirm his nickname, 'Breakthrough Bruchmüller'.

Bruchmüller's plan began with silent registration and consisted of seven phases, six of them between 0400 and 0940 hours, the jump-off time. The seventh was a creeping barrage. He defined the targets to be hit, the intensity to be achieved, the explosive/phosgene gas mixture to be used, and the duration of each phase. Training for the attack, 'Operation Michael', was intensive and thorough. Steadily Ludendorff built up his strength. By the night of 20 March the German superiority in infantry was four to one, and the more than 6,000 guns standing by for Bruchmüller's overture were a larger assembled force of arms than those of the British on the Somme on 1 July 1916, the British at El Alamein in October 1942 and the Allies against Saddam Hussein in February 1991 all added together: *Der Tag* was about to dawn.

The Battle

At 0930 hours on 21 March 1918, after five hours of Bruchmüller's itemised bombardment, 3,500 mortars opened rapid fire on the British front line defences. Five minutes later in thick mist the storm troopers advanced. 5th Army communications had been destroyed, battalion positions and redoubts were cut off and by passed. Not only did the defenders know little about what was happening, they could see little. By nightfall, the Germans had penetrated the forward zone on both 4th and 5th Army fronts and were consolidating in the battle zone. Gough withdrew his right wing seven miles to behind the Crozat Canal (shown on modern maps as the St Quentin Canal between Ham and Chauny) and asked the French for permission to blow the railway bridges. They refused.

   The following morning the Germans continued their assault, the mist still protecting them. By the end of the day the Fifth Army's centre had been broken and all of its meagre reserves committed. On the night of 22 March Gough decided that he must pull his remaining forces behind the line of the River Somme and make a stand there (see Map 305). The line held for three days but the German tide would not be denied. The Fifth's retreat continued. On 23 March German long-range railway guns started to shell Paris. The French considered pulling back to defend their capital and Haig looked at the possibility of abandoning the Fifth Army and moving the Third Army north to protect the Channel Ports. But the German advance was slowing. Their roads forward were clogged with traffic and constantly harassed by the RFC. Their soldiers, who had been on short rations for many months and whose clothing and equipment was of poor quality, were overwhelmed by the richness of captured British food and supplies and engaged in wholesale looting. Rudolph Binding, the German writer who took part in the advance, recorded in his diary on 28 March, 'There were men driving cows... others who carried a hen under one arm... men carrying a bottle of wine under their arm and another open in their hand... men staggering… men who could hardly walk... the advance was held up and there was no means of getting going again for hours.'

On 26 March, in emergency sessions, Clemenceau, Foch, Milner, Haig and others conferred under the chairmanship of President Poincaré at Doullens. The initial mood of impending defeat was shattered by Foch, who proclaimed, 'I will never surrender.' Haig promised Poincaré that he would hold Amiens and when Foch was appointed Supreme Commander of the Allied Forces on the Western Front, Haig willingly acquiesced to the position of Number Two. The headlong retreat of the Fifth Army, however, needed a scapegoat. Ignoring the fact that Gough had warned of his shortage of men both for fighting and for preparing defences, had warned of the too-extended frontage that he had to hold, had warned of the certainty of the location of the coming attack and had asked repeatedly for reinforcements, he was relieved of his command. Two days later Rawlinson took over from him in the field with the HQ staff of the Fourth Army. On that same day the German advance was virtually spent. The Third Army north of the Somme threw back the German efforts against Arras. Ten miles in front of Amiens, just to the east of the village of Villers Bretonneux, the tired Germans were fought to a standstill by the 1st Cavalry Division.

On 3 April Gough met Haig before returning to England. The meeting was brief. Haig said that the orders for Gough's removal had not come from him, that there would be an enquiry into the actions of the Fifth Army and its Commander and that Gough would have 'every chance' to defend himself. Haig concluded by shaking hands. 'I'm sorry to lose you Hubert,' he said. 'Goodbye'.

Already Australian troops, rushed down by Haig from the north, were arriving around Villers Bretonneux. When the Germans attacked again at dawn on 4 April it seemed momentarily as if the village must fall, but an Australian bayonet charge tipped the scales. The forty miles advance was over.

The Germans paused to gather their strength. At GHQ Haig realised that the situation was critical and asked Foch to take over some part of the front held by the British and Commonwealth forces. Foch agreed to move a large French force towards Amiens and on 11 April Haig, worried about the morale of his tired and overstretched troops, issued his 'Special Order of the Day' which was addressed to 'All Ranks of the British Army in France and Flanders'.

In the dawn mist of 24 April the 4th (Ger) Guards Division and the 228th Division supported by thirteen tanks came down the hill from Villers Bretonneux towards Amiens. Again the Australians took them on, pinching out the village on the morning of Anzac Day, 25 April, just hours after the first ever tank-versus-tank battle. The advance was over. Amiens was safe and the Germans switched their attention to Flanders. But the signs were there that the end was nigh.

Three days earlier the Australians had buried Baron Manfred von Richthofen, the 'Red Baron', at Bertangles, with full military honours. An Australian anti-aircraft battery claimed the victory - so did the Canadian pilot, Capt Roy Brown, and the dispute continues to this day. Von Richthofen had had eighty kills and was a symbolic figure of German military prowess. His death was a great blow to military morale at a time when back home workers' strikes were crippling the German economy.

An extraordinary insight into the desperate attempts to stem the German tide is portrayed in **R.G. Sherriff's** play, *Journeys End*. It is set in an officers' dugout near St Quentin between 18-20 March 1918. The attack is anticipated, and a suicidal raid is undertaken into enemy lines to secure a prisoner for intelligence purposes and, because it is written from personal experience - Sherriff served with the East Surreys and fought in the battles of St Quentin and the Somme Crossings throughout March and April 1918 - it is searingly realistic. First produced in December 1928 at the Apollo Theatre it starred the unknown actor Laurence Olivier in the pivotal role of the company commander, Capt Stanhope. A brilliant revival, produced by David Grindley, and with the most superb cast who seem to 'be' rather than to act their roles, was put on in the Playhouse Theatre, London in 2004/5. The raw feelings and authentic sets and sound effects transcended the outmoded language and attitudes of '14-18' to project a genuine empathic experience.

The German offensive, codenamed 'Operation Michael', continued to beat elsewhere along the Allied line, but on 8 August came the 'Black Day' of the German Army. The Fourth Army of British, Australian, Canadian and a few attached Americans, achieved complete surprise by opening their counter-offensive at 0420, and co-ordinated artillery, infantry, tanks and air force to such effect that 16,000 prisoners were taken that day.

It was the beginning of the final **'100 Days'** that led to the Armistice of 11 November 1918.

Part 2. The American, Canadian and French Sectors:

The Kaiser's Offensive of 21 March 1918 had reached almost to Amiens. On the D1029 St Quentin-Amiens road their advance was stopped by the **Australians** at Villers Bretonneux and some three miles south the **Canadian** Cavalry held the Germans at Moreuil, while 8 miles still further south the **Americans** were to have their first large-scale assault, as an American formation, at Cantigny. Then on 8 August the **Allied** counter-offensive known as **'The Hundred Days'** began.

This Itinerary looks at a part of the Somme battlefield that, compared to the area associated with the actions of 1916, is rarely visited. The Kaiser's Offensive which began on 21 March 1918 made its greatest gains in this area and what we look at here are some of the Memorials and Cemeteries associated with the international efforts that finally brought the Germans to a standstill. We examine briefly each of the nations involved in bringing the German advance to a stop south of the D1029 Villers Bretonneux-Amiens road.

The Americans

The United States entered the First World War on 6 April 1917. Relations between Germany and America had been strained by the sinking of the Lusitania on 7 May 1915, when over 120 Americans died, and by indiscriminate German use of submarines against unarmed merchant shipping. Things were brought to a head by the publication of the 'Zimmerman Telegram'. Supposedly sent from the German Embassy in Washington to the German Embassy in Mexico, it proposed that, in the event of war between America and Germany, an alliance be formed with Mexico and that Mexico should be allowed to 'reconquer her lost territory in Texas, New Mexico and Arizona'. Feelings in America ran high against Germany, despite theories that the telegram was a fake engineered by British Intelligence and, finally, President Wilson declared war.

On 26 May 1917 Major General John. J. Pershing was appointed to command the American Expeditionary Force and he landed at Boulogne on 13 June 1917 with a small advance party. Two weeks later elements of the First Division (later to be known as 'The Big Red One') began landing at St Nazaire. After the war a splendid Memorial was erected there to commemorate the Division's arrival but it was destroyed by the Germans in the Second World War. A full size replica was erected in 1989.

America had no experience of the 'new' war that was being fought in Europe and units were distributed amongst Allied formations in order to gain experience (e.g. see the Carey's Force entry on page 234). The first American deaths occurred at Bathlemont (south-east of Metz) on 3 November 1917 when three men serving with the French were killed. However it remained a key part of American policy that their forces should operate as a whole, as an 'American' force.

In March and April 1918 the 'Kaiser's Offensive' (sometimes called by the French 'The Second Battle of the Somme') hammered against much of the Western Front with large gains along a line from Péronne to Montdidier (see map on page 305). Pershing put all his troops under General Foch in order to help to counter the German threat and the American First Division entered the front west of Montdidier, the first time that a complete American division had been so used. Given the task of taking the high ground around Cantigny the Division's 28th Infantry attacked at 0645 on 28 May 1918, taking the town that day and never losing it, despite heavy German counter-attacks over the next two days. The American action was acclaimed as a great success and its significance is remembered by three Memorials at Cantigny – one commemorating the National significance of the event, another remembering the First Division and the most recent to the 28th Inf Regt - a fine statue of a Doughboy. In Chicago the 1st Division Museum is in Cantigny Park and has more than 100,000 visitors a year – see www.cantigny.org

The Canadians

When the war began in August 1914 Canada automatically joined on Britain's side and within weeks its small regular army of barely 3,000 men had been swelled by over 32,000 volunteers. In October a convoy of some 30 ships carrying the Canadian Expeditionary Force set sail for the two weeks journey to England, being joined en-route by a ship carrying the Newfoundland contingent that insisted upon remaining independent.

Not until December 1914 did the Canadians get to the front line, their first troops being the Princess Patricia's Canadian Light Infantry formed almost entirely from ex-regular British soldiers. Two months later the 1st Canadian Division arrived and in September 1915 the 2nd Division landed in France. Much as General Pershing would later demand for his Americans, the Canadians insisted that their troops should remain together as a Canadian force and thus the Canadian Corps was formed, being joined in

December that year by the 3rd Division.

During 1915 the Canadians were in action around Ypres and in 1916 they were on the Somme. In 1917 they had their remarkable success at Vimy Ridge (qv) and at the beginning of 1918 the Canadian Cavalry Division faced the advancing Germans at Moreuil south of the D1029. It is that action that we look at here. On the 'Images of a Forgotten War' website, of the National Film Board of Canada, by following the 'Wartime/Battles/August Offensive 2', links, one is taken to a short film of Canadian cavalry gathering before the assault.

The French

The Kaiser's Battle in the south was directed along a rough line from Péronne to Amiens against General Byng's 3rd Army and General Gough's 5th Army. Both British Armies fell back, the 5th in the south suffering particularly badly. As the German drive towards Montdidier developed during the day General Pétain gave orders that French troops should support the British right and forces under General Humbert, part of General Fayolle's Army Group (he had commanded the French 6th Army that attacked south of the Somme on 1 July 1916), were rushed forward in lorries, joining the battle the following day.

French air ace, René Fonck

The German advances continued, however, and on 26 March at Doullens all Allied forces were placed under the command of General Foch, superseding Pétain. Two days later General Pershing told Foch, 'All we have is yours'. On 27 March Montdidier fell but the German progress had been stalling as French resistance south of the Somme gathered pace and now, almost forty miles from their supply bases and exhausted, the Germans stopped to gather breath. It was in this area from the end of March to the end of June that René Fonck, the French air ace, claimed some 18 of his 75 victories.

THE APPROACH ROUTES

These are the suggested routes to the Somme from the Channel or Paris.
Please read this section carefully before you leave so that you can plan the most appropriate route for you. This will depend on your chosen base. Basically the Eastern Approach comes into the battlefield from the east at Péronne via the *Historial* Museum; the Western Approach enters at Amiens. The Central Approach goes directly to Albert.

Extra Visits are suggested from the direct basic routes that will make your journey more interesting, provided you have the time.

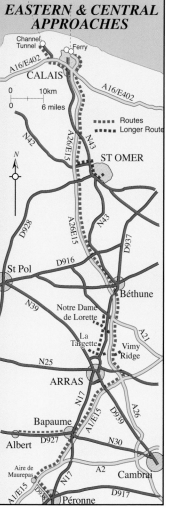

EASTERN & CENTRAL APPROACHES

NOTE FOR ALL APPROACH ROUTES

Remember that most of these are toll roads, the toll booths being signed as *Péages*.
On arriving in France SET YOUR MILEOMETER TO ZERO. Five miles equate to 8 kilometres.
a. From Calais Ferry Port *take the A16 signed Paris/Reims. After 4.4 miles take the A26/E15 signed St Omer/Lens/Arras/Paris (and if all else fails initially keep following Paris signs).*
b. From Eurotunnel. *After emerging, pass on your left a **Petrol station (GPS: 50.93480 1.81769)**. Follow signs through a series of roundabouts to A16 and deduct approx 8 miles from the total mileages now given. Initially follow signs to A26/Péage and Paris.*
c. If arriving by air or train into Paris and thence by car *take the A1 to Assevillers and either turn right to start at the Historial at Péronne on the D1029 or left on the D1029 or the Autoroute A29 to Amiens and pick up the Approach routes as appropriate.*

THE EASTERN APPROACH

1. This is the Quickest Basic Route to Péronne if you are making it your base or starting point from that end of the battlefield with a visit to the *Historial* Museum.
Approximate driving time, without stops: 1 hour 40 minutes.
Approximate distance: 100 miles.
At 24.4 miles on the A26 is the first *Péage* station. Take a ticket.
At 55 miles the Loos battlefield, marked by twin slag heads (the famous 'Double Crassier') can be seen on the left.
At 56 miles Exit 6.2, signed to Liéven/Lens/Douai is passed.
[IT IS AT THIS POINT THAT THE LONGER ROUTE (SEE BELOW) MAY BE STARTED.]
At 60 miles the Memorial to Jacques Defrasse (qv) may be seen to the right.
At 62.4 miles the Vimy Memorial (qv) may be seen to the left.
At 69.5 miles at the motorway junction take the A1/E15 signed Arras/Paris.
Continue on the A1.
At 86 miles Exit 14 is passed.

[IT IS AT THIS POINT THAT THE CENTRAL APPROACH ROUTE (SEE BELOW, Map page 29) MAY BE STARTED.]

At 94.3 miles is Exit 13-1.

> *Take this exit from the A1 at the Aire de Maurepas, signed Albert/Péronne, take the D938, signed to Péronne and the Historial.*

At the first roundabout is a large sculpture entitled *Lumières d'Acier* (Steel Lights), an imaginative comment on the war by sculptor Albert Hirsch, with an explanatory signboard (only seen if you look back as you start along the D938!). Cross the Canal du Nord, enter Péronne, follow signs to the *Historial* (beware of fierce speed bumps as you enter the town) and park in the square in front of the Museum.

• *Historial de la Grande Guerre/RWC (100 miles, Map I /40, GPS: 49.92885 2.93245)*

This costly and ambitious project, which aims to show World War I in an entirely new light and act as a centre for documentation and research, was funded by the Department of the Somme, and opened in 1992. At the main entrance is a Ross Bastiaan bronze bas relief Plaque inaugurated by the Australians in 1993.

Its façade is the medieval castle, behind which is the modern building, designed by H.E. Ciriani.

At first considered by some to be somewhat intellectual and exclusive, the Museum started to become more accessible and relevant to the area under the influence of Director, François Bergez. François has now moved on to become Director of Tourism for the Somme Département and has been succeeded by the enthusiastic and dynamic Hervé François, who has some exciting plans for the four years of the WW1 Centenary. The Museum re-opened in March 2014 after extensive work on what will be an on-going project of renovation and change of emphasis over the 4 years of the Centenary. Progressively the great halls will illustrate the history of the Castle itself, the pre-war years and build up to War, its conduct and participants, and finally the Armistice, the trauma legacy of the war and the post-war reconstruction period. These are illustrated through the skilful combination of original artefacts and art works with modern technology. The beautiful courtyard contains a vaulted brick hall whose renovation was funded by the Australians which concentrates on their actions round Péronne and Mont St Quentin (qv, where there is an Australian Remembrance Trail, a map of which may be collected here). There is a new informative video presentation near the entrance, formidable documentation centre,

Historial de la Grande Guerre, the entrance

Floor display, Historial, Péronne

Replica Saint Chamond Tank, Historial courtyard before moving to Thiepval Museum

comfortable 'Internet Café' and well-stocked boutique. Changing temporary exhibitions.

To further the *Historial*'s aim to commemorate the Great War through artistic and cultural events, a major 'artwork', 'The Garden of the 6th Continent', designed by horticultural engineer Gilles Clément was inaugurated on 2 July 2014 beside the *Historial* with an international ceremony and concert.

The *Historial* works closely with the *Comité du Tourisme de la Somme* (CDT) and the *Conseil Générale de la Somme* on projects to preserve and promote the Somme battlefield by acquiring historic sites, putting up descriptive signboards in sites of particular interest (indicated with CGS/H in the text of this book) and signs for a *Circuit de Souvenir* (Remembrance Route). It directs the Centre at Thiepval and the new Museum attached to it (qv). Also, in conjunction with the CDT and the *Musée Somme* at Albert, it produces a list of approved guides/hotels, b+bs to the area (**'Somme Battlefields' Partners', qv**) and offers special entrance fees to the two museums.

For progress, information and events programme, see www.historial.org.

Entrance fee payable (+ new advantageous ticket covering several other museums). Closed: annually mid-Dec to end Jan. Open: Low season 0930-1500, closed Wed. High season: Every day 0930-1800. Tel: + (0) 3 22 83 1418. E-mail: info@historial.org

• *Péronne/RWC*

The town is well worth a closer look. It has been a fortified town since the Roman invasion and the massive ramparts were built in the ninth century (of which only the Brittany Gate now remains intact). Besieged and heavily damaged in 1870 in the Franco-Prussian War and invaded by the Germans in August 1914, it became to the Germans what Amiens was to the British – a centre of activity and leisure. Many dramatic German notices and posters appeared around the town, some preserved in the *Historial*. The most famous is that which was put up on the Town Hall on 18 March 1917 - '*Nicht ärgern, Nur wundern!*' ('Don't be angry, only wonder') left by the Germans as they retreated to the Hindenburg Line. The Warwicks retaliated with their own sign, affixed to a lamp-post, '1/8 Warwicks Entered Péronne at 7 a.m. 18/3/17'. The town was re-occupied by the Germans during the March Offensive of 1918 and retaken by the 2nd Australian Division on 2 September 1918. Their divisional flag is in the Town Hall, which every day at noon and at 1800 hours plays the *Poilu*'s favourite song, *Le Madelon* on its carillon and beside the Town Hall is the Roo de Kanga! The church of St Jean still bears marks of bullets and shells on its walls. Damaged again in 1940, the town bears two *Croix de Guerre* and the *Légion d'Honneur* in its coat of arms. It is twinned with Blackburn, which adopted it after

World War I and funded the rebuilding of a bridge over the Somme (qv). The town's War Memorial is unusual as it shows the figure of a belligerently gesticulating woman, Marie Fouré, 'Picardy cursing the War'.

(Alternatively Péronne and the Historial may be visited on Itinerary Four.)

2. A LONGER ROUTE with more to see. [Much of this Approach is covered in more detail in Holts' Western Front – North Guide.]

Follow the Basic Route from Calais to Exit 6.2 (note that this was previously 6.1!) on the A26. (56 miles).

New International WW1 Interpretative Centre, Souchez, Notre-Dame de Lorette & French Memorials/Museum RWC/OP/Cabaret Rouge CWGC Cemetery, Czech & Polish Memorials, La Targette–Museum, CWGC Cemetery & French National Cemetery, Neuville St Vaast–German Cemetery, Lichfield Crater CWGC Cemetery, Vimy Ridge Canadian National Memorial, trenches, tunnels and Memorials/WC

Take Exit 6.2, the junction with the A21. Immediately after the péage fork right from the A21 onto the D301 signed to Bruay la B., Aix Noulette. Take the first exit signed Aix Noulette, Béthune on the D937.

Continue through Aix Noulette, past the junction with the D51 to the **Auberge de Lorette** (uncategorised, 5 bedrooms. Tel: + (03)21 72 25 25) *on the right and stop on the left by the Memorial.*

The **Memorial is to the 158th Régiment d'Infanterie (GPS: 50.40882 2.73190),** erected by survivors of the Lorette sector. Before it is the tomb of **Sous Lieutenant Jean R. Léon**, age 22, 26 May 1915, of the **28th Régiment**, *Légion d'Honneur, Croix de Guerre.*

Walk up the track marked 'privé' to the left to the large memorial on the right.

The **Memorial (GPS: 50.40926 2.73376) is to Sous-Lieutenant Jacques Defrasse** age 23, 16 June 1915 of the **174th Régiment** and the men of the 3rd Company, killed in the assault on the *Tranchée des Saules* (which was roughly on the site of the track leading to the memorial). One side bears a message from the General commanding the Division praising Cadet Defrasse's courage in the assault on *La Tranchée de Calonne* on 3 May 1915. The other side bears a message from the Corps commander detailing Defrasse's promotion to Sous Lieutenant. He had only just put his rank stripes on his tunic (to be seen in the Museum at Notre-Dame de Lorette) when he was killed.

The Memorial is clearly visible to the right when driving past on the A21.

Return to your car and continue. On the left is the

Tomb of Sous-Lt J. R. Léon

Memorial to 158th Regt d'Inf

Memorial to Sous-Lt J. Defrasse

Lens Centre d'Interpretation de la Première Guerre Mondiale, Souchez (GPS: 50.40121 2.73889)

This new **WW1 Intrepetative Centre of the First World War**, (covering 1,200 square metres, of which 650 are dedicated to the stark anthracite building) was open to the public on 7 June 2015. The ambitious project cost €6.1million and was funded by the State, the French MOD, the Region and the *Département*. Designed by architect Pierre-Louis Faloci, it uses the latest modern technology - video, audio etc, some of which can be used via smart phones. It describes in chronological order the seven main stages of the conflict in the area. There is access to the personal stories and artefacts of the men commemorated on the International Circle of Death Memorial at N-D de Lorette (see below), an Exhibition space and boutique. Open: 1000-1800 in summer and 1000-1700 in winter. Closed Mon and 3 weeks in Jan. Admission Free. Audio-guide €3.00.

Tel: + (0)3 21 74 83 15/21 67 66 66. E-mail: info@tourisme-lenslieven.fr Website: tourisme-lenslieven.fr

Follow signs for parking and entrance. Beyond the Centre the Loos Double *Crassier* is clearly visible.

On the roadside past the Centre is
The *Art Deco* style white building (now repainted with new images) which was the old European Centre for Peace.

Turn right and drive up the hill to the Memorials.
Opposite is the **Estaminet A l'Potée de Léandre.** Regional dishes. Tel: + (0)3 21 45 16 40.

Turn right and drive up the hill to the Memorials.
This road to N-D de Lorette has been widened

Lens Interpretation Centre, Souchez

to include a walking route with interesting **Information Stations** en route as one ascends. On the left are panoramic views and on the right pillars with haunting images of *Poilus*.

Notre-Dame de Lorette Commemoration Area. GPS: 50.40012 2.71941

At the entrance to the area there is a fine statue to **General Maistre and 21st Army Corps,** erected in 1925.

This vast French National Cemetery, containing 40,057 burials of which 20,000 have individual graves and the rest are in eight ossuaries, is on the site of bitter and costly fighting by the French in 'the Battle of Lorette' from October 1914 to October 1915. It is dominated by an imposing Basilique (with vivid SGWs showing important highlights of the war) and 52m-high memorial lantern which contains a crypt in which are unknown soldiers and déportés from the wars in 1939-45, Indochina (1945-54) and North Africa (1952-62). An extraordinary personality was commemorated here in September 1994 – Louise de Bettignies - who worked for both the French and British Intelligence Services, and was imprisoned by the Germans, dying in Cologne on 27 September

Haunting Poilu faces, en route to Notre-Dame de Lorette.

1918. See http://www.cheminsdememoire.gouv.fr/en/louise-de-bettignies

The 200 steps of the lantern may be climbed for a superb view over the battlefield and its rotating light can be seen for more than 40 miles around.

Between the two edifices is an eternal flame. This is rekindled and the *Tricolore* is raised each Sunday morning after the 1030 Mass in the Basilica. There are sixty-four Russians, one Belgian and one Rumanian graves. The first grave on the left as you enter the cemetery is that of **General Barbot of 77th (French) Div**, whose impressive divisional Memorial is in Souchez village. He was killed here on 10 May 1915. The whole area is manned by volunteers from the dedicated *Gardes d'Honneur de Lorette*, from 0900-1630 in March, until 1730 in April and May, until 1830 in June-August and then until 1630 again until 11 November.

To the left of the entrance to the Cemetery is an **Orientation Table** erected in May 1976 by *Le Train de Loos*. It points to Vimy Ridge and to the ruined church of Ablain St-Nazaire (qv), preserved as a memorial in the valley below.

International 'Circle of Death'. This ambitious and important **International Monument** was inaugurated at 1100 on 11 November 2014 by French President François Hollande, German Chancellor Angela Merkel and British Prime Minister David Cameron. It comprises a vast circular wall (thought to be the largest ever constructed), designed by

Lantern Tower, Notre-Dame de Lorette

Parisian architect Philippe Prost, which carries the names, in alphabetical order, of some **580,000 soldiers** (294,000 British Empire; 174,000 German, 106,000 French; 2,300 Belgian plus Czechoslovakian, Polish, Portuguese, Rumanian and Russian) killed in French Flanders and Artois – Allies and Enemies together. It is sobering to **look for your own name** – there are three complete panels for Smith alone for instance. The impressive wall is seen as a symbol of fraternity and an expression of peace. The monumental task of assembling the names was straightforward for the British & Commonwealth names, using the meticulous CWGC records, but the German names were more difficult to discover as many of their records were destroyed in WW2. Amongst the French names are the North African Colonial Forces.

The Circle is permanently illuminated at night using solar panels. Its horizontal form of the wall contrasts and balances with the perpendicular of the lantern tower and the circular shape creates a space between heaven and earth, a technical work of art in durable, weather resistant fibre-reinforced concrete. The budget for the project was €6.5million.

Entrance free. ***Opening times*** vary according to season, on average from 0900-1730 summer and 0830-1615 winter.

International Circle of Death.
Look for your own name

On the far side of the Cemetery from where you are parked (you can drive round to it if you wish) is the excellent **Museum,** now known as *Le Musée Vivant* [**Living Museum**] **(GPS: 50.40159 2.71581)**. The Museum is constantly being improved, both with its growing number of fascinating exhibits and its appearance. The owner, M. David Bardiaux (who also owns the Museum at La Targette, visited later) acquired many of the artefacts from the old demolished Artisan Museum and has placed the original stone *bas relief* frieze on a wall leading to the entrance. On the ground below it is a rose garden in season and a concrete ramp for wheel chair access leads to the entrance. The building beyond, which houses the old Museum's Diorama and stereoscopic pictures, has a room where students may take their picnics.

The Museum recreates the daily life of the soldier on the Artois front, containing many interesting and realistic dioramas with sound effects in French, English and German, and collections of artefacts retrieved from the original battlefields or donated by families of veterans. They include the tunic of Jacques Defrasse (qv), which should not be missed. Another interesting item is a German 420 calibre 'Big Bertha' shell.

Behind the Museum is an extensive recreated battlefield area with trenches, shell holes, barbed wire and many items of artillery.

Open every day (except 12 Dec - 2 Jan): 0900-2000. Tel: + (0)3 21 45 15 80. Entrance fee payable.

Beside it is the now smart Bar/Restaurant/**Salon de Thé, L'Estaminet de Lorette**, Tel: (0)3 21 45 29 07. It sells regional products and home-made patisseries. **Open** every day 0930-1830. Closed Dec/Jan/Feb.

When all other eating options in the area are shut this pleasant restaurant can usually be relied upon. It serves hot food until well after 1400 hours and then snacks and pastries.

In front of the Museum is a Memorial to **Sous Lieutenant Henri Merlin**, age 24, **10th Chasseurs à Pied**, 3 March 1915. His citation by the General commanding the 10th Army describes how he fought until his position was overrun by the enemy, made sure that his surviving comrades escaped and then committed suicide rather than retreat.

Return down the hill.

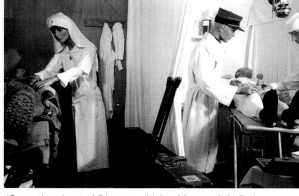
'Operating theatre' Diorama, 'Living Museum', N-D de Lorette.

The tip of the Vimy Memorial may be seen ahead to the right, and the Loos battlefield to the left.

Turn right to Souchez.

On leaving the village is a fine bronze statue and **Memorial to General Barbot (qv) and the 77th Division with Plaques to General Stirn**, 1871-1915 and **General Plessner**, 1856-1914. **GPS: 50.38628 2.74438**

The nearby imposing N. African Campaign (1952-64) Memorial was raised in 2002 by the survivors to their fallen comrades. It consists of large white archways joined by a pathway in which there is an eternal flame, flagpoles and a sunken pool. The names of the dead are inscribed in white on a black Memorial wall reminiscent of the Vietnam Memorial in Washington DC.

Here around Souchez, particularly in the area of the local cemetery, was some of the fiercest fighting during the 1914/15 Artois battles. The Germans had fortified all the houses and built a number of strong points – the cemetery, the Cabaret Rouge – and armed them with machine guns. The heights of Notre-Dame de Lorette (visible on a good day behind the General's statue) seemed to dominate the French positions at the end of 1914, much as Monte Cassino seemed to dominate the way to Rome in 1944. During the second Artois battle from May 1915 the intensity of the struggle to clear 'the bloody hill' of Lorette, the village of Souchez and to gain Vimy Ridge, reached depths of horror and destruction only paralleled at Verdun. Even with Lorette under control Souchez stood in the way of a secure assault upon Vimy and it was not until 26 September 1915 that the village was finally re-taken. It had been in German hands for a whole year. On 23 September 1920 the village was awarded the Croix de Guerre.

Continue.

Memorial to Gen Barbot and others, 77th Division, Souchez.

[N.B.] Some 100m beyond the sign for Cabaret Rouge CWGC Cemetery is a small Plaque (erected in 2002 by the Arras Souvenir Français) on the left marking the exact site of the famous **Cabaret Rouge (GPS: 50.38267 2.74302)**, a small estaminet, named from the red bricks from which it was constructed.

Plaque on the site of Cabaret Rouge.

Continue to the cemetery on the right.
Cabaret Rouge CWGC Cemetery (GPS: 50.38069 2.74158) was started by the British 47th Division in March 1916 and used by fighting units including the Canadian Corps until September 1918. To the east were dugouts used as Battalion HQ in 1916 and communication trenches ended here. This large Cemetery (with nearly 8,000 burials) was enlarged by concentration of graves from the nearby battlefields after the Armistice. It was from here that the **Canadian Unknown Soldier** was taken on 25 May 2000 from Grave 7, Row E, Plot 8 (and which now bears a headstone explaining the ceremony) and removed to the Tomb of the Unknown Warrior at the foot of the National War Memorial

Entrance to Cabaret Rouge CWGC Cemetery

Former grave of the Canadian Unknown Soldier, Cabaret Rouge CWGC Cemetery.

in Ottawa, Canada. To the right under the imposing entrance arch is a Plaque to the designer of the cemetery, **Brigadier Sir Frank Higgins**, CB, CMG, ARIBA, who was Secretary to the IWGC 1947-1956. His ashes were scattered here after his death on 20 November 1958 (as were his wife's in 1962).

Continue towards Neuville St Vaast.

On the right is the **Czech Memorial and Cemetery (GPS: 50.36589 2.74474)**. The Czechs joined the French Foreign Legion in Paris in 1914 and fought with the Moroccans in the May 1915 Artois Offensive as part of the French 10th Army. The Memorial refers to the attack of 9 May 1915 on the German strongpoint at Hill 140 in Thélus. The hill was taken but the Czechs had 80% casualties. The Memorial was erected in 1925 and behind it are graves from WW2 (including a Captain Aviator, complete with photograph, from 1940).

Across the road is the

Polish Memorial. The Poles were also part of the Foreign Legion and took part in the same attack on Hill 140. The Memorial was inaugurated on 9 May 1935, twenty years after the battle.

Continue to the crossroads in the centre of la Targette village. On the left is

La Targette Torch in Hand & Other Memorials (GPS: 50.35474 2.74827).

The Memorial was completed on 20 October 1932 and commemorates the rebirth of the village, totally destroyed in May 1916. It is reminiscent of the concept explored in John McCrae's famous poem *In Flanders Fields* – 'To you we throw the torch – Be yours to hold

Above: Torch in hand Memorial, la Targette

Above: Polish Memorial, Neuville St Vaast

Right: Czech Memorial and Cemetery, Neuville St Vaast

it high'. Beside it are **Memorials to Lt Millevoye & Sous-Lt Mouette d'Andrezel.**

On the opposite corner is the private **La Targette Museum**, owned by David Bardiaux (who also owns the Notre-Dame de Lorette Museum). It contains a superb collection of uniforms, Allied and German gas masks, weapons and artefacts and has several well-presented scenes of trench, aid post and dugout life.

Open every day 0900-2000 (except Xmas & New Year). Tel: + (0)3 21 59 17 76. Entrance fee payable.

Continue on the D937, La Targette CWGC Cemetery will be signed just a few metres off the road to the right.

[At the junction with the D55 and the D937 is the **Relais St Vaast**. Tel: + (0)3 21 58 58 58. Open Mon-Fri lunch time and Fri & Sat evenings. Annual Holiday mid-Aug. Specialities Pizza and Grills.]

Turn right to the cemetery on the right.

La Targette CWGC Cemetery (GPS: 50.35056   2.74881), described in the Register as "known until recently" as Aux Rietz Military Cemetery, was begun at the end of April 1917 and used by Field Ambulances and fighting units until September 1918. One third of the burials are of Artillery Units. They also include 295 Canadians, 3 Indians and 3 South Africans. There is one WW2 burial. Adjoining it is

La Targette French National Cemetery. The perfectly symmetrical pattern of lines of white crosses, which changes from each angle, stretches up the slope to three ossuaries.

La Targette CWGC and French Cemeteries.

Built in 1919 it is formed exclusively from concentrations from the surrounding battlefield and other small cemeteries. It contains 11,443 burials (including 3,882 unknown) from WW1 and 593 French, 170 Belgian and 4 Poles from WW2.

Return to the D937 and turn right. Continue to the sign to the German Cemetery on the left.

Neuville St Vaast (Maison Blanche) German Cemetery/WC/GPS: 50.34334 2.75216

This is on the site of the heavily defended German position known as 'The Labyrinth', graphically described by French writer Henri Barbusse and English writer Henry Williamson. It contains 37,000 burials with 8,000 in a mass grave. In the centre is a stone monument erected by the old comrades of the **4th Hannover Inf Regt, No 164** with the inscriptions *Ich hatt einen Kameraden Ein Bessern findst du nicht* (I have a comrade whose better you could not find) and *Sei getreu bis in den Tod* (Stay true, even unto death). There are WCs to the left of the entrance and **Information Boards** in three languages which describe the renovation of 1975-1983 by the *Deutsche Kriegsgräbefirsorge* when it was reopened again to the public.

Opposite is a farm known as La Maison Blanche, the original of which gave its name to this sector.

Memorial to German 164th Regt, Neuville St Vaast German Cemetery

Beneath it is an amazing network of tunnels and chambers known as the **Maison Blanche Souterraine**. Originally a chalk quarry, it was probably used as a refuge in the 19th Century (some graffiti would appear to be c1861) and later as a storage facility for the farmer. Although technically part of the vast 'Labyrinth' system, there is no evidence that it was used by the French or the Germans in the heavy fighting of 1915. It was however certainly used by the Canadian Corps as an underground barracks behind the reserve line in their preparations for the assault on Vimy Ridge of April 1917. (It was later again used as a shelter for Belgian Refugees in May 1940. After WW2 the *souterraine* was used as a dump by the current farmer and rubbish filled the *puit*, almost blocking the entrance.)

The Canadians refer to the 'Maison Blanche Caves' in the *History of the 15th Bn, CEF (48th Highlanders of Canada)* and now they form part of the Canadian *Souterrain Impressions Project*. It started in 2009 when Zenon Andrusyszyn, Canadian founder of CANADIGM saw a TV programme about the Caves and the Canadian carvings in it. They are of an exceptional quality and skill (notably those executed by Pte A.J. Ambler who is understood to have been a stone carver before he enlisted).

The Project aims to preserve these carvings by documenting, scanning and duplicating them and exhibiting them in travelling exhibitions throughout Canada to commemorate the Centenary of the Battle of Vimy Ridge in 2017. They will then be permanently exhibited in a Canadian museum.

The entrance to the Caves had been rediscovered by a French archaeologist, Dominique Faivre, in 2001. In 2006 Judy Ruzylo, a film researcher, negotiated access to the Caves to film them and at this stage the respected and experienced Durand Group became involved. They formed an agreement with the proprietor to protect access* to the Caves and were permitted to undertake extensive archaeological researches, clearing out the garbage, improving the safety underground, installing lighting etc and mapping the extent of the *souterraine*. They assisted the Canadians in laser scanning the carvings in 3D. A YAP film, *'Vimy Underground'* was duly made in which Ambler's son, Alex, and other family members were shown Pte Ambler's extraordinary work. (Alex died the following year, age 93).

NOTE. The entrance to the Caves is on private land and may not be visited under any circumstances by individuals who are not part of an authorised group. DO NOT ATTEMPT TO FIND THE ENTRANCE! The only way to see these remarkable Caves is by joining an official tour organised by the Durand Group (Contact : Lt-Col Phillip Robinson (pgrobinson@telco4u.net), sometimes in conjunction with other experienced underground archaeologists, such as Andy Robertshaw (andy@dtsmail.net)

The wonderful work achieved by the Durand Group in the area over many years is detailed in the book Phillip wrote with Nigel Cave, *The Underground War. Vimy Ridge to Arras*, Pub Pen & Sword 2011.

Return to La Targette crossroads. From La Targette crossroads take the turning to the right signed to the Canadian Memorial. Continue through Neuville St Vaast to the sign (easily missed) to the right to Lichfield Crater. Turn.

15TH Bn Can 48th Highlanders carving, Maison Blanche Souterrain

Lichfield Crater CWGC Cemetery.

Lichfield Crater CWGC Cemetery (GPS: 50.36020 2.77731) is one of the most unusual on the Western Front. It is in one of two mine craters (the other being Zivy crater) used by the Canadian Corps Burial Officer in 1917 for bodies from the Vimy battlefield who all died on 9 or 10 April 1917. It was designed by W. H. Cowlishaw and was originally called only by letters and numbers – CB 2A. The grassed circular cemetery is essentially a mass grave and contains only one headstone (to **Pte Albert Stubbs,** S Lancs Regiment, age 25, 30 April 1916) found after the Armistice. It is surrounded by beautiful stone and flint walls and the Cross of Sacrifice is on a raised level. Below it is a Memorial wall on which are the names and details of 41 Canadians soldiers who are buried here. There are also 11 unidentified Canadians, 4 completely unidentified men and 1 unidentified Russian.

> *Return to the main road, turn right and continue to the well-signed entrance to the Vimy Ridge Canadian Memorial Park.*

NOTE. you are now travelling in the direction of the well-planned and successful Canadian attack on Vimy Ridge, strongly fortified and held by the Germans for the first three years of the war, despite several brave and costly attempts by the French to take it. Following a well-timed artillery barrage the attack went in at daybreak on 9 April 1917 with all four divisions of the Canadian Corps fighting together for the first time under General Byng. By mid-afternoon they had taken the entire 14km long ridge except for Hill 145 (the highest point upon which the Memorial now stands) which they captured three days later. The price was 10,602 casualties, 3,598 of whom were killed.

• *Vimy Ridge Canadian National Memorial & Park/WC*

On 25 April 1915 allied landings were made in Gallipoli. The ANZAC forces landed in the wrong place and were caught and held by the Turkish defenders on a narrow beach below high cliffs where, in essence, they were to remain until withdrawn nine months later. The extraordinary courage and resolution of the ANZAC soldiers, depicted mostly in the writings of C.E.W. Bean, the official Australian historian, led to the Gallipoli campaign becoming a focal point in the developing character of that young nation. Here too, at Vimy, was a 'National Army' fighting its first battle, the Canadian. In a way the fighting for, and the capture of, Vimy Ridge, might be seen as Canada's Gallipoli. Their achievement was remarkable and their pride in what they achieved thoroughly deserved. The importance of Vimy to the self-awareness of Canada is evident in that it is at the highest point of the Ridge that they have placed their most important Memorial, which is visited later.

In 2001 a massive programme of restoration of all Canada's Memorials in Belgium and France began. At $(Can)20 million, Vimy is by far the most important project – 20% of the original stone needed replacing, name panels needed re-engraving, the drainage system needed renewing. Work (which included the renovation of trenches and tunnels) was completed for the official opening date of 9 April 2007, the 90th Anniversary of the Battle. The pristine Memorial was re-inaugurated in an impressive ceremony by HM Queen Elizabeth in the presence of the Canadian and French Prime Ministers, an estimated 5,000 Canadian students, Canadian war veterans and serving soldiers.

As part of the commemorations on 9 April 2007 **Pte Herbert Peterson** of the 49th Bn, Can Inf was reburied with full military honours in nearby La Chaudière CWGC Cemetery. Peterson, who was commemorated on the Vimy Memorial, was killed on 9 April 1917 but his body was lost and then rediscovered, with another body, in 2003 at a construction site some 2 kms from Vimy Ridge. Scraps of uniform, a cap badge and other debris were found with the remains and there followed three years intensive historical, forensic and archaeological research which finally resulted in the identification by means of DNA matching. Members of Peterson's family were present at the moving funeral ceremony. During the extensive work the Welcome Centre was moved to the area near the tunnels/craters/trenches, which is where the visit begins.

Drive through the Park to

The Vimy Welcome Centre (GPS: 50.37197   2.76973) has informative panels and photographs, some trench periscopes, a circular audio-visual presentation of the battlefield in English, French and German and a small book stall. Here enthusiastic and well-informed bi-lingual Canadian student guides are based. There is fierce competition in Canada amongst young people who wish to be guides, most of whom are either students or graduates. Each year a new cadre is selected and shared with the Memorial Park at Beaumont Hamel on the Somme. In 2013 the Canadian Government allocated $5 million towards the construction of a permanent Visitor Centre to replace this temporary building. Construction will be completed in time to mark the 100th anniversary in April 2017. The Vimy Foundation, a charity founded in 2005 to promote Canada's war legacy, will also conduct a fundraising campaign to complete the project.

Open every day (except two weeks around Christmas) 1000-1800 May-Oct, 0900-1700 Nov-April. Guided tours available May-November. Tel: + (0)3 21 50 68 68. E-mail: vimy.memorial@vac-acc.gc.ca Website: www.virtualmemorial.gc.ca. There are WCs next to the Centre.

In front of the Centre is **the Lions Club International Memorial.**

The underground tour (which must be booked through the Centre – well in advance for groups) goes through part of the Grange Crater tunnel system but for security reasons only in groups accompanied by guides, for which there is no charge. A trip into the tunnel, which begins near the Canadian flag, generally lasts about 25 minutes and should not be taken by anyone who is at all claustrophobic. It is cold underground and often wet and slippery.

Beyond the tunnel, clearly signed, are the preserved trench lines formed with concrete sandbags. Work on preserving this area began in the late 1920s and was still going on in 1936 when the Vimy Memorial was unveiled. The first trenches are the Canadian line, and sniper posts, firesteps and duckboards are plain to see. Just over the top of the Canadian parapet is one of the features that makes Vimy so extraordinary – a huge mine crater.

When the British took over this 'quiet sector' from the French, (after the Artois battles of 1914/15 both sides settled for a mutually uncomfortable existence devoid of set-piece attacks) peace gave way to conflict. Fighting patrols were sent out to take enemy prisoners, raids were launched, 'nuisance' bombardments began and underground too the warfare intensified. Tunnel after tunnel was driven under the enemy trenches, packed with explosives and fired, producing huge craters. The crater immediately beyond the Canadian line is 'Grange' The effectiveness of the mine warfare is evident in a report from the German 163rd Regiment. 'The continual mine explosions in the end got on the nerves of the men. One stood in the front line defenceless and powerless against these fearful mine explosions.'

Both sides attempted to sabotage each other's mining by burrowing under the other's galleries and blowing them up. Miners had to stop and listen at regular intervals for the sound of enemy digging and then make fine judgements

The Grange Tunnel, Vimy

about just where the other's tunnel was and what he was about to do. The tension must have been heart-stopping. Dark cramped conditions, foul air to breathe, hot and probably wet too, trapped mole-like underground – it needed special qualities just to remain sane. Tunnels were frequently dug at different levels. Near Souchez mining went on at 110 ft and 60 ft down, and some tunnels were over 1,000 yards long. One, called 'Goodman', was more than 1,800 yards. Grange was a sophisticated tunnel 800 yards long with side-bays for headquarters, signal offices, water points, etc. and standing room. It was meant for the movement of troops. Six miles or more of such tunnels were dug before the battle. Tunnels to be used solely as a means of reaching the enemy lines in order to place explosives under them were frequently crawling-size only. There is yet another surprise in store for the visitor because just across the crater, on the opposite lip, are the German trenches.

It was a remarkable feat for the Canadians to do so well here. The whole attack had been rehearsed day after day at unit level on a full-scale replica behind the front. Short, reachable objectives were marked on maps as lines – black, red, blue and brown - attacking formations only moving on or through as each line was established. The Canadians went in ten battalions abreast, fighting, for the first time as a national contingent, and working steadily forward from objective to objective. Left to right in line the Divisions were: 4th, 3rd, 2nd and 1st. The Canadian 2nd Division was strengthened by the attachment of 13 Brigade from the British 5th (Imperial) Division the remainder of that Division being left in reserve.

The 0530 hours pre-assault bombardment, which had been started by the firing of a big gun from behind Mont St Eloi, was of such intensity that it was impossible to distinguish the sound of individual explosions. Those present felt that if they could reach up into the air they would touch a wall of sound. The plan was that the guns would lift at intervals and the infantry would then walk forward as if behind a curtain of steel. Gus Sivertz, serving with the 2nd Canadian Mounted Rifles, later recalled, 'We didn't dare lift our heads, knowing that the barrage was to come flat over us and then lift in three minutes. I don't think anyone was scared... instead one's whole body seemed to be in a mad macabre dance. It was perhaps the most perfect barrage of the war, as it was so perfectly synchronised. Then suddenly it jumped a hundred yards and we were away,' (*Vimy Ridge* – Alexander McKee). Flying over the assault was **Major Billy Bishop VC** (the Canadian aviator who became an Hon Air Marshal of the RCAF after the war) who wrote,

> 'The waves of attacking infantry as they came out of their trenches and trudged forward behind the curtain of shells laid down by the artillery were an amazing sight. These troops had been drilled to move forward at a given pace and from this timing the "Creeping" or rolling barrage which moved in front of them had been mathematically worked out', (*Winged Warfare*).

In fact the timing for the infantry was that they should move 100 yards in three minutes. If they were to go too fast then they would run into their own artillery fire, if they were too slow then the barrage would get too far ahead of them and they would lose its protection.

The timing of the Canadian attack went even further. The four Canadian divisions had 35 minutes to reach the Black Line, then 40 minutes there to re-organise, then 20 minutes to get to the Red Line. There the attack was to narrow to a two division front and, after two and a half hours there, reserve brigades of the 1st and 2nd Divisions were to push on to the Blue Line, re-organise there for 96 minutes and then carry on just beyond the crest of the ridge to the Brown Line which in theory would be at 1318 hours. It was an extraordinary plan. A common military maxim is that 'No plan survives contact with the enemy' and the more complicated a plan the more likely it is to go wrong. There are many examples of too complicated plans going wrong particularly when they involve precise timings. A prime instance took place 27 years later on 6 June 1944 at OMAHA beach when American General Huebner's precise instructions did not survive contact with events. However, it worked for the Canadians in 1917 and they deserved it to do so but they had to have an added factor – luck. Perhaps one does make one's own luck and, as President Lincoln apparently said, 'Give me lucky generals'.

The Grange position was defended by companies of the German 261st Reserve Regiment of the 79th Reserve Division. When the fighting was over the 261st Regiment had lost 86 killed, 199 wounded and 451 missing – a total of 736 men. The Canadian assault here was made by 7th Brigade of the 3rd Division and alongside, to the north, 111th Brigade of the 4th Division. One of the Canadians waiting in the Grange tunnel at 0530 hours described the sound of the opening barrage as 'like water on a tin roof in a heavy thunderstorm'. Around the Grange crater area there are many other craters with names like Durand, Duffield, Patricia, Birkin and Commons, as well as paths leading off into the woods.

It was long believed that each of the trees in the park represented one of the 66,655 Canadian soldiers (their dead for the entire war) listed on the Memorial and that they came from Canada. In fact they are Austrian firs, three containers of whose seeds arrived by train after the war as part of Germany's reparations price. Beneath the trees, shell-holes, craters and lines of trenches in the Park are a series of German and allied tunnels which were packed with mines and then exploded. The 100-hectare Park is full of unexploded and highly volatile materiel and most areas are out of bounds. There is a constant threat of erosion to this historic site, presenting great problems of preservation to the Canadian Ministry of Veterans Affairs which administers it. Much dangerous work has been undertaken by the **Durand Group** (qv) to render known unexploded mines harmless to the thousands of visitors who walk and drive over them each year.

Sadly one of the group's founders, **Lt Col Mike Watkins**, was killed in 1998 when one of the tunnels they were excavating collapsed. There is a **Memorial Plaque** to him at the entrance to the Grange subway.

Drive out of the car park area and turn right signed to the Memorial. En route you will pass signs to the following:

Canadian Cemetery No 2, Givenchy Road Canadian Cemetery and Givenchy-en-Gohelle Canadian Cemetery. Map 14/16

Continue to the main car park. It is opposite the **Moroccan Memorial (GPS: 50.37919 2.76990)** see below.

Canadian National Memorial/WC

Here are Canadian Guides ready to assist you – and occasionally buggies are available for the disabled. There is a toilet block on the right before you go up the main path.

As you walk towards the Memorial you are looking at the rear of the monument. When the Canadians decided to erect a national Memorial here to replace the divisional Memorials placed after the battle, they invited competitive designs and 160 were submitted. The winner, who said that the design came to him in a dream, was a Toronto sculptor, Walter Seymour Allward (who also designed the Superintendent's house opposite). The two tall pylons symbolize Canada and France and between them at the front, carved from a single 30-ton block of stone, is a figure of Canada mourning for her dead. She overlooks the Douai Plain and the Loos Battlefield.

Below the figure is a sarcophagus carrying a helmet and laurels and a Latin inscription commemorating the 60,000 Canadians who died during the Great War. On the wall of the Memorial are the names of 11,285 Canadian soldiers who were killed in France and who have no known grave. The 90 ft high Memorial stands on Point 145, the highest point of Vimy Ridge. The base was formed from 12,000 tons of concrete and masonry and 6,000 tons of Dalmatian stone was used for the pylons and the figures, of which there are twenty, all 12 ft high. Construction began in 1925 and Allward's aim was, he said, to produce 'a structure which would endure, in an exposed position, for a thousand years – indeed, for all time'.

When the Memorial was unveiled on 26 July 1936 (it took four years longer to build than at first estimated) it was in the presence of King Edward VIII, his only overseas official engagement as King. Also present was M. Victor Maistriau, the Burgomaster of Mons, which had been liberated by the Canadian Corps on 11 November 1918. He carried with him the personal flag of Lt General Sir Arthur Currie who had commanded the Corps. The General presented his flag to the town of Mons and it is now in the Museum there. The area between where you are and the Memorial was estimated to have been filled with 100,000 pilgrims, of whom 8,000 had come from Canada. These had left Canada on 16 July 1936 in five of Canadian Pacific's steamers, sailed to Antwerp, stayed overnight in Armentières and then on to the unveiling ceremony on Sunday 26 July. The pilgrimage, which was organised by the Canadian Legion, continued to London where ceremonies were held at the Cenotaph attended by British Prime Minister Stanley Baldwin.

Return to the car park. Opposite is

The **Moroccan Division Memorial**, commemorating the Division's achievements during the second battle of Artois on 9 May 1915. Bronze panels around the stone monument list the ORBAT of the Division (motto *Sans peur, sans pitié* – without fear, without mercy)

Twin pylons, Vimy Memorial

Memorial to Canadian Artillery, Thélus

Moroccan Memorial, Vimy National Park

Canada mourning for her dead,
Vimy Memorial

and also recognise the contribution of other foreign forces, including the Jews, Greeks, Sudanese and Czechs.

Return past the Canadian Cemetery No 2 signs etc and turn left following signs to Vimy for 1.2 miles to a small track to the left which may – or may not – be signed to the Canadian 3rd Division Memorial. Park.

[N.B.] By following some 200m up the track the concrete cross of the **3rd 'Canadian' Division Memorial, GPS: 50.36887 2.78417** is reached. It was erected to the men of the Division who fell in the defence of the line from 23 October 1916-15 February 1917 and the attack on Vimy Ridge of 9 April 1917. It is on the centre line of the Divisional attack (which came from the area of the Welcome Centre, aiming in the direction of Thélus (next stop). In the centre of the 1,500 yards wide line was the 2nd Canadian Mounted Regiment who were searching for the German position at la Folie Farm, which was some 150 metres due east of the Memorial. The Divisional Commander, Maj-Gen Lipsett, had commanded a Battalion during the gas attacks near Ypres in April 1915. The Division would go on to liberate Mons on 11 November 1918.

Memorial to 3rd (Canadian) Division, Vimy Ridge

Continue through the battle-scarred woods of the Park and at the T junction turn right signed Arras/A26 on the N17.

Pass the **Canadian Artillery Memorial, GPS: 50.35616 2.78983** (unveiled by General Byng on 9 April 1918) on the left at Thélus crossroads. This was one of the few Memorials to be inaugurated during the War.

Drive under the motorway and rejoin the A26/E15 direction Reims/Paris and continue with the main itinerary, being careful to take the A1/E15 Paris/Amiens fork to the right when the motorway splits.

THE CENTRAL APPROACH (SEE MAP PAGE 29)

It may be considered useful to start one's tour of the Somme battlefield by visiting the *Historial* at Péronne (planned to be 'The Gateway to the Somme Battlefields') as in The Eastern Approach above. However, this involves a considerable detour from the area considered to be of greatest British interest, which centres around the town of Albert, and a direct route to that town is therefore proposed for those with limited time.

The Quickest Basic Route from Calais Ferry Port/Eurotunnel to Albert

Approximate driving time, without stops: 1 hour 45 minutes. Approximate distance: 100 miles.

Follow the instructions for The Eastern Approach to Exit 14 on the A1.

*From the A1 at approximately 86 miles take Exit 14 signed Bapaume. In the town follow signs to Albert on the ring road and then take the D929 which leads directly to **Albert**.*

THE WESTERN APPROACHES

1. The Quickest Basic Route from Calais Ferry Port/Eurotunnel to Amiens if you are making your base or starting point from that end of the battlefield.

From Calais Ferry Port take the A16/A26 signed Paris/Reims. After 4 miles fork right signed Boulogne on the A16.

From Eurotunnel (Exit 42) join the A16 and deduct 8 miles from the total mileage.

Continue on the A16 round Abbeville to Amiens.

Approximate driving time: 1 hours 30 minutes. Approximate distance: 113 miles

2. A Longer Route with more to see

If you can set aside a day and wish to make the Approach an interesting and pleasurable experience, with frequent stops along the way, the route to **Amiens is via Wimereux, Boulogne, Etaples, Montreuil, Hesdin, Doullens, Louvencourt, Warloy Baillon, Querrieu to Amiens, with an alternative route via Bus les Artois, the Château of Val Vion, Vert Galand and Bertangles.**

SET YOUR MILEOMETER TO ZERO.

***From Calais Ferry Port** take the A16/A26 signed Paris/Reims. After 4 miles fork right, signed Boulogne on the A16.*

***From Eurotunnel** (Exit 42) join the A16 and deduct 8 miles from the total mileage. Continue on the A16.*

At Exit 43 on the A16 (7.2 miles) is the good shopping facility at Cité Europe.

At Exit 38 (13.7 miles) the *Cimetière Canadien* is signed.

At 22.6 miles take Exit 33 then the D242 signed Wimereux-Nord. Continue over the first roundabout and over the railway to the large, ornately landscaped roundabout, with a 'Mermaid'. Take the D242 exit signed Cimetière Sud, take the first turning left and follow those signs to the entrance on the left at the bottom of the hill.

The CWGC plot is a walled enclosure within the main cemetery wall.

Open: 1 Nov-31 March 0800-1700, 1 April-31 Oct 0800-1900.

• *Grave of Lt Col John McCrae, CWGC Communal Cemetery, Wimereux (24.8 miles, GPS: 50.77394 1.61333)*

To the left of the CWGC cemetery entrance is a Plaque bearing some biographical details about **McCrae**, erected by the Ontario Heritage Foundation and Ministry of Culture & Recreation. Below it has been added a blue **Plaque to RBL Standard Bearer John Munn**, who during many years perpetuated the memory of Col McCrae on 11 November. Standing with one's back to the Plaques the Napoleon column (see below) is visible at 11 o' clock. Some lines from McCrae's famous poem, *In Flanders Fields*, are inscribed on the Memorial Seat set in the internal wall to the right of the cemetery. The headstone (near the Cross of Sacrifice) of this compassionate Canadian Medical Officer is laid flat, as are all of the headstones in this Cemetery, designed by Charles Holden. **Lt Col John McCrae** died on 28 January 1918, at No 14 General Hospital of complications to pneumonia and was buried here with full military honours. His appointment as Consulting Physician to the First British Army had just been announced. There is a shelter with Visitor Book and Cemetery Report at the bottom of

Plaques to Lt Col John McCrae & John Munn, Wimereux Comm CWGC Plot

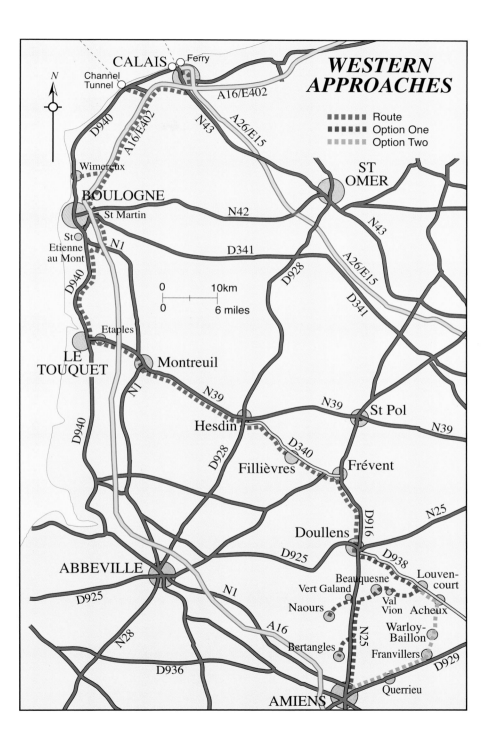

Grave of Lt Col John McCrae, Wimereux CWGC Cemetery

the plot, which being attached to a hospital, segregates the burials by rank, including QA Nurses.

The row of burials above the CWGC plot contains some interesting **British Private Memorials**, e.g to **Winifred Constance Lockwood**, wife of Cdr E.M. Lockwood RNVR, Hawke Bn RND; '**Constance Eugenie 'Barry', husband and infant Hugh** 25 April 1915'; **Capt Cameron Lamb, DSO**, 2nd Border Regt, 29 Dec 1914, youngest son of Sir John Cameron Lamb; **Samuel Pickard, IWGC 2** Nov 1920.

Continue to the bottom of the road and turn right uphill, picking up signs on the D242 back to the 'Mermaid Roundabout' and thence to the A16. Rejoin it and continue directions to Boulogne.

At Exit 32 the imposing **Colonne de la Grande Armée** may be seen on the right. Surmounted by a figure of **Napoleon**, whose back is pointedly turned towards Britain, it commemorates the Assembly of Napoleon's Army as it prepared to invade Britain in 1804 and the first issue of the *Légion d'Honneur* on 19 May 1802. It was financed by subscription of Napoleon's soldiers to honour their Commander. (One of the authors remembers 'subscribing' to a memorial. The Commanding Officer announced that his officers would donate a day's pay but that it was entirely voluntary. Anyone not wishing to donate had to put his name on the mess notice board.)

Continue on the A16 to Exit 31, 33.6 miles.

[N.B.] At this point a visit could be made to **Boulogne Eastern CWGC Cemetery (GPS: 50.72480 1.62172)**, by taking Exit 31, continuing on the D341 signed to Boulogne Centre and turning left and left again following green CWGC signs on Rue de Dringhien to the entrance on the right through a lovely stone shelter. Here is buried the poet **Capt the Hon Julian Grenfell, DSO**, famous for his poem Into Battle, written in April 1915 near Ypres. He was then wounded on 12 May, sent to the base hospital here at Boulogne where he was nursed by his sister, Monica, and died of his wounds on 26 May 1915 (Plot 2, Row A, 15). Also buried here is **L/Cpl Jesse R Short** (Plot 8, Row 1, 43), shot for his role as ringleader in the Etaples Mutiny (see below). Short's headstone bears the ironic personal inscription, 'Duty called and he went forward. Ever remembered by his wife and children.' His death certificate gives as the Cause of Death 'Shot by Sentence'.

Grave of poet Julian Grenfell, Boulogne Eastern CWGC Cemetery

---

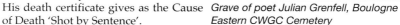

Continue to Exit 29 and take the N1 signed Abbeville/Boulogne Centre. Keep following Abbeville par RN [Route Nationale] on the D901. At the T junction with a château to the

*left, bear right on the D901 and keep to the right following signs to St Etienne au Mont/
le Touquet on the D940. Continue through Pont de Briques and on leaving St Etienne
au Mont stop by a striking pagoda which can be seen in a cemetery on the hillside to the
right.*

• Chinese Memorial in the St Etienne au Mont Communal Cemetery (39.2 miles, GPS: 50.66938 1.63523)

The Memorial is at the top of the Cemetery, through the French local burials and
surrounded by Chinese graves. It was erected by their comrades in December 1919 in
memory of the Chinese labourers who died on service during World War I and are
buried in this cemetery, which is on the site of No 2 Labour Gen Hospital. The 168 WW1
graves are from 1917 to 1919. In this fascinating cemetery there are also three graves of
the SA Native Labour Corps from September/October 1917 and three Chinese sailors
from **HMT *Montilla*** (launched in February 1917, later renamed *Gaelic Star*) from October
1918 – a Donkeyman, a Fireman and a Greaser – who died of 'flu. There are members of
the RASC Canteens, a **Major Houssemayne du Boulay**, DSO, RE of the RAMC Labour
Corps and 3 RAF graves from 31 August 1944. In the civilian cemetery that one passes
through is the grave of **Mme Rufin**, 'Victim of the Bombardment of St Omer, 28 April
1942'.
[For more information about the Chinese Labour Corps, see *Holts' Ypres Battlefield Guide*.]
  Continue towards Etaples on the D940, passing Camiers on the left.
It was there that the stockade of the Etaples base court-martial prison and detention
camp was situated. Here the various delinquents, deserters and absentees that hid in the
dunes as they attempted to get back to Blighty were rounded up. Many of them were
desperate men, some of them out and out criminals who preyed on the soldiers training
at the Bull Ring with gambling games and robberies.
  Continue towards Etaples and stop at the large cemetery on the right.

St Etienne-au-Mont CWGC
Cem, Chinese Memorial

Unusual headstone of a Chinese sailor, St
Etienne-au-Mont Cemetery

• Etaples CWGC Military Cemetery/Bull Ring (49.6 miles, GPS: 50.53568 1.62442)

The large Cemetery (of 11,436 burials and covering 59,332 square metres) which overlooks the railway line and the Bay of the River Canche originally contained soldiers, sailors, airmen and civilians from the UK, Canada, Australia, New Zealand, South Africa, British West Indies, Newfoundland, India, USA, Belgium, China, Germany and Portugal (who were later re-interred), with eleven Special Memorials. Set apart at the left (as one enters) of the left hand shelter is a row of Chinese Labourers. The burials were made by ward, therefore officers and other ranks are segregated. Several nurses are buried here. The Cemetery was started in May 1915. Its striking entrance complex with fine stone flags was designed by Sir Edwin Lutyens.

The Cemetery overlooks the vast area of dunes that was occupied by extensive hospitals (eleven general, one stationary, four Red Cross and a convalescent depot, which could collectively cope with 22,000 wounded or sick), stores, a railway, and the infamous 'Bull Ring' training ground, site of the *Monocled Mutineer*' episode. The ringleader, **L/ Cpl Jesse Short**, who had served in France since November 1915, was tried, found guilty, shot for mutiny on 4 October 1917, and is buried in Boulogne East CWGC Cemetery (see above). **Vera Brittain** served as a VAD in No 24 General Hospital in 1917 and mentions the mutiny in *Testament of Youth* (a major film based on the memoirs appeared in January 2015). She sometimes nursed the Portuguese officers and, rather to her bewilderment, the Germans. Among the many harrowing and tragic experiences she endured in the wards, the haunting Last Post, with its 'final questioning note' inspired her to evermore 'sacrifices and hardships' and to write a poem called '*The Last Post*', published in her 1917 collection *Verses of a V.A.D.*

In his fictional account of his own war-time experiences, *The Golden Virgin*, Henry Williamson describes how the hero, Phillip Maddison, arrives at Etaples ('What a —-—ing hole') in 1916, for three days training en route for the Somme. The Bull Ring 'lay beyond a sandy road past hospitals and rows of bell tents, upon an open area of low sandhills where trenches were dug, bayonet-fighting courses laid out, with Lewis gun and bombing ranges'. He recalls the 'scores of sergeant-instructors … the barrack-square drill … physical jerks; firing of rifle-grenades, throwing of Mills bombs; filing through a gas-chamber, wearing damp P. H. helmets … under coils and over knife-edge obstacles of barbed wire, down into the trench, to stab straw painted crudely grey and red.' Most Bull Ring trainees remembered the brutality of the experience. Robert Graves in *Goodbye to All That* also describes bayonet practice and the words of the instructors with 'their permanent ghastly grin. "Hurt him, now! In the belly! Tear his guts out! … Now that upper swing at his privates with the butt. Ruin his chances for life! No more little Fritzes!"'.' Like Williamson, Graves was 'glad to be sent up to the trenches'.

In 1922 King George V visited Etaples during his Pilgrimage tour. In anticipation of the visit Mrs Matthew of the Bear Hotel, Devizes, wrote to the Queen and asked her to place a bunch of forget-me-nots on the grave of her son, **Sgt Alpheus Thomas William Matthew**, RASC. The Queen was unable to go to Etaples and gave the letter to the King and asked him to put the flowers by the headstone. This he did. Sgt Matthew is buried at XLVII .C.5. Actually he died after the end of the war, on 9 December 1918.

In L1.C.1 at the top of the cemetery to the left, is the headstone of '**Florence Grover, wife of Pte A. Grover**, 26 November 1918, age 21, one of the 19 women buried in the Cemetery.' She died of pneumonia after going over to France to nurse her wounded husband who survived her until 17 December, age 23. He is buried in XLV11.E.5. Another of the 4 Non World War combattant dead is **George William Riley**, died of peritonitis 11 March 1919, age 52, XLV.C.12. He was in charge of the Lena Ashwell Concert Party. As well as the amateur regimental concert parties that sprang up, professional companies also toured behind the lines to raise morale and provide a little light relief to the horror and monotony of WW1 trench life. Most were light-hearted performances but Lena Ashwell's company also performed Shakespeare. [In 1916 it was planned to issue a copy of Shakespeare's works to each wounded soldier in memory of Lord Kitchener]. Ashwell, who married the Royal Obstetrician, Sir Henry Simpson, was convinced that such shows helped to alleviate shell shock and by the end of the war she had 25 companies touring the camps. She was awarded the OBE and died in 1957. It was a Lena Ashwell Concert Party in April 1918 that inspired Siegfried Sassoon's evocative poem, which could so easily apply to a concert party at Etaples:

Concert Party (Egyptian Base Camp)

They are gathering round…
Out of the twilight; over the grey-blue sand,
Shoals of low-jargoning men drift inward to the sound –
The jangle and throb of a piano … tum-ti-tum…
Drawn by a lamp, they come
Out of the glimmering lines of their tents, over the shuffling sand.

O sing us the songs, the songs of our own land,
You warbling ladies in white.
Dimness conceals the hunger in our faces,
This wall of faces risen out of the night,
These eyes that keep their memories of the places
So long beyond their sight.

Jaded and gay, the ladies sing; and the chap in brown
Tilts his grey hat; jaunty and lean and pale,
He rattles the keys … some actor-bloke from town …
God send you home; and then A long, long trail…
I hear you calling me; and Dixieland …
Sing slowly… now the chorus … one by one
We hear them, drink them; till the concert's done.
Silent, I watch the shadowy mass of soldiers stand
Silent, they drift away, over the glimmering sand.

Continue. After .3 mile to the right is the renovated ***** Hotel Kyriad** Tel: +(0)3 21 89 99 99, letouquet@kyriad.fr Open all year but restaurant closed at lunch-time Oct-April.

Continue into Etaples following signs to Centre Ville/A16 on the D940 (51.2 miles).
Along the north bank of the mouth of the River Canche are a variety of delightful fish restaurants, notably **Aux Pêcheurs d'Etaples**, Tel: +(03) 21 94 06 90, etaples@ auxpecheursdetaples.fr which closes promptly at 1400 hours at lunchtime! Closed Sunday evenings. It is very popular and therefore advisable to make a reservation in advance.

Continue along the quay.
To the left from the Anchor roundabout and on the left before the Town Hall in the main square, Place Gen de Gaulle, is the **Musée Quentovic (GPS: 50.51397 1.63781)** in which there is a small exhibition on the **Bull Ring Camp**. Tel: +(03) 21 94 02 47 for opening hours. Closed Tues. High Season July & Aug.

Return to the Anchor Roundabout and take the D939 signed to Montreuil/A16. Continue to Montreuil. Turn right and follow signs to Centre Ville and then right up a road which becomes cobbled following Ville Haute signs. Continue to the Place du Théatre.

• Montreuil/Gen Haig Statue/RWC (59.8 miles, GPS: 50.46144 1.76047)

From March 1916 to April 1919 the old walled town with its encircling ramparts housed the British GHQ, General Haig staying in the nearby Château de Beaurepaire (about 2 miles south on the D138 near St Nicholas). In the market square, in front of the theatre, is a post-World War II replica of an equestrian statue of Haig on Miss Ypres (who, on closer examination, appears to have undergone a sex change). The statue was raised by national public subscription in memory of Marshal Haig and of the collaboration between the British and French armies, and Franco-Britannic friendship. Montreuil is an ideal

Gen Haig on Miss Ypres, Montreuil

place for a lunch break or stopover, with several interesting restaurant possibilities around the square itself. An alternative is Hesdin, near the Agincourt battlefield.

Continue through the Square following signs to Hesdin and at the first small roundabout turn onto the D138, which becomes the N39. Continue to the bottom of the hill and take the D138E4 just before the motorway. Continue to the T junction and turn right on the D349, signed to Hesdin. Continue, with the River Canche and a single track railway line to the left, along a winding and scenic route. [If in a hurry take the D939 to Hesdin.]

On approaching Hesdin on the D349 continue to the crossroads with the D928 (signed right to the A16) and go straight over, into Marconne on the D349, and keep on it to St Pol. At the junction turn right signed Frévent on the D340. Continue to Galametz.

In the centre of the village to the right is a **Memorial to François Lesur**, FFI, (84 miles, **GPS: 50.32781 2.13901**). *Groupe de Fillièvres, age 19, 'abbatu lâchement'* ('killed in a cowardly fashion' – actually shot in the back) by the Germans on 3-9-44. Erected by his brothers.

Continue following the path of the Canche to Fillièvres. On leaving the village watch out for the green CWGC signs to the right. Follow them along a picturesque and winding small road to the cemetery on the right.

• CWGC British Cemetery, Fillièvres (86.2 miles, GPS: 50.31093 2.16593)

Begun in June 1918 by 46th CCS and later used by 6th Stationary Hospital, the Cemetery contains 81 WW1 burials and 19 WW2. In it are some interesting burials, including **Lt E. F. Baxter, VC** of the King's Liverpool Regt, 18 April 1916, age 30. Near Blairville Baxter dug out the detonator from a 'bomb', which fell with its pin withdrawn, and smothered it, saving many lives. Later he led a storming party, helped the last man

Headstone of Lt E.F. Baxter, VC, Fillièvres Brit Cemetery

Memorial to François Lesur, Galametz.

over the parapet after bombing enemy dugouts and was never seen alive again. Also **Lt-Col Gerald Cornock-Taylor, CBE,** Deputy Director of the Graves Registration and Enquiries, 14 February 1919. A variety of regiments and corps are represented, including the Royal Marine Light Infantry, the RAF and the ASC Canteens and one New Zealand burial of World War I.

Continue through Conchy-sur-Canche and Boubers-sur-Canche to the turning to the left on the D111 at Ligny- sur-Canche.

[N.B.] By going straight over at the roundabout and turning left on the D111, crossing the River Canche, and by following the green CWGC signs along a narrow, winding country lane, the tiny but immaculate **Ligny-sur-Canche British Cemetery (GPS: 50.29361 2.26427)** may be reached. (It is a 2-mile round trip.) The beautiful wooden entrance gate is set between stone benches and inside two tightly-packed lines of headstones stretch to the Cross of Sacrifice. The Cemetery, designed by W.H. Cowlishaw, which contains 80 burials, mostly from August/September 1918, is enclosed by a fine stone wall. The care and attention lavished on this small and rarely-visited cemetery 'in the middle of nowhere', typifies the dedication of the Commonwealth War Graves Commission.

The lovely entrance to Ligny-sur-Canche Brit Cemetery

The road now becomes the D941. Continue into Frévent, following Toutes Directions, and at the roundabout turn right following Amiens/Doullens signs on the D916, then go straight over at the next roundabout signed to Arras/Amiens/Doullens Centre on the D925. Then at the next roundabout take the D916 to Doullens. Continue to the next roundabout signed Arras to the left and A16 Amiens to the right. Take the second exit up a small road, Ruelle Merlin, signed Calvaire Foch. Drive uphill to the Calvary at the top.

• Foch Memorial Cross (104 miles, GPS: 50.15720 2.36035)

Foch was familiar with Doullens, having set up his HQ here in the early days of the war. He returned again in the last year and this Memorial, with *bas reliefs* of Foch and his *Poilus* by Albert Roze, erected in 1921, recognises that fact, although no inscription remains.

Return to the roundabout and take the N25 signed Amiens and take the first turning to the left, then turn right following the green CWGC signs to

• Doullens Communal Cemetery Extension (104.9 miles, GPS: 50.15476 2.34969)

The military graves are in the local cemetery which is **Open:** 1 Feb-30 April 0830-1830, 1 May-10 Nov 0730-1900, 11 Nov-31 Jan 0830-1730.

From the summer of 1915 to March 1916 Doullens was at the junction of the French Tenth Army on the Arras Front and the British Third Army on the Somme. The Citadelle was a large military hospital and the railhead was used by both armies. From March 1916 the Arras front became British and 19th Casualty Clearing Station came to Doullens, followed by the 41st, 35th, 11th CCS. At the end of 1916 they gave way to 3rd Canadian Stationary Hospital and from June 1918 the 2/1st Northumberland CCS arrived. From February 1916 to April 1918 British medical units continued to bury in French Extension No 1 of the cemetery until it contained 1,142 UK, 78 New Zealand, 69 Australian, 36 Canadian, 4 Newfoundland, 3 South African, 2 British West Indies, 1 British Civilian, 1 Guernsey, 13 German and 469 French burials. In March/April 1918 the German advance threw severe strain on the Canadian Stationary Hospital. The extension became full and Extension No 2, on new ground, had to be opened. It contains 321 UK, 27 New Zealand, 23 Canadian, 23 South African, 1 Australian, 1 Chinese Labourer and 87 German POWs. Like Etaples, another 'hospital' cemetery, the burials are in rank, according to ward. An interesting conjunction of graves has **2nd Lt James A. Donnelly** of the RFC, killed on 31 March, the last day of the RFC, and in the next-but-one grave **Lt Ronald Stonehouse**, RAF, killed on 1 April 1918, the day that the RAF

Foch Memorial Cross near Doullens

Bas relief of Foch and soldiers, 1921

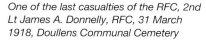

One of the last casualties of the RFC, 2nd
Lt James A. Donnelly, RFC, 31 March
1918, Doullens Communal Cemetery

Side by side in death and killed on the same
day, 25 April 1918. German and British
headstones, Doullens Communal Cemetery

was officially formed. **Brigadier H. T. Fulton, CMG, DSO,** *Croix de Guerre,* of the New
Zealand Rifle Brigade who served on the Indian Front and in South Africa, died here of
wounds on 29 March 1918. Side by side are the German **Moritz Demant,** 9/J.R. 184 and
Pte C.A. Jennings, Notts & Derby, both killed on 25 April 1918. Also side by side [I.B.
28 & 29] lie **Lt Edgar Meath Martyn,** age 25, 19th Battalion 2 Can Mounted Rifles and **Lt
Francis Leopold Mond,** age 22, RFA, both of 57th Sqn RAF, who were shot down on 15
May 1918 and to whom there is a Private Memorial at Bouzencourt. Originally the wrong
headstones were put on these graves (see Itinerary Three for their full story). There is
a row of French Colonial troops which also contains Muhammad Beg, 29th Lancers
(Deccan Horse), 6 November 1916 and Kala Khan of the RFA, 23 May 1918. There are also
some British burials from World War II (mostly from 20 May 1940) and a large French
World War I plot at the top of the Cemetery, with a Private Memorial to Georges Martelle,
10th RIF, killed on 17 August 1916 at Belloy (qv).

*Return to the N25 and turn left. Continue over the traffic lights and turn right signed
to Doullens Centre. Continue, passing the* **Tourist Office** *(see Tourist Information) on the
left and at the T junction turn left following signs to Salle de Commandement Unique to
the Town Hall and park.*

• *Unified Command Room, Doullens/RWC (105.9 miles, GPS: 50.15705 2.34110)*

The first-floor room in the impressive town hall in which Marshal Foch was created
Allied Supreme Commander on 26 March 1918, has been preserved, with the original
furniture (with place names still around the table) and a stained glass window depicting
the players in the drama, including Poincaré, Clemenceau, Pétain and Foch, Haig, Wilson

Stained glass window depicting the scene in the Unified Command Room, Doullens, on 26 March 1918

and Milner. It is flanked on either side by magnificent paintings by Jonas showing scenes of the historic day. The conference was called at a time of extreme danger to the Allies. The German offensive had swept like an incoming high spring tide over the old 1916 battlefield and the Allies' backs were truly against the wall. 'Do you want peace today or victory tomorrow?' asked the old tiger, Clemenceau, of Haig as they arrived outside the town hall. Haig maintained that he wished to continue to fight, but desperately needed French support. He offered to put himself under command of Foch, a move since suspected by some as a clever ruse to prevent Prime Minister Lloyd George from sacking him because of the success of the German offensive, code-named 'Operation Michael'. Only Gough of Haig's Army Commanders was absent, and he was busy keeping the Fifth Army together in the face of the enemy's assault, which had started five days before. Despite an earlier February conference at Doullens, when Gough had warned Haig of the danger facing the Fifth Army, Gough was to be the scapegoat for the March Retreat. Henry Wilson, CIGS, insisted that Gough be removed and Haig concurred – perhaps another act of self-preservation.

Neither the Belgians nor the Americans were present on the 26th, but two days later General Pershing visited Foch and put '… all that I have … at your disposal. Do what you like with them.'

Foch had been appointed Supreme Commander charged with, 'co-ordinating the action of the Allied Armies on the Western Front' whether the Belgians liked it or not. The plan worked. The entrance hall is covered in commemorative plaques of World Wars One and Two.

Open: 0900-1200 and 1400-1800, Mon-Fri (Thurs to 1645) and Sat 1000-1200. For more information contact the **Tourist Office** on Tel: + (0)3 22 32 54 52. Email: Contact@doullens-tourisme.com

Return to the crossroads with traffic lights and go straight over on the D938 direction Acheux, crossing the D11/D1 en route, and continue to Louvencourt. Drive through the village, past the church and the crucifix at the top of the hill and take the small road to the right.

• Louvencourt Military Cemetery (115.6 miles, GPS: 50.08924 2.50366)

This unusual cemetery has a row of experimental French headstones along the wall (the area was originally a French medical centre) dating from the end of the French occupation of this sector in June/July 1915. Then the British Field Ambulance established itself here, and British burials commenced. During the 1 July 1916 battle, Louvencourt was only 6 miles behind the front line. The Somme battles carried medical units further east until in April 1918 the German offensives pushed the line back to its old position. The 1918 graves here are due to the climax of that fighting. That same year the Imperial War Graves Commission decided upon the sites of the first three permanent cemeteries to be built after the war. They were Le Tréport, Forceville and Louvencourt. It was originally intended that the Commission's three principal architects, Blomfield, Baker and Lutyens, should build one cemetery each, but in the event Blomfield designed all three and completed them by the middle of 1920. They cost more than the £10 per grave that had been allowed – the War Stone alone cost £500 to make, move and install – and financial lessons learnt were applied to future construction, **e.g.** in small cemeteries the War Stone would be omitted.

The cemetery contains the grave of **2nd Lt Roland Leighton** of the 1/7th Worcesters who died of wounds on 23 December 1915, aged only 20. A brilliant scholar (he attended Uppingham School) and budding poet, he was engaged to Vera Brittain. In 1920 she made a pilgrimage to visit his grave and the areas where he fought. There are often violets on his grave, in tribute to the poem Roland wrote to Vera entitled *Villanelle*, whose starting lines are,

> *Violets from Plug Street Wood*
> *Sweet, I send you oversea.*

He enclosed four violets with the poem, which Vera still had, dry and pressed, in 1933 when she wrote her wartime story *Testament of Youth*, which charts their relationship. Later research indicates that Leighton was beginning to have doubts about their future together. Also buried here is **Brigadier General Charles Bertie Prowse, DSO** of the SLI,

Left: Headstone of Roland Leighton, Louvencourt Mil Cem

Below: Experimental French headstone, Louvencourt Mil Cem

mortally wounded in the area of the German position, the Quadrilateral (where Serre Road No 2 Cemetery is today, Map D24) on 1 July 1916, when in command of 11th Brigade. His body was moved here after the war. Prowse Point in 'Plugstreet' Wood in the Ypres Salient, now the site of a CWGC Cemetery, was named after him.

Note the singular lack of personal messages here, over and above the usual New Zealand headstones.

The final advance of 1918, which came towards you, stopped on 11 November barely 5 miles further ahead.

Here there are two ways in which to complete the journey to Amiens:

OPTION ONE

Via Val Vion, Vert Galand and Bertangles. Approximate driving time: 1 hour.
Approximate distance: 19 miles.

SET YOUR MILEOMETER TO ZERO.
Return to the crossroads with the D1/D11 and turn left on the D11 towards Beauquesne.
Continue to the next crossroads and turn right signed Beauquesne on the D31.

• *Val Vion Château (6 miles, GPS: 50.08480 2.41887)*
This is visible half a mile later to the left along a track bordered with chestnut trees. The view is of the back of the château (sometimes described in contemporary accounts as

being the Château de Beauquesne) where famous photographs of Haig, King George V and members of their entourages were taken, standing on the staircase which can be seen from this point without disturbing the owners (relatives of Mme Potié, former Mayor of Thiepval). Haig had moved his advanced HQ here prior to the opening of the July 1916 Somme battle and was also variously visited by Joffre, Foch, Weygand, Pres Poincaré and Lloyd George. He was still there in April 1918 when the château came within range of the German artillery. The château was demolished by a bomb in 1940, and this is an exact post-war replica.

Val Vion Château, with the famous staircase

Continue to Beauquesne to the T Junction with the D23. Continue past the church and take the first right onto the D31. Follow signs to Candas, and at the junction with the N25 turn left. Ahead on the left are the buildings of Vert Galand Farm.

• *Vert Galand Aerodrome Site (10.4 miles, GPS: 50.07005 2.32354)*
This is spelt as 'Galant' on modern maps and Maurice Baring also uses the 't'. The farm buildings were used as a mess and administrative buildings by the RFC and RNAS Squadrons based at the aerodrome. During the Somme battle of 1 July, 60 Sqn,

Site of Vert Galand Aerodrome

commanded by 'Ferdy Waldron', flying Morane Bullets, was stationed there. On 3 July Maurice Baring visited Vert Galand and 'saw Ferdy Waldron go up. But this time he did not come back.' **Maj Francis Fitzgerald Waldron**, 11th Hussars, attd RFC, was one of the pioneers of the RFC and at one time held the height record for the Army. He was killed in aerial combat and is buried in Ecoust-St-Mein CWGC Cemetery (qv) to the north-east of Bapaume. Baring also saw **Major Hubert Dunsterville Harvey-Kelly, DSO** of the Irish Regiment and RFC take off for his last flight on 29 April 1917. This ... gayest of all gay pilots ... always took a potato and a reel of cotton with him when he went over the lines. The Germans, he said, would be sure to treat him well if he had to land on the other side and they found him provided with such useful and scarce commodities. He was the first pilot to land in France, reported Baring. Sadly the commodities did not help him — Harvey-Kelly died in captivity, having been shot down by Richthofen's six red Albatrosses. He is buried in Brown's Copse Cemetery, Roeux near Arras. His Squadron (60th) was taken over by Capt R. R. Smith-Barry, who in late 1917 went on to found the Special School of Flying at Gosport. 'The Man Who Taught the World to Fly' dramatically cut down casualties during training and his methods are still being used to this day. On 7 May 1917, **Capt Albert Ball, VC, DSO and 2 Bars, MC**, of 56 Sqn was posted as missing on a flight from Vert Galand. He is buried in Annoeullin Communal Cemetery German Extension near la Bassée. Baring had a room at Val Vion (see above) for his HQ during the first days of the July Somme battle.

 Continue.

> **[N.B.]** At this point there is a sign to **Naours**, Cité Souterraine to the right on the D117. (GPS: 50.03424 2.8080). These huge underground caverns and tunnels, some of which date back to the third century, were rediscovered in 1887. They were used by the Picards to shelter from the dangers of many wars, including World War I, and make a fascinating visit. British units, including the 10th Gloucesters, were billeted in the village prior to the Battle of the Somme and there is much graffiti (particularly Australian) inscribed on the walls of the caves. The Germans occupied the cavern from 1942-44.
>
> **Open:** Times vary! Tel: +(0)3 22 93 71 78. E-mail: contact@citesouterrainedenaors.fr Website: www.grottesdenaours.com]

Continue on the N25 and at the D97 junction after Villers-Bocage turn right to Bertangles. Continue through the village following signs to Vaux-en-A and fork right on rue du Moulin at a sign to the left to Vaux-en-A. Continue to the cemetery on the left.

• Bertangles Cemetery (Map Side 1/5, 17.8 miles, GPS: 49.97264 2.29405)

To the right of the entrance is a CGS/H Signboard and a brief account of the Red Baron's burial.

Manfred von Richthofen, the top German Ace (with eighty kills), was buried here on 22 April 1917, by the Australians, with full military honours. In 1925 his remains were moved to the German Cemetery at Fricourt, and later transported to his family home in Schweidnitz. P. J. Carisella in his book *Who Killed the Red Baron* claims that only the skull was moved and that he unearthed the rest of the Red Baron's skeleton in Bertangles in 1969 and presented it to the German Military Air Attaché in Paris. Pictures published in magazines like *I Was There* show the edge of a brick entrance post and a hedge behind the grave. The hedge and gate post are still there, so

Bertangles Cemetery gates, looking from the site of von Richthofen's grave.

the grave site, not marked in any way, can roughly be identified as being about fifteen paces into the cemetery and fifteen paces to the right, where there is a distinct depression in the grass. There is one CWGC headstone in the cemetery – that of **2nd Lt J. A. Miller, RFC**, killed on 28 March 1918, age 24. Miller was born in Hawaii and his parents lived in California.

Return through the village, past the junction with the rue de Villers Bocage on the rue de Croissy and continue to the N2. Continue to AMIENS Ring Road (approx 19 miles).

OPTION TWO

Via Bus-les-Artois, Warloy-Baillon and Querrieu. Approximate driving time: 1 hour. Approximate distance: 25 miles

SET YOUR MILEOMETER TO ZERO

From the cemetery return into Louvencourt and take the first turning right after the church on Rue de Bus. Continue bearing right past a small Y fork before green farm buildings and immediately fork left at next Y fork. Continue into Bus-les-Artois. Continue to the T junction. Turn right and immediately stop by the local War Memorial. Behind it is

• Memorial to the Leeds Pals and Leeds Rifles (Map Side 1/2b, 2.4 miles, GPS: 50.10385 2.53933)

This Portland stone **Memorial** was unveiled on 30 June 2006 to commemorate the men of the Leeds Pals (the 15th (Service) POW W Yorks Regt) who had spent the night of 30 June 90 years before singing songs such as *On Ilkley Moor baht 'at* at an impromptu concert in the village before setting off to participate in the 1 July 1916 attack. Members

NZ WW1 graffiti on Bus-les-Artois church

Memorial to the Leeds Pals and Rifles, to the rear of the War Memorial, Bus-les-Artois

of The Great War Society recreated the event at the inauguration. During their attack on Serre (qv) the Pals lost 13 officers (2 more dying of wounds later) and 209 ORs (24 later dying). They include professional cricketer **Lt Major** (his forename) **William Booth** and **Pte Horace Iles**, who had enlisted aged 14. Both are buried in Serre Road No 1 (qv).

Around the exterior rear walls of the church *(GPS: 50.10364 2.54221)* further on to the left, with its immaculately tended churchyard, there remain the traces of graffiti from 1840s and on through WW1 from the successive battalions that passed through the village. Among them are the names of two Leeds Pals from June 1916.

Continue to the T junction and turn left on the D176. At the next T junction turn right signed to Bertrancourt on the D176 and then at the War Memorial turn right on the D114 signed to Acheux and green CWGC sign to Bertrancourt Mil Cemetery. Continue into Acheux and at crossroads turn left on the D938 signed Albert/Amiens.

After the Acheux exit sign there is a **Monument to Martyrs of the Picardy Resistance 1940-45** on the left. (GPS: 50.06780 2.542210)

*Continue, passing signs to **Forceville Comm Cem + Extension** to the right.*

> **[N.B.] Forceville Comm Cem + Extension** is approached by a grassed path which runs from the end of Forceville Local Cemetery on the right to the CWGC plot at the back (GPS: 50.06213 2.55262). One of the first three Cemeteries to be built after the War, it was designed by Sir Reginald Blomfield and contains 304 burials (3 buried in the adjoining Communal Cemetery) including 7 Germans. This section was taken over from the French in 1915 and used by Field Ambulances from Feb-July 1916 (the graves in Plot II are from the Somme offensive of July/Aug 1916). Buried here is **Pte John Lewis**, age 21, 5th Dorsets, shot here on 19 April 1917 for desertion with his pal, Pte W Anderson (see Putowski & Sykes, *Shot at Dawn*).

*Continue, passing a sign to **Hedauville Comm Cem Extension** to the left. Continue to the crossroads, turn right on the D919 to Warloy Baillon and continue to the cemetery on the right.*

• *Warloy-Baillon Communal Cemetery & Extension (Map Side1/4, 11.2 miles, GPS: 50.01298 2.52920)*

Here are the Graves of Lt Col P. Machell and Maj Gen E.C. Ingouville-Williams. These two exceptional officers are buried in what is a cemetery of particular beauty – especially in the late spring/early summer. The main cemetery was used between October 1915 and 1 July 1916, and contains forty-six British and Commonwealth graves and 158 French graves. It adjoins the local cemetery. The extension, in what was originally an apple orchard, was used from July to November 1916 and contains 1,331 WWI, 2 WWII and 18 German graves. It was designed by Sir Reginald Blomfield.

Headstone of Maj-Gen E.C. Ingouville-Williams, Warloy-Baillon Comm Cem

Lt Col Percy Wilfrid Machell, CMG, DSO, served with the Nile Expeditionary Force 1884-5, joined the Egyptian Army in 1886, was Inspector-General of the Egyptian Coastguard, Adviser to the Egyptian Minister of the Interior, 1898-1908, received countless Egyptian Decorations and when World War I broke out, helped the 5th Earl of Lonsdale (known as the 'Yellow' Earl, and of Lonsdale Belt fame) to raise and train his own battalion (the 11th, Service) of the Border Regiment. He was killed on 1 July 1916, leading his battalion's attack on the Leipzig Salient at the age of 54. Machell had married into a distinguished and talented family. His wife, Lady Valda, was the daughter of Admiral HSH Prince Victor of Hohenlohe Langenburg, GCB, RN, nephew of Queen Victoria. Her sisters, Lady Feodora and Lady Helena were both accomplished artists/sculptresses. Lady Helena, who served during the war with the British X-ray Section in France and on the Italian front and who was awarded the Italian Medal for Military Valour, designed the beautiful 37th Division Memorial at Monchy (depicting three soldiers back to back) a replica of which stands in the grounds at Sandhurst. Lady Feodora sculpted a small bronze of the 28th August 1914 '*Stirrup Charge*' of St Quentin which we illustrate and explain in our *Western Front – North* Guide Book. Their brother was Major General Lord Albert Edward Wilfred Gleichen KCVO, who commanded the 37th Division 1915-16, then commanded the Intelligence Bureau and Department of Information. The bronze plaque which for many years stood at the foot of Machell's grave was stolen in the early 1990s.

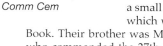

Headstone of Lt Col P. Machell, Warloy-Baillon Comm Cem

Maj General E. C. Ingouville-Williams ('Inky Bill') who commanded 34th Division (which suffered such heavy casualties around la Boisselle on 1 July) was killed by a shell at the Queens Nullah near Mametz Wood on 22 July 1916, after reconnoitring the area and while walking back to his car at Montauban. He too was 54 and had served with the Buffs. His funeral here was held with considerable pomp for a war-time burial.

Another distinguished veteran officer buried here is Lt-Col Thomas Mowbray Martin, Camp commandant of 8 Corps, age 56, killed 20 May 1915. He was decorated in the Nile Expedition and the South African War.

There are two IWGC workers' headstones here: Ed Jones served during the '14-

Memorial to WW2 Airmen Lucas and Pinkney

'18 War, joined the Commission as a Gardener Labourer in 1920 at a salary of £2.00 and was killed in a motor accident on 17 March 1940. Griffith Jones was born in 1922 and served with the Commission from 1936 until he resigned on 2 March 1940. He died on 24 July 1947. One wonders if they were brothers, although no evidence can be found to substantiate this.

Two soldiers buried here served under aliases: Sgt W.H. Hughes, age 25, 5th Can Mounted rifles, 14 October 1916, served as B. Anderson. Pte Ewen Mackinnon, age 28, 8th Can Inf Regt, 28 September 1916, served as D. Dow.
Continue to the junction with the D179. On the right is
Memorial to Pilot Officer K.R. Lucas, 145 Sqn, 1919-1940 and **Capt D.E. Pinkney**, RA, attd 662 Sqn, 1919-1944 **(GPS: 50.01231   2.52707)**. This black marble Memorial bears images of their planes. Beside it is an Information Board. Lucas's Hurricane was shot down by Gruppenkommandeur Gerhard Homuth who was credited with 63 victories when he himself went missing on 2 August 1943 on the Eastern Front. Both British airmen are buried in Warloy-Baillon Cem Ext above.

Continue on the D919 to Vadencourt and then turn left by the church on the D23 through Franvillers, passing a sign to Contay Brit Cemetery.

[N.B.] Contay British CWGC Cemetery (GPS: 49.99871 2.48277). Designed by Sir Reginald Blomfield, this is a gloriously beautiful sight in summer. It was started in August 1916 for the casualties from 49th CCS, followed by 9th CCCS. Then in April 1918 it was used by 38th and other Divisions until August 1918. It contains 1,133 WW1 burials.

Continue to the crossing with the D929. Turn right on the D929 signed to Amiens. DO NOT TAKE THE QUERRIEU BYPASS but immediately turn left on the D929A to Lahoussoye.
Continue over the river to the château entrance on the right.

• *Querrieu Château (20.7 miles, GPS: 49.93876 2.43208)*

Here Rawlinson had his Fourth Army Headquarters from the beginning of 1916. From here he organized the 'Great Push' of 1 July 1916, and watched the progress of the battle from the heights above the village that he called 'The Grandstand' and to where he took Haig to observe the barrage on 27 June. The King visited the château with Balfour in August and there are many well-known pictures of him presenting decorations to soldiers, British and French, in the grounds. The Prince of Wales installed his HQ here in 1918 and was an occasional visitor after the war. During World War II the château

Querrieu Château

was again used as a headquarters – this time by the Germans and Guderian, Goering and Rommel all passed through it. The château is owned by the Count and Countess of Alcantara and they have many photographs and other mementoes of their home during World War I. The elegant château, dating from the eighteenth century, was rebuilt after being burnt down in the Siege of Corbie in 1636 and extensively redesigned under Louis-Philippe in the nineteenth century. It has always played host to a string of glittering personalities, from the aristocracy and the world of the arts. **Open** to the public 7 July – 25 August (closed Mon) and *Patrimoine* Weekend. Guided visits 1400 and 1700. Group visits by appointment 1 June-15 September. Tel: + (0)3 22 40 14 09. E-mail: ydalcantara@orange.fr

Henry Williamson, in his novel, *The Golden Virgin*, describes what must have been a typical occurrence in many towns and villages behind the lines – a 'bioscope' showing of a Charlie Chaplin film and a concert party, both housed in barns at Querrieu. 'Some of the actors dressed up as girls, with varied types of wigs' and garish makeup. 'Each herded man in the audience was fascinated, filled with longing ….' But the star turn was the actor, Basil Hallam Radford of the Kite Balloon branch of the RFC, 'famous before the war for his song *Gilbert the Filbert*'. In it Radford, known simply as 'Basil Hallam', created the comic figure of 'the Knut' – a languorous upper class twit. Sadly he was killed when the balloon in which he was observing broke away, and, having thrown all the papers overboard, he tried to descend by his parachute. It failed to open, however, and he received fatal injuries. He died on 28 August 1916, and is buried in Couin British CWGC Cemetery near Gommecourt. Ironically, balloonists were the only members of the RFC then to be issued with parachutes. Initially it was thought that if pilots had them they would be too eager to abandon their expensive, and hard-to-replace, machines.

Continue and immediately turn left following green CWGC signs to the Cemetery.

• *Querrieu British CWGC Cemetery (Map Side 1/9, 20.9 miles, GPS: 49.93499 2.42975)*
This Cemetery was started in 1918 by the divisions taking part in the defence of Amiens in March 1918. It contains 102 UK, 84 Australian, 1 Chinese and 12 German burials. Here is buried **Lt Col Christopher Bushell**, DSO, VC, commanding the 7th (S) Battalion, the Queen's Royal West Surrey Regiment. His VC was won on 23 March 1918, west of the St Quentin Canal when he personally led C Company of his battalion, in a counter-attack, in the course of which he was severely wounded in the head but continued to carry on, walking in front, not only of his own men, but those of another regiment as well, encouraging them and visiting every portion of the lines in the face of terrific machine-gun fire. He refused to go to the rear until he had to be removed to the dressing station in a fainting condition. There is also a most unusual **Private Memorial** in the cemetery which bears the inscription, 'Well done. Pray for 31691 **Dr [Driver] J.P. Farrell**, 9th Battery FA, AIF, killed in action May 28th 1918, age 20 years'. Around the broken column that surmounts his grave is the legend, 'For God and Australia' and 'Erected by his sorrowing Mother, Ulverstone, Tasmania'. In 2013 the cross surmounting the Memorial was missing.

Continue to the Amiens Ring Road on the D929 (approximately 30 miles).

Private memorial to Driver J. P. Farrell, Querrieu British CWGC Cemetery

ITINERARY ONE

• **Itinerary One** starts at the Town Hall Square in Albert, heads directly towards the German front line along the main axis of the 1916 British attack and then swings north to follow the front line across the River Ancre and ends in Arras.

• **The Route:** Albert – Machine Gun Corps & other Plaques, Town Hall, Golden Madonna, Musée Somme 1916, Bapaume Post CWGC Cemetery; Tara-Usna Line; Tyneside Memorial Seat; La Boisselle – site of Glory Hole Tunnels, Lochnagar Crater and Memorials, 34th Div Memorial, 19th (Western) Div Memorial; Ovillers – CWGC Cemetery; Pozières – British CWGC Cemetery, Fourth, Fifth Armies Memorial, KRRC Memorial, Australian 1st Div Memorial, RB Plaque, Gibraltar Blockhouse; Mouquet Farm RB Plaque; Thiepval – Carton de Wiart VC, Plaque, Visitor Centre and Museum, Memorial and Cemetery, 18th Div Memorial; Connaught and Mill Road CWGC Cemeteries; Ulster Tower, Memorials and Visitors' Centre; Hamel – Essex Regt Plaque on Church; Beaumont-Hamel - Newfoundland Memorial Park, Visitor's Centre, Trenches and Memorials; Mesnil-Martinsart - RIR Memorial; Auchonvillers - Ocean Villas Guest House, Museum, Tea Rooms, Cellar, Trenches, Conference Centre & Estaminet, Auchonvillers Mil CWGC Cemetery; Beaumont-Hamel - Argyll & Sutherland Highlanders Memorial, Beaumont-Hamel Brit CWGC Cemetery, Hawthorn Crater, 51st Highland Div Flagpole, Beaumont-Hamel Church; Redan Ridge No 3 CWGC Cemetery; Serre Road No 2 CWGC Cemetery; Braithwaite Cross; Memorial near site of Wilfred Owen's Dugout; French Memorial Chapel; French National Cemetery; Serre Road No 1 CWGC & Serre Road No 3 CWGC Cemeteries; Sheffield Memorial Park and Memorials; Queen's CWGC Cemetery; Luke Copse CWGC Cemetery; 12th Bn York & Lancs Memorial, Serre; Ayette Indian & Chinese Cemetery; Arras Centre & Memorials, Boves, NZ Tunnellers' Memorial, Wellington Quarry, Faubourg d'Amiens CWGC Cemetery & Arras Memorial, *Mur des Fusillés*.

• **Extra Visits** are suggested to Authuille - Ancre CWGC Cemetery, Salford Pals 15th, 16th, 17th Bns/HLI,/Northumberland Fus Plaques, SOA Sgt Turnbull; Dorset Memorial, Lonsdale CWGC Cemetery, Leipzig Salient; Beaucourt - RND Memorial, SOA Lt Col Freyburg, VC; Bois d'Hollande, Cpl A. Burrows & other Plaques; Sucrerie Military and Euston Road CWGC Cemeteries; Hébuterne Bradford Pals Mem; the Gommecourt Salient – Owl Trench, Rossignol Wood CWGC Cemeteries; Rossignol Wood bunker; SOA Rev T. Bayley Hardy VC; Redan Ridge - Waggon Road & Munich Trench Brit Cemeteries; Gommecourt Wood New CWGC Cemetery; SOA Capt L. Green VC; CWGC HQ, Beaurains; Point du Jour CWGC Cemetery; 9th Scottish Div Memorial.

• **[N.B.]** The following sites are indicated:
Albert - Demarcation Stone and Station, 1944 Resistance Plaque; Ovillers – Breton Calvary, Site of Ulverston Street Trench; Pozières – 'Dead Man's Road' & Chalk Pit; Hawthorne Ridge No 1 CWGC Cemetery; Auchonvillers – Mem to 13th Bn, RIR, Auchonvillers Comm Cemetery; Redan Ridge No 2 CWGC Cemetery.

• **Planned duration**, without stops for refreshment or Extra Visits: **12 hours**.

• **Total distance: 40 miles**.

• Albert Town Hall Square/0 miles/10 minutes/RWC/Map J14/15/GPS: 50.00109 2.65145

The town takes its name from Albert, Duke of Lynes, whose property it became some time after 1619. Noble links remain to this day and the current pretender to the French throne, the Comte de Paris, can still count 'Marquis d'Albert' among his titles. The town's motto is Vis Mea Ferrum (my strength is in iron), reflecting the iron works that once gave it its prosperity. Previously it had been called Ancre (even Encre before 1610) after the river which flowed through it (right below the Basilique). The original station was built in 1846 and Albert became an important rail link, vital to the growing metallurgy industry and the burgeoning pilgrim tourist business (20,000 pilgrims arrived on 27 April 1862 alone). In 1914 Albert had 7,343 inhabitants. By 1919 it had 120.

Fierce fighting around Albert began in the early months of the war, the first enemy shelling being on 29 September 1914. Albert was a major administration and control centre for the Somme offensive in 1916, and it was from there that the first press message was sent announcing the start of the 'Big Push'. By October 1916, when the Somme offensive had pushed the German guns out of range, the town was a pile of red rubble. Yet it still offered some attractions to the troops fresh from the front line as a place of rest and rough entertainment. The YMCA Club charged 15 francs a day (for four meals and a bed), which John Masefield said was 'just 5 francs a day less than the mess at Amiens'. He was dismayed when the club

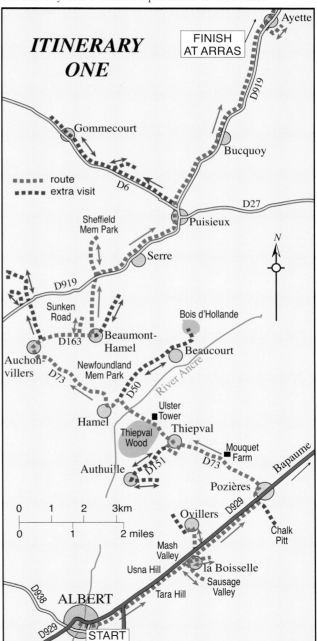

was forced to close on 31 March 1917 to make way either for a hospital or another HQ. The 'Bonza' Theatre operated near the old station. Some civilians drifted back in 1917 and attempted to salvage their homes and businesses. General Byng made the town his HQ while planning the November 1917 attack on Cambrai. Then, in a rude awakening on 26 March 1918, during their final offensive, Albert was taken by the Germans. It was re-taken by the British on 22 August, the East Surreys entering the town at bayonet point.

After the Armistice, the Imperial War Graves Commission established its Somme headquarters in a collection of huts joined by duck-boards along the Bapaume road. There were architects, stone masons and carpenters, landscapers, gardeners and wardens or 'caretakers' as the cemetery guardians were originally called. They were recruited from the willing ranks of ex-servicemen who undertook the often dangerous, always harrowing work of re-interring their 'pals' from isolated graves and reburying them in the beautiful garden cemeteries that were being created with help of experts from Kew and the services of the country's best architects. Mobile teams of workers, with a cook and the inevitable dog, would be driven out each Monday with basic camping equipment to the isolated, ravaged areas of the old front line. Affectionately known as 'travelling circuses', they completed their work with extraordinary despatch and cheerfulness.

The plan to declare the area a *Zone Rouge* (too dangerous to rebuild, like some of the battlefields around Verdun) was strongly resisted by the inhabitants of Albert. Its reconstruction was helped by the city of Birmingham (hence the street name, rue de Birmingham) which funded a ward in the new hospital, and Bordeaux, and it also became a centre for pilgrims – it was claimed that over 160 small cafés existed to serve them. The conducting of battlefield tours by motor vehicle became a thriving industry.

As early as 1917, John Masefield in his classic description, *The Old Front Line*, prophesied,

"To most of the British soldiers who took part in the Battle of the Somme, the town of Albert must be a central point in a reckoning of distances. It lies, roughly speaking, behind the middle of the line of that battle. It is on the main road, and on the direct railway line from Amiens. It is by much the most important town within an easy march of the battlefield. It will be, quite certainly, the centre from which, in time to come, travellers will start to see the battlefield where such deeds were done by men of our race."

That still holds today, and the town has two traditional hotels – the 3-star **Hôtel de la Paix** (qv), 43 rue Victor Hugo, run by Jean Luc Richard, redecorated in 2013, 9 bedrooms with en-suite facilities, popular restaurant and the base for the Friends of Lochnagar, Tel: +(0)3 22 75 01 64, e-mail: hoteldelapaix-albert@voila.fr The *Logis de France* **Hôtel de la Basilique**, run by M et Mme Petit, 10 rooms, restaurant closed Sun night & Mon, Tel: +(0)3 22 75 04 71, e-mail: contact@hoteldelabasilique.fr opposite the Basilique as its name implies, also has its faithful regulars. They are joined by the modern, 23-bedroom 3-star **Best Western Royal Picardie** on the D929 Amiens Road, room service, fitness centre, restaurant, Tel: +(0)3 22 75 37 00, e-mail: royalpicardie@wanadoo.fr and the handily sited 3-star Ibis, with 57 air-conditioned rooms, 'business corner', restaurant, on the roundabout with the D929/D938, Tel: +(0)3 22 75 52 52, e-mail: h6234@accor.com - so that more tourists can stay in this, the heart of the British sector.

At a superficial glance the rebuilt red-brick town may appear unlovely, but a quiet, observant stroll around its streets is rewarding in its glimpses of a certain *Art Deco* charm, revealing delightful tiled pictures and patterned brickworks in its varied façades.

Machine Gun Corps Plaque, Albert Town Hall

Park in the Square. Walk to the town hall steps and face the building.
The town hall, in splendid Flemish Renaissance style, with an *Art Deco* interior and stained glass windows that show the town's economic activities, was opened by President Lebrun in 1932. Inside is a plaque commemorating the reconstruction of the devastated war area. To the left of the steps, on the external wall, is a **Plaque to Resistance fighters, the Armies of Liberation and Gen de Gaulle**. At the bottom of the step to the left is a **Bust to Emile Leturq,** 1870-1930, mayor during the reconstruction. To the right is a **Plaque** commemorating the more than 60,000 casualties suffered by the **Machine Gun Corps** during 1914-18. It was unveiled at Easter 1939 by **Lt Col Graham Seton Hutchison, DSO, MC**, artist and author of many books including *Pilgrimage*. The Colonel had been with 100 MG Coy during the attack on High Wood on 15 July 1916. Another Memorial to the Corps, formed in October 1915, is the figure known as "The Boy David" (designed by Derwent Wood) at Hyde Park Corner in London.

[N.B.] 1. On the outskirts of the town to the left of the D4929 as it crosses the railway, is a well-preserved **Demarcation Stone (Map J28, GPS: 49.99887 2.63728)**. The British defensive line ran roughly north to south through here taking advantage of the railway line as a defensive position. The line held during the German March 1918 offensive.

Albert Demarcation Stone on D4929

2. At the bottom of the road from the Basilique is **Albert Station (GPS: 50.00548 2.64451)**, rebuilt in *Art Deco* style. To each side of the main entrance are charming tiled pictures of the surrounding countryside. The picture to the right is captioned, *Circuit du Souvenir* and shows sites on the battlefield such as the Thiepval Memorial and the *Historial* at Péronne. The main hall in the station houses a Potez 36 FHZN aeroplane in commemoration of Henry Potez, born in Albert, who founded the aircraft factory at Méaulte which became Aerospatiale. The plane, restored in 1957, had been flown by notables such as Saint-Exupéry, the French World War I ace and writer of *Vol de Nuit*, and was last flown on the hundredth anniversary of Henri Potez's birth in 1991.

Albert Station and the 'Circuit du Souvenir' tiled picture at the entrance

Return to your car. Drive down rue Jeanne d'Harcourt and park in the square outside the Basilica.

In the square and around Albert a series of 10 statues by local sculptor Olivier Briquet are progressively being installed: Australian, English (2 with different uniforms,) Scottish, French, (2 with different uniforms), Nurse etc…

Beside the **Hôtel de la Basilique** (qv), at 9 rue Gambetta, is the '**Office de Tourisme** du Pays du Coquelicot' (Poppy Country). Tel: +(0)3 22 75 16 42. e-mail: officedetourisme@paysducoquelicot.com. Website: www.paysducoquelicot.com. At the rear is a large hall containing exhibits such as fine maquettes of Albert's most important buildings. Battlefield tours available, including one of the Basilique.

The site www.somme-100th-anniversary.com details the Pays du Coquelicot's plans for a variety of events and commemorations for the 4 years of the 100th Anniversaries of the Great War in the area.

On the corner opposite the imposing Basilique, under the shadow of the emotive

Albert Square Piper Statue

Albert Square Digger Statue

golden figure of the Madonna is the handy **Le Brasserie Hygge**, Tel: + (0)3 22 75 47 12. Varied menu, reasonable prices, quick service. **Open:** Mon-Sat 1200-1430 and 1830-2200. Closed Sunday.

• *The Golden Madonna, Basilique, Albert/0.2 miles/10minutes/Map J11/ GPS: 50.00373 2.64753*

The golden figure of the Virgin Mary holding aloft the baby Jesus stands on top of the church, known as *la Basilique, of Notre-Dame de Brebières* (Our Lady of the Ewes). Before the war thousands of pilgrims came to see another statue in the church which gave the basilica its name. Legend has it that this statue was found in the Middle Ages by a shepherd looking after his flock in a meadow. It was credited with miraculous properties and attracted large numbers of pilgrims. In 1834 Pope Gregory XVI accorded an indulgence to pilgrims who visited the statue and successively grander churches were built to house it, culminating in the 1890s basilica. This was surmounted by the 5-metre high Golden Madonna (reached by climbing 238 steps) which was coated with 40,000 sheets of gold leaf. The numbers of pilgrims continued to increase and in 1898 Pope Leo XIII dubbed Albert 'The Lourdes of the North'. In January 1915 German shelling toppled the statue to a perilous-looking angle below the horizontal, but it did not fall. Visible to soldiers of both sides for many miles around, and giving the bizarre impression that the Virgin was about to hurl the baby Jesus into the rubble below, the statue gave rise to two legends. The British and French believed that the war would end on the day that

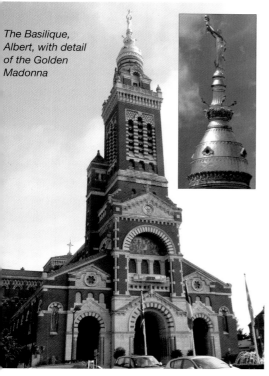

The Basilique, Albert, with detail of the Golden Madonna

the statue fell (and it is said that the Allied staff sent engineers up the steeple at night to shore up the statue to prevent raising false hopes). The Germans believed that whoever knocked down the statue would lose the war. Neither prediction came to pass. During the German occupation from March to August 1918 the British shelled Albert and sent the leaning Virgin hurtling to the ground. The figure was never found (perhaps it was despatched to Germany in the salvage effort to make new weapons).

Today's basilica is built to the original 1897 designs, with a splendid gilt replica of the Madonna and Child on its 70-metre high spire that glints in the sun for miles around. The inhabitants of Albert vetoed the idea that she should be replaced in her famous war-time pose (the subject of many postcards, silk and board, embroidered handkerchiefs, painted plates and statues). It contains a magnificent marble pulpit, mosaics, paintings and statues by the sculptor Albert Roze.

Beneath it, with its well-marked entrance to the side, is a museum.

Entrance to Musée Somme 1916, Albert, showing
Tommy Statue

Tunnel entrance, Musée
Somme, Albert

• *Musée Somme 1916, Albert/40 minutes/Map J13*

This interesting and well-presented Museum, officially reopened on 8 October 1994, is constantly being improved and updated and is well worth a visit.

It has been made in the 250 metre long subterranean tunnels under the Basilica and other parts of the town. They date from medieval times and were used by locals as shelters in times of conflict (including as air raid shelters in WW2). From the entrance hall one descends 61 steps to the 10 metre deep tunnel. To either side of the main corridor are 25 realistic scenes of 1914-18 trench and dugout life – British, French and German - and artefacts. Sound and light effects add to the experience. Visitors emerge into the light in a new extension at ground level where there is an air-conditioned conference room seating up to 80 people with large screen and projector for films and internet work stations (which can be used by students for picnics etc), a well-stocked boutique for books, maps and souvenirs. Drinks and snacks available. Beside it is an impressive 'Gallery of Heroes' in 'Fort Newhaven Hall', dedicated to nine individuals who distinguished themselves during the war (e.g. German artist Max Pechstein, Canadian Medic Col John McCrae, Aviator Sadi Lecointe, Musician George Butterworth) each with a fine portrait by Mafil and personal stories on the reverse.

Guided visits available in French and English. Run by the pleasant and helpful team under President Thierry Goulin with the charming Christine at the entrance.
Open: every day 1 Feb to 15 Dec 0900-1200 and 1400-1800, June-Sept 0900-1800. Entrance fee payable. Tel: +(03) 22 75 16 17. Fax: +(0)3 22 75 56 33. Email: <u>musee@somme1916.org</u> Eng website: <u>www.somme-trench-museum. co.uk</u> Fr website: <u>musee-somme-1916.eu</u>

Boutique, Musée
Somme 1916, Albert

Visitors emerge, into the pleasant arboretum public gardens, formerly the gardens of the château (the red brick walls of which can still be seen), rented to the town by the Comte de Toulouse in 1717, thence up steps back to the square. At the top of the steps is a splendid **Mural by Albert Mac Carton**, showing the Basilique with the Madonna, leaning perilously, and the figures of allied soldiers. In the small garden below it is a Plaque to commemorate the inauguration of the mural on 29 June 1996.

> [N.B.] One can also enter the new wing here through the gardens at the other side via the wrought iron gates that lead from rue Jules Ferry. **GPS: 50.00152 2.64623**
> Opposite the gate, on House No 54, is a **Plaque to Léandre Deflandre, Resistance Chief, killed by the Germans on 23 July 1944.**

Mural by Albert Mac Carton, Albert

Drive up the rue de Birmingham, turn left and leave Albert on the D4929, signed Bapaume/A1 Lille/ Cambrai.

The D4929 heads north east, straight as an arrow, as befits a Roman road, for Bapaume, 19km away. Barely 3.5km away along the road is the village of la Boisselle, which marked the German front line in 1916. The road passes Bapaume Post Cemetery and rises to a crest just before the village, a crest from which the 34th Division set off at 0730 on 1 July 1916 to attack la Boisselle. The ground to the left of the road was in 8th Division's area and the ground to the right in 34th Division's. Behind was Albert, under constant German bombardment, teeming with supplies, its cellars full of troops who emerged at night into the streets with their transport and moved up to and over the crest along deep communication trenches and then fanned out into assault trenches in the valley below to await the whistle to go over the top. On their way,

'Here and there, in recesses in the trench, under roofs of corrugated iron covered with sandbags, they passed the offices and the stores of war, telephonists, battalion headquarters, dumps of bombs, barbed wire, rockets, lights, machine-gun ammunition, tins, jars and cases. Many men, passing these things as they went 'in' for the first time, felt with a sinking of the heart, that they were leaving all ordered and arranged things, perhaps forever,' reported Masefield. In some sectors men even passed rows of coffins.

Drive to the second roundabout.

Here there is the **Ibis Hotel** (qv) in the grounds of which there is the 4-metre high figure of a British Tommy (GPS: 50.00973 2.67228) clambering out of a trench with his rifle, the initiative of the Somme Museum in 2005, when it proved somewhat controversial.

Continue, following signs to Cambrai/Lille on the D4929 and stop at the cemetery on the right.

• Bapaume Post Mil CWGC Cemetery/1.3 miles/5 minutes/Map J16/GPS: 50.01186 2.67381

This Cemetery, one of the first to be completed in the sector in 1924, lies on the western slope of Tara Hill, and here the divisional boundary crosses the road and swings well left to include the hill known as Usna, 1,000m away to the northeast. Both hills were in the 34th Division area. In the cemetery, which was begun in July 1916, lie more than a hundred Northumberland Fusiliers of 34th Division, two battalion commanders of the Tyneside Scottish Brigade (**Lt Cols William Lyle, age 40 and Charles Sillery**, age 54, both killed on 1 July 1916) and soldiers of 38th (Welsh) Division, which recaptured the position on 23 August 1918. In Plot I Row G there is an interesting group of burials: **2nd Lt C. Edwards**, E Yorks, 29 January 1917, age 28, has the personal message, 'He responded to Lord Kitchener's appeal, August 1914'and 2nd Lt J.E.F.T. Bennett, R Warwicks, 24 July 1916, has the soldier's decoration the MM.

He lies near **Maj Sir Foster H.E. Cunliffe, Bart**, Rifle Bde, 10 July 1916, age 43. Altogether there are 410 burials (181 Unknown), including Canadians, Australians and a South African. It was designed by Charles Holden.

Continue to the top of the crest.

• Tara-Usna Line/1.7 miles/Map J16-17

The crest, which runs from Tara Hill on the right-hand side to Usna Hill on the left-hand side, overlooks the village of la Boisselle, 900m straight ahead. It may be possible to spot Ovillers CWGC 2,500m away at 11 o'clock and the Lochnagar mine crater 1,500m away at 1 o'clock. Moving in the direction in which you are travelling, four battalions of Northumberland Fusiliers – all Tyneside Scottish, part of 102nd (Tyneside Scottish) Brigade, itself part of 34th Division – advanced towards the German lines at la Boisselle on 1 July. On the left-hand side of the road the 1st and 4th battalions moved forward,

Headstone of Lt Col W. Lyle, Bapaume Post CWGC Cemetery

side by side in extended line, and two minutes after them, in column of platoons, to the right-hand side of the road, came the 2nd and 3rd battalions.

They had climbed out of their assault trenches in the valley ahead of you moments after the explosion of huge mines at la Boisselle. But although the men had been promised that the opposition would be disorganised by the artillery bombardment and the mines, it was not so. The Germans emerged from deep dug outs, set up their machine guns and mowed down the British infantry advancing as if on parade across the open ground. On the left-hand side no advance was made, the German trenches were not reached and casualties were around 60%. On the right-hand side, where casualties were marginally less, around 50%, a small part of the German line was captured some 700m south-east of the village.

Continue to bottom of hill. On the right is the handy **Poppy Restaurant**, Tel: +(03) 22 75 45 45. *Excellent food with good price range of menus.*

Fork right on the D20 and immediately park.

Tyneside Memorial seat, la Boisselle, and detail of bas relief

• *Tyneside Memorial Seat, la Boisselle/2.1 miles/5 minutes/Map J17/GPS: 50.01846 2.687727*

The curved seat is on the left. Situated close to where the opposing front line trenches crossed the D929, it was unveiled by Marshal Foch, and was the first permanent Regimental Memorial to be erected along the road. It commemorates the attack of the 102nd (Tyneside Scottish) Brigade and their follow-up brigade, the 103rd Tyneside Irish. The latter, storming through the remnants of the 102nd, penetrated beyond the German lines in small parties to the east of the village, but no permanent gains were made astride the road. Their losses matched those of the 102nd.

Opposite, across the D929, after about 100m, is the site of what was the best-known crater in la Boisselle of the mine in Y Sap, blown at the same time as Lochnagar, but now filled in. In his novel, *The Golden Virgin*, based on his personal war-time experiences, Henry Williamson describes a visit to the 1,300ft-long gallery that led under the German fort of the same name, whose charges were to be blown at Zero Hour on 1 July. It left a crater 165ft in diameter, throwing up a high lip which afforded protection under which the infantry were able to reform. It caused little damage to the enemy as the area had been evacuated prior to the explosion. After the war, locals erected a hut by the great hole from which they sold postcards of the two craters at la Boisselle and on the other side of the road, not far from today's **Poppy Café**, was the Café de la Grande Mine.

Continue along the Rue de la 34ième Division, signed to La Grande Mine, for some 100m.

Glory Hole/2.2 miles/Map J18/GPS: 50.01835 2.68897

On the right-hand side can be seen a small fenced-off area of craters known as the Glory Hole (Map J18), which was immediately behind the German forward trenches. Williamson paints a word picture of it as a place of dread, 'a boneyard without graves' of British and German corpses, and unexploded British shells. At that time it made 'a gap of five hundred yards in the British lines, an abandoned no-man's-land of choked shaft and subsided gallery held by a series of Lewis-gun posts'.

Fears that the craters were to be filled in and built over were allayed and a major archaeological excavation was undertaken here in 2011 which uncovered a fascinating *souterrain* complex, now unfortunately halted and no longer visitable. For more details see www.laboisselleproject.com/

However there are new initiatives to preserve and hold events here. See the sign placed by the Friends of the Glory Hole (Ilot): http://www.ilotdelaboisselle.com/decouvrir/les-amis-de-l-ilot.html

More research is being undertaken by the Somme Tourist Director, the Breton François Bergez, about the Breton regiments that fought in the area in 1914. There was

much aerial activity over the Somme on 1 July. Cecil Lewis, serving with the RFC, describes in his book *Sagittarius Rising*, 'We were to watch the opening of the attack, co-ordinate the infantry flares (the job we had been rehearsing for months) and stay over the lines for two and a half hours.' Continuous, overlapping patrols were due to run throughout the day. The patrol was ordered to 'keep clear of La Boisselle' because of the mines that were to be blown. From above Thiepval he watched as,

Cratered ground, The Glory Hole

"At Boisselle the earth heaved and flashed, a tremendous and magnificent column rose up into the sky. There was an ear-splitting roar, drowning all the guns, flinging the machine sideways in the repercussing air. The earthy column rose, higher and higher to almost four thousand feet."

Turn right on the C9 signed La Grande Mine and 100m later fork left on C102. Continue and park at the crater.

• La Boisselle/Lochnagar Crater/2.7 miles/25 mins/Map J19-24 OP/GPS : 50.01605 2.69723

On entering the site one passes through large stone curbs and 'knife-rests' then along duckboards and a hedge which completely surround the site. The land containing the crater was purchased in 1978, and is maintained privately, by Englishman Richard Dunning (Tel: 01483 810651, E-mail:Richard.dunning@uwclub.net. See Website: www.lochnagarcrater.org for enquiries about the 'Friends of Lochnagar') as a Memorial to all those, of both sides, who fought in the Battle of the Somme. Thus the fate of the other large craters at la Boisselle – of being filled in and built upon – was averted. Richard, who is intensely aware of the historical and spiritual value of the crater, of its ability to shock and evoke the violence of war through its sheer size, raised a simple 12ft high Cross made from church timber originating on Tyneside, replaced with a new green English cross when the original was blown down in 2010. The Cross, with the inscription, 'Lochnagar Crater Memorial 1914-1918 In Remembrance – *A la Mémoire*', is the focal point of the well-attended annual ceremony of remembrance that takes place here every 1 July at 0730 hours. On that day beautifully carved wooden panels which depict the insignia of all the units who took part in the battle, carved by Tim Rogers, are placed around it. There is also a ceremony here on 11 November. All are welcome, but you should contact

Richard if you wish to lay a wreath. Please be aware that the July ceremony is becoming increasingly popular (some 3,000 participants in 2014) and parking is problematical; shuttle buses ply from the village. **SPECIAL LIMITATIONS APPLY FOR THE 100TH ANNIVERSARY COMMEMORATON AND ENTRY WILL BE BY INVITATION ONLY – APPLY TO THE FRIENDS FOR DETAILS.** The road from the village has been widened and there is a turning circle for coaches at the far side of the crater. Much work has recently been undertaken by the wonderful 'Friends of Lochnagar' with the help of the CWGC, to enhance the feeling that one is entering a very Special Memorial area and a 'living' Garden of Remembrance.

When standing at the rim and peering down into its vast depth it is difficult to grasp quite how large this crater is. Note that as the crater is subject to increasing erosion it is strictly forbidden to clamber down into it. Please also remember that the area still contains the remains of many of those killed by the explosion and it is therefore a burial ground. Indeed wooden crosses at the bottom of the crater stood out starkly against the white chalk for many years after the war. Several memorials have progressively been erected in the area. One is a **Stone in memory of Tom Easton**, a private in the 2nd Battalion of the Tyneside Scottish. Below it is a **Plaque to 129364 Gnr Noon**, W.G., B/160 RF 34th Div 1916-1919, 1895-1963. To its left is a **Memorial Seat** on which a Plaque simply states, 'Donated by Friends who visit in memory of friends who remain'. A further **Plaque to John Giles**, founder of the WFA, has been added. A brick shelter has been erected to house the Lochnagar Crater Memorial Visitors' Book (which please sign). It is estimated that there are now over 400,000 visitors to the crater each year (and, encouragingly for future remembrance, many of them are schoolchildren). On the far side of the impressive gaping hole of the crater is a **Memorial Seat to Harry Fellows**, 1896-1987, ex-12th Northumberland Fusiliers, who fought on the Somme, erected by his son, Mick. The seat was bought from the proceeds of Harry's moving poetry. Installed for the 2015 ceremony is the **Lochnagar Stone** - a beautiful 2cwt piece of granite from the very top of Lochnagar mountain - polished, inscribed and brought over by the local RAF Mountain Rescue. It is about 30 yards from the walkway towards the far right hand corner. The new semi-circular **Nurses' Memorial Bench** was also unveiled on July 1st - hand-made by Friend Vinny (who constructed the walkway) and faces the nearest nurses' first aid post in the direction beyond Bécourt Wood.

Nearby is a **Seat to the Grimsby Chums**, Saturday 1 July 1916, erected in July 1999. From this seat you have the best OP vantage point from the crater's rim.

Stand with your back to the Seat facing the Cross.

OP. Take the Memorial Cross as 12 o'clock. Just to the left and beyond is the spire of la Boisselle Church and just to its left on the skyline is the Thiepval Memorial, 4,000m away. On a clear day its flags can be seen. A further 4,000m away beyond Thiepval is Beaumont Hamel. At 11 o'clock is the road up which you have driven which runs roughly parallel to, and beside, the German front line trench. At 2 o'clock on the horizon is a long line of poplars. At their left hand end is the wireless mast at Pozières, 4,200m away, which stands on the D929 opposite the Australian Memorial at Pozières Windmill, always a useful reference point around the battlefield and visited on Itinerary 2. In front of the trees, 900m away, is Gordon Dump Cemetery at the north-eastern end of Sausage Valley. The valley curves around from behind you 500m away, and from there to your right-hand side up to the cemetery, which is positioned close to a battlefield track junction once known as Gordon Post. The valley was named 'Sausage' after a German spotter balloon which was flown in the area and the christening of the opposite valley across the D929 as 'Mash' was inevitable.

Above: *The Crater, early morning*

Below: *Commemorative Plaques to 3 brothers, 2 of whom went down on HMS Hampshire with Lord Kitchener.*

Above: *Contact QR Post*

Memorial made of Granite from Lochnagar (Scotland) placed by local RAF Mountain Rescue Association, 1 July 2015

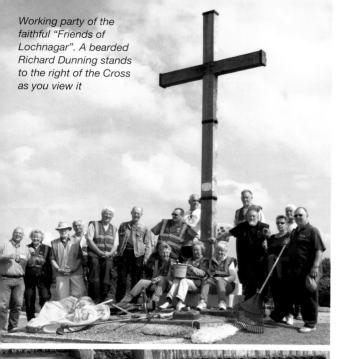

Working party of the faithful "Friends of Lochnagar". A bearded Richard Dunning stands to the right of the Cross as you view it

Sister
Ellen ANDREWS A.R.R.C.
Territorial Force Nursing Service
58 (W.Riding) C.C.S. Lillers
23 March 1918
Lochnagar Crater

Pte
T.G. TURRALL V.C.
10 Bn Worcestershire Reg
C. La Boisselle 3 July 1916
1885 – 1964
Lochnagar Crater

Lt Gen
A CARTON de WIART V.C. D.S.O
8 Bn Gloucestershire Reg
VC La Boisselle 2/3 July 1916
1880-1963
Lochnagar Crater

Stoker
TTETT
Hampshire
1916
Crater

G/21680 Pte
A.H PETTETT
The Queen's Regiment
Sept 1960
Lochnagar Crater

10495 Pte
A. INGHAM
Manchester Regiment
Shot at Dawn 1 December 1916
One of the first to enlist
Lochnagar Crater

At the going down of the sun...

3/8323 Pte
S. STANNARD
7 Bn Yorkshire Regiment
1 July 1916
Lochnagar Crater

Above: *Commemorative Plaques to 2 VCs; a soldier killed on 1 July 1916; a Nursing Sister; a Soldier "Shot at Dawn"*

Thus the general shape of the German front line to the north may be seen: i.e. Beaumont Hamel to Thiepval, Thiepval to the Glory Hole (by the poplars at 10 o'clock) and from there up the road to where you are now standing. At 7 o'clock the Golden Madonna at Albert should be visible on an average clear day, at 10 o'clock in the dip is the Poppy Restaurant and the crest, 1,000m away, running to behind the Glory Hole, is the Tara-Usna line, from which the Tynesiders advanced towards la Boisselle and where you now stand.

Continue round the crater to the cross to the right of the path.

"... Private Turrall picked up his rifle and opened fire on the bombers"

This simple **wooden Cross is in Memory of 22/1306 Pte George Nugent**, Tyneside Scottish, Northumberland Fusiliers. His remains were found at this spot by Friends clearing the area on 31 October 1998. George Nugent was reinterred in Ovillers CWGC Cemetery (qv) on 1 July 2000.

Mine warfare had been carried on in this area well before July 1916 and there were many craters in No Man's Land. In June, along the Western Front as a whole, the British had blown 101 mines and the Germans 126. In this area some of the shafts dug, from which tunnels then reached out to the enemy line, were over 100ft deep with tunnels at up to four levels. When dug, the mine here was called Lochnagar, and it was started by 185th Tunnelling Company and packed with two charges of 24,000lb and 36,000lb of ammonal. It was exploded, along with sixteen other British mines along the Somme front, at 0728 on 1 July, and the circular crater measured 300ft across and was 90ft deep. Debris rose 4,000ft into the air and, as it settled, the Tyneside attack from Tara-Usna began.

Following the failure of that attack, the 10th Worcesters were ordered to move up from beside Albert to make an assault at dawn on 2 July. So chaotic were conditions in the communication trenches that the battalion got lost, and the attack did not go in until 3 July. The Worcesters took the crater area and the village, **Private Thomas George Turrall** winning a **VC** in the process, (a Gilbert Holiday drawing commemorates the action) but the battalion lost a third of its fighting strength and the Commanding Officer was killed.

An increasingly popular memorial feature is the opportunity to sponsor small rectangular Plaques to individuals with WW1 connections (especially to those who fought on the Somme) on the edges of the wooden planks which make up the Crater's surrounding path (apply to the Friends as above for details). Samples of these are illustrated.

Return to the Rue du 34th Division and turn right on what is now Rue Georges Cuvillier (Mort pour la France).

Immediately on the left is the **Old Blighty Tea Rooms**, run by John and Alison Haslock. It is near the site of the café that existed here in the 1920s run by an old British soldier with his French wife. There are some interesting WW1 exhibits in the attractive tea room which serves drinks and light refreshments. There is a small terrace and parking area. Tel: +(0)3 22 64 09 16. E-mail: old_blighty@hotmail.com Website: wwwoldblightysomme.com The large room is available for small groups as a lecture/meeting/function room. Open: Thurs-Mon 1030-1700, Tues: 1200-1600, other times by appointment. Battlefield tours available by prior appointment.

It was in la Boisselle on 2-3 July that the extraordinary Belgian-born officer, **T/Lt Col Adrian Carton de Wiart** (qv), commanding the 8th Gloucesters, won his VC for forcing home the attack while exposing himself fearlessly to the enemy simultaneously controlling the commands of three other battalion commanders who had been wounded. He himself was wounded many times before and during WW1 (he had lost his left hand at Ypres and his left eye in S Africa and wore a dashing black eye patch) and went on to become Lt-Gen Sir Adrian Carton de Wiart, KBE, CB, CNG, DSO, with many foreign awards and distinguished service that took him to Poland, Norway, Yugoslavia, Italy and China in WW2. Well-connected, he had married Countess Federica, eldest daughter of Prince Karl Ludwig Fugger Babenhausen of Klagenfurt in 1908 and married for a second time in 1951 at the age of 71. He died on 5 June 1963 having written his memoirs, Happy Odyssey. He was the model for Brig-Gen Ritchie-Hook in Evelyn Waugh's Sword of Honour trilogy.

Continue towards the church, passing a splendid Poilu memorial on the left. Stop beside the octagonal remains of a water tower as the buildings stop and walk up the path to the left.

• 34th Division Memorial/3.3 miles/10 minutes/ Map J7/GPS: 50.02123 2.6937

This handsome Memorial, comprising a figure of Victory (who, a few years ago, lost the laurel wreath she was brandishing) on a stone base, which commemorates the Division's deeds in the area on 1 July 1916, the first battle in which it was engaged, also incorporates the Division's striking chequerboard emblem. Below the statue the composition of the Divisional Units is inscribed. There is an identical memorial (but with its laurel wreath complete) at Mont Noir in the Ypres Salient (Ypres Map K1). Ovillers CWGC Cemetery may be seen on the slope behind the statue.

Return to the church. Stop at memorial in front of it.

• 19th (Western) Division 'Butterfly' Memorial/3.4 miles/5 minutes/Map J6/GPS: 50.02054 2.69522

34th Div Memorial, la Boisselle

This Memorial, whose divisional emblem of a butterfly is engraved at the top, commemorates their casualties of 2 July-20 November in la Boisselle, Bazentin le Petit and Grandcourt. The Divisional Units are inscribed on the base. It was the 19th that finally took the village on 4 July. The Division has another memorial at Oosttaverne in the Ypres Salient (Ypres Map M19).

Return to the D929 by turning right behind the Poilu. Turn right on the D929 and after 200m, turn left and follow signs to Ovillers CWGC Cemetery.

• Ovillers CWGC Cemetery/4.3 miles/10 minutes/Map J4/5/GPS: 50.02847 2.69221

This Cemetery contains 3,265 burials of soldiers (and sailors of the Royal Naval Division) from the UK, Canada, Australia, South Africa, New Zealand and France (there are about 120 French graves), of which 2,477 are unidentified. It was started as a battle cemetery behind a Dressing Station and was in use until March 1917. After the Armistice, graves from Mash Valley and Red Dragon Cemeteries, as well as many temporary graves from the surrounding battlefields, were concentrated here. There is a Special Memorial inside the front wall to thirty-five soldiers originally buried in Mash Valley whose graves were subsequently lost. It also contains the grave of **Capt John C. Lauder** of the Argyll & Sutherland Highlanders, killed by a sniper (a Scottish newspaper in the 1980s hinted that it may have been a British one – young Lauder was not a universally popular officer) on 28 December 1916. His distraught father, Sir Harry Lauder, visited the 'brown

19th (Western) Div Memorial, La Boisselle

mound' of his son's grave, with its temporary wooden cross, in June 1917. At that time there were 500 graves in the Cemetery. Sir Harry was on a strenuous tour, which took him from Folkestone via Boulogne, to Vimy Ridge, Aubigny, Tramecourt, Arras, Athies, le Quesnoy, Doullens, Albert (where he commented on the Leaning Virgin, still clinging to her perilous position) and thence to Ovillers. He gave concerts to entertain the troops at each stop, often coming under fire. Lauder called it the 'Rev Harry Lauder, MP Tour', and it was a tremendous morale-raiser. It is chronicled in his book *A Minstrel in France* published in 1918, which describes his love of, and pride in, 'My boy, John', which parallels Rudyard Kipling's feelings for 'My Boy, Jack', his son Lt John Kipling, killed at Loos in September 1915. It was as a result of the shattering blow of his son's death that Lauder wrote *Keep Right on to the End of the Road.*

Pte George Nugent (qv) whose remains were found at the Lochnagar Crater in 1998, was reinterred here, with full military honours and in the presence of members of his family, on 1 July 2000. His personal message reads, 'Lost, found, but never forgotten.' In the French plot are several of the Breton soldiers who were killed in the actions of December 1914, when the French held the sector.

In October 1916 the 2nd/5th Gloucesters moved from their reserve position on Aubers Ridge to the Somme, serving at Grandcourt, Aveluy and Ovillers. With them was the poet and musician, Ivor Gurney, and here he wrote one of his most disquieting poems, *Ballad of the Three Spectres:*

As I went up by Ovillers
In mud and water cold to the knee,
There went three jeering, fleering spectres,
That walked abreast and talked of me.

Above: Ovillers CWGC Cemetery

Left: Headstone of
Capt John C. Lauder

Right: Headstone
of Sgt C.C.
Castleton, VC,
Pozères Brit
Cemetery

Left: Sir Harry
Lauder, whose son
is buried in Ovillers
CWGC Cemetery

One prophesied a 'Blighty one' for him – correct, as in September 1917 he was gassed at St Julien and sent home. The second predicted that he would die in 'Picardie', which he did not do. The third, and most fearsome prediction, was:

He'll stay untouched till the war's last dawning

Then live one hour of agony.

It could be said that the mental turmoil in which Gurney lived for the last fifteen or so years of his disturbed life were indeed one long hour of agony.

In the village of Ovillers after the war a Nissen hut stood on the site of the church, proclaiming 'This was Ovillers Church'. At one time a memorial to the miners, whose tunnels riddled the slope leading up the village, stood in Ovillers. The rebuilt village sits on the site of the old light railway, the bath house and the encampment known as Wolfe Huts. Gurney would have been pleased to know that after the war, Gloucester paid for two wells in Ovillers.

On 1 July 1916 the German front line ran from la Boisselle past the right hand edge of the cemetery and on towards Thiepval.

[N.B.] 1. To the left here is a cart track (which may be driven up if the ground is extremely dry, otherwise it is a 10-minute return walk) signed **Calvaire Breton**.

It leads to an imposing memorial **Calvary** (**Map J5a, GPS: 50.03178 2.6905**) with an imaginative *bas relief* of crosses with an inscription around the base to 'les braves du 19 RIF, 7 dec 1914' and the words *'Je n'abandonne pas mes bretons'*, which has been refurbished, thanks to the instigation of François Bergez (qv). It is also in memory of **Capt Henby Baillard** and **Lt Augustin de Boisanger** who fell here and **André Pitel**, the Regiment's Adjutant. In the first year of the war this sector was mostly manned by men from the west of France - la Vendée and Brittany.

Breton Calvary Memorial, with detail, Ovillers

[N.B.] 2. Site of Ulverston Street Trench.

As Albert is twinned with Ulverston there was much interest in the inauguration in 2006 (the 30th Anniversary of the Town Twinning and the 90th of the battle) of the site of the trench, part of a system of trenches named after north-eastern towns. Here the King's Own Royal Lancaster Regt and the Seaforth Highlanders (including the poet Lt E.A. Mackintosh) were stationed in the autumn and winter of 1915. The Royal Berks and 2nd Middlesex fought here in July 1916. Main instigators of the project were the historian Michael Stedman with Paula Kesteloot who had been researching the movements of men from her home county, Lancashire. The site may be reached by walking up the sloping track away from the Memorial and just over the crest turning left along a track which is on the line of the old trench which is behind Ovillers Cemetery – some 800 metres in all. At the crest of the track where you turn left, there is a splendid **OP:** at 9 o' clock – the Golden Madonna at Albert, at 11 o' clock – The Leipzig Salient, at 12 o'clock - Thiepval Memorial, with Thiepval church at the end of the trees to the right, at 3 o' clock Pozières Wireless Mast and Church, at 5 o' clock 5th Army Memorial, Pozières.

Turn round and return to the junction with the road that leads to the D929 to the right (up which you drove). Return to the D929, turn left signed Bapaume.

As you drive to the crest of the Pozières Ridge the Thiepval Memorial may be seen 2,800m away to the left.

Continue to a large cemetery enclosure beside the road on the left. Stop.

• Pozières British Cemetery and 4th & 5th Armies Memorial/6.2 miles/15 minutes/Map J8/9/GPS: 50.03371 2.71565

The Memorial is the wall that surrounds the cemetery. It is to men of the Fifth and Fourth Armies who have no known grave, and was designed by W. H. Cowlishaw of the (then) Imperial War Graves Commission. It relates to the period of the final German assault of March 1918 and over 14,600 names are inscribed on the wall. Among these the Rifle

Memorial to 4th & 5th Armies, Pozières, seen from the Chalk Pit

Brigade, the Durham Light Infantry and the Machine Gun Corps each have over 500. The Manchesters have almost 500, including **Lt Col Wilfrith Elstob** (qv), CO of their 16th Bn who won the **VC** at Manchester Hill Redoubt near St Quentin on 21 March 1918. The cemetery contains over 2,700 burials, from the UK, Australia and Canada, including **Sgt Claude Charles Castleton**, 5th MGC, AIF, who won the **VC** on 28 July 1916 in this area.

Continue about 300m. Park near a memorial cross on the right.

• KRRC Memorial/6.6 miles/5 minutes/Map H10/GPS: 50.03668 2.72134

The Kings Royal Rifle Corps had two battalions in the original BEF and raised twenty more during the war. There is a similar memorial in the Ypres Salient at Hooge (Holts' Ypres Map I31) and another in Winchester.

Continue to small road to the right.

[N.B.]This was known as **Dead Man's Road** and runs through a depression once known as Smyth Valley. At the end of this narrow, rough track with very sharp stones (negotiable by car only if dry) is the **Chalk Pit (GPS: 50.02938 2.72046)** where on 15 July 1916 the 8th East Lancs with the remnants of the 11th R Warwicks gathered as they were repulsed by the enemy in their drive from Contalmaison towards Pozières. Battalion HQs were established in the pit under heavy artillery fire and at 1400 hours **Major-General Ingouville-Williams** (qv), commanding 34th Division, made a visit to assess the situation. He ordered a further bombardment and assault

to take place at 1700 hours. This was met by heavy machine gun fire but the East Lancs managed to dig in some 300 yards short of the village. The following day the weary men were relieved and their wounded evacuated to a dressing station in Contalmaison. During the attack the 112th Brigade sustained 1,034 casualties, of which the 8th East Lancs had 365. It was the Kitchener Battalion's first battle of the war.

The Chalk Pit, Pozières

Turn left almost immediately, signed up a small road to the Australian 1st Division Memorial.

• Australian 1st Division Memorial/1993 RB Plaque & Gibraltar Blockhouse/6.7 miles/15 minutes/Map G47/48/GPS: 50.03778 2.72196

The obelisk Memorial sits on the forward slope of Pozières Ridge, the ground rising to its crest 500m away as the D929 continues on through the village towards Bapaume. At the Memorial entrance is a low bronze, Ross Bastiaan (qv) *bas relief* Plaque, unveiled by the Australian Minister for Veterans' Affairs on 30 August 1993 and sponsored by AMPSOC. There are interesting Information Boards beside the Memorial with details of the Australian Remembrance Trail stops around the village, another being at the entrance to Dead Man's Road. There are now two distinct trails: the Short one is a 2 km

Gibraltar Blockhouse, Pozières

Australian 1st Div Memorial, Pozières

circuit within the village itself, the Longer one extends to 10kms around the village and they have a 'totem'-like marker – see Mouquet Farm, the next stop on this Itinerary). Details of the routes are available in a leaflet from the *Albert Pays du Coquelicot* **Tourist Office** (qv) – see the App 'Australians at Pozières 1916'.

Beyond the obelisk the Thiepval Memorial can be seen on the horizon. The ridge was a major feature, furiously contested by both sides and, with Thiepval towards its northern end, it sits like a barricade across the D929. It was a formidable obstacle, with its fortified cellars, network of defensive trenches and twin OP blockhouses. One, called **Gibraltar**, is in the bank to your right as you drive up to the Memorial and it has been cleared by the CGS/H to make its entrance easily visible. The other was at The Windmill - see Itinerary Two. There are informative signboards, a large car park and a wooden viewing platform (which gives the German viewpoint and indicates points of interest). The entrance to the blockhouse has been protected and entry is forbidden.

Following the collapse of the night attack offensive which began Part 3 of the Somme Battle on 14 July, four unsuccessful assaults were made on Pozières. The first attack was made by the British 48th Division on the left (Pozières Memorial) side of the D929 and the 1st Australian Division on the right (KRRC Memorial) side, the Australians having moved up from Albert and then through Sausage Valley. The attack went in thirty minutes after midnight on 23/24 July. The main trench, known as Western Trench, of the German garrison, the 117th Division, ran parallel to and on the left beside the small road you have just driven up. The trench and the village were taken on 24 July, but the Germans still held the crest of the ridge (marked by the tall wireless mast) and counter-attacked. Although the Australians held on, after three days the division had lost over 5,200 casualties and had to be relieved. The subsequent actions are summarised in Itinerary Two, Pozières Windmill entry.

Continue to the T junction by the village war memorial. It is surmounted by the cockerel emblem of France. Opposite is the school and Mairie.

Turn left. After approx 100m, shells and other battlefield relics are piled in the garden against the house on the right owned by private collectors.

Continue along the D73 road.

Ovillers is to the left, 2,500m away. This road roughly follows the route of the German Second Line to Thiepval, which can be seen ahead.

In anticipation of the extra traffic along this road during the Centenary years, it was widened and resurfaced.

Continue to the Memorial Plaque on a bend on the right roughly half way between Pozières and Thiepval.

• Ross Bastiaan Memorial Plaque, Mouquet Farm/8.1 miles/10 minutes/ Map H15/GPS: 50.04943 2.70818)

This is on the site of **Mouquet Farm** (known to Tommy as Mucky Farm and to the Aussies as Moo Cow Farm) on the right. A farm has been rebuilt close to the original site. On 10 September 1997 the Plaque was unveiled here by the Australian Deputy Prime Minister, Mr Tim Fisher. It commemorates the Australians who fell in August/September 1916 in the struggles for Thiepval and is sited close to the line of the German 'Constance' Trench. Here is a 'totem' marker for Australian Remembrance Trail stop No 23.

Continue to Thiepval village. Follow signs to the Visitor Centre.

The village was virtually wiped out in the war and the present small cluster of church, houses, school/Mairie and farm is

Ross Bastiaan Plaque, Mouquet Farm behind, Australian Remembrance Trail Marker No 23

far smaller than the original thriving village. To the right of the church entrance is

• Plaque to Lt-Gen Sir Adrian Carton de Wiart, VC, KBE, CB, CMG, DSO/ 8.9 miles/5 minutes/Map G44b/GPS: 50.05378 2.68813

Instigated by Lt-Col J.P. Schellekens, Chairman of the Belgian National Remembrance Committee, the Plaque was inaugurated on 2 July 2006. This extraordinary soldier and personality won his VC at la Boisselle (qv) commanding the 8th Gloucesters on 2/3 July 1916. The ceremony was attended by the British Ambassador to Belgium, Regimental, Belgian and local dignitaries (including Mme Potié, then-Mayor of Thiepval) and members of the Belgian and Irish branches of the Carton de Wiart families, including la Comtesse Renée-Victoire de la Kéthulle de Ryhove and de Wiart's grandson, the war correspondent Anthony Lloyd.

Continue, following signs to the Visitor Centre car park.

Plaque to Lt-Gen Sir Adrian Carton de Wiart, VC, KBE, CB, CMG, DSO, Thiepval Church

• *The Thiepval Visitor Centre & Museum/9 miles/30 minutes/Map G44a/ GPS: 50.05237 2.68814*

NOTE that this memorial site has undergone major changes during the Centenary years.
1. New Museum. This is being built in the ground between the existing Visitor Centre and
the Memorial and consists of three exhibition rooms.

Room 1 will feature the original of the remarkable Frieze by Joe Sacco which depicts the lives of soldiers fighting in the area in 1916 in vivid detail (a book showing the Frieze is on sale in the Centre.) Beneath the glass floor are artefacts found during the excavation.

Room 2 features the Missing – British, French and German - on the Thiepval Memorial in particular, with personal stories and illustrations.

Room 3 concentrates on the War in the Air with a

The exterior, Thiepval Visitor Centre

replica of the Red Baron's Fokker and stories of the Aces. It links the Unknowns with the 'famous'.

In the centre is a Saint Chamond Tank replica. It was a French heavy tank, production of which began in mid-1917.

The Foundation Stone was laid on 20 June 2015 by dignitaries from the Franco-British Committee.

The Visitor and Education Centre was opened here in September 2004 by one of its Patrons, HRH the Duke of Kent. The nearly £2 million required was funded half by British donations and half by the *Conseil Général de la Somme* and EU Regional Funds

and is supported by Madame Geneviève Potié, then-Mayor of Thiepval. It is the inspiration of Sir Frank Sanderson who felt that modern-day visitors should have some background information about what happened at this historic site and also have a place of rest and refreshment. He fund-raised energetically to find the 50% from some 2,000 different donors and worked with determination to see the challenging project through with the French builders. The idea was regarded as somewhat controversial by purist regular visitors who feared that the building would detract from the classical Lutyens Memorial and that the proliferation of information centres in the area was tending to create a Somme 'theme park'.

Missing of the Somme display, Thiepval Visitors Centre

Boutique, Thiepval Visitors Centre

Sensitive to these feelings the designers have created a discreet sunken building with a glass façade and original Lutyens bricks which is shielded by trees and which blends into the environment. The Centre has now been accepted as an informative and convenient facility and is very popular with visitors. It is managed by Vincent Laude and his helpful bi-lingual team led by Dawn and is served by a new road leading to a large car and coach park. The Centre contains a book shop, refreshment and toilet facilities, as well as offering historical Information Panels (by Professor Peter Simkins, Brother Nigel Cave and author Michael Stedman) and a databank to enable visitors to trace where relatives – Allied and German – are buried or commemorated. Part of the exhibition is devoted to personal details of some of the 72,000 men who are commemorated on the Memorial and there is a striking and very moving montage of some of their portraits. Another section is devoted to Sir Edwin Lutyens. There is access to the Debt of Honour websites, video displays, a small theatre and a superb panorama of the surrounding area as in 1916. There are facilities for student groups and for bus drivers.

An accurate 1:25 scale model of the Lutyens Memorial stands inside the entrance. It was constructed by Andrew Ingham and Assocs.

During the excavations, the Durand Group (qv) established that no significant vestiges of the war were disturbed other than a few shells and the remains of six Germans which were taken in charge by the German authorities.

In June 2006 the hard-working Charity Committee handed over all administration to the *Historial* at Péronne and the CWGC undertook the landscaping and maintenance of the surroundings.

Open: 1 May-31 Oct 1000-1800 and 1 Nov-30 April 0900-1700. Closed for two weeks over Christmas and the New Year. Free admission. Tel: +(0)3 22 74 60 47. Fax: +(0)3 22 74 65 44. Email: thiepval@historial.org Website: www.historial.org There is a series of Information Boards outside the entrance.

From the Centre walk along the short path to the entrance to the Memorial.

The house opposite the entrance was built in the 1980s by the then-Mayor, Madame Potié, on the site of the cottage of the old guardian for many years, Monsieur Poprawa, and serves as a staging and command post for ceremonies. It has now been acquired by the Somme. To the left of the entrance to the Memorial are the gardeners' huts and garages for the CWGC section, for many years supervised by Arthur Leach. Arthur was the son of Serre Road No 2 gardener, Ben Leach, who during World War II hid, and then sent on their way to the Spanish border, several Allied airmen.

• *Thiepval Memorial & Cemetery/9.1 miles/25 minutes/Map G46/45 OP/ GPS: 50.05122 2.68792*

NOTE. In December 2014 the CWGC announced that an 18-month project to restore the Thiepval Memorial, one of its most iconic structures, would begin in Spring 2015. Representing one of the most important pieces of restoration work to be undertaken by the organisation for some time, the facelift will ensure that both the monument and surrounding landscape are ready for the Battle of the Somme Centenary in July 2016. It includes making the Memorial watertight and replacing the drainage system. Work not completed before the Anniversary commemorations will cease and restart afterwards. As Thiepval will be the venue for a major 1 July 2016 Ceremony the project is also being supported by the UK Government.

The Thiepval Memorial

Outside the entrance is a CGS/H Signboard. The structure is both a battle Memorial and a Memorial. As the former it commemorates the 1916 Anglo-French offensive on the Somme and as the latter it carries the names of over 73,000 British and South African men who have no known grave and who fell on the Somme between July 1916 and 20 March 1918. The Australian Missing are commemorated on the Villers Bretonneux Memorial, the Canadians on the Vimy Ridge Memorial, the Indians at Neuve Chapelle, the Newfoundlanders at Beaumont Hamel and the New Zealanders at Longueval. The Memorial, 150ft high, which dominates the surrounding area, was designed by Sir Edwin Lutyens and has sixteen piers on whose faces the names of the Missing are inscribed. It stands on a concrete raft 10ft thick, built 19ft below ground – the solution of surveyor Major Macfarlane to the problems of building over the warren of tunnels and dugouts that formed part of the German second line. It is the largest British war memorial in the world and was unveiled on 31 July 1932, by HRH the Prince of Wales in the presence of the President of the French Republic. The event was not without controversy. At the time ex-servicemen were suffering from the mass unemployment that was to lead to the general depression. Where was the land 'fit for heroes to live in', promised by Lloyd George? Bruce Bairnsfather, the creator of Old Bill, used his popular folk hero to express his views in an article in the *Daily Herald*. Would not the money used to create this splendid edifice not have been better spent in caring for the men without limbs, without minds, living a twilight existence in the Star and Garter Home? Yet posterity might feel that it is appropriate to have an enduring focal point for remembrance for those who gave their lives for their beliefs – to remind us that they were fighting for our peaceful future. 'The Thiepval Arch will stand as firmly as the Empire whose sons it commemorates', wrote H. A. Taylor hopefully in his enduringly interesting *Good-bye to the Battlefields*, in 1928. The war correspondent, Sir Philip Gibbs, wrote of Thiepval in a 1916 despatch, 'It is historic ground. A hundred years hence men of our blood will come here with reverence as to sacred soil.' How accurate this prophecy has proved to be.

During the mid-1980s the Memorial underwent some drastic changes. It had to be refaced with sturdy Manchester red house brick stock, owing to the deterioration of the original attractive, but soft, rust-coloured bricks selected by Lutyens, and the handsome semi-circular hedge, which was such a striking feature around the lawns in front of the memorial, was killed in the winter frosts of 1984/5 and had to be removed. Another major refurbishment was carried out in January-February 2007 on the twenty-one flat roofs of the memorial.

Walk through the entrance into the 40-acre park.

The path heads directly towards the tip of the Leipzig Salient, marked by an isolated copse of tall trees, 1,000m away and from which one can walk to the Lonsdale CWGC Cemetery (see Extra Visit on page 99 and **WALK NUMBER 1** page 319). The path points almost exactly at the Golden Madonna in Albert, 6.4km away.

[N.B.] In the summer of 2014 a sensitive and imaginative public art work, 'The Lost Men, France', by South African artist Paul Emmanuel, was installed at the edge of the CWGC area just as this path starts. It was a reflection of 'impermanence and forgetting' and also a statement drawing attention to the fact that black South African names were excluded from the Thiepval Memorial. The artist used photos of parts of his own body upon which were superimposed random names, without rank, nationality or ethnicity, of soldiers lost on the Somme. These were mounted on fine material which hung on a line of poles and blew with the wind in a haunting manner. See www. the-lost-men.net]

'The Lost Men, France' [The Lost Men].

Walk to the War Stone.

Among the names commemorated on the Memorial – each important to those who mourn it – are the brilliant musician **Lt George Butterworth MC**, of the 13th Bn, DLI (qv), killed on 1 August 1916; **Major Cedric Charles Dickens** (qv), descendant of the great novelist, killed on 9 September 1916; **Pte Watcyn Griffith,** killed in Mametz Wood on 10 July 1916, while carrying a message from his famous brother, author Wyn Griffith; **Lt William Ker** of Hawke Bn, RND, mentioned in A. P. Herbert's moving tribute to his fallen comrades, Beaucourt Revisited; **Lt Thomas Kettle**, Royal Dublin Fusiliers, the Irish poet and former MP; **Lce Sgt Hector Hugh Munro** (qv) of the 22nd Royal Fusiliers, the author Saki, killed by a sniper on 14 November 1916, at the age of 46, in the area of what is now Munich Trench Cemetery; **Cpl Alexander Robertson** of the 12th Yorks & Lancs, the same battalion as fellow poet, John William Streets (qv) and, like him, killed on 1 July 1916; some unfortunate men 'shot at dawn' – **Pte Cairnie** of the 1st Scots Fusiliers, **Pte Farr** of the 1st W Yorks, **Pte Skilton** of the 22nd Royal Fusiliers; **Victoria Cross winners T/Capt Eric Frankland Bell** of the 9th RIF, **Pte William Buckingham** of the 2nd Leicesters, **T/Lt Geoffrey Cather** of the 9th RIF, **Pte 'Billy' McFadzean** of the 14th RIR, **Rifleman William Mariner** of the 2nd KRRC, **T/Lt Thomas Wilkinson** of the

Private Memorial to Lt Geoge Butterworth near his name on the Thiepval Memorial

7th LNL and **Sgt Maj Alexander Young** of the Cape Police, SAF. **Pte Reginald Giles**, 1st Gloucesters once thought to be **only 14 years old**, but research by Jessica Wise proved that he was in fact 19.

Demonstrating the impact this battle made on one school, there are 17 Old Salopians named on the Memorial.

Behind the Memorial is a **small Anglo-French cemetery**, which symbolizes the joint nature of the war. Its construction was paid for equally by both Governments and 300 dead of each nation are buried there. On the base of the Cross of Sacrifice in the cemetery is the inscription 'That the world may remember the common sacrifice of two and a half million dead there have been laid side by side soldiers of France and of the British Empire in eternal comradeship'.

Stand beside the War Stone with your back both to it and the cemetery. Look straight ahead over the far wall and between the avenue of trees. That is 12 o'clock.

At 9 o'clock through the arch is the obelisk of the 18th Division memorial and behind it on the crest is the area of the Schwaben Redoubt. At 12 o'clock in the middle ground is Mouquet ('Mucky') Farm and behind it, running right to left across your front, is the Albert-Bapaume road. On that road, but just concealed behind the right-hand avenue of trees, is the Pozières Wireless Mast, probably the most useful reference feature on the battlefield. The Pozières Ridge/Thiepval Plateau feature running towards you from beyond Mucky Farm and the area up to and including Thiepval were not finally cleared until September. On the 15th, Part 4 of the Somme battle had opened with the tank attack from right to left along the horizon at 12 o'clock, that area having been taken by the Australians in August. Mucky Farm fell on 26 September and Thiepval to the Essex, Middlesex and Suffolk county regiments of 18th Division on the 27th. Throughout the whole period of German occupation to 1916, the village was garrisoned by the 180th Württemberg Regiment. It fell again to the Germans on 25 March 1918 and was recaptured by the 17th and 38th (Welsh) Divisions on 24 August 1918.

How To Find An Individual Name On The Thiepval Memorial

Using the Register Books which are kept in the pillars of the Memorial, first look up the regiment of the name that you are searching for. These are listed in alphabetical order. Within each regiment, ranks are listed in order of seniority. Within each rank, names appear in alphabetical order. Regiments are not broken down by battalion, with the sole exception of the London Regiment. The number of the pier and the letter of the face on which the names of casualties from each regiment appear, are shown on pages 14-18 of the Cemetery Report Introduction.

The memorial has sixteen piers, or columns, on which all the names are inscribed. Each pier is numbered and each face is lettered. The number allocated to each pier and the letter allocated to each face of the piers are shown on the plan on page 13 of the Memorial Report Introduction. The reports are vital to this operation. Ideally, you should ascertain the pier number and face letter of the name you are looking for in advance of your visit by visiting the CWGC Debt of Honour website (qv).

Return to your car. As you drive out of the car park, a memorial obelisk is seen to the left at the D151 junction ahead.

18th Division Memorial with Thiepval Church behind

• *18th Division Memorial/9.3 miles/5 minutes/Map G44/GPS: 50.05264 2.68566*

This obelisk to the victors of Thiepval is a replica of the one in Trônes Wood (Itinerary 2) and bears the same exhortation: 'This is my command, that ye love one another'. It gives the order of battle of the brigades which made up the division and the division's battle honours. When standing in front of the memorial there are open views behind it of Thiepval Wood, the Connaught Cemetery, Mill Road Cemetery and the Ulster Tower.

Extra Visit to the Salford Pals Memorial & 15th, 16th & 17th Battalions Highland Light Infantry Memorial, 16th Northumberland Fusiliers Plaque and Seat, Authuille (Map G42a,b,c, GPS: 50.04305 2.66907), SOA of Sgt Turnbull VC (Map G49, GPS: 50.04305 2.66907), Dorset Memorial/Lonsdale CWGC Cemetery (Map G43, GPS: 50.04127 2.68485) Round-trip: 3-6 miles. Approximate time: 30 minutes.

Turn left on the D151 and follow the road down into the village of Authuille and stop at the Plaque, next to the Poilu local memorial on the right.

The **Salford Pals Memorial** was unveiled on 1 July 1995, by members of the Lancashire Fusiliers Association, the Lancashire & Cheshire Branch of the WFA and the Mayor of Authuille in a simple and moving ceremony. The site was chosen as, of the four Pals Battalions raised in Salford during 1914 and 1915, three of them (the 15th, 16th and 19th Lancashire Fusiliers) fought in this area against fortress Thiepval in the opening days of the Battle of the Somme from 1 July 1916. Their initial attack was met by a determined defence from twenty-five machine guns and soon the lanes around Authuille were filled with the dead and dying men from the dockyards, coal mines, textile mills and engineering works of Salford. Many are buried in the nearby cemeteries of Aveluy Wood

Salford Pals Memorial, Authuille

(Lancashire Dump) (Map G41) – where **2nd Lt Francis Kennard Bliss**, brother of the composer Arthur Bliss, is also buried – and Authuille (Map G42). Others are commemorated on the Thiepval Memorial. Opposite is a **Memorial Seat** presented to the village by the City of Glasgow in March 2003.

Continue to the Church on the right.

1 July 1996, the 80th Anniversary of the opening day of the Battle of the Somme, saw the unveiling of a long overdue **Memorial to three Battalions of the Highland Light Infantry** – the 15th (Glasgow Tramways), 16th (Boys' Brigade) and 17th (Glasgow Commercials – which included men from Strathclyde University and affiliated schools). At a memorial service to the 17th Bn held in Glasgow Cathedral on 8 July 1917, the Bn Padre, Rev A. H. Gray ended his address by asking for a special memorial for the fallen and with the words;

"From a hundred lonely graves in that foreign land – from the spots where they fell and which now are sacred spots for us – our dead are asking us when we mean to erect that monument. From trench and shell hole where death found them, their voices call – young, musical voices, the voices of boys still in their teens, the voices of martyrs on life's threshold. Scarce a wind can blow that will not waft to you these voices. And they ask a better

Britain as their monument. They ask it of you and me. Shall we not go from this place resolved to build it?"

On coming across this account three-quarters of a century later, Glaswegian Charles McDonald, of the Thistle and Poppy Society, was so moved that he resolved to take the appeal for a monument literally

Memorial Plaque to 15th, 16th & 17th Glasgow Bns, HLI, with brass Plaque below inaugurated by the `Thistle and Poppy Association, Authuille Church

Unveiling of Plaque to 15th Bn Northumberland Fusiliers, Authuille Church, by (l) Ian Johnson and (r) CEO NE Chamber of Commerce, James Ramsbotham

and started to raise funds. His original idea was to erect a female figure representing 'Mother Glasgow', with three children representing the three battalions. When it became clear that this would not be achieved in time for the eightieth anniversary, Charles decided on a simple black marble Plaque engraved with the regimental crest, a tribute to the three battalions and the poignant words of the Rev Gray. The Memorial is on the church at Authuille, from where the battalions made their assault on Thiepval Ridge on 1 July 1916. Below is a brass Plaque blessed in Glasgow Cathedral on 23 June 1996 and inaugurated on 30 June 1996, the 80th Anniversary, by the Deputy Mayor of Glasgow.

On 27 June 2015 a Plaque in the Church and Memorial Bench nearby to the 16th Bn, Northumberland Fusiliers was inaugurated. The project was initiated by Ian Johnson, author of *Newcastle Battalions of World War One*, and the £20,000 required was also funded and supported by the Newcastle Branch of the Fusiliers' Veterans' Association, Newcastle City Council, the Somme Remembrance Association, and the Authuille Council. The Plaque commemorates the members of the Battalion 'who manned the trenches in Authuille from early 1916 and who valiantly attacked the Thiepval Defences on 1 July'. The ceremony was attended by Gateshead MP, Ian Means, dignitaries from Newcastle and Authuille. 'Jordie' songs were played by the Samarobriva Pipe Band.

Turn round and return to a sharp right turn on the 'C' road, signed to Ovillers and the Londsale Cemetery.

This is the route the Salford Pals took in their attack on the Thiepval fortress. The road runs round the tip of the Leipzig Salient to the left and there are superb views on reaching the crest. This area was the **SOA of Sgt James Youll Turnbull VC** of the Highland Light Infantry. On 1 July 1916 his party captured an important enemy post which was then bombarded by the enemy throughout the day. Turnbull held on as several parties were wiped out and replaced around him, but was himself killed later in the day in a 'bombing' counter-attack.

Continue to a track (not driveable) to the left **(GPS: 50.04297 2.68015)**.

This leads to the **Leipzig Salient**, and a short distance up the path on the right there is (perhaps no longer) a beautiful **Private Tribute** in the form of a wreath in the centre of which is an encapsulated account of **Pte Henry Parfitt**, 1st Wilts, kia 7 July 1916, and commemorated on the Thiepval Memorial and other family members killed in the Great War, placed by his great nephew.

Continue to the path to the cemetery to the right.

Private Memorial to Pte Henry Parfitt, Leipzig Salient

As you walk, the 1916 front lines were roughly 200 yards apart astride the path, the German to the left. At the corner of the path is a fine **Obelisk Memorial** to the men of the **Dorset Regiment** who have fallen on battlefields as far afield as France, India and present day Iraq. It was instigated by Maj Tim Saunders, ex Devon & Dorsets, now military historian, supported by the Dorset & South Wilts WFA, the local Cadets and many other contributors, who raised the required £23,000. The Somme Remembrance Association with the Mayor of Authuille arranged the purchase of the land for a token €1.00. The 8 ft high cream stone Monument was sculpted by Zoe Cull and Alex Evans. It carries the battle honours of the Regiment and their badge on the back. A quote from Thomas Hardy, "Victory Crowns the Just", is carved beneath the County Crest. It was unveiled on 7 May 2011 in an impressive ceremony conducted by Rev Nick Wall in the presence of the Lord Lt of Devon, the Pres of the Devon & Dorset Regt Old Comrades' Association, Bugle Major Cox, many contributors, local dignitaries and the family of L/ Sgt John Dobson, buried in Lonsdale Cemetery (1 July 1916, age 36).

Before 1 July the 1st Bn of the Regiment was in reserve at Blackhorse Dugouts, adjoining Authuille Cemetery. They attacked in the second wave, and moved up through Authuille Wood where they came under heavy machine gun fire. They dashed from the wood as enemy fire redoubled and the Drum Major played the regimental March on his flute as some 150 men reached the front line. They attacked the trenches opposite and to the south of the Leipzig Salient. They were then driven back but were left holding the Salient. The Dorsets suffered between 450 and 490 OR casualties and 23 Officers, about half of them falling between the Wood and the site of this Memorial.

Continue up the grass path to the side of the Monument to

Memorial to the Devon & Dorset Regiment, Authuille, with Bugle Major Tony Cox

Lonsdale CWGC Cemetery. GPS: 50.04008 2.68241. It was named after the Earl of Lonsdale, who recruited a 'Pals' unit, the 11th Bn, the Border Regiment, which attacked the Leipzig Salient from this point on 1 July. It contains the grave of **Sgt Turnbull VC** (see above). The battalion's CO, **Lt Col Percy Machell** (qv), was killed here on 1 July 1916. This interesting officer served in Egypt and the Sudan and had been Military Adviser to the Egyptian Ministry of the Interior during 1898-1908 (Simkins, *Kitchener's Army*). Machell is buried in Warloy-Baillon Communal Cemetery Extension (qv, Map S1/4).

The Cemetery, designed by Sir Herbert Baker, makes an excellent vantage point from which to study the attack on the Leipzig Salient. It was started in the spring of 1917 after the German withdrawal to the Hindenburg Line when the battlefield was cleared of the sad bodies which still lay there from the 1 July battle. Several small cemeteries were created, including this one, originally Lonsdale Cemetery No 1 which contained the 96 bodies buried in the current Plot I, the majority of them being men of the 1st Dorsets and 11th Borderers. After the Armistice the burials from the other small cemeteries were concentrated here and there is now a total of 1,542 burials, 816 Unknown, with a Special Memorial to 22 casualties 'known to be buried here'.

Return to the 18th Div Memorial and pick up the main itinerary.

Lonsdale CWGC Cemetery, Authuille

Turn right (towards the church).

Thiepval Château, once an imposing building with an elegant façade containing twenty-four windows, used to stand on the left of this road. Before the war it gave employment to the majority of the villagers living in its shadow, but it was never rebuilt.

In January 2013, the Abbott and Holder Gallery, London, put on an exhibition/sale of 62 watercolours by artist Albert Heim (1890-?), commissioned by Lieutenant General Theodor von Wundt (1858-1929). Wundt commanded the 6,500 Württemberger men of the 51 Reserve Infantry Brigade from 2nd August 1914 to 1st October 1916, during most of which time the Brigade was on the Somme battlefield between Ovillers and Beaumont Hamel and centred at Thiepval. The watercolours record the General's life, mostly before the British offensive of July 1st 1916, while he was quartered first at Courcelette,

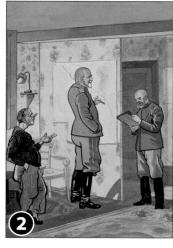

1. Ruins of Thiepval Chateau (briefly Lt-Gen Wundt's HQ in Sept 1914)
2. L-Gen Wundt beside map of the Albert sector as the morning news arrives
3. The Artist, Albert Heim, above trench between Ovillers and Beaumont Hamel
4. Festivities in cave, Courcelette. Gen Wundt seated on right, his dog, Moritz, on the floor
5. German Staff Officer in a trench – same perception on both sides

then at Miraumont and at work on the Sector's battlefields. It is remarkable that a busy Lieutenant General should have commissioned such a personal record and they may have been painted with publication in mind. He certainly had a great sense of humour as many of the images of him are less than flattering caricatures.

For images of all 62 paintings (whose price range was mostly between £1,000-£2,000) and biographical details of Heim and Wundt, see www.abottandholder-thelist.co.uk/heim/

Continue. After 200m turn left at the crossroads onto the D73, signed to Beaumont Hamel Memorial Park. Continue.

On 1 July this road was mostly in No Man's Land, running roughly parallel with the British front line about 150m to your left and the German line up to 300m to your right.

• *Connaught & Mill Road CWGC Cemeteries/10 miles/20 minutes/Map G29/36/GPS: 50.05890 2.68089*

Connaught Cemetery was begun in the autumn of 1916, and after the Armistice the burials from ten or so other cemeteries nearby were concentrated here. Of the more than 1,200 soldiers, sailors and Royal Naval Division Marines in the cemetery, the majority

fell in the 1916 Somme offensive – many of them Ulstermen – and over half are unknown. A further measure of the chaos and destruction on the battlefield, in which men simply disappeared, is that for one-third of the 1,268 buried not even their units are known. The Cemetery was designed by Sir Reginald Blomfield.

Behind the Cemetery is Thiepval Wood, known today to the locals as Authuille Wood, and not to be confused with the wood of the same name just south-east of the village of Authuille. The Somme Association (qv) have acquired this area which is of such historic interest to the Irish as well as to the British Regiments which also occupied it. They have cleared paths and the area around the crater where **Billie McFadzean's** act of gallantry won him the **VC** and there are recreated trench lines and Information Panels. In 2004 three small

Above: Trench lines, Thiepval Wood

metal Crosses were erected here as Memorials to the 36th Ulster Div, followed in 2006 by a larger wooden Cross. They were inspired by Pte McFadzean's heroic action and an annual ceremony is held here on 1 July. Apply to the Ulster Tower (next stop) for a visit.

Opposite the Cemetery is a track leading to **Mill Road Cemetery** which was begun in Spring 1917 and enlarged after the Armistice with concentrations from nearby small cemeteries. It sits just forward of the main German position (1 July 1916) on the crest. The area is so riddled with tunnels that subsidence still occurs and many of the headstones in the cemetery are laid flat. There are some 1,300 burials (815 Unknown), including Ulstermen from 1 July and 18th

The path to Mill Road CWGC Cemetery

Above: *School group at Connaught CWGC Cemetery, Thiepval behind*

Left: *Members of the Ulster Volunteer Force at the dedication of the Wooden Cross, Thiepval Wood*

and 39th Division men from later attacks. The notorious Schwaben Redoubt extended beyond the same ridge. Monsieur Poprawa (see above) recalled his team of horses falling into the great chasms of the underground chambers as he ploughed the area when the land was restored to agriculture between the wars. The Cemetery was designed by Sir Herbert Baker.

Continue and park by the entrance to the memorial on the right.

• *Ulster Tower Memorials & Visitors' Centre/10.1 miles/30 minutes/RWC /Map G31/33/34/35/37/OP/GPS: 50.06067 2.6769*

Outside the entrance gate is a CGS/H Signboard about the 36th Ulster Division. Stand with your back to the gates. Straight ahead at 12 o'clock is Thiepval Wood (now shown on modern French maps as Authuille Wood). At 7 o'clock is Mill Road Cemetery. At 9 o'clock is Connaught Cemetery and beyond it the Thiepval Memorial. At 2 o'clock on the horizon is Beaumont Hamel Memorial Park. At 3 o'clock is a small track leading down to

St Pierre Divion village in the Ancre Valley. Two hundred yards down the track, on the right, are the remains of a German machine-gun post (Map G32) which was sited in the German second line trenches. At 1 o'clock on the far slope beyond the Ancre is Hamel Church and between 2 and 3 o'clock above the first horizon is the church at Beaumont Hamel. The Divisional boundary on the Ulster's right ran along the line of the road from Authuille past Thiepval Church and on the left along the line, and inclusive of, the River Ancre. Within those boundaries the Division was to advance.

On 1 July the Ulsters walked, and then charged, from the forward edge of Thiepval Wood, across the road, up past where the tower stands and on via Mill Road to the crest and beyond. They were the only soldiers north of the Albert-Bapaume road to pierce the German lines. Some say that their achievement was due to a mixture of Irish individualism and religious fervour. Whatever the reason, it was a magnificent feat of arms. Within hours five lines of German trenches had been overwhelmed. Some small parties of 8th, 9th and 11th Royal Irish Rifles penetrated into and beyond the Schwaben Redoubt itself, some even into the village of Grandcourt, but unsupported by advances on their left or right, shelled by their own artillery, exposed to enemy machine guns on their flanks and subject to fierce counter-attacks, they were forced to withdraw at the end of the day. Fourteen hours after the assault began the lines finished virtually where they started but the Irish, unlike most, had won the race at 0730. If the rest of the Fourth Army had advanced at the same speed it is certain that the outcome on 1 July would have been totally different. An eye witness of the Irish action wrote:

"Then I saw them attack, beginning at a slow walk over No Man's Land and then suddenly let loose as they charged over the two front lines of the enemy's trenches shouting, 'No Surrender, boys' … perhaps the Ulstermen, who were commemorating the anniversary of the Boyne, would not be denied."

1 July is the anniversary using the old calendar. This is an ideal viewpoint for several literary connections.

Edmund Blunden, serving with the 11th Royal Sussex Regiment, established an ammunition dump near Hamel, the village seen due west over the River Ancre and the railway line. Armed with a copy of his realistic and vivid account of his war experiences, *Undertones of War*, with its supplement of the best of Blunden's war poems, one can identify Jacob's Ladder (Map G28), Kentish Caves and Brock's Benefit, described in *'Trench Nomenclature'* –

Genius named them, as I live! What but genius could compress
In a title what man's humour said to man's supreme distress?

In *The Ancre at Hamel: Afterwards* he describes, on a subsequent visit to the area, the river and his searing memories of the comrades who fell around it,

The struggling Ancre had no part
In these new hours of mine,
And yet its stream ran through my heart;
I heard it grieve and pine,
As if its rainy tortured blood
Had swirled into my own,
When by its battered bank I stood
And shared its wounded moan.

The beautiful Cemetery seen on the upward slope of the valley is the Ancre Cemetery.

It is on the site of the RND's successful but costly attack of 13 November 1916, and in it lie some casualties of the operation. A.P. Herbert, of Hawke Battalion, lost some well-loved comrades. His grief for them is expressed in the haunting poem *Beaucourt Revisited*, written when the battalion returned to the Ancre in 1917 and very similar in feeling to Blunden's poetic reminiscences,

> And here the lads went over and there was Harmsworth shot,
> And here was William lying – but the new men knew them not.
> And I said, 'There is still the river and still the stiff, stark trees;
> To treasure here our story, but there are only these;'
> But under the white wood crosses the dead men answered low,
> 'The new men know not Beaucourt, but we are here, we know'.

Harmsworth is **Lt the Hon Vere Harmsworth** of Hawke Bn, son of the newspaper magnate, Lord Rothermere, who was killed on 13 November 1916, and is buried in Ancre CWGC Cemetery (qv). William is **Lt W. Ker**, also of Hawke Bn, and who died on the same day, but who is commemorated on the Thiepval Memorial. To read the poem while overlooking the scene of its action is an extremely emotional experience.

Visit the memorial and Visitors' Centre.

This is a replica of the tower known as Helen's Tower on the estate of the Marquis of Dufferin and Ava at Clandeboye in County Down, where the 36th (Ulster) Division trained before coming to France. The tower has had an interesting and checkered existence since it was built in 1921, the first official commemorative monument to be completed on the Western Front. It was inaugurated by Sir Henry Wilson. In the late 1920s and '30s when the cemeteries and the memorials (other than Thiepval) were completed, visitors averaged about 300-400 per day. A former Ulster Division Sgt-Major, William MacMaster, and his wife lived in the one-room-per-floor apartment in the tower and acted as guardians. At that stage, there were preserved trenches behind the tower, around which MacMaster guided his visitors. One is reminded of Philip Johnstone's marvellously satirical 1918 poem *High Wood*, in which a guide conducts a group of tourists around the battlefield:

> … this trench
> For months inhabited, twelve times changed hands;
> (They soon fall in) used later as a grave.
> … Madame , please,
> You are requested kindly not to touch
> Or take away the Company's property
> As souvenirs; you'll find we have on sale
> A large variety, all guaranteed.

Macmasters, it is said, however, guided his pilgrims with genuine feeling. After World War II a succession of guardians came from Ireland, but the loneliness of the job often seemed to induce a desire to over-party with the local community, resulting in subsequent recall. After many years with no resident in the tower, Ulster started to take an active interest in this focal point of their sacrifice in the Great War and in 1991, the 75th Anniversary of the 1 July battle, **Princess Alice** re-dedicated the tower. A **Plaque commemorates the occasion**, and a splendid cake representing the tower was made for the event by the women of Ulster. Another **Memorial to the 36th (Ulster) Division Victoria Cross winners, Capt Bell (1 July 1916), 2nd Lt Emerson, Lce Cpl Seaman, Fusilier Harvey,**

The Ulster Tower

2nd Lt de Wind, Rifleman McFadzean (1 July 1916), Rifleman Quigg (1 July 1916), Lt Cather (1 July 1916) and 2nd Lt Knox was also erected. **The flagpole** was donated by the women of Ulster. A striking, but somewhat controversial, black marble Memorial obelisk with gold lettering was erected outside the tower grounds on 12 September 1993 (Map G30). Raised by voluntary donations, it is known as the '**Orange Order Memorial**', and it is dedicated to the thousands of Orange Institution members who gave their lives during WW1. On 1 July 1999 it was moved to an enclosed area to the right rear of the Tower and re-dedicated. Beside it is a **bench dedicated to the VCs of the Orange Order** from the Orange Brethren. The Order is the oldest and largest Protestant Order and Members of the Order from the Dominions and the USA, as well as from the home country, responded to the call to arms, some 50,000 from Canada alone, encouraged by Bro Sir Samuel Hughes, Canadian Minister for War. The first Australian member to be killed in the war was Able Seaman Bro William George Vincent who was killed in Papua New Guinea in the first Australian action of the war.

By 1994 **the Somme Association** (qv), based in Newtownards (Tel: 028 91823202, e-mail: sommeassociation@btconnect.com Website: www.irishsoldier.org) was established under Royal Patronage, and undertook to 'co-ordinate research into Ireland's part in the First World War and provide a basis for the two traditions in Northern Ireland to come together and learn of their common heritage'. It took over care of the tower, declaring it to be Northern Ireland's National Memorial. It was beautifully restored in 2011.

On 1 July 1994 a smart new Visitors' Centre was opened behind the tower, offering refreshments, books, maps and souvenirs for sale, some interesting displays charting Ireland's part in the Somme Battle, and a 12-minute video. It has excellent, clean toilets and was enlarged in 2006. Its welcoming and dedicated Custodians were, for many years, Teddy and Phoebe Colligan whose daughter, Carol Walker, is the CEO if the Somme Association.

Open every day except Monday, 1 March-30 Nov 1000-1700 (May-Sept 1000-1800). Tel: +(0)3 22 74 87 14.

Guided tours of Thiepval Wood, preferably by prior appointment, Tues-Sun at 1100 and 1500. No fee but donations are appreciated. Add another 25 minutes if you take the tour.

Behind the centre is a small copse which has preserved its 1916-18 contours, with trench lines and shell holes.

In the tower itself, the Memorial Chapel is full of commemorative plaques, pictures of Irish actions, flags and standards, a Visitors' Book and a **Private Memorial to Lt W. J. Wright**, 14th RIR, killed 2 July 1916, which was removed from Thiepval Wood the better to preserve it. The memorial details do not tie up with CWGC records which list **Lt M. J. Wright**, 14th RIR who was killed on 1 July 1916. He is commemorated on the Thiepval

Above: *The Memorial Chapel of the Tower*

Left: *The Orange Order Memorial*

memorial. Of particular interest is a reproduction in oils by Carol Graham RVA of the painting which shows survivors of the Ulster Division's attack on the Schwaben Redoubt on 1 July repulsing a counter-attack on a trench outside Grandcourt. Its title is the Royal Irish Rifles' motto, *Quis separabit?* The painting was donated by the artist's father, Mr A. N. Graham. On the wall are the lines,

Helen's Tower Here I Stand
Dominant Over Sea and Land
Sons' Love Built Me and I Hold
Ulster's Love in Letter'd Gold.

In 2013, during the widening of the road, the remains of two bodies were found, one just outside the hedge of the Connaught Cemetery, the other just by the wall of the entrance to the Tower. One has been identified from his metal ID discs as Sgt David Harkness Blakey of the 11th Inniskilling Fusiliers with his kit, rifle and bayonet, but to this date the other has not. The two soldiers were reburied with full military honours in Connaught Cemetery on 8 October 2015.

Return to your car and continue downhill.

Teddy & Phoebe Colligan, who for many years welcomed visitors to the Centre

You are driving down Mill Road which descends into the Ancre Valley. Ahead on the skyline is the Beaumont Hamel Newfoundland Memorial Park, which at a distance looks like a wood. Cross the river. To the right is the site of the mill which gave the road its name.

Cross the railway.

Extra Visit to the Ancre British Cemetery (Map G21, GPS: 50.06768 2.66803), the RND Memorial & SOA Lt Col B. C. Freyburg VC at Beaucourt (Map G24, GPS: 50.07810 2.68391) Private Memorials to Pte Amos & Pte Farrell, Cpl Austin (Map G11, GPS: 50.08395 2.69498) Round-trip: 4 miles. Approximate time: 30 minutes

Turn right and continue to the cemetery on the left.

Ancre British Cemetery was constructed on the site of No Man's Land at the time of the RND 13 November 1916 attack. It is a concentration cemetery and also has burials from the 1 July 1916 attack by the Ulster Division and the 3 September attack by 39th Division. There is a bronze laurel wreath **Plaque** on **Lt Vere Sidney Tudor Harmsworth, RNVR's** grave (Map G22), presented by Hungarian Scouts in

gratitude for the stand by the *Daily Mail* on the restitution of Hungarian territory after the war. Here, too, is buried **Capt E. S. Ayre**, one of four Newfoundland cousins killed on 1 July (qv).

A track to the right of the Cemetery gives an excellent overview of the cemetery and the area of the RND attack of 13 November. This attack was launched at 0545 in thick mist behind a creeping barrage on a 1,200yd-front running north from the Ancre. The final objective line lay just beyond Beaucourt village, the first German trench line being roughly along the high ground on the track to the right of the cemetery. The RND start line was approximately where the road from the Ulster Tower meets the railway line. The right-hand battalion, the Hood, commanded by Lt Col B. C. Freyburg, (who had single-handedly created a dummy diversionary attack on the Turkish lines at Bulair during the Gallipoli campaign) moved quickly forward and cleared the entrances along the Ancre to the

Headstone & Plaque, Lt Vere Harmsworth, Ancre British CWGC Cemetery

enemy tunnels that ran to Beaumont Hamel. In the centre, casualties were heavy, the Hawke Battalion having almost 400 within 30 minutes and the fighting became confused both there and alongside the 51st Highland Division to the north. It was decided that the attack should be renewed the following day. At dawn on 14 November the final assault on Beaucourt was personally led by Freyburg. The garrison of 800 surrendered but Freyburg was wounded for the third time, and this time seriously. 'For his conspicuous bravery and brilliant leadership as Battalion Commander' he was awarded the VC. Although the attack was eventually successful, the price was high – the Naval Brigades had almost 3,000 casualties. Also taking part in what was known as 'The Battle of the Ancre', was the 22nd

Bn, Royal Fusiliers. Serving with them was the 46-year-old **Lce Sgt Hector Hugh Munro**, better known as the author **Saki**. Despite his age and history of ill-health, Munro had enlisted in the ranks on 25 August 1914, refusing a commission. After a year's service in France, he was hospitalized with malaria, but discharged himself on 11 November 1916, when he heard that a 'show' was soon to take place. Saki was hit by a sniper on 14 November, just after uttering the words, 'Put that bloody cigarette out' to a man who had just lit up.

In August 1928 the British Legion and the British Empire Service League organised a massive pilgrimage to Flanders and the Somme. Earl Haig was to have led the mourners, but died on 29 January, so Lady Haig was at their head. The Prince of Wales, Patron of the Legion, joined the throng in Béthune. After visiting Flanders, the party travelled to the Somme via Notre Dame de Lorette and Vimy Ridge, being billeted with local people (a logistic nightmare to arrange in itself) and travelling by train. They were lubricated by 31,500 bottles of beer and mineral water and by 26,000 quarts of tea, brewed by French Army Field Kitchens, and devoured 23,500 slices of both ham and cake. The women in the party upset the calculations – that they would drink three bottles of mineral water to one of beer, by consuming half and half! On 6-7 August 10,000 pilgrims arrived at Beaucourt Station by train-loads of 500 at intervals of 10-15 minutes and then wandered off in groups by foot, charabanc and 'excellent Citroen cars' to the Ancre Cemetery, the Ulster Tower and the Newfoundland Park. The cemetery already looked much as it does today, the Ulster Tower stood out bare and granite on the crest, but the Thiepval Memorial was not to be unveiled for another four years. Among the sadness was the unfailing humour of the Tommy. 'I wonder if my blinkin' leg is still up there?' mused a one-legged veteran, looking up to Beaumont Hamel. 'Well, I dunno; Somebody's bin muckin' abaht 'ere since I was 'ere larst', commented another.

Continue along the road, passing the derelict station on the right.

Gare de Beaucourt was the station at which the pilgrims arrived, and some sheds from that period still remain. The travellers were lured back to catch their return trains by the promise of tea, which they took in a field adjoining the station. The Legion report on the Pilgrimage claimed that several times during the two days 1,500 pilgrims were entrained and despatched on three different trains in the space of 10 minutes! A supremely evocative picture of this area just before the war and during the Somme Battle of 1 July 1916 is given in the fictional account by Sebastian Faulks in *Birdsong*.

Continue into Beaucourt-sur-Ancre.

The **RND Memorial** may be seen on a bank to the left on entering the village. In this area is the SOA where Lt Col B. C. Freyburg (later **Lt Gen Freyburg, GCMG, KCB, KBE, DSO, 3 bars, GOC New Zealand Forces 1939-45, Governor General of New Zealand 1946-52) won the Victoria Cross** while commanding Hood Battalion on 13 November 1916.

Continue through the village on the D50.

Royal Naval Division Memorial, Beaucourt

Private Memorials to Cpl Burrows and to Pte Austin, with Pte Amos to the right, Bois d'Hollande

After about half a mile, a track to the left skirts a small wood (Bois d'Hollande). Approximately two-thirds of the way up the wood and some 10m inside is a small wooden cross on a large tree. It bears a brass **Plaque to Pte D. Amos**, 15258, 9th Bn N Staffs, who died on 21 November 1916 at this location. Beside it is a much more recent **Plaque to Pte Henry Austin**, N Staffs, 20/21 Nov 1916, aged 23. Nearby on another tree is an original **Plaque to Cpl A.L. Burrows**, 7th Bn S Staffs, 23 Nov 1916, aged 20. Be warned – they are not easy to find. They are all commemorated on the Thiepval Memorial and the CWGC give Austin's death as 24 November 1916. All were killed in the final phase of the Somme offensive, the Battle of the Ancre, when V Corps drove a salient forward along the river into the German lines.

Turn round (there is turning area at the top of the wood) and return to the railway crossing and pick up the main itinerary.

Turn left and follow the signs to the Newfoundland Memorial Park up the D73 to the right. Continue uphill to the tiny church on the left. Park.

Plaque to the Essex Regt, Hamel Church/11.5 miles/5 minutes/Map G21a/ GPS: 50.06517 2.65998

The Plaque commemorates the 1st Bn of the Regiment who suffered severely in the attack with the 29th Division over what is now the Newfoundland Memorial Park. It was instigated by Ted Bailey, whose remarkable grandfather took part in that attack. The full story can be found by contacting Ted on info@tedbailey.co.uk and the Regimental Association: http://www.chelmsford.gov.uk/essexregimentmuseum The Memorial, supported by the Regimental Association and local Councils, was unveiled in June 2014. It also commemorates the 2nd, 9th and 13th Bns who suffered losses on the Somme. The two original battalions of 1,000 men each were re-established twice after being virtually wiped out.

Continue to the Newfoundland Park entrance and stop in the large car park on the left.

Here there is a signboard of welcome and a reminder to respect the site.

In the distance in a field to the left (but approached from a track from Mesnil) is **Knightsbridge Cemetery** (**Map G26, GPS: 50.06756 2.64373**) in which is buried **2nd Lt W. D. Ayre**, another of the family of four Newfoundlanders killed on 1 July 1916 (qv).

• *Newfoundland Memorial Park/Visitor's Centre/12 miles/50 minutes/ OP/Map G20/19/18/17/17a/16/15/14/13/12/GPS: 50.07214 2.64756*

The park covers 84 acres and was purchased by the then Government of Newfoundland as a memorial to the soldiers and sailors of Newfoundland. It was officially opened by Earl Haig on 7 June 1925. There are a number of Memorials and Cemeteries in the park, as well as preserved trench lines which have been maintained in their original shape, the Visitor's Centre and the Director's house. In the late 1920s, the 'warden', Billy Brown, a Newfoundland veteran, lived in a log cabin. At that stage the preserved trenches in the park contained duckboards, and the wreckage of an aeroplane, boxes of hand grenades and many other relics littered the battlefield. The great Pilgrimage of

Plaque to 1st Bn Essex Regt, Hamel Church

August 1928 visited here too, and members were photographed holding rifles and shell cases and wearing tin hats. They were much impressed by the 'defiant' Caribou and the 'indomitable' Highlander Memorials (see below) that were already well-established in the Park.

Walk into the park.

The regular visitor of many years will have noticed that since the opening of the **Visitor's Centre** and the increase in visitors (230,000 in 2014), especially of students, the nature and atmosphere of the park has changed - from a true battlefield to a Memorial Park. This has been necessary to protect the precious and vulnerable trench lines and craters from the erosion caused by the sheer volume of feet walking on them. Therefore areas which were freely visitable are now protected by strong wire fences, some electric. Duckboards and wooden bridges have also been constructed in and over the trenches.

At each side of the entrance are **Plaques** erected in 1997 confirming that the Park, initiated in 1922, is now a Canadian Historic Site and Monument. Plaques describe how the idea was conceived by Padre Thomas Nagle and the construction was under the direction of R. H. K. Cochus, landscape artist, from funds raised by the Government and the women of Newfoundland. There is a dispenser to the left for self-guided tour leaflets. A path to the right leads to the **Visitor's Centre**.

This typical Newfoundland wooden building was opened in July 2000. It contains a recreated living room, complete with working stove and contemporary artefacts.

The Visitors' Centre, Newfoundland Memorial Park

Preserved trenches

Hunters CWGC Cemetery, Newfoundland Memorial Park

Canadian student Guide

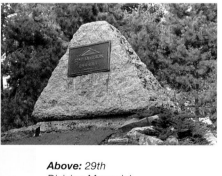

Above: *29th Division Memorial, Newfoundland Park*

Left: *The Highlander, 5st Highland Div Memorial*

The grieving Newfoundland Caribou

The exhibits are imaginatively and sensitively mounted (some on a large board in the shape of a ship), with many personal photographs, letters and other ephemera. A continuing story follows a dwindling band of 32 Newfoundland soldiers through the Great War on the Western Front and in Gallipoli. There are excellent toilet facilities. In the same way as at Vimy, the Centre is manned by knowledgeable Canadian students (often actual Newfoundlanders) who compete for the honour and who give guided tours of the Park. Coaches should book ahead. Tel: + (0)3 22 76 70 86. E-mail: beaumonthamel.memorial@vac-acc.gc.ca Website: www.veterans.gc.ca The Centre is **open every day:** 0900-1700. Closed Christmas and New Year's Day. Guides are available from January to mid-December. The Park is open 24 hours a day, 365 days a year.

The attack on 1 July was in the direction in which you are walking. The assault division was the 29th, which had done so well in Gallipoli, and whose previous General, Hunter-Weston, was now its Corps (VIII) Commander. Some 1,350m ahead of you, beyond Y Ravine at the bottom of the park, on a curve in the German lines, a massive mine of 40,600lb of ammonal was placed by 252nd Tunnelling Company, 75ft under a German redoubt known as **Hawthorn**. Believing that it would be to his soldiers' advantage, Hunter-Weston had the mine blown at 0720, ten minutes before the infantry went over the top. It was not to their advantage. On the contrary, it only served to give the Germans a warning of imminent attack. The first brigade that went in, the 87th, was cut down and the 88th was ordered up. One assault formation of the 88th was the 1st Battalion of the Royal Newfoundland Regiment. They made their attack across the area of the park you are now entering. It lasted less than half an hour. The Newfoundlanders had done all they could, wrote the divisional commander later, 'because dead men can advance no further.' Every officer who went forward was either killed or wounded. Of the 801 men who went into action, some authorities say that only 68 members of the battalion were not wounded, one of the highest casualty counts for any regimental unit on 1 July. Among those killed here were three members of the Ayre family (qv). **2nd Lt Gerald W. Ayre** is commemorated on the Newfoundland Memorial below the Caribou (qv).

The Durand Group (qv), under Lt Col Phillip Robinson, have undertaken much archaeological and historical research here at Beaumont Hamel Park and in unit records, which offers alternative figures for the wounded and missing. Confusion is simply one of the states of war and this is particularly true of casualty figures, e.g. Are the 'attached personnel' accounted for? Was the recent draft allowed for? Did more survivors turn up after the roll call? Did everyone actually take part in the fighting? Whatever the precise number of casualties, the Newfoundlanders suffered greatly on 1 July. The 29th Division had an overall casualty percentage on 1 July of about 26%. The Newfoundlanders had a rate of about 65% but Robinson believes that the 10th Battalion of the West Yorkshire Regiment at Fricourt had an equivalent rate of about 70%. Nevertheless the achievements of the Newfoundlanders were recognised by King George V in December 1917 when he gave the regiment the title 'Royal.'

The first **Memorial** to be seen is that to **29th Division**, its distinctive red badge displayed on a stone cairn, which is on the left of the path a few metres from the entrance. Then almost immediately on the left is the bronze box containing the Visitors' Book and registers and a plaque on the right carrying a **verse by John Oxenham**.

Continue on the path to the Caribou and climb to the top.

The Caribou was the emblem of the Newfoundland Regiment and there are three more identical bronzes in France commemorating other regimental actions – at Gueudecourt (Itinerary Three), Masnières (Cambrai 20 November 1917) and Monchy le Preux (Arras

14 April 1917). It is a most poignant Memorial – the animal appears to be baying for her lost young – as well as a striking piece of sculpture. On the parapet around the Caribou are orientation arrows which identify various parts of the battlefield, including the **three British Cemeteries** in the park. On the left is **Hawthorn Ridge No 2** (containing 214 burials from 1 July 1916), and the attractive, circular **Hunters** (containing 46 men buried in what had been a large shell hole), on the right **Y Ravine** (containing 366 burials, including Newfoundlanders from 1 July and RND from November 1916). At the base of the mound on which the Caribou stands are **three bronze Plaques** on which are named **591 officers and men of the Royal Newfoundland Regiment** (including **2nd Lt W. D. Ayre**), 114 of the Newfoundland Naval Reserve and 115 of the Newfoundland Mercantile Marine who lost their lives during the war and have no known grave. To the right of this group is a separate **bronze Plaque** to the **staff of the Imperial Tobacco Company of the 1st Newfoundland Regiment**. To the left a **Plaque** to commemorate the **200th anniversary of the Royal Newfoundland Regiment** was unveiled on 1 July 1995.

When we began our battlefield touring there was no Visitor Centre here and the only annual 1 July ceremony was one which we arranged with the local Souvenir Francais and the then Superintendant. We held it in front of the Caribou and had both British and French veterans in attendance. Today there is a regular official ceremony on 1 July usually around 1100 hours, and if you wish to attend it is wise to check the details of timings ahead of your visit.

Also visible are the **'Danger Tree'**, a twisted skeleton of an original trunk which marks the spot where casualties were heaviest on 1 July (about a third of the way to Y Ravine) and in the distance at the bottom of the slope, the handsome kilted **Highlander of the 51st Highland Division**, standing on a platform of Aberdeen granite. The bronze figure commemorates the action of the Division in taking Beaumont Hamel and the natural feature of Y Ravine on 13 November during Part 5 of the Somme Battle. Sculpted by G.H. Paulin of Glasgow, it was unveiled on 28 September 1924 by Marshal Foch and has a Gaelic inscription which translates 'Friends are good on the day of battle'. Four hundred people travelled from Glasgow for the ceremony, including an impressive Guard of Honour of several Scottish Regiments. There was also a French Guard of Honour.

In his book *The 51st Division War Sketches*, published in 1920, divisional artist Fred Farrell shows a splendid drawing of '7th Gordons Clearing 'Y' Ravine'. The Germans took advantage of this natural shelter and riddled the banks of the ravine with tunnels and deep, comfortably furnished, well-provisioned dugouts. Booty from these and other strong German defensive positions taken during the attack, included 'tinned beef from Monte Video, Norwegian sardines, cigarettes (including Wills' Gold Flake), cigars and many thousand bottles of excellent soda and of beer' (Regimental History). More mysterious were the 'piano, some ladies' dancing slippers, silk stockings, and petticoats'. The Jocks deserved their perks. Casualties sustained represented 45% of those who took part in the attack. In the days that followed, the remnants of the division were detailed to clear the battlefield, which still bore the skeletons (picked clean by the thousands of rats which swarmed over the area) of casualties from the 1 July 1916 attack. 152nd Brigade alone buried 669 bodies in the Cemeteries at Mailly Maillet and Auchonvillers. It was an un-nerving task even to these hardened soldiers.

Between the Highlander and the Ravine (about 20m deep) is a **Celtic Memorial Cross** commemorating the Division's casualties at High Wood in July 1916.

Keeping to the authorised pathways, examine the trench lines (marked as 'British Front Line' and 'German Front Line') and craters, which still contain some battlefield debris. Walking briskly it takes 10 minutes to get to Y Ravine.

Return to your car and continue past a CWGC sign to the right.

[N.B.] This is to **Hawthorn Ridge Cemetery No 1. (Map G2, GPS: 50.08151 2.6492)**, approached by a track driveable part-way by car, but do not attempt to drive if it is wet and muddy as you may get stuck. As one reaches a junction at the crest of the track which overlooks the Cemetery, in the distance on the upward slope two small Cemeteries may be seen. They are Waggon Road and Munich Trench British CWGC Cemeteries (qv).

Hawthorne Ridge No 1 contains 152 UK burials (half of them Unknown) including many public schoolboys of the 16th Middlesex and a Newfoundland burial. It was made by V Corps in 1917 when they cleared the area of bodies from the 1916 Somme battles.

Hawthorne Ridge Cemetery No 1, Auchonvillers

Continue to the crossroads.

[N.B.] By turning left here signed to Mesnil-Martinsart on the C6, then on the D174, and continuing to the T junction in Mesnil-Martinsart, on the left on the wall of the *Mairie* is a **Memorial to 23 men of 11 Platoon of C Coy 13th Bn RIR**. They were killed or died later as a result of a shell on the evening of 28 June. The black marble Plaque, funded by the Somme Association, was inaugurated by the Rev Ian Paisley on 30 June 2007 (**Map G28a, GPS: 50.05370 2.64728**). The German advance of 1918 stopped just short of the village.

En route to Mesnil-Martinsart two bunkers may be seen to the right of the road (GPS: 50.07257 2.63249/50.07204 2.63207). These were probably part of a defensive position known as Fort Anley.

Above: Bunker on road between Auchonvillers and Mesnil-Martinsart

Left: Memorial to 23 men of 'C' Coy, RIR, Mesnil-Martinsart

At the crossroads take the D73 signed Mailly Maillet and enter Auchonvillers.

[N.B.] **Auchonvillers Communal Cemetery** is to the right at the crossroads. It contains fifteen CWGC burials with red sandstone headstones, mostly of 1st Borders from 6 April 1916 in a plot to the left. To the right is a white CWGC headstone to **William Brown** of Newfoundland, 1896-1954. Brown (qv) was the guardian at the Newfoundland Memorial Park (qv) where he worked with Padre Nagel (qv) in reburying Newfoundland's dead. A Sgt-Maj in the British Army he escorted the catafalque of the Unknown Warrior to the UK (see *Known Unto God. In Honour of the Missing during the Great War* by Frank Gogos and Morgan Macdonald)

Red sandstone CWGC headstones in Auchonvillers Communal Cemetery

Auchonvillers (obviously 'Ocean Villas' to Tommy) was described by Blunden as 'a good example of the miscellaneous, picturesque, pitiable, pleasing, appalling, intensely intimate village ruin close to the line …' 'The French', he felt, had modelled it 'comprehensively as a large redoubt, complete with a searchlight. There were many dugouts under houses and in the gardens, but of a flimsy, rotted and stagnant kind; the Somme battle had evidently swamped all old defence schemes.' With just over 500 burials, it was started by the French in 1915.

Continue to the Guest House on the left.

• *Ocean Villas Guest House/Tea Rooms /Museum/Conference Centre/12.9 miles/30 minutes/Map G1a/GPS: 50.08013 2.63119*

Run by Avril Williams, who bought this attractive but originally derelict site and has been progressively improving the facilities over the years until it now offers four en-suite twin rooms and a self-catering apartment sleeping up to 6. Currently the tea room, with a glassed terrace extension, caters for groups (who must book in advance) and individuals and can serve breakfasts, lunches, teas, pre-booked packed lunches and dinners. Around the walls are many interesting items, including a tribute to **Prof Richard Holmes** (a frequent visitor, who died in April 2011), who also has a Memorial Seat in the attractive garden. A book stall offers books, maps and souvenirs.

Open daily: 0830-1800 (but flexible!). Tel: +(0)3 22 76 23 66. E-mail: avwilliams@ orange.fr Website: www.avrilwilliams.eu An original trench line has been excavated at the rear and other work is in constant progress, including behind the Museum (see below) by members of the RAF Regiment, REME and many other willing volunteers,

Its well-preserved cellar was used as a dressing station. A dividing wall was built in 1914 by the French, and half was used as a ward, and still shows the marks where bunks were attached to the wall, the other half being used as a surgery/makeshift operating theatre. There

Ocean Villas Tea Rooms

Avril Williams and son, Mark in the Museum

Beautiful local War Memorial, Auchonvillers

are many scratched or carved names from 1916, mostly of members of the RIR, both patients and stretcher bearers. A tunnel, now bricked up, led into the cellar, the entrance to which was protected by a gas curtain. Avril has many interesting personal items and artefacts found in the cellar or in the garden and sells books and maps relating to the Somme battles.

A major project was to create a Museum in the large complex of farm buildings across the road for the extensive WW1 and WW2 collection of uniforms, artefacts, ephemera etc which she bought from André Coilliot of Beaurains, built up over some 60 odd years and which has already been extended. André was a staunch supporter and organiser of *Souvenir Français* (qv). A later acquisition was the stunning collection of some 300 trench art shell cases. These are on permanent loan from owner, 9-year old Charlie, grandson of Steve and Sharon Clements who regularly come to Auchonvillers to clean them! Charlie gives talks to his local school about the collection. The Museum was extended in 2015, using fine display cabinets obtained when the Woolwich Museum closed.

On the exterior wall of the Museum is a Wall of Remembrance where members of the public can buy 'bricks' (or plaques) in remembrance of soldiers who fought in the Great War. Any profit will fund the Museum, which we had the honour to unveil on 1 July 2008 and which has developed into a fascinating and well-maintained museum. It will be run as an official charitable organisation. **Open:** daily 1000-1600. There is also a recently developed **Learning/Conference Centre** for students and an '**Estaminet**' for events and entertainment, with kitchen, bar, shower facilities etc.) Battlefield guides, a programme of lectures by experts (such as Prof Peter Simkins and Andy Robertshaw), bicycle hire are all available.

*Continue, passing on the right the female statue of the **local War Memorial**.*
Continue to the crossroad and turn left on the D73 signed to Mailly-Maillet. Follow signs to the cemetery which is approached up a grassy path to the right through a farm yard.

• Auchonvillers Military CWGC Cemetery/13.5 miles/10 minutes/Map G1/GPS: 50.08004 2.62617

The Cemetery, entered through a graceful hedged, circular patio, was designed by Sir Reginald Blomfield. It was begun by the French in June 1915, was used by field ambulances and fighting units, such as the 51st Highlanders, in November 1916 until burials ceased on the German withdrawal in 1917. Further burials were added after the Armistice and there are now 528 burials, 468 identified. The French graves were later removed.

Auchonvillers Mil CWGC Cemetery

The Cemetery Report rewards careful reading. It lists men of many Regiments, including RND, Newfoundlanders and New Zealanders, with ages ranging from 17 to 47. **Clifford Vallance**, Herts Regt, age 35, 26 September 1916, served as J. Brown; **Sgt William Edward Lynn**, 1st Royal Irish Fusiliers, age 21, was one of four brothers who were killed in the war; **Pte Richard Dale Lovett**, Middx Regt, age 46, 'left his coffee estate in India' to come to Britain to enlist; **William Henry Davies**, Drake Bn, RND, 13 July 1918, had the MM + Bar. The Visitors' book, in July 2013, went back to 2009 and contained many family members' signatures.

Return to the crossroads and continue on the D174 signed to Beaumont Hamel. 350m later the road forks with the D174 left and the D163 straight on.

Extra Visit to Sucrerie Military Cemetery & Euston Road Cemetery/ Bradford Pals Mem, Hébuterne/Map D7/6/5a. Round-trip: 3.0 miles. Approximate time: 40 minutes.

Take the left fork towards Hébuterne and continue to the crossroads with the D919. Turn left and 200m later right along a rough, tree-lined track (you are advised to leave your car and walk to the cemetery or risk getting stuck if it is at all damp) following CWGC signs.

Sucrerie Military Cemetery (GPS: 50.09581 2.6232) is situated on what was one of the routes from Colincamps to the front line on 1 July and later Somme battles and where mass graves were prepared for the casualties. In it, in a row of officers, is **Lt Col the Hon L. C. W. Palk, DSO**, CO of the 1st Hampshires, who lost all twenty-six of their officers and 559 of their men on 1 July. Lt Col Palk, obviously a fan of the cartoonist, Bruce Bairnsfather, exhorted his battalion that this was the greatest day the British army had ever had, dressed himself in his best uniform, donned white gloves and led his battalion HQ across No Man's Land. Lying mortally wounded in a shell hole, he turned to another man lying near him and said, 'If you know of a better 'ole, go to it'. Ironically one of the trenches leading forward to the front line was named 'Cheeroh Avenue'.

Return to the crossroads, and immediately turn left. At the next fork take the left hand road, the D129E, and stop at the cemetery on the left on the D4129.

Euston Road Cemetery (50.10186 2.61975), like Sucrerie Military Cemetery, was constructed on one of the main routes from the rear areas to the front line this one being Railway Avenue. Here the Bradford Pals added shovels and picks to their already heavy load on the evening prior to the attack. The area at the last fork was known as Euston.

Many of the burials are from 1 July 1916, many of them of 'Pals', notably that of the exceptional war poet, **Sgt John William Streets** of the 12th 'Sheffield Pals' Battalion of the York and Lancs.

Streets broke the mould of the perceived image of the 'golden' poet from a public school and of the officer class. He was born, the eldest of twelve children, to a Derbyshire miner, whose profession he followed from the age of 14. A sensitive boy, he loved the countryside, literature and art. Indeed his main dilemma, on deciding to quit the mine, was whether he should become a writer or an artist. With the encouragement of a perceptive teacher Streets taught himself Latin, Greek and French and from an early age wrote poems of exceptional literary ability. The outbreak of war solved his dilemma. He enlisted on 6 September 1914 at the age of 29. Throughout his training in the UK, Will continued to write poetry and send snippets home in the regular letters he wrote to his mother. The poetry and letters showed signs of the malaise common to many poets – intimations of mortality. In the case of the poets from World War I, however, the premonition was based on the growing casualty figures. In December 1915 the battalion moved to Egypt for training, but arrived too late to participate in the action at their ultimate destination – Gallipoli. In March 1916 the 12th Battalion arrived on the Somme and the poetry continued, still, despite worsening conditions, in an heroic and patriotic mode. Recognition was just beginning for this self-taught bard (he had been published in *The Poetry Review* and a compilation called *Made in the Trenches*) when the carnage of 1 July cut short his life. The battalion had moved into assembly trenches behind John Copse (see below) and Streets was wounded soon after their attack began. He was seen going to the assistance of another seriously wounded man and then disappeared. At first there was some hope that he was simply missing, as his body was not immediately found. It was later identified, and he is buried here in Euston Road Cemetery. Coincidentally, Streets' twin brothers were serving with the RAMC at the dressing station in the Basilica at Albert. One of them sent home Will's 'worn, red-covered pocket-books' with 'jottings in it of stray ideas or phrases that occurred to him for stories or for verses'. Adcock included a chapter on Streets in his book of soldier poets, *For Remembrance*, and his slim collected works were published in May 1917 by Erskine Macdonald as *The Undying Splendour*. His posterity was assured. The inscription on his headstone, 'I fell, but yielded not my English soul; that lives out here beneath the battle's roll', is a quotation from his own work. Another soldier poet of the 12th Battalion Yorks & Lancs, **Corporal Alexander Robertson**, was killed in the same attack as Will Streets. He is commemorated on the Thiepval Memorial.

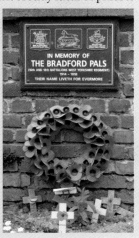

Return to the fork and turn left direction Hébuterne. Continue to the church. Beside it, near the Poilu Memorial, is the

Bradford Pals Memorial (GPS: 50.12449 2.63728). The simple brick Memorial with its Plaque commemorating the Bradford Pals has a poignant story. In 1995 a Bradford couple, Eric and Joan Kenny, finding no

Memorial to Bradford Pals, Hébuterne

Memorial to the Bradford Pals during a visit to the Somme, determined to raise one. Hébuterne was chosen for its site as it was midway between the villages of Gommecourt and Serre where so many of the Pals were lost on 1 July, and because of the support from the local Mayor. The Kennys worked hard at fund-raising despite Joan's terminal cancer and eventually gained some support from Bradford Metropolitan Council, who insisted that the Memorial bore their coat of arms. Finally it was unveiled in June 2002 though only Eric was able to attend because sadly Joan died before the event. Eric died soon afterwards. Their story inspired David Whithorn of the GWS (qv) to continue their work of commemorating the Bradford Pals.

Return to the junction with the D163 (D176.)

Continue.
To the left of the road was the British position known as 'The Bowery'.
After 800m stop at the memorial on the bank on the left.

• Argyll & Sutherland Highlanders Memorial, Beaumont Hamel/14.8 miles/10 minutes/Map G4/GPS: 50.08572 2.64853
Unveiled in 1923 by the Duke of Argyll, this imposing Celtic cross commemorates and gives details of the war service of the 8th Argyllshire Bn, Princess Louise's Argyll & Sutherland Highlanders, the 51st Highland Division, the 61st Division, and the 15th Scottish Division: 'Mobilised Service from 4 August 1914 to 12 November 1919. Service

Argyll & Sutherland Highlanders Memorial and Sunken Road. **Inset:** *Malins filming just before the attack on 1 July 1916.*

in the field from 1 May 1915 to 11 November 1918: 3 years and 195 days. Killed in Action: officers 51, NCOs and men 831. Wounded: officers 105, NCOs and men 2,527'. The Gaelic inscription translates as 'The complete heroes of the Great War, the braves who went before us'. 'Cruachan' is the war cry of the Campbells. The Memorial stands at the entrance to the Sunken Road, where the 'Official War Office Kine-Matographer', Lt Geoffrey H. Malins, attached to Maj Gen H. de B. de Lisle's 29th Division (part of Hunter-Weston's VIII Corps) from 28 June, to film The Battle, filmed men of the 1st Lancashire Fusiliers on 1 July. This end the Road was known as Hunter Trench and some 500 yards to the north west near a chalk feature known as White City Malins filmed, 'with shaking hand, as … for all the world like a gigantic sponge, the earth rose in the air to the height of hundreds of feet. Higher and higher it rose, and with a horrible, grinding roar the earth fell back upon itself, leaving in its place a mountain of smoke.

Turn round and return to the crossroads with the D919, turn left signed to Beaumont and follow the main itinerary.

His historic, and much-shown, sequence of the great Hawthorn mine going up at 0720 hours on 1 July, was the high point of his film *The Battle of the Somme*, first shown to an invited audience in London on 10 August and seen by thousands when it was put on general release at the end of the month. Prior to The Battle of the Somme, front-line pictures were rarely published. In 1916, however, the Press Bureau asked for tenders for the exclusive right to reproduce, as postcards, pictures taken by official photographers at the front. The *Daily Mail* tender was accepted, half the profits to go to military charities, with a minimum payment of £5,000. On 6 September seven sets of six postcards were put on sale. Card No 13 in Series II shows the Hawthorn explosion. The complete set of cards is available on a DVD which can be obtained from Tony Allen, tonyallen43@hotmail.com

The filled-in entrances to underground tunnels and dugouts can be discerned by the eagle-eyed to the right of the bank in the Sunken Road. Other entrances have also been filled in in the steep chalk cliffs to the left of the road as one leaves the village towards Beaucourt.
The short circular **WALK Number 2** can be taken from here. Distance: 1.5 miles. Duration: 35 minutes. See page 320

Standing at the memorial and looking due south across the D163, a copse can be seen on the skyline. This is the Hawthorn Crater. To the left is a path leading to a cemetery.

• *Beaumont-Hamel British CWGC Cemetery/5 minutes/Map G3/GPS: 50.08591 2.64981*
There are two long lines of graves, many unknown, others from 1 July 1916 and early 1917. There is one German grave.

Continue on the D163. To the right is a sign leading to Hawthorn Crater up a steep path through the fields. *Park and walk up the path between fields.*

• *Hawthorn Crater/14.1 miles/15 minutes/Map G6/GPS at path 50.08488 2.65088*
The double crater, which appears as a figure-of-eight from the air, is now enclosed by wire, and filled with hawthorn and other thick undergrowth. A sergeant who had worked on the tunnel described the 'exploding chamber' as 'as big as a picture palace, and the gallery was an awful length. It took seven months to build, and we were working

under some of the crack Lancashire miners'. The tunnel leading to the mine prepared for 1 July was 75ft deep and 1,000ft long, with a charge of 40,600lb of ammonal. It had been prepared by 252nd Tunnelling Company. It was fired 10 minutes early and formed a crater 40ft deep and over 300ft wide at its largest diameter. Although the German redoubt here was totally destroyed, no advance was made and another attack was launched on 13 November when a 30,000lb charge was blown under the old crater which the Germans had fortified. The mine was successfully blown at 0545 (the figure-of-eight shape of the crater is due to the two explosions) and the 51st Division advanced steadily along its whole front in the general direction that you are travelling.

Continue into Beaumont Hamel.

At the crossroads in the village, on the left, is a flagpole. Stop.

• *51st Highland Division Flagstaff/15.2 miles/5 minutes/Map G8/GPS: 50.08421 2.65621*

The original flagstaff bore a plaque recording its presentation on 28 September 1924 by the officers, NCO's and men of the 51st Highland Division to the inhabitants of Beaumont Hamel to commemorate the recapture of the village by the division on 13 November 1916. It was an integral part of the Division's remembrance with the Highlander statue at Y Ravine (qv) and unveiled just before the statue. The flagstaff fell into disrepair and Derek A. Bird, Chairman of the Scotland (North) Branch of the WFA, raised the money to erect a new flagpole and stone. On 13 November 2006 the new, 12 metre high flagpole and Morayshire stone with bronze plaque and three small granite plaques with the emblems of the WFA, Beaumont and *Souvenir Français* was inaugurated in the presence of local dignitaries and a contingent of the Khaki Chums. A new *Tricolore* and Scottish Standard were also presented to the village to be flown on each anniversary thereafter. Just 18 months earlier a new Highlander statue was unveiled at Château St Côme to commemorate the Division's part in the Normandy campaign in the Second World War. The story is told in detail in our *Normandy D-Day Guide book*.

The renovated 51st Highland Div Flagpole with detail of the Plaque, Beaumont Hamel

In their regimental history it is reported that the village was 'famous for its manufacture of powder-puffs' before the war!

Continue. Turn right to the church and park.

• Beaumont-Hamel Church Stained Glass Fragment/15.3 miles/5 minutes /Map G7/ GPS: 50.08379 2.65625

A small fragment of stained glass with the head of a sweet Virgin Mary is incorporated in the plain coloured glass window of the church to the left of the entrance. A plaque records that it was found in the ruins of the original church in 1914 and returned in 1962 by Lt Georg Muller of the German 99th Infantry Regiment and re-installed by villagers Monsieur and Madame Welferinger-Letesse, who worked with devotion for Souvenir Français and joined us in our 1 July 'Caribou' ceremonies for many years.

Returned WW1 stained glass fragment, Beaumont Hamel Church

Return to the D163.

Extra Visit to Waggon Road (Map D27)/OP & Munich Trench British/(Map D28) CWGC Cemeteries on Redan Ridge/OP Round-trip: 1.6 miles. Approximate time: 25 minutes

Drive straight over and continue uphill on the narrow road, following green CWGC signs to the cemeteries.

The vantage point from the crest of the ridge gives such a good overall view of the 1 July 1916 battle, that this diversion is highly recommended. Binoculars are essential. The extraordinary feeling of remoteness, of peace and of beauty experienced in these cemeteries also make the journey rewarding.

To the right on the crest is **Waggon Road, V Corps Cemetery No 10 (GPS: 50.09218 2.66368)** , which contains 195 UK burials, 36 unidentified. Forty-nine of the burials are of men from 11th (Lonsdale) Battalion, the Border Regt, which attacked on the Ancre in July (qv) and also in November 1916. Waggon Road was the name given to the road running north towards the village of Serre from **Beaumont Hamel Station.** Go to the cross and stand facing the entrance gate. That is 12 o'clock. The skyline to the front, left to right, gives the axis of the British attack on 1 July. To the left at 11 o'clock is the church spire at Auchonvillers on the British start line. The shape of the battle can now be followed by finding these points: at 12 o'clock is the Cross of Sacrifice of Serre Road No 2 Cemetery. This is the site of the German front line defensive position known as The Quadrilateral. At 9 o'clock is the Newfoundland Memorial Park and both the Caribou and the Kilted Highlander Memorials can be seen. At 7 o'clock is the copse at the end of the Leipzig Salient and the Thiepval Memorial. At 2 o'clock is the

Waggon Road CWGC Cemetery

Memorial to the Sheffield Pals on the Serre Road. The road up which you have driven runs due north just behind the German front line of 1 July, with the British line about 600m to the left.

Continue.

To the left is **Munich Trench, V Corps Cemetery No 8 (GPS: 50.09444 2.66326)**, with the legend 'Beaumont Hamel' inscribed on the gatepost. The 126 burials, of which 28 are unknown, are arranged in three lines of graves, enclosed by a hedge. The grass path leading to this isolated cemetery is immaculate, witness to the dedication of the CWGC in that little-visited sites are as lovingly cared for as are those that are more accessible. Indeed, in October 1995 the visitors' books for these two cemeteries dated back to 1975.

Turn round and return to the D163. Rejoin the main itinerary.

Turn left and return to the flagpole. Take the small road uphill to the right (Rue de la Montagne).

[N.B.] At the top **Redan Ridge Cemetery No 2 (GPS: 50.08892 2.65262)** is signed to the left (Map G5a). It is on the site of 'Watling Street', 100m west of the old German front line and has 279 burials of 2nd, 4th and 29th Divs.

Continue to the cemetery on the left.

• Redan Ridge CWGC Cemetery No 3/15.7 miles/5 minutes/Map D26/GPS: 50.09103 2.65386)

This lovely little cemetery contains only fifty-four graves, mostly of 2nd Div from 1 July and 13 November 1916 and thirteen special memorials. It is on the site of German front line trenches known as Frontier Lane.

Beyond, on the crest, is **Redan Ridge No.1 CWGC Cemetery (GPS: 50.9298 2.65212)**.

Continue to the D919. Turn left and continue to the large British cemetery on the left.

Redan Ridge No 3 CWGC Cemetery

French Memorial Chapel & Serre Road No 1 CWGC Cemetery from Redan Ridge

• *Serre Road CWGC Cemetery No 2/Val Braithwaite Memorial/16.7 miles/20 minutes/Map D24/23/GPS: 50.09664 2.65131*

Designed by Sir Edwin Lutyens, this is one of three Serre Road Cemeteries. They were begun by V Corps in the spring of 1917, over-run by the Germans in March 1918 and re-taken in August. There are over 7,100 burials in this concentration cemetery, making it the largest British Cemetery on the Somme battlefield. It contains some German graves and that of Private A. E. Bull, 12th Yorks & Lancs, who has a Private Memorial

in Sheffield Park (qv). It was in the gardener's hut in this cemetery that CWGC worker Ben Leach hid two RAF pilots when visited by Germans inspecting German graves during World War II. At the roadside outside the cemetery wall is a private memorial to Lt V. A. Braithwaite, MC, a regular officer of the SLI, son of Gen Sir Walter Braithwaite, KCB, Chief of the General Staff in Gallipoli, where his son served as his ADC. Besides winning one of the first MC's of the war at Mons, Braithwaite had twice been mentioned in Despatches. In his Gallipoli Memories Compton Mackenzie remembers with

The imposing entrance to Serre Road No 2 CWGC Cemetery

affection the unsophisticated, 'tall, sunburnt young Wykehamist'. He was killed on the first day of the Somme battle, (though on the Thiepval memorial the date is given as 2 July) along with his commanding officer, adjutant and fourteen other officers in the battalion. Their attack had been made along the line of the road towards you, and to its left, against the German stronghold known as Quadrilateral Redoubt, which was on the site of the cemetery.

Turn round and continue back up the D919 towards the chapel on the right.

• *Memorial to 3 Soldiers Found Near Probable Site of Wilfred Owen's 1917 Dugout/16.9 miles/5 minutes/Map D21a/GPS: 50.09786 2.653521*

Beyond Braithwaite's Cross, before the French Chapel, and to the right of the road, is the probable site (first located by researcher Philip Guest) of 'the advanced post, that is a "dugout" in the middle of No Man's Land' described by the poet Lt Wilfred Edward Salter Owen of the 2nd Bn, the Manchester Regt, in a letter to his mother of 16 January 1917, where he suffered 'seventh hell'. Here one of Owen's most powerful poems, The Sentry, was inspired by an incident when a sentry was blown down the dugout steps by the force of a shell blast and blinded. The man's terror and distress: 'O sir, my eyes – I'm blind – I'm blind, I'm blind', would haunt Owen.

V. A. L. Braithwaite private memorial, with Serre Road CWGC Cemetery No 2 in the background

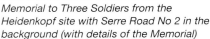

Memorial to Three Soldiers from the Heidenkopf site with Serre Road No 2 in the background (with details of the Memorial)

A few days later the battalion moved to billets in Courcelles (a village slightly further behind the lines than Colincamps) from where Owen wrote home on the 19th, describing his close encounter with a gas shell. This incident was probably the inspiration for the episode in one of his best-known poems, *Dulce et Decorum Est:*

Gas! GAS! Quick, boys! – An ecstasy of fumbling,

Fitting the clumsy helmets just in time …

But they were not in time for one poor lad who virtually drowned 'under a green sea'. Like the blind sentry, Owen saw the gas victim 'In all my dreams'. Owen was killed a week before the Armistice and is buried in Ors CWGC cemetery.

In October 2003 the group *'No Man's Land: the European Group for Great War Archaeology'* investigated the site at the Heidenkopf or Quadrilateral (filmed by the BBC for their Ancestors series) but had to close the dig before the dugout had been positively identified. They did, however, find the remains of 3 soldiers, one of the 1st King's Own (Royal Lancaster) Regt and two Germans. After some brilliant research by Alastair Fraser and Volker Hartmann in Germany with Ralph Whitehead in America, one of the Germans, found with several artefacts and a corroded identity disc, was identified as Jakob Hones of the 121st Wurttemberg Res Inf Regt and an amazingly full personal and family history was discovered. Hones was reburied in the German Cemetery at Labry near Verdun. The full story is told on Alastair's website, www.fylde.demon.co.uk/fraser.htm

In 2006 the Memorial was inaugurated to commemorate the three soldiers.

• *French Memorial Chapel & German Memorial/17.1 miles/5 minutes/Map D21/22 /GPS: 50.09928 2.65609*

In the porch of this sadly neglected chapel there are two interesting memorials. One is to a remarkable man, Maistre Joseph de la Rue, who founded the memorial. He seems to have been the French equivalent of 'Woodbine Willie' (the Padre, Geoffrey Studdert-Kennedy). A professor of history before the war, he became Chaplain to the 243rd and 233rd RI during 1914-18, was Chaplain to the Army in 1939-45, and Chaplain to the Galliéni Group in 1940-3, *Chevalier de la Légion d'Honneur, Médaille Militaire* and *Croix de Guerre.* Below his

Bavarian Res Inf Regt No 1 memorial, Serre Chapel

French National Cemetery, Serre from Redan Ridge

imposing plaque is a small, modern Plaque, one of the few German memorials on the Somme, to the memory of comrades of the Bavarian Reserve Infantry Regiment 1 who were killed at Serre.

Walk over the road.

• French National Cemetery Serre-Hébuterne/10 minutes/Map D17/20

Created in 1919 for the dead of the 243rd RI of the 10-13 June battles of 1915 it was enlarged in 1923 for other dead of the 243rd and 327th RI. It contains 834 burials, of which 240 are in the mass grave. Note the Muslim headstones among the creamy-white crosses. At the top of the Cemetery is an impressive memorial, with a bronze bas relief, to the men of 233rd, 243rd and 327th RI from Lille. A black Plaque lists the regiments engaged here at the Ferme de Toutvent from 7-13 June 1915. The farm which was about a kilometer behind the present cemetery, had been taken and fortified by the Germans in 1914 and in a set piece attack at 0500 hours the French set out to take it back from the Bavarians who were holding it. This they did in an action which won the 93rd Regiment the Military Cross.

Continue to the next cemetery on the same side of the road.

• Serre Road CWGC Cemetery No 1/17.2 miles/5 minutes/Map D18/GPS: 50.09981 2.65726

This was begun in May 1917 by V Corps but was enlarged after the Armistice by the concentration of over 2,000 graves from other parts of the Somme battlefield. There are some 2,100 burials, including 71 French soldiers. On 1 July it was the Leeds and Bradford Pals who attacked here, i.e. the 15th, 16th and 18th West Yorks. The Cemetery was seen in the 2006 film *Mrs Henderson Presents*.

Continue 100m. Park off the road by the beginning of the track, Chemin des Cimetières, leading to the left signed Luke Copse, Railway Hollow, Queen's and Serre Road No 3 Cemeteries. Walk along it. If it is very dry you may consider driving up it as far as the first cemetery on the right, but be aware of farm vehicles.

• Serre Road No 3 CWGC Cemetery/5 minutes/Map D15/GPS: 50.10363 2.6565

This tiny Cemetery contains eighty-one burials (mostly of W Yorks from 1 July) and four Special Memorials.

Continue. As the path curves to the right, an enclosed wooded area is on the left. Walk in.

Serre Road No 3 CWGC Cemetery

• *Sheffield Memorial Park & Memorials/Railway Hollow CWGC Cemetery/25 minutes/Map D12/31a/13b/13c/13d/13e/16/GPS: 50.10607 2.65546*

Originally there were four small copses in this area, named after the Apostles, Matthew, Mark, Luke and John. The remnants of them now merge into one wooded area based on Mark, in which is the park, where, as at Beaumont Hamel, craters and trench lines have remained undisturbed by agriculture and have been allowed to grass over naturally.

'I am the grass; I cover all', wrote the American poet Carl Sandburg and graphically described the potent work of that benign plant which covered bodies from Austerlitz,

Above: Barnsley Pals Plaques

Left: Sheffield Memorial Park: Accrington Pals Memorial

Memorial to 13th, 14th Bns York & Lancs, Sheffield Memorial Park

Railway Hollow CWGC Cemetery, Sheffield Park

Chorley Pals Plaques left and right

Waterloo, Gettysburg, Ypres and Verdun. Here it covers some of the trenches from which the Pals from the northern towns received their baptism of fire as part of Kitchener's New Army. The **Accrington Pals** (Map D13b, a symbolic broken brick wall), the **Chorley Pals** Y Co (Map D13a, a plaque on a tree), the 13th/14th York & Lancaster, **Barnsley Pals** (Map D13e, a smart black marble monument with coloured badges and on the tree a small black plaque naming the sponsors, including Sir Nicholas Hewitt and the Barnsley Chronicle) and the **Sheffield Pals** (Map D3d, a brick Memorial gateway with commemorative plaques) have all placed memorials here to their sacrifice. On a tree to the left is a small Plaque to **Alister Sturrock**, I July 1994. A wooden cross bears a plaque in memory of **Pte A. E. Bull** of the 12th York & Lancs, killed here on 1 July 1916, whose body was found on 13 April 1928 and who is now buried in Serre Road No 2 CWGC Cemetery. At the foot of the slope at the rear of the park is **Railway Hollow CWGC Cemetery** (Map D12) containing 107 UK burials (mostly York & Lancs of 1 July, plus 2 French graves). It is situated on the line of the old military railway which ran through here. Leading here was a long communication trench called Northern Avenue which began just above Colincamps some 2 miles away to the west.

Emerge from the park and walk to the cemetery straight ahead.

• Queen's CWGC Cemetery/5 minutes/Map D14/GPS: 10568 2.65643

This Cemetery contains 311 burials, mostly from July and Nov 1916, with a large number of Accrington Pals who attacked from their trench, now within the park, on 1 July.

Return to the entrance to the park, turn right.

• Luke Copse CWGC Cemetery/5 minutes/Map D11/GPS: 50.10777 2.6592

This small Cemetery (seventy-two burials) contains men of the Sheffield City Battalion who attacked here on 1 July, including brothers L Cpl F. and Pte W. Gunstone, and has a memorial to men of the 2nd Suffolks who fell here on 13 November 1916.

The three cemeteries, Serre Road No 3, Queens and Luke Copse, all lie just on the No Man's Land side of the British line of 1 July. At 0720 the assault troops of 31st Division climbed out of their trenches to file through the passages cut in their own wire, intending to lie in No Man's Land before advancing together to capture the village of Serre. It was their first time in battle. They were immediately subjected to heavy machine-gun fire from Serre village and bombarded by both field and heavy artillery. At 0730 when the leading waves stood up in order to advance, the fire increased and hardly any troops reached the German front trench, barely 400m away. Those that did were either killed or taken prisoner. The 31st Division contained four Rifle Battalions from Hull, one from Leeds, two from Bradford, one from Accrington, one from Sheffield, two from Barnsley and one from Durham. These were 'Pals' battalions, made up of volunteer soldiers hailing from a single town or village, or even a single factory or football team. They worked together, lived together, joined up together and frequently died together, devastating whole communities back home at a stroke.

Return to the main D919 road. Continue towards Serre. Park by the memorial on the left

• 12th Bn York & Lancs Memorial/Serre Village/ 17.7 miles/5 minutes/ Map D19/GPS: 50.10351 2.66892

This was raised by Sheffield to her Pals, known as the Sheffield City Battalion. Sheffield adopted Serre after the war. A glance at the 140m contour lines on the Holts' map shows the predominating position held by the Germans in this village, which they had prepared as a fortress. At this northern end of the Fourth Army sector there were no significant gains at all during the Somme fighting. Following the July failures by the 4th and 31st Divisions, the 3rd and 31st tried again on 13 November to no avail. The Memorial is located here because during the unsuccessful assault on Serre on 13 November 1916, some British troops briefly entered the village and found bodies of men of the 12th Bn still lying where they had fallen in July. Eventually on 24 February 1917 the Germans withdrew from Serre and the 22nd Manchesters moved in the following morning.

Continue on the N919 signed to Arras, to Puisieux.
Like Serre, this was abandoned by the Germans on 24 February 1917 in their retreat to the Hindenburg Line.
Continue to the junction left in Puisieux with the D6.

12th Bn York & Lancs Memorial, Serre

Extra Visit to Owl Trench CWGC Cemetery, Rossignol Wood CWGC Cemetery & Rossignol Wood Bunker, SOA Rev Bayley Hardy, VC. Round trip: 7.6 miles. Approximate time: 45 minutes
    Turn left up the D6 following green CWGC signs.
The British attack of 1 July had included a diversionary assault (from your left) by Sir Edward Allenby's Third Army on a German salient at Gommecourt. Its object was to divert attention away from the main thrust astride the Albert-Bapaume Road. The task was given to 56th Division, a London and Middlesex territorial force under General Hull and 46th Division from the Midlands. Beginning early in May, great pioneer works were begun behind the British lines. Headquarters were built, roads, railways and pipe lines laid and even a new front line dug some 400m in front of the old one. These preparations so caught the Germans' attention that on 1 July three divisions-worth of artillery hammered the British attack. Many Tommies believed that the enemy knew exactly when to expect them. 56th Division took the German front line (roughly the road you are driving along) and more, but lost it all by the end of the day. 46th Division to the north was unable to advance at all, and was thus incapable of supporting its neighbour. General Stuart-Wortley was relieved of command less than a week later. In this area the D6 runs roughly parallel with the German line, which from Rossignol Wood CWGC Cemetery onwards was about 400m to your left and was in 56th Division's area. The line bent sharply to the right 400m beyond Gommecourt village, this northern part being in 46th Division's area, with the assault being down the D6 from Foncquevillers directly towards the village.

    Continue to **Owl Trench (Map D10, GPS: 50.12866 2.66443)**, the first cemetery you reach on the left. This tiny cemetery contains only fifty-three burials, from 31st Division's attack on

The isolated Owl Trench CWGC Cemetery

the German rearguard in February 1917 during their retreat to the Hindenburg Line. The burials, many of W Yorks (many Bradford 'Pals'), are mostly three to a grave, therefore the cemetery looks even smaller than it actually is.

Continue a few hundred yards further.

Rossignol Road CWGC Cemetery showing German Headstones

On the left is **Rossignol Wood Cemetery (Map D9, GPS: 50.12962 2.66552)**. This was begun on 14 March 1917 by the N and S Staffs and used again in August 1918 by the New Zealanders. It has thirty-four UK, seven New Zealand and seventy German graves, i.e., considerably more German than British graves.

Continue to the next junction and turn right towards the wood. Stop at the first corner of the wood and walk south some 100m along the edge to an obvious indentation.

A few metres inside **Rossignol Wood**, with a clear line of old trenches leading to it, is a **German bunker (Map D30, GPS: 50.13182 2.66987)**.

Near it one of the most exceptional Padres of World War I won the Victoria Cross. The **Rev Theodore Bayley Hardy** spent the day of 5 April 1918 there comforting a badly wounded man injured in the 8th Lincolnshires' attack on the wood. At dusk he returned to ask for a volunteer to help him bring back the wounded man, and a sergeant, G. Radford, helped him to bring the man to safety. The Padre then continued to tend the wounded under fire and later in the month at Bucquoy, on 25, 26 and 27 April, again acted with such self-sacrificing heroism to save others' lives that he was nominated three more times for the Victoria Cross. Radford was awarded the DCM, and Hardy went on to add the DSO, MC and DCM to his VC. That month he was also appointed Chaplain to King George V, who presented him with his VC in 1918 (an event immortalised by the artist Terence Cuneo).

Despite pleas to accept a safe appointment at Base, Hardy – who had almost refused to accept his VC, but agreed when it was pointed out by Col Hardyman, CO of the Somersets, that if he did refuse it would only 'be advertising yourself all the more' – continued in the front line. On 11 October 1918 the 8th Lincolns and the 8th Somersets were crossing the River Selle at Briastres when the Padre was shot through the thigh. Evacuated to No 2 Red Cross Hospital at Rouen, he died on 18 October, less than a month before the end of the war. He was 55 years old and the most decorated noncombatant of the conflict.

Return to the main road and turn right.

German Bunker, Rossignal Wood, with discernible trench lines

On the right, opposite Gommecourt Park, was the fortified position known as Kern Redoubt, or the Maze.
Continue through the village to the final cemetery on the road.
Gommecourt Wood New Cemetery (**Map D2**, **GPS: 50.14342 2.63956**) contains 682 UK burials, 56 New Zealanders and 1 Australian. There are ten special memorials. On the right-hand wall inside the Cemetery is a Memorial **Plaque to 46th N Midland Division** (Map D1).

Memorial to 46th (North Midland) Div, Gommecourt Wood New CWGC Cemetery

Immediately to the S of the Cemetery is the **SOA** of **Capt John Leslie Green VC** (Map D3). On 1 July 1916, **Captain John Leslie Green of the RAMC**, attd 1/5th Battalion the Sherwood Foresters, although himself wounded, rescued an officer who had been wounded and was caught up in the enemy wire, with grenades constantly being thrown at him. He dragged him to a shell hole where he dressed his wounds, and had almost succeeded in bringing the man to safety when he was killed. Capt Green is buried in Foncquevillers Military Cemetery (Map A4)

Return to the N919 at Puisieux, turn left and pick up the main itinerary.
NOTE: that if further itineraries are to be followed, you may wish to finish Itinerary One here and return to your base on the Somme. If returning to one of the Channel Ports, the remainder of Itinerary One is directly *en route.*
Continue in the direction of Arras through Bucquoy, whose church is an interesting example of Art Deco architecture (qv), to the fork with the D7 at the edge of the village of Ayette. Take the fork to the right and immediately turn left up a small and very narrow track. Note that there is no turning area at the end, so this is an opportunity to practise your reversing skills.

• Ayette Indian & Chinese Cemetery/23.7 miles/10 minutes/Map B2/GPS: 50.17574 2.733209

This unusual Cemetery, which has a pagoda-shaped shelter but no Cross of Sacrifice, contains ten soldiers of the Indian Army, forty-two men of the Indian Labour Corps and twenty-seven of the Chinese Labour Corps (whose inscriptions bear a selection of the standard English inscriptions – see St Etienne au Mont on the Western Approach, page 51), one German prisoner and six Chinese Labour Corps (French). The Indian and Chinese headstones bear inscriptions in their own languages.
Continue on the D919 to Beaurains.

Ayette Indian & Chinese Cemetery

Extra Visit to the Commonwealth War Graves Headquarters at Beaurains/GPS: 50.25756 2.78123 /Round trip: 2 miles. Approximate time: 15 minutes

At the outskirts to the town turn right, following the green CWGC signs to the imposing low brick building on the right (Rue Angèle Richard, 62217 Beaurains).

This is the administrative headquarters for the Commission in France, and cemetery registers are held for all the cemeteries in the area. Behind are workshops from which carpentry, masonry, engraving, ironwork and gardening repairs and maintenance are organised.

The offices are open during normal working hours, Monday to Friday, with a break for lunch. Telephone ahead if you wish to consult a register or enquire about a burial. Tel: +(0)3 21 21 77 00, e-mail: france.area@cwgc.org or use the CWGC Debt of Honour website, www.cwgc.org (qv) in advance of your visit to find the information you are seeking. Copies of the Commission's excellent themed information pamphlets on a variety of topics are available here, as are poppy wreaths and sprays.

Return to the main itinerary.

Continue to the centre of Arras on the N17, following signs to Gare SCNF and park as near as possible to the railway station.

• *Arras Centre/Town Hall & Boves/33 miles approx miles/60 minutes/ Map 14/23/GPS: 50.28747 2.78166*

NOTE: From here your mileage and timings will vary depending upon exactly where you can park and if you walk or drive to the Town Hall.

Arras suffered considerable damage from long-range shells – the German front line was only some two miles east of the town. In 1916 the British took over from the French and in the days preceding the April 1917 offensive the war correspondent Philip Gibbs vividly described the scene in the damaged town: the Highlanders playing their pipe bands, the soldiers in their steel helmets and goatskin coats who resembled 'medieval men-at-arms', the dead horses lying thick on the Arras-Cambrai road, the long queues of wounded men waiting for treatment in the old Vauban Citadel – 3,000 of them on one day alone... Men and materiel poured through the town in huge numbers in the preparation for the offensive.

On the wall of the station are **Plaques to Station Workers** (SNCF) killed in the War 1 and WW2 and the **Red Cross** in 1940.

Opposite the railway station on the central area is the **Arras War Memorial**, with some fine *bas reliefs* of various aspects of the Great

Arras War Memorial

War, which shows scars from the Second World War. All around the square are numerous Cafés and Hotels (see **Tourist Information**, page 339). The town has been a centre of trade and population since ancient times. It was fortified by Vauban who built the citadel. It was briefly over-run by the Germans in September 1914 but then held by the French until March 1916 and then the British until the end of the war.

The **British 56th (1st London) Division's** part in the fighting is commemorated by a **Plaque** on the wall of the Chapel on rue du Saumon, some 200 yds due north from here. **GPS: 50.28885 2.78063**

The **Town Hall/Boves.** This is a five minute walk from the station area (follow signs to *'Les Places'*, or you may decide to drive and park under the Grand' Place). The Squares have delightful Flemish baroque facades and many restaurants. Through the Town

Plaque to 56th (1st London) Div, Arras

Hall (with its impressive belfry, started in 1463, rebuilt between 1924-1932) is access to the *'Boves'* – the caves and tunnels dating from the fourteenth century that were enlarged and extended during the 1914-18 war. The soft, porous stone underlying Arras was tunnelled in deepest secrecy for 18 months before the April 1917 offensive when narrow-gauge railways were constructed to carry away the spoil. The tunnels, christened after British towns – 'Glasgow', 'Manchester' etc, were reinforced with pine logs supporting the heavy cross timbers of the roof and led to cavernous chambers. Generating stations to produce electricity were installed and miles of wiring were used in the hundreds of yards of tunnels that linked the ancient cellars, crypts and quarries. Not only were the undergrounds used as hospitals and shelters, but also to transport vast bodies of troops and material safely to the start line trenches of the offensive in open country. The **Tourist Office** in the Town Hall is **open** 21 April-16 September Mon-Sat: 0900 - 1830; Sun: 1000-1300 and 1430-1830. 1 Jan-20 April and 17 Sept-31 Dec: Mon 1000-1200 and 1400-1800; Tues-Sat 0900-1200 and 1400-1800; Sun 1000-1230 and 1430-1830. A visit to the *Boves* and tours of the surrounding battlefields may be booked here. Tel: + (0)3 21 51 26 95. E-mail: *arras.tourisme@wanadoo.fr* Website: *www.ot-arras.fr* It will be useful to pick up a town plan here, lists of any commemorative events in the vicinity and more information about accommodation and restaurants.

Return to your car. Take the N17 on Ave du Maréchal Leclerc, direction Bapaume. After crossing over the railway bridge the road then leads into the Ave Ferdinand Lobbedez. Continue almost exactly half a mile after the bridge to the junction with rue Alexandre Ribot to the Memorial on the left.

Memorial to New Zealand Tunnellers and Wellington Quarry/34.0 miles/45 mins/Map 14/24/GPS: 50.28040 2.78285

The striking Monument which simulates a section of a tunnel, was designed by Arras artist, Luc Brévart. It is made of white stone and railway sleepers (reminiscent of those used by the NZ Tunnellers) with bronze components, such as a NZ tin hat, a pick and a map of New Zealand. It honours the 41 NZ Tunnellers who lost their lives here and the 151 who were wounded. They included Maori and Pacific Islanders of the ZN Pioneer Battalion.

Beside the Memorial is the old 'Défence Passive' building. This was the name for the **quarry** in which the local inhabitants sheltered during the bombings of May 1940 and the building was used as a power/water supply zone for the underground quarries, originally dug in the Middle Ages. These were the basis for the network of underground quarries linked up by the NZ Tunnellers in preparation for the April 1917 Battle of Arras and which eventually could house 24,000 soldiers as they waited for the surprise offensive to start on 9 April at 05.30. The section underground here was known as **Wellington Quarry** in WW1.

New Zealand Tunnellers Memorial, Arras

Its imposing entrance is in the adjacent Rue Delétoile which should be signed from here. There is a large car park. A **Memorial Wall** listing the Regiments of the 1st, 3rd and 5th British Armies involved in the battle leads the visitor to the entrance.

Wellington Quarry, Arras.

Open: every day from 1000-1230 and 1330-1800 except 25 Dec and the three following weeks. **Contact:** as Tourist Office above. This is a fascinating and atmospheric visit. Accompanied by a guide and an audio-guide available in several languages, the visitor descends 20m in a glass lift to the living and administrative quarters. Most poignant are the many examples of signs and carved and painted graffiti (also from the period of WW2), examples of letters and photos. A film sets the scene.
Return to the Place Maréchal Foch and follow signs to the Citadelle/Motorway and on the town ring road, Boulevard Gen de Gaulle, just south of the junction with the N25 to Doullens, is

• *Faubourg d'Amiens CWGC Cemetery/Arras & RFC Memorials to the Missing/Mur des Fusillés/approx 40 miles/45 minutes/Map 14/22/GPS: 50.28667 2.76048*

Despite the name of the Cemetery, this is the **Arras Memorial**. It takes the form of a wall carrying almost 36,000 names of the Missing of the battles around Arras. On it are the names of the First World War poet **Capt. T.P. Cameron Wilson** of the Sherwood Foresters, **Lt Geoffrey Thurlow** of the same regiment – one of Vera Brittain's coterie of friends, and **Captain Charles McKay** and **Private David Sutherland** of the Seaforths. David was the subject of Lt. E. A. Mackintosh's searing poem, *In Memoriam*, which describes his death during a trench raid on 16 May 1916 in which McKay also took part.

Also commemorated here is **2nd Lt Walter Daniel John Tull**, Middx Regt, 25 March 1918, age 29. Tull was one of Britain's first black professional footballers and, despite his poor background, also its first black Army Officer. Tull was admitted to an orphanage in Bethnal Green when both his parents died and was signed up by Tottenham Hotspur in 1908. In 1909 he suffered appalling racial abuse during a match and was transferred to Northampton Town. On the outbreak of war he enlisted in the 17th (1st Football) Bn of the Middx Regt, was promoted to sergeant in 1916, was invalided home with trench fever at the end of the year and went to the officer cadet training school at Gailes in Scotland – despite the fact that 'Negroes' were specifically excluded from commanding as officers. In 1917 he went to the Italian Front as a 2nd Lieutenant in the 23rd (2nd Football) Bn of the Middx Regt and was MiD in the Battle of the Piave. In 1918 he returned to France

The Arras Memorial to the Missing

Arras Flying Services Memorial

Mur des Fusillés Execution Post

and was killed in No Man's Land near Favreuil. In the mid-1990s a campaign was started to use Tull's inspiring story to help black recruitment in the British Army and to defuse racial discrimination in the world of football and on 11 July 1999 the **Walter Tull Memorial and Garden of Rest** was opened at Sixfields Stadium, Northampton. Tull will be featured during the 100th WW1 Anniversaries.

Three members of the Banks Brass Band, **Pte Tom Ryding**, MGC, 12 March 1918, **Pte Robert Blundell**, KLR, 3 May 1917 and **L/Cpl Robert Brookfield**, KSLI, 18 March 1918 are commemorated here. Members of the current Banks Band (accompanied by members of Blundell's family) made a pilgrimage in 2012 and played in tribute at the Arras Memorial.

The wall encloses the Cemetery, begun in March 1916, and which contains 2,700 burials. At the back are separate small rows for Hindus, Mohammedans and Sikhs. Just within the entrance wall, in a space once occupied by the graves of French soldiers, is the **Royal Flying Corps Memorial**. It takes the form of a column surmounted by a globe. The flight of doves encircling the globe is following the path of the sun on 11 November 1918. It carries the names of over 1,000 personnel of the **RNAS, RFC** and **RAF** personnel missing on the Western Front, **including VCs Major Lanoe Hawker and Major E. ('Mick') Mannock.** Also commemorated here is **Lt Donald MacGregor**, the Red Baron's 63rd victim, shot down on 30 November 1917 during the Cambrai battle and **Capt J.V. Aspinall** whose name was originally over the grave of Capt F.L. Mond in Doullens Cem Ext (see page 57).

Beyond the Memorial the '*Mur des Fusillés*' is signed. This is a 1 mile round trip which leads to a poignant area where between July 1941 and July 1944 the Germans shot over 200 Frenchmen, including some liberated in the 'Operation Jericho' Amiens prison raid of 1944. A concrete marker indicates the Execution Post and Memorial Plaques commemorate those who were killed (many of them Miners, dating from 1942 and June 1944). Entry to the area is controlled by a gate which closes at dusk and you must park before the barrier and walk the last section around the old Citadel walls.

• *End of Itinerary One OR*

Extra Visit to Point-du-Jour Military Cemetery/9th Scottish Division Memorial. GPS: 50.31377 2.83578. Round trip: 10 miles. Approximate time: 20 minutes

Continue north on the ring road and follow signs to A26/Douai onto the D950 dual carriageway. Then take the D42e through Athies following green CWGC signs to the Cemetery finally along a rough track to both cemetery and memorial.

The Cemetery, designed by Sir Reginald Blomfield, is in the village of Athies, in the Valley of the Scarpe, which was captured by the 9th (Scottish) Division (including the S African Brigade) on 9 April 1917 and remained in Allied hands for the remainder of the war. The **9th Scottish Division Memorial** was moved here some 5 years ago from its dominating position about half a mile away as it was deemed dangerous of access from the busy dual carriageway. In the form of a large Cairn, it is surrounded by stone boundary markers with the names of units in the Division and bears the legend, 'Remember with Honour the 9th Scottish Division who fell on the Fields of France and Flanders, 1915-1918. Served Well'. The Cairn and surrounding stones echo those which commemorate the 1746 Battle of Culloden.

9th Scottish Div Mem
with Point du Jour CWGC
Cemetery

Point-du-Jour ('Daybreak') was the name of a house on the St Laurent-Blangy-Gavrelle road which had been strongly fortified by the Germans and which was captured by 34th Division on 9 April. Two cemeteries were made on the right of the road between St Laurent-Blangy and Point-du-Jour and one of them (No 1) developed into the present cemetery. Used from April to November 1917 and again in 1918 it contained 82 graves at the Armistice (now part of Plot I). It was then enlarged as remains were brought in from the surrounding battlefields. It now contains 786 WW1 burials, 52 UK Navy, 264 UK Army, 2 Airforce and 378 UK Unknown, 5 Canadian and 9 Unknown, 2 New Zealand, 66 S African and 8 Unknown and 3 UK 1940. There are 3 French plus 3 Unknown burials. There are 22 Special Memorials and 6 Memorials to casualties buried in other cemeteries but whose graves have been destroyed.

Here are buried **Lt Colonel F.S.N. Savage**, DSO and twice MiD, age 36, who commanded the 11th Battalion, the R Warwicks, had served in the S African Campaign as a boy, fought at Ypres in 1914, at Neuve-Chapelle, Fromelles and Festubert in 1915, Arras in 1917, was wounded at Festubert and killed on 23 April 1917 and **Lt Colonel C.J. Burke**, DSO, age 35, of the RIR, who went to France in 1914 as commander of No 2 Squadron RFC, and served with the 1st East Lancs, killed on 9 April 1917.

More recently the Cemetery has been used for the burials, for example in June 2002, of the 23 soldiers of the Lincolnshire Regiment (the Grimsby Chums) found in January 2001 in St Laurent-Blangy (through which you have just driven). They lie together in a row in front of which are the graves of the five soldiers of the 15th Royal Scots found in June 2001 and re-interred later in the month, including **Pte Archie McMillan**.

Boundary Marker to 63rd & 64th Fd Coys, RE

ITINERARY TWO

Itinerary Two starts at the Town Hall Square in Albert, turns east along the old 1916 front line of the British right flank, then heads north through the woods – Mametz, Bernafay, Trônes, Delville and High – to the Albert-Bapaume Road at Courcelette. It ends in Pozières.

• **The Route:** Albert – Communal Cemetery Extension, French National Cemetery; Dartmoor CWGC Cemetery; Fricourt – CWGC British Cemetery, Church Memorials, New Military CWGC Cemetery, German Cemetery; 38th (Welsh) Div Memorial, Mametz Church; 38th (Welsh) Div Dragon Memorial; 12th Manchesters Memorial; Donald Bell, VC Memorial; McCrae's Bn Memorial, Contalmaison Château Cemetery; Harry Fellows' Grave; Flat Iron Copse CWGC Cemetery; site of the 14 July 1916 cavalry charge; Caterpillar Valley CWGC Cemetery; New Zealand Memorial to the Missing; Bristol's Own Cross; Longueval Road CWGC Cemetery; Bernafay Wood CWGC Cemetery; Liverpool & Manchester Pals Memorial; Capt Monclin Private Memorial; Pommiers Redoubt; Dantzig Alley CWGC Cemetery and Memorials; Manchester Regt Memorial; Shrine Corner; Devonshire CWGC Cemetery; Gordon CWGC Cemetery; Carnoy CWGC Cemetery; Franco-British Memorial, Maricourt; 18th Div Memorial, Trônes Wood; SOA Capt Chavasse VC+Bar; Guillemont Rd CWGC Cemetery; 16th Irish Div Memorial; French 265th Inf Memorial; 20th Light Div Memorial; Private Memorials to Capt Dickens and Lt Irwin; Private Memorial Lejoindre and Pfister; Delville Wood – CWGC Cemetery, Memorials, Museum and Visitors' Centre; Footballers' Memorial, Pipers' Memorial, Longueval; SOA 'Billy' Congreve VC; New Zealand Memorial; Cameron Highlanders/Black Watch Memorial; 47th (London) Div Memorial; 20th Bn RF Tree; Glasgow Highlanders Cairn; London Cemetery and Extension; Martinpuich – 47th Div/German Memorials, Bunker; Courcelette – Adanac Military CWGC Cemetery, Canadian Memorial; Pozières – Tank Corps Memorial, Australian Windmill Memorials, Butterworth Memorial, Sunken Road and 2nd Canadian Cemeteries, Tommy Café.

• **Extra Visits** are suggested to: Capt Dodgson Private Memorial; 'Nine Brave Men' Private Memorial; Capt Wallace Private Memorial; Pte Tomasin Private Memorial; Point 110 Old and New Military Cemeteries; area of Sassoon's Raid; Maltkorn Farm; Private Memorials to Capt Cochin and Boucher & Lapage; Private Memorial Lt Marsden-Smedley; Dickens Cross.

• **[N.B.]** The following sites are indicated: Maricourt - Fr 224th RI Lt Brodu Memorial; Fricourt – Site of Le Tambour; Courcelette – 15th Bn Can Inf 48th Highlanders Memorial; Pozières – Site of Butterworth Trench.

• **Planned duration**, without stops for refreshments or Extra Visits: **9.5 hours.**

• **Total distance: 39.5 miles.**

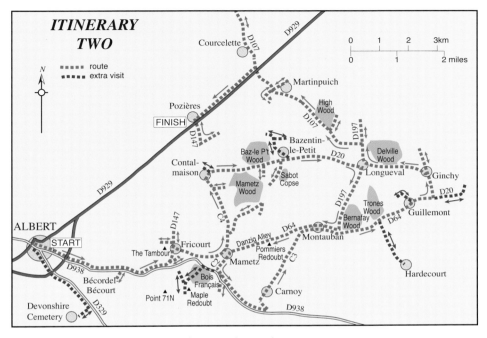

ITINERARY TWO

- ▪▪▪▪ route
- ▪▪▪▪ extra visit

N

Courcelette

Martinpuich

Pozières

FINISH

High Wood

Bazentin-le-Petit

Baz-le P't Wood

Delville Wood

Contal-maison

Longueval

Ginchy

Mametz Wood

Sabot Copse

Trones Wood

Bernafay Wood

Guillemont

ALBERT

START

Fricourt

The Tambour

Danzig Alley

Pommiers Redoubt

Montauban

Mametz

Hardecourt

Bécordel-Bécourt

Bois Français

Point 71N

Maple Redoubt

Carnoy

Devonshire Cemetery

0 1 2 3km
0 1 2 miles

• **Albert Town Hall Square/0 miles/RWC/Map J14**

Leave the Square on rue Jean Guyon signed to Bray on the D938/ A1 Paris. En route keep to the left of the town war memorial, signed Péronne. Fork left on the D938 direction A1/Historial on rue 11 Novembre and continue to the cemetery on the right.

• **Albert Communal Cemetery Extension/0.5 miles/10 minutes/Map J29/GPS: 49.99921 2.65248**

This was established during the first part of the Somme fighting, known as the Battle of Albert. It was used by fighting units and field ambulances from August 1915. In August 1918 5th CCS was established here. Plot II was made by 18th Div. There are 618 UK graves, 202 Canadian and 39 Australian, 12 unknown and 2 BWI. There are many interesting burials here, including communal graves for thirteen 10th Essex soldiers blown up by a German mine at la Boisselle in November 1915 and eleven soldiers of the 41st Siege Battery killed by a shell when unloading ammunition in July 1916. There are also two **Brigadier-Generals – Henry Frederick Hugh Clifford DSO**, CO of 149th Bde, 50th Division, killed on 11 September 1916 by a sniper from Delville Wood while inspecting advanced assembly trenches, age 49, son of Maj Gen the Hon H. H. Clifford VC, KCMG, CB, and **Randle Barnett-Barker DSO**

Headstone of Pte Cocks with photo of him with his wife and baby

and Bar, CO of 99th Bde, 47th (London) Division killed at Gueudecourt on 24 March 1918. There is also a Special Memorial to four men and a WW2 Plot containing 17 Known and 8 Unknown burials

Next to the British military plot is a sad plot with what appears to be CWGC headstones. This is a local paupers' graveyard and the headstones are damaged stones discarded by the Commission. The area was over-run by the Germans in the March 1918 offensive and re-taken by the 8th East Surreys on 26 April.

In the civilian cemetery there is a plot at the back enclosed by a high hedge. It contains crosses marking the graves of the **Breton soldiers** killed in 1914/15/16. Among them is the **Adjutant of the 19th RIF, Jules Boccard**, 7 February 1915, who was the probable successor to André Pitel, commemorated on the Breton Calvary at Ovillers (qv). Outside the plot is a grey marble stone inscribed *A Nos Soldats Bretons.*

Continue on the D938 over the roundabout.

Breton Plot, Albert Comm Cemetery

• *French National Cemetery, Albert/0.9 miles/15 minutes/Map J30/GPS: 49.99627 2.66288*

On the left is this large concentration cemetery from the Somme battlefield with 6,290 burials (including three British, one of whom is a Chinese Labourer, 5 December 1918, who only has a number (33295), not a name, inscribed on his headstone, and two Polish). 2,879 of them are in four mass graves (including two of the British). Here is buried, in grave No 352, **Lt Robert**

Left: *Cross of Lt R. Brodu, 224th RI (qv)*

Below: *French National Cemetery, Albert*

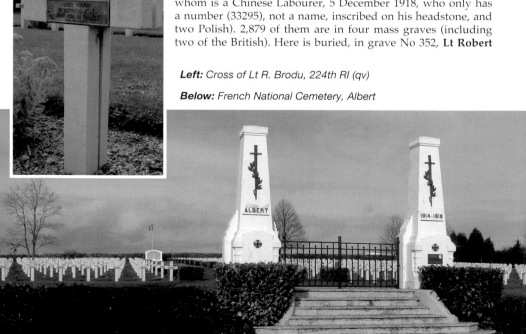

Brodu (qv), *Legion d'Honneur, Croix de Guerre* of the 224th RI, killed near Maricourt on 17 December 1914.

> *Continue over the roundabout, following signs to Péronne/Historial and A1 and continue past the junction with the C2. Take the first small road to the right following CWGC signs to Dartmoor, Cemetery.*

• *Dartmoor CWGC Cemetery/2.2 miles/15 minutes/Map J37/GPS: 49.99181 2.68851*

Originally Bécordel-Bécourt cemetery, this was begun in August 1915 and its name was changed in May 1916 at the request of the Devonshire Regiment. Behind the British lines of July 1916, the area nearby was used by XV Corps Main Dressing Station from September 1916. A notable burial among the total of 768 (632 UK, 71 Australian, 59 NZ, 4 Canadian, an Indian and an unknown) is **Lieutenant Henry Webber** who, aged 67, is believed to be the oldest soldier killed in action during the war. Born on 3 June 1849, he graduated from Oxford and then entered the Stock Exchange. He was a well-known figure in his home town of Horley, having served both as a Justice of the Peace and Chairman of the District Council. After the war broke out, Webber put much effort into helping the recruiting drive and pestered the War Office to allow him to join up, despite his age. In May 1916 he was appointed a Temporary Lieutenant in the 7th Bn, the S Lancs Regt and joined the regiment in France. Webber, who had been a member of the Surrey Stag Hunt, and therefore a good horseman, became the First Line Transport Officer to the Battalion, and it was after taking rations to the battalion in Mametz Wood on 21 July, that he was killed by a shell while talking to his CO. Three of his sons served in the army as officers and all survived. This exceptional old gentleman was honoured by being mentioned in Despatches and his family received messages of condolence from the king. Also buried here is **Pte J. Miller**. Pte Miller, who, despite being shot clean through the stomach from behind, delivered an important message, falling dead at the feet of the officer to whom he delivered it. He won a posthumous **VC** and the citation is in the cemetery report. Also buried next to each other **are father and son Sgt George and Cpl Robert Frederick Lee**, of 156th Bde RFA, killed on 5 September 1916. This area, too, was taken by the Germans in March 1918 but was retaken by 12th Division on 24 August.

Headstone of Lt Henry Webber, 67, Dartmoor CWGG Cemetery

> *Return to the D938, turn right and continue in the direction of Fricourt.*

The British attack on 1 July was made in the direction you are travelling, by a brigade of the 17th (Northern) Division, led by the 7th Battalion Green Howards. Due to a misunderstanding, they attacked 15 minutes or more after the zero hour of 0730, and suffered badly from German machine gun fire.

> *On entering the village, turn left at the crossroads onto the D147 direction Pozières. Stop 200m later on the left.*

• Fricourt Brit CWGC Cemetery (Bray Road)/Green Howards Memorial/3.5 miles/10 minutes/Map J38/39/GPS: 49.99524 2.7115

The 1 July British front line crossed the D938 road at about where you turned left, and Fricourt village was just inside the German lines so the cemetery is about halfway between the two. The village had been fortified by the Germans, using the cellars in the houses to provide shelters up to 45ft deep. 'One at Fricourt had nine rooms and five bolt-holes', wrote John Buchan, 'it had iron doors, gas curtains, linoleum on the floors, wallpaper and pictures on the walls, and boasted a good bath-room, electric light and electric bells. The staff which occupied it must have lived in luxury'. But according to John Masefield, 'although the ... stairs with wired treads, the bolting holes, the air and escape shafts, the living rooms with electric light, the panelled walls, covered with cretonnes of the smartest Berlin patterns, the neat bunks and the signs of female visitors, were written of in the press, ... it was not better fitted than other places on the line.' While the Christmas Truce around Plugstreet and Frelinghien south of Ypres is well known, the fact that a truce happened here at Fricourt is not. Just before midday on the 25th December 1914 German soldiers came unarmed towards the French XI Corps trenches and met with a positive response. However local Commanders ordered their soldiers back to the trenches and three German soldiers who had reached that far were taken prisoner. Regimental accounts from both sides suggest that it was the others that started the attempt at the truce. Full hostilities were resumed that evening.

The Cemetery was used by the 7th Yorkshires (Green Howards) between 5 and 11 July and, at the end of an avenue of twenty headstones of men who died on 1 July, a **memorial Celtic cross** to the regiment has been placed in the far right-hand corner of the cemetery which names all those of the Regiment who fell in the area on 1 July 1916. Two-thirds of the 130 or so burials belong to the 7th Green Howards, the Alexandra Princess of Wales'

Memorial to Green Howards, Fricourt Brit CWGC Cemetery

CHEMIN DE CROIX
OFFERT EN SOUVENIR
DU MAJOR RAPER

Station of the Cross
dedicated to Maj Raper,
Fricourt Church

Own Yorkshire Regiment, and fifty-nine of them are believed to be in a mass grave in the centre of the cemetery, originally a shell-hole. One grave of note is that of **Major R. G. Raper** of the 8th S Staffs, who was killed on 2 July 1916. He was originally buried in a private grave, marked by his family after the war. The village of Fricourt, perhaps because his body was singled out in this way, made a cult of Roper, naming after him the road that leads from the attractive village *Poilu* war memorial to the village church. *Continue to the Poilu. Take the fork to the right along rue du Major Raper to the church and park.*
If the church is locked, ask at the café opposite. This is closed on Wednesdays, in which case enquire at houses around the square for the keyholder.

• *Fricourt Church Memorials/3.8 miles/10 minutes/ Map J41/GPS: 49.99911 2.71657*

The Raper family gave funds to the church, which was rebuilt during 1928-31, and the Stations of the Cross are dedicated to **Major Raper**. There is also a Plaque to the 494 officers, 8,421 WO's and soldiers of the 17th (Northern) Division who gave their lives in France and Belgium during the 1914-18 war, and a Plaque to **Sgt Pierre Louis Viget** of the French 156th Régiment d'Infanterie who died in Fricourt on 3 October 1914, decorated with the *Médaille Militaire, Croix de Guerre* and Gold Star.

Return to the Poilu. Turn right on the D147 towards Contalmaison. As you drive you are in German-held territory with their front line about 300 yards to your left. Some half a mile on the left is a sign to Fricourt New Military Cemetery. Turn up the track and drive, with extreme caution, as far as you can, according to weather conditions. Walk the final few metres.

• *Fricourt New Military Cemetery/4.5 miles/15 minutes/Map J40/GPS: 50.00124 2.70812*

This Cemetery was made in No Man's Land between the British and German front lines of 1 July by the 10th Bn, the W Yorkshire Regiment (which had one of the highest casualty rates of 1 July). They attacked at 0730 and by 0900 only one officer and 20 men remained uninjured.

Headstone of Lt A.V. Ratcliffe, poet, with private memoral, Fricourt New Mil Cem

Of the 210 burials, 159 are of the Regiment, including the 29 year old poet, **Lt Alfred Victor Ratcliffe** (who had been training to be a barrister) and **16 year old Pte Albert Barker**. There is 1 New Zealand grave.

[N.B.] From the Cemetery the cratered site of **The Tambour** (see Fricourt CWGC Brit Bray Road Cem below) may be seen to the left (GPS: 49.9982 2.7043), surrounded by bushes (it is actually on private ground). Behind it on the skyline is the Bois Français and there Lt Ratcliffe was killed. There were machine-gun positions and redoubts on this crest behind the village. Mine warfare had been initiated in the area by the French in 1915 and this was taken over by 178th Tunnelling Company who had shafts up to 115ft deep leading to the crest .Three mines were placed in the Tambour (the French word for 'Drum) area for the 1 July offensive and one failed to explode. The plan was to pinch the Fricourt salient out of the line by taking la Boisselle on its left and Mametz to its right. The village was carried after 36 hours of fighting and 1,500 German prisoners were taken. The area was lost to the Germans in March 1918 and re-taken on 26 August.

Return to the D147. Turn left and continue to the cemetery on the right and park in the designated area on the left.

• *Fricourt German Cemetery/4.7 miles/10 minutes/Map J34/GPS: 50.00434 2.71432*

Outside is a detailed Information Board. There are 5,056 marked burials, plus 11,970 in mass graves at the rear of the cemetery. The black metal crosses mark up to four burials, the names being inscribed on both sides of the arms of the crosses. The headstones mark Jewish graves. The remains of **Baron Manfred von Richthofen** were removed to this cemetery from his original burial place at Bertangles (qv). In 1925 they were moved again to the family home at Schweidnitz in eastern Germany by his brother Bolko. He was buried here in Section 4, grave 1177, now occupied by **Sebastian Paustian**, in the ninth grave in the second row in the right hand corner. The iron gate to the cemetery carries the five crosses emblem of the VDK which is a version of the original sketch for

Entrance to German Cem, Fricourt

a symbol which was made in 1926, although the organisation itself was founded in 1919 as a charity. See page 332.

The discrepancy of one between the total number of burials given above and the figures given at the entrance to the cemetery may well be because of the removal of von Richthofen's remains.

Turn around and take the first left towards Mametz and turn left at the T junction on the D64 signed to Mametz.

Between Fricourt and Mametz the British line for 1 July ran roughly parallel to the road you are taking and some 750m away to the right. The assault troops were a mixture of New Army and regulars of 7th Division and within the first hour they had taken the German front line trenches, which ran some 250m to your right, watched by **Siegfried Sassoon**, a 2nd Lt in the RWF. The village of Mametz held out until mid-afternoon and then fell.

Continue to the church on the left.

• *38th (Welsh) Division Memorial, Mametz Church/5.3 miles/10 minutes/ Map 34a/ GPS: 49.99705 2.73512*

If the church is locked, telephone the custodian on Tel: 03 22 15 47 75, or enquire at nearby houses.

The handsome marble Memorial, emblazoned with a magnificent red dragon, is on the left-hand wall just before the altar. The inscription is in Welsh, French and English. It reads, 'Dedicated to the Glory of God this tablet in memory of the 38th (Welsh) Division of the British Army is committed to the pious care of the sons of France in whose land they repose in everlasting alliance.' The villagers of Mametz feel very involved with their Welsh Allies and there are always fresh flowers below the memorial. The Welsh reciprocate the feeling. Mametz was 'adopted' by Llandudno after the war.

Continue to the crossroads in the village.

In the green opposite is a **CGS/H Signboard** about the Welsh memorial.

Turn left on the C4 following signs to the Mémorial Gallois/38th (Welsh) Division Memorial on the C4, direction Contalmaison. After half a mile turn right, following green CWGC signs to the Welsh Memorial. Continue to the fork and go right to Mémorial Gallois.

You are now passing the area of the **Queen's Nullah**. Here the author of Up to *Mametz*, **Lt Llewelyn Wyn Griffith**, who served with the 15th RWF, but was attached to the staff during the attack on Mametz Wood, saw walking wounded streaming to the ADS sited in a

38th (Welsh) Div Memorial, Mametz Church

dugout in the bank in the Nullah after the Division's first attack on the wood on 5 July. Here too **Major General E. C. Ingouville-Williams**, commanding 34th Div, was killed by a shell on 22 July after reconnoitring the area and while walking back to his car at Montauban. He is buried in Warloy-Baillon Communal Cemetery (see page 64).

Fork left, following signs to Mémorial Gallois.

Note soon the sharpness of the cliff to your right. To the left is Death Valley.

Continue and park at the foot of the magnificent Welsh Dragon. Walk up the steps.

Welsh Dragon Memorial, Mametz, encircled by the Samarobriva Pipes & Drums Band

- **38th (Welsh) Division Red Dragon Memorial/7.9 miles/15 minutes/Map K39/GPS: 50.01363 2.75593**

This most emotional of all the Western Front Memorials was designed by sculptor-in-iron, David Petersen. It was erected mostly through the tireless fund-raising and organisational efforts of the Cardiff Western Front Association. The exuberant, winged red dragon spits fire and grasps the enemy's barbed wire in its powerful claws. The Welsh inscription means, 'Let us respect their endeavours. Let our memories live on.' It was unveiled at a grand ceremony on 11 July 1987 and, although not an official National Memorial, is the focus of Welsh remembrance on the Somme. Beside it is a bronze tablet with the ORBAT of the 38th Division, a sketch map and summary of the two attacks on the Wood in July 1916. In 1994 the site was cleared through the initiative of Major Tony Swift of UK Movements and Liaison Staff who found clear traces of the World War I light railway system between the Memorial and the Hammerhead (part of Mametz Wood and so-called because of its shape). The line ran alongside the Nullah (the name was probably picked up by soldiers while serving in India – in Hindi it means a ravine or gully) and onward past Trônes Wood and Guillemont to Combles.

In 2013 the Welsh Government pledged £7,000 to add to the money being raised by the S Wales branch of the WFA for the restoration of the area. The Dragon has now been beautifully restored by the sculptor and the surrounding area improved by the CWGC. There is another dragon on the Pilkem Ridge north of Ypres. It was unveiled in August 2014 as a Welsh National Memorial.

This is a perfect site from which to contemplate the sacrifice of the Welsh, overlooking as it does the notorious Hammerhead feature of the wood. One can almost hear the strains of *Jesu lover of my soul* ... to *Aberystwyth* sung by the 'genuine Taffies' on the right of the line, wafting over as they waited to go in to the attack, as did the poet **David Jones** who (like **Wyn Griffith**) served here with the London Battalion of the RWF. To a first approximation, the dragon faces the wood, as did the attacking Welsh. On the morning of 7 July 1916, one week after the first day of the Battle of the Somme, two British divisions began a pincer attack on Mametz Wood, a German stronghold held by the Prussian Guard. The two divisions were the 17th (Northern), attacking from the west, and the 115th Brigade of the 38th (Welsh), commanded by Brigadier-General H. J. Evans, attacking from the east. The attack, in bald military terms, was a failure. German machine guns, sited in Acid Drop Copse (which the 17th Division attacked), Flat Iron and Sabot Copses and in the Hammerhead (attacked by the 16th Welsh Cardiff City Battalion and the Gwent Battalions of the SWB) apparently unaffected by the preparatory artillery bombardment, inflicted heavy casualties upon the attackers approaching across the open ground. Battlefield communications broke down and a covering smokescreen failed to appear. At the end of the day neither division had even reached the wood, let alone captured it. The divisional commander, **Maj-Gen Ivor Philipps**, a peace-time MP and Lloyd George appointee, who was 'ignorant, lacked experience and failed to inspire confidence' (Maj Drake-Brockman, quoted by **Colin Hughes** in his definitive account of the action *Mametz*) was finally relieved of his inappropriate position.

Three days later, at 0415 hours on 10 July, the two divisions were ordered in again. The main thrust this time was towards the southern face of the wood by the Welsh – a frontal assault. The leading battalions were the 13th Welsh (2nd Rhonddas), the 14th Welsh (Swansea Battalion) and the 16th RWF (Caernarvon and Anglesey Battalion), reinforced by the 15th. Despite the hail of German small arms fire they made it to the wood. The struggle became increasingly bitter in the thick undergrowth beneath the splintered trunks. More and more battalions of the small men from South Wales were committed to the struggle until almost the whole division was in among the trees and the brambles. According to David Jones 'General Picton was of the opinion that the ideal infantryman was a south Welshman, five feet four inches in height'. Siegfried Sassoon, however, handing over Quadrangle Trench to them, had called them a 'jostling company of exclamatory Welshmen ... panicky rabble ... mostly undersized men' and felt that 'As I watched them arriving at the first stage of their battle experience I had a sense of their victimisation.' Ideal soldiers or victims, they fought with determination. The bloody contest, often bitter hand-to-hand fighting, continued for two days until, on the night of 11 July, the Germans withdrew, driven out from the north of the wood. At one stage 'friendly' artillery rained down on the desperate Welshmen. Wyn Griffith was commanded by Brig-Gen Evans to send messengers to the Queen's Nullah to stop this 'sheer stupidity'. One of the runners he despatched was his young brother, Watcyn. Watcyn got through with his message but was hit by a shell as he tried to return. 'I had sent him to his death, bearing a message from my own hand in an endeavour to save other men's brothers', wrote the distraught Wyn Griffith. Pte W. Griffith is commemorated on the Thiépval Memorial (qv).

The cost to the 38th (Welsh) Division, proudly raised by Lloyd George and inadequately officered by his cronies and protégés, was high – some 4,000 men were killed or wounded. Although they did capture the wood they came under severe criticism for having taken five days to do so, and in 1919 Lt Col J. H. Boraston, co-author of *Sir Douglas Haig's Command*, effectively accused them of a lack of determination which prevented a significant Fourth Army advance on the Somme. It was a stigma not expiated until their successful attack on the Pilckem Ridge of 31 July 1917. This Haig called 'the highest level of soldierly achievement' in the Preface to the Division's History.

The epic struggle is described in what is most probably the war's most original work of literature, David Jones's *In Parenthesis*. Like **Philip Johnstone** in the poem *High Wood* (qv), Jones anticipates future battlefield tours. Wounded and encumbered by his rifle he decides to 'leave it for a Cook's tour to the Devastated Areas and crawl as far as you can and wait for the bearers'. Officer **Robert Graves** and Private soldier **Frank Richards**, both serving with the 2nd Bn the RWF, describe the horror of mopping up in the wood on 15 July, a few days after the attack. 'Not a single tree in the wood remained unbroken', wrote Graves in *Goodbye to All That* as he charged through 'the wreckage of green branches', past 'bloated and stinking' corpses. Richards recalled in *Old Soldiers Never Die*, 'We rested in shell holes, the ground all around us being thick with dead of the troops who had been attacking Mametz Wood.'

(At this point you have the option to walk, or if it is exceptionally dry, drive to Flat Iron Copse CWGC Cemetery some 800m further along the track. Otherwise it will be covered later in the Itinerary.) The wood to the right beyond the Dragon was named Caterpillar Wood because of its shape.

Return to the C4 and turn right.

To your right is Death Valley, followed shortly by the small Quadrangle Wood. To your left is Bottom Wood. Continue towards the village of Contalmaison, park by the civilian cemetery on the right and walk through it to the rear wall.

• *Memorial to 12th Manchesters/10 miles/10 minutes/Map K21/ GPS: 50.01894 2.73258*

This impressive Memorial is to the 1,039 Officers, NCOs and men of the 12th Bn, the Manchester Regt who fell in World War I. It was erected by relatives and the Old Comrades Association. Beyond the cemetery is Acid Drop Copse (see the account of the attack on Mametz Wood above). From the front of the Cemetery Peake Wood CWGC Cemetery (see page 151) may be seen in the valley below.

There is also a WFA Memorial here.

Memorials to 12th Manchester Regt, Contalmaison

Continue to the memorial on the bank to the right.

• *Memorial to 2nd Lieutenant Donald Simpson Bell, VC, Bell's Redoubt/10.2 miles/5 minutes/Map K20a/GPS: 50.01999 2.73091*

On 9 July 2000 this handsome Memorial was unveiled to **Donald Bell**, the first professional footballer to enlist in November 1914, by members of his family and the present Green Howards Regiment. Bell worked his way through the ranks and was commissioned into the 9th Battalion Princess of Wales's Own Yorkshire Regiment (now the Green Howards). On 5 July the 8th and 9th Battalions were ordered to take a

1,500m long position known as Horse Shoe Trench between la Boisselle and Mametz Wood. The attack started at 1800 hours and the trench, with 146 prisoners and two machine guns, was captured. Then a German machine gun began to enfilade the 9th Battalion. Bell, supported by a Corporal and a Private, rushed the gun position. He shot the gunner and blew up the remainder with Mills bombs. He then bombed the nearby trench, killing over 50 of the enemy. Bell died five days later performing a similar act of gallantry. He is buried in **Gordon Dump CWGC Cemetery** and there is a Memorial to him in St Paul's Church, Harrogate. In 2010 his VC was sold for £210.000.

On September 1916 Trench Maps the area is marked as 'Bell's Redoubt'.

Continue to the junction with the D147.

Memorial to 2nd Lt Bell, VC, Contalmaison

Memorial to Capt Frances Dodgson, Contalmaison

Extra Visit to Private Memorial to Capt Dodgson (Map J27) Round-trip 1.0 miles. Approximate time 15 minutes/GPS: 50.02177 2.72435

Turn left on the D147, drive downhill and after some 500m park (ahead is Peake Wood CWGC Cemetery, Map J26) and walk up the small farm track to the right.

The small stone Memorial is some 500 paces up and to the right of the track. In 1919 Dodgson's mother visited the area where he was known to have been killed and found the original cross marking the burial site up-ended. She organised the erection of this stone Memorial from a local stonemason, which bore the inscription, "In Memoriam, Francis Dodgson, Captain, 8th Yorks Regt who fell here 10-7-16." He is buried in Serre Road No 2 Cemetery. His brother Captain Guy Dodgson was badly wounded in November 1918 and died three days after the Armistice. From this point the Pozières Memorial may be seen straight ahead on the horizon and to the right is Contalmaison Church tower.

Turn round and return to the junction. Pick up the main itinerary.
Continue right on the D147 to the Church. Beside it is

• Memorial to McCrae's Battalion/10.4 miles/5 minutes/Map K20b/GPS: 50.02245 2.72988

Dedicated on 7 November 2004 this 10ft high cairn of Elgin stone commemorates the remarkable **Battalion of Lt Col Sir George McCrae**, the 16th Royal Scots, who on 1 July 1916 briefly captured the German strongpoint known as Scots Redoubt in the ruins of Contalmaison. Their story is told on superb bronze plaques on the cairn showing the 34th Division's chequerboard insignia, a cartoon that was the regimental Christmas card for 1916, the figure of St George, details of the Heart of Midlothian Football Club's sacrifice, a commemoration of the 15th Royal Scots and an account of the unveiling and local co-operation. Jack Alexander, who inspired the erection of the cairn, describes the action here as 'the deepest penetration of the enemy line anywhere on the front that morning' and after the war great plans for memorial cairns and pilgrimages between Edinburgh and Contalmaison were planned but came to naught. The full story of Sir George and his brave battalion and Jack Alexander's efforts to resurrect 1920 memorial plans was told in the Spring 2004 edition of *The New Chequers* , the Journal of 'The Friends of Lochnagar'.

Cairn to McCrae's Bn, Contalmaison

There is also a bronze Plaque and an Orientation Board of the battle behind the memorial and opposite is a pleasant small grassed rest area with bench and table plus a small information office.

Turn left at the junction and stop at the CWGC sign to the right.

• Contalmaison Château CWGC Cemetery/10.5 miles/10 minutes/Map K20/GPS: 50.02372 2.72926

This is one of the most attractive cemeteries on the Somme. Surrounded by a mellow brick-topped flint wall and framed by trees it is approached by a well-tended grass path. It contains the grave of **Pte William Short** of the 8th Battalion, the Yorkshire Regiment, who died on 6 August 1916 in Munster Alley trench where he continued to throw grenades at the enemy despite being mortally wounded. For this gallant action he was awarded a posthumous V**ictoria Cross**.

Return to the junction and turn left on the D20 following signs to Bazentin and Longueval.

After some 500m you will be driving along the edge of Mametz Wood. The wood was owned by the late and much-loved Comte de Thézy who gave a plot of land for the burial of Harry Fellows. It is now owned by his nephew.

Continue to the far, north-east corner of the wood and, if not muddy, turn right down the small track to a metal gate and stop. Park and walk 150m into the wood. The grave is on the right. Be careful not to disturb the game birds that are raised in the wood.

• Grave of Harry Fellows/11.3 miles/10 minutes/Map K22/GPS: 50.02540 2.75127

The headstone is like a CWGC headstone, but with a curved top, and is in a small glade. It bears the inscription 'This tree is dedicated to the memory of 13587 L/Cpl H Fellows, 12th Battalion, Northumberland Fusiliers, 1914-1918, whose ashes are buried in this wood. Died 1st September 1987 Aged 91', followed by some lines from one of his own poems:

> Where once there was war,
> Now peace reigns supreme,
> And the birds sing again in Mametz.

Continue to the green CWGC sign pointing right to Flat Iron Copse Cemetery. Drive carefully down the track, passing Sabot Copse on the left, and park by the entrance gate.

Grave of Harry Fellows, who died 1 September 1987, Mametz Wood

• Flat Iron Copse CWGC Cemetery/12.4 miles/15 minutes/Map K23/GPS: 50.01979 2.75844

Sir Herbert Baker designed this cemetery which contains some notable burials. It had been begun by the 3rd and 7th Divisions on 14 July 1916 as they cleared Mametz Wood (which is immediately behind the rear wall of the cemetery) after its capture by the 38th. There are over 1,500 burials, including three pairs of brothers. Two of the pairs are Welshmen, killed in the July attack on Mametz Wood – **Lts Arthur and Leonard Tregaskis** and **L/Cpl H and Cpl T. Hardwidge**. The Tregaskis brothers were in the 16th (Cardiff City) Welsh and were killed on 7 July, the Hardwidges were in the 15th (Carmarthenshire) Welsh Regiment and were killed on 11 July. Both sets of brothers died when one attempted to help his wounded brother.

Privates Ernest and Herbert Philby served with the Middlesex Regiment and were both killed on 21 August 1916. The **Victoria Cross** winner buried here, **Sgt Edward Dwyer** of the 1st East Surreys, is particularly interesting. He won his award 'for conspicuous bravery and devotion to duty at Hill 60 [in the Ypres Salient] on 20 April 1915' and

was used back in Britain to help the recruiting effort by giving talks about his experiences. In December 1918 a memorial medallion, paid for by Fulham schoolchildren, was unveiled in Fulham Library by Lt Gen Sir Francis Lloyd. Dwyer was born in Fulham. Dwyer's wife, 'Billie', continued to serve in France as a nurse after his death. In the 1980s Pavilion Records of Sussex produced a remarkable pair of records (now in cassette and CD forms) (GEMM 3033/4) which feature original recordings from the 1914-18 period. Track 2, side 2 of the first record is a monologue by Sgt Dwyer, most probably the only contemporary recording of a

Headstone of Cpl Edward Dwyer, VC, Flat Iron Copse CWGC Cem

First World War VC in existence. To the right as one enters is a Special Memorial to the nine graves behind it (the majority of them of the Rifle Brigade), men all killed in 1916 and originally buried in Mametz Wood Cemetery, whose graves were destroyed in later battles.

Return to the D20. Turn right. Continue some 600m to the crossroads with the D73 in Bazentin le Petit.

Extra Visit to Private Memorials: 'Nine Brave Men', (Map K6), GPS: 50.034547 2.761127 & Capt Wallace (Map K7)
Round trip: 1.7 miles. Approx time: 15 minutes.

Turn left on the D73, passing a sign to Bazentin le Petit Communal Cemetery (Map K8) on the right and, after the church, a sign to Bazentin le Petit Military CWGC Cemetery (Map K5) to the left.

During the July Somme battles **Captain N H Radford** of the Royal Welsh Fusiliers was sent to a windmill just east of the Communal Cemetery here, to act as Forward Liaison Officer. His job was to relay messages both forward and to the rear. The windmill was a regular German artillery target because it was clearly marked on contemporary trench maps, **(GPS: 50.03193 2.77129)** so it was in a bad state. Good battlefield communications are essential at all levels of command to send instructions and to receive orders. Captain Radford had little luck. He recalled: –

> 'At the beginning of the morning attack, the enemy barrage cut the wires. The barrage smoke made lamp signalling impossible even if adequate preparation had been made for it. The wireless set provided was for transmission only, so it was not known if messages were being received. The supply of runners was soon exhausted and was not replaced. At noon I went to Brigade to report the futility of it all'.

Continue.

As the road bends sharply to the left there is a Memorial in the corner, refurbished in 1989 by 82nd Junior Leaders Regt RE. It is to **nine men of 82nd Field Coy RE** who were killed on 29 July 1916. The names of the men are listed on the front of the Memorial and on the rear is a somewhat faded plaque which tells their story, placed by Sgt S.R. Brooks who was part of the renovation party which also included Capt J. Dargavel, Cpl Moffat and Sgt J. Moores. The company had been formed by Captain R.F.A. Butterworth in Bulford in 1914 and went with him to France, suffering severely in the July 1916 battles. On 29 July Sections 3 and 4 went on a wiring party to Bazentin where they came under murderous H.E. and machine-gun fire. Knowing the work was vital, Lieutenant Howlett (with No 4 Section) and CSM Deyermond (with No 3

Memorial to 'Nine Brave men' of 82nd Fd Coy RE, Bazentin

Section) carried on, though 6 men were killed and 19 wounded out of a total of 40 men. Three men had been killed in similar circumstances the previous night and their commanding officer (to be promoted to Lt Colonel in October) christened them the 'Nine Brave Men'. 'One lived in such close touch with the lads in those days that one knew every man personally, and very often intimately', wrote this caring officer. 'Choate was a first-rate carpenter and a most lovable man, Ellison just a boy from a North Country workshop, Vernon a fitter and a fine stalwart fellow'. He personally wrote to each of the next of kin and promised that one day he would go back and raise 'a little stone to their memory'. Butterworth was then moved ('with great regret') to take up his new job as CRE of 16th Division in the Messines sector. There he had a block of granite engraved and waited for an opportunity to take it to the Somme. This he did in November 1917 when, with his Adjutant, Capt Stradling, and two Sappers, (as he later wrote in the Sapper Magazine of October 1923 when he was serving in Hong Kong) they 'constructed our small tribute of affection and respect to the memory of our nine brave comrades', using bricks collected from the debris lying around.

The nine are listed on the Memorial but looking them up on the CWGC Debt of Honour website it seems that two of them are mis-spelt. Tregidgo (listed as Tredigo) is commemorated on the Thiepval Memorial, as are Choat, Joiner, Havilland, Blakeley, Robotham and Vernon. Ellisson (listed as Ellison) is buried in Caterpillar Valley and Higgins in Bécourt CWGC Cemeteries.

The story of 82 Squadron RE, from 1914-2001, has been put on a CD by Captain Simon Mann, 2i/c of the Squadron when it was disbanded in December 2001. All its property and history have been moved from Arborfield to Chatham and the Squadron will be reformed as a Bomb Disposal Unit.

Take the track to the right.
At the end of it, up the bank to the right is the cairn, (refurbished on 23 October 1994, with help from the WFA) surmounted by a **Calvary, to Capt Houston Stewart Hamilton Wallace** of the 10th Worcester Regiment who was killed on 22 July 1916. After the war Wallace's aunt, on his mother's side, began a search for his body in order to place

Memorial to Capt Wallace and detail (left), Bazentin

a memorial to him (his parents had already died) and having located this spot renovated an existing Calvary in his memory. Capt Wallace is commemorated on the Thiépval Memorial.

Behind it, on the skyline, is High Wood, which could be reached by walking along the grassy track ahead.

Return to the crossroads and rejoin the main itinerary.

Thistle Dump CWGC Cemetery

*Continue on the D20 signed Longueval, to a green CWGC sign to **Thistle Dump Cemetery**, Map K10, on the left, with High Wood behind it.*

• *Site of the 14 July 1916 Cavalry Charge/13.9 miles/Map K10/GPS: 50.02944 2.78519*

The small track to the cemetery continues past it, runs effectively due north and emerges on the D107 Longueval to Martinpuich road at the south-east corner of High Wood. The valley that it crosses is Caterpillar Valley. The attack that began at 0325 on the morning of 14 July (broadly from the direction of Mametz) opened with a bombardment that General Haig, back at his HQ at Val Vion (qv), heard and commented was 'loud', and achieved total surprise. Some three miles of the German second line, from Bazentin le Grand to Longueval, were taken by the middle of the day. 7th Division, opposite High Wood, discovered to their surprise that the wood was empty and General Watts, the GOC, urged XV Corps HQ to allow him to press the attack on the wood. Corps insisted that the attack should wait until cavalry arrived. Only a small force – the Deccan Horse and one squadron of the 7th Dragoon Guards – was available and that was moving up slowly from south of Albert. Not until after 1900 hours was the attack eventually launched, by which time the Germans had re-entered the wood. Thus, when the cavalry charged, pennants flying and lances glittering in the evening sun, few survived to reach the wood. (Their route was up the slope to the left of the track.) The wood was not taken. A second, frontal, infantry assault on High Wood was planned by 100th Brigade for early on 15 July and the assault battalions – the 1st Queens, the 9th HLI (Glasgow Highlanders) and the 16th KRRC – moved up Death Valley, past Flat Iron Copse and deployed into Caterpillar Valley ready for the assault. The attack began in a heavy mist. German machine guns took a heavy toll as the troops struggled up the slope towards the wood and at 1000 hours the Brigade reserve, the 2nd Worcesters, was quickly committed, their line of advance being along and then to the left of the track. Fighting in the wood became hand-to-hand and after 24 hours only the south-west corner of the wood was in British hands and the four battalions of the Brigade had over 1,300 casualties. It is possible to walk the path of the charge and the Worcesters' attack.

Continue to the large cemetery on the right. Park.

• Caterpillar Valley CWGC Cemetery & New Zealand Memorial to the Missing/14.4 miles/15 minutes/Map K24/25/OP/GPS: 50.02626 2.79195

The area was captured by the 12th Royal Scots and the 9th Scottish Rifles on 14 July. Lost again in the Kaiser's March Offensive of 1918, it was recovered on 28 August 1918

by the 38th (Welsh) Division. The vast Cemetery, second only to Serre Road No 2 (which, technically speaking, is not in the Département of the Somme), contains 5,197 UK burials, 214 New Zealand, 98 Australian, 19 South African, 6 Canadian and 2 Newfoundland, with 38 special memorials. The majority are unknown.

On the left-hand wall is the **New Zealand Memorial to the Missing**, following their decision to list their missing in cemeteries near where they fell. Others are in Buttes New, Polygon Wood; Cité Bonjean, Armentières; Grevillers; Marfaux; Messines Ridge and Tyne Cot. They are not listed on the Menin Gate. 1,205 are listed here.

On 6 November 2004 in an impressive ceremony at the New Zealand Memorial at Longueval, attended by Maori, New Zealand and French Service personnel and dignitaries, the remains of an **Unknown Soldier** were removed from the Cemetery and handed over by the CWGC to the New Zealand authorities. His remains were then flown by Boeing 757 to Wellington where they arrived at the Parliament on 10 November. There they were presented with the Unknown Warrior's

Headstone of former grave of New Zealand Unknown Soldier, Caterpillar Valley CWGC Cemetery

medals, which included the 1914-1918 NZ Star, the British War Medal, the Victory Medal and the RNRSA Badge in Gold, instituted in 1920, previously only awarded to Monarchs, Governors-General, Prime Ministers and those who have dedicated their lives to the

well-being of Veterans. He was the 60th and only posthumous recipient.

The coffin was then interred in a fine new custom-built Tomb of stone and bronze at the National War Memorial, designed by Kingsley Baird. The ceremonial programme surrounding this event was probably the largest commemorative programme ever undertaken in New Zealand. A new headstone was placed on the grave in Caterpillar Valley. The **Unknown Warrior**, one of 9,000 New Zealand soldiers of overseas wars who have no known grave, was chosen from this cemetery as this was the area

New Zealand Memorial, Caterpillar Valley CWGC Cemetery

where the greatest number of New Zealand regiments and battalions are known to have fought. The act represents a renewed desire to honour the WW1 dead in New Zealand. In September 2000, 5 New Zealanders executed for mutiny or desertion were pardoned under a new Act, 'Pardon for Soldiers of the Great War'.

The Cemetery stands on the Longueval Ridge and is an excellent vantage point. Stand with your back to the entrance. Straight ahead at 12 o'clock is the New Zealand Memorial on the skyline. At 1 o'clock is a calvary. At 2 o'clock is the church of Longueval and behind it Delville Wood. At 3 o'clock at the D107 road junction is the Bristol's Own Cross. Ahead, between the road and the New Zealand Memorial, is Caterpillar Valley. At 11 o'clock is High Wood, at the left hand edge of which is London CWGC Cemetery. At 10 o'clock in the Valley is Thistle Dump CWGC Cemetery. Just before 10 o'clock is the wireless mast at Pozières and at 9 o'clock the Bazentin Woods. From the shelter at the rear of the cemetery, Montauban Church is straight ahead at 12 o'clock and at 1 o'clock on the skyline is the memorial cross to French soldier Capt H. T. de Monclin on the D64. At 10 o'clock is Trônes Wood, at 11 o'clock is Bernafay Wood and at 3 o'clock Mametz Wood.

Continue on the D20 to the junction with the D107 to the left and park.

• *Bristol's Own Cross/14.6 miles/5 minutes/Map K29/GPS: 50.02514 2.79716*

This Memorial was raised by British and French volunteers under the leadership of Dean Marks.

Inspired by an old photograph showing Bristol veterans standing beside a cross on the Somme, Dean investigated and found that the cross in the picture had disappeared during World War II. He determined to replace it and helped by friends, members of the

Bristol's Own Cross, High Wood behind

Detail of Plaque

WFA, Bristol Civil Authorities and others he set to work. In the seventieth anniversary year of the Battle of the Somme, Dean, his two-year-old daughter Amy, his father Roy, the Mayor of Longueval and a party of helpers put up the new cross. It stands where the 12th Battalion Gloucestershire Regiment set off to battle and commemorates those who fell around Longueval and Guillemont between July and September 1916.

Continue to the crossroads with the D197. Turn sharp right, signed Montauban, and continue to a cemetery on the left after some 500m.

• Longueval Road CWGC Cemetery/15.4 miles/5 minutes/Map K28/GPS: 50.01916 2.79877

Cleared by the 5th Division in July 1916, the start point for the 8th Black Watch's assault of the 14th on Longueval, used as a Dressing Station from September 1916, lost in the Kaiser's spring 1918 offensive, this area was finally retaken by the 38th (Welsh) Division on 28 August 1918. The Cemetery contains 182 UK, 22 Australian, 7 Canadian, 7 New Zealand, a Newfoundland and a German burial, with three special memorials. To the right of the road ahead is the distinctive shape of Montauban church spire, ahead is Bernafay Wood and to the left Trônes Wood.

Continue to the next cemetery on the right.

• Bernafay Wood CWGC Cemetery/16.1 miles/5 minutes/Map K27/GPS: 50.01194 2.79338

The area was taken by the 9th (Scottish) Division on 3-4 July 1916 with little loss of life. A dressing station was then set up here. This same division was driven from the wood in the Kaiser's Offensive on 25 March 1918. They recaptured it briefly but it was the 18th Division who finally regained it on 27 August 1918. It contains 793 UK burials, 122 Australian, 4 South African, 2 New Zealand, an Indian and 32 special memorials.

Continue. At the crossroads with the D64 turn right, signed Montauban. At the first crossroads in the village, stop.

• Liverpool & Manchester Pals Memorial/17.1 miles/5 minutes/Map K40/GPS: 50.00634 2.78316

Graham Maddocks, author of *Liverpool Pals*, led a committee that raised funds for this memorial, designed by Derek Sheard and inaugurated on 1 July 1994 at an Anglo-French ceremony attended by bands from the RAF and 43rd RI from Lille. The Pals were part of 30th Division that took the village on 1 July 1916.

Memorial to Liverpool & Manchester Pals, Montauban

Continue into the village, past the church with its distinctive spire on the right, to the Mairie.

On the wall is a **Plaque commemorating the village's twinning with Maidstone in 2014 (GPS: 50.00620 2.77846).**

Continue on the D64 to a memorial cross on the right.

Montauban-Maidstone Twinning Plaque.

• *Private Memorial to Capitaine de Monclin/17.5 miles/10 minutes/Map K38/OP/GPS: 50.00447 2.77156*

This Private Memorial (the cross which was visible from the back of Caterpillar Valley Cemetery) is to **Capitaine Henri Thiéron de Monclin** and his soldiers of the 5th Coy of the French 69th Inf Regt, who were killed on 28 September 1914.

Monclin was a professional soldier who enlisted in 1902 and served with the Zouaves in North Africa. Though wounded he maintained control of his men during a difficult withdrawal but was later killed. He was awarded the Croix de Guerre.

This spot makes an excellent observation point.

This entire ridge, of the D64 from before Montauban to the far edge of Mametz village, was taken on 1 July 1916, the biggest advance of the day. Take the Pozières wireless mast, visible straight ahead, as 12 o'clock. The Golden Madonna at Albert is at 10 o'clock, the Thiépval Memorial is at 11 o'clock, High Wood is at 1 o'clock, Caterpillar Valley Cemetery is at 2 o'clock to the left of Longueval Church and immediately to the left is the New Zealand Memorial, apparently level with it, but actually beyond the area of Caterpillar Valley which is in dead ground between them. Delville Wood is at 2 o'clock to the right of Longueval Church.

Capitaine de Monclin Private Memorial with High Wood on the left horizon

Continue along the D64. After about half a mile stop by a track leading to the right.

• *Pommiers Redoubt/18.1 miles/5 minutes/Map K between 38 and 36/GPS: 50.00126 2.75462*

Nothing now remains of this position (except occasionally piles of fertiliser!) which was so important during the July-September 1916 battles, the objective of 54th Brigade (the 7th Bedfords and 11th Royal Fusiliers) on the opening day. The redoubt, and White Trench beyond (the start line for the 10 July attack of the 38th Division on Mametz Wood) were taken by the afternoon, as was the village of Mametz. The redoubt, named after the apple trees which grew along the ridge, was used by Brig-General Evans as his temporary 115th Brigade HQ during the 10 July attack on Mametz Wood. 'What's it like at Pommiers Redoubt?', asked Lieutenant (soon to be acting-Captain and then Brigade Major as his superior officers became casualties in the Wood) Wyn Griffith of his Brigade Signalling Officer who had just returned from the HQ. 'Just like any other hole in the ground', replied Taylor. But the redoubt was a typically complicated German system of dugouts and its position commanded excellent views over the wood. It was used again by 2nd KOSBs after the attack on High Wood, and then by 10th West Yorks and the 8th KRRCs in September, by which time it had become a busy, and very muddy, camp site.

Continue. Stop at the cemetery on the right.

• *Dantzig Alley CWGC Cemetery & Memorials/18.8 miles/15 minutes/*
Map K37, 3, 36/OP/GPS: 49.99943 2.74371

Danzig Alley Trench, which gave the Cemetery its name (but note the different spelling),
ran parallel to the D64 at this point and was part of 7th Division's (the 22nd Manchesters)
objective on 1 July 1916. They achieved it
at approximately 0800 hours. The direction
of the attack was broadly towards you, left
to right, from the area on the other side of
the road and involved an advance of some
1,000 yards up the slope from the British
front line.

The large Cemetery (it contains 1,923
UK, 17 New Zealand, 13 Australian, 10
Canadian, 3 South African burials and
87 special memorials (many from 1 July),
was begun soon after the battle and by 11
November 1918 it contained 183 graves
– all now in Plot I (see map in Cemetery
report). After the Armistice, eight or
more other cemeteries were concentrated
here. On the left-hand wall by the box
containing the Cemetery Report and
Visitor's Book is a memorial plaque to the
RWF on the Somme 1916-18. At the back
of the cemetery overlooking open country,
is a memorial seat erected by 14th (S)
Battalion the Royal Welsh Fusiliers of the
38th Welsh Division raised in Anglesey
and North Wales who had their baptism of
fire in the second attack on Mametz Wood.
It bears an inscription in Welsh from one
of the regiment's most famous sons, the
bardic poet **Pte Ellis Humphrey Evans**

14th (S)Bn, 38th (Welsh) Division Memorial
and seat, Dantzig Alley CWGC Cemetery

who, although he too was a North-Walian, served in the 15th (London) Battalion (as did
Wyn Griffith and David Jones). Evans, whose bardic name was **Hedd Wyn**, was killed
on 31 July 1917 on the Pilckem Ridge (qv). The translation reads,

> Distance cannot make you forgotten,
> The children of those dear hills,
> Heart and heart remain together
> Even when separated.

On a clear day the view from the wall which incorporates the memorial is truly
remarkable and binoculars are recommended. At the extreme left is the water tower in
Mametz. In front is a valley, known by the soldiers who had to cross it under enemy fire
as Death Valley, which runs left to right between the cemetery and the various woods
and copses ahead. The feature stretches from Fricourt, 2,000m away beyond the water
tower, to High Wood, 5,000m away at 2 o'clock. Take 12 o'clock as straight ahead facing
the spire of Contalmaison church which should be visible on the sky-line. The water

tower is at 9 o'clock and the Golden Madonna at Albert can sometimes be seen at 10 o'clock. Just to the left of 12 o'clock on the skyline the Pozières Memorial to the Missing may be seen and further right on the skyline at the tip of the finger of wood that points left from the main wood in view, is the wireless mast at Pozières Windmill. The bulky wood with the finger is Mametz Wood, and where it disappears behind the near fold in the ground to the right is the beginning of Caterpillar Valley where, in the late afternoon of 14 July the 7th Dragoon Guards and the Indian Cavalry of the Deccan Horse gathered for their charge on High Wood (see Historical Summary, Part 3 and page 156 Their target is just visible to the extreme right on the skyline. About halfway between the cemetery and the wood is White Trench, from which the Welsh attacked on 10 July. The ground then drops sharply down a steep cliff to the Willow Stream. However poor visibility may be, it will be possible to appreciate how German machine guns sited in the woods beyond Death Valley dominated the open ground, and how wise a decision it was to move up at night for the attack of 14 July.

Continue to the crossroads in Mametz and stop.

• Manchester Regiment Memorial/19.1 miles/5 minutes/Map K34/GPS: 49.99787 2.73762

This Memorial Plaque was erected by the Cheshire and Lancashire Branches of the WFA in memory of the 20th, 21st, 22nd and 24th Battalions of the Manchester Regiment who, as part of 7th Division, 'successfully freed this village on the morning of 1 July 1916'. Pointing to the right at the corner is a green CWGC sign to the Welsh Memorial (Mémorial Gallois).

Turn left on the C2 following signs to Carnoy, then fork right downhill towards the D938. Some 500m later pass a civilian cemetery on the right and stop by the 150m sign. Look left along the small track.

Memorial to Manchester Regt, Mametz

• Shrine Corner/19.5 miles/5 minutes/Map K/OP/OP/GPS: 49.99348 2.73401

You are now looking towards the rear of the German front line some 250 yards ahead with the British front line the same distance further on. Straight ahead is a valley – the Vallée St Martin – and a house with the word Mametz painted on its side which was the old railway station (it may be hidden in a small batch of trees). Take that as 12 o'clock. At 1 o'clock is the tip of the Golden Madonna, visible along a bare skyline. At 10 o'clock (not straight ahead of you or even demolished). on the forward slope the other side of the valley, is a wood with a track running up the left-hand side. In the wood is the Devonshire Cemetery on the site of a trench occupied by that Regiment prior to 1 July. To one officer in the Devons, Vallée St Martin gave off a foreboding of death. By extraordinary coincidence his name was Martin too – **Captain D. L. Martin**. He was convinced that a German machine gun, sited just about where you are now at the base of the shrine (a crucifix), would decimate his company as they left their trench for the 'Big Push'. Martin was an artist and made a 'Plasticine' model of the 20th Brigade area, when at home on leave shortly before the attack, which reinforced the danger the machine gun presented. So good was the model that it was used in briefings by the Brigade Commander and HQ 20th Infantry Brigade circulated a secret letter to its units instructing Commanding

Officers to 'arrange for all officers to inspect this model at 0900 hours on 22 June'. But the message of the danger presented by the machine gun was not heeded. Haig did not encourage questioning from his subordinates and even the most intelligent soon learned that to do so might mean being dégommé (literally unstuck) or "limoged", or what was known in the Boer War as "stellenbosched" – that is being relieved of one's command and sent back to an unattractive dead-end post. The suppression of any hint of lack of enthusiasm for a plan spread down through all levels. Captain Martin's doubts were not passed any higher. In the event he was right. As the Devons made their way to and through the remnants of the wood, Mansel Copse, the gun opened fire and you can see how exposed they were.

Continue downhill on the road that was called Shrine Alley to the D938 junction.

Extra Visit to Private Memorial to H. Tomasin (Map J44, GPS: 49.98974 2.71721), Point 110 New CWGC Cemetery (Map J45, GPS: 49.98431 2.71929), Point 110 Old CWGC Cemetery (Map J43, GPS: 49.98634 2.71918) & Siegfried Sassoon's Raid on Kiel Trench. Round-trip: 3 miles. Approximate time: 25 minutes

Turn right on the D 938 and turn left, following signs to Point 110 Old & New Military Cemeteries. Drive uphill through the woods – Bois Français to the right and Bois Allemand to the left. Stop at the top. Walk down the track to the right and 150m down is an entrance into the wood.

It leads to the large tomb, decorated with shells, of French soldier H. Tomasin of the 26th RI, Class of 1900 who was killed while taking a message to the Officers of the Regiment holding the trenches in the Bois Français, 20 September 1914. The site is surrounded by hawthorn trees. At this point the front lines were only some 50 yards apart. The grave is just behind the British front line.

Return to your car and continue straight ahead, following green CWGC signs to the cemetery on the right.

Point 110 Old Military Cemetery was begun by French troops in February 1915 and continued by the Dorsets and other British units from August 1915 to September 1916. The French graves were later removed to the Albert French National Cemetery. Now it contains a hundred soldiers from the UK, and three unknowns.

Walk towards the further cemetery.

The cemeteries are built on what was known as King George's Hill in September 1916. 'Point 110' refers to the contour on which they were thought to stand (although they are actually on the 100 contour!) Approximately half way between the two is a track which leads to the right down to the D147 road in the valley. At this point **Siegfried Sassoon's** raid may be studied. A copy of his *Memoirs of an Infantry Officer, Part One, Section III* to hand will help to follow the precise course

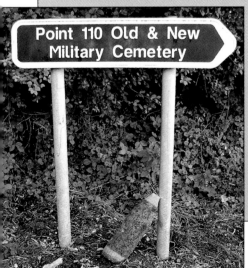

CWGC sign to Point 110 Old & New Military Cemeteries

Grave of French soldier, H. Tomasin, Bois Français

of the raid. It started from Point 71N, where the track to the right meets the road. The objective was 'to enter the enemy loop on the edge of the crater (there were a number in Bois Français); to enter Kiel Trench at two points; to examine the portions of the trench thus isolated, capture prisoners, bomb dug-outs, and kill Germans.' At 1030 on the night of 25 May 1916 Siegfried accompanied the raiders to his CO's HQ at Maple Redoubt. The redoubt was about 150 yards to the west of Point 110 Cemetery. Kiel Trench lay over the ridge, approximately half way between Maple Redoubt and the old railway house from which you started the diversion. The raid did not achieve its objectives and Sassoon's favourite Corporal, O'Brien, was mortally wounded. (He is buried in **Citadel New Military CWGC** Cemetery, Map M4.) 'I would have given a lot if he could have been alive', wrote Sassoon, 'but it was a hopeless case .... But when I go out on patrol his ghost will surely be with me.' For his part in the raid Sassoon was awarded the MC. 'He remained for 1.5 hours under rifle and bomb fire, collecting and bringing in our wounded. Owing to his courage and determination all killed and wounded were brought in', reads his citation.

Point 110 New Military Cemetery. Here is buried **2nd Lt David Cuthbert Thomas** of the 3rd Bn RWF, friend of both Sassoon and Graves, killed on 18 March 1916, age 20. Graves dedicated a poem, *Goliath and David: For D.C.T. killed at Fricourt, March 1916*, to him. The Cemetery was begun by 403rd RI in May-July 1915. It was continued by British units in February-July 1916. The twenty-six French and two German graves it originally contained have been removed and it now contains sixty-four UK, twenty-seven of whom belong to the 20th, 21st and 24th Manchesters, whose memorial plaque is in Mametz. Look uphill past the top left-hand corner of the cemetery and that is the direction of Sassoon's raid towards Kiel Trench.

Return to the junction with the D938 and rejoin Itinerary Two.

Turn left on the D938 signed to Maricourt and Péronne. 300m later fork right up the track to the car park and walk up the remainder of the track to the cemetery.

• *Devonshire CWGC Cemetery, Mansel Copse, Mametz/20.0 miles/10 minutes/Map K45/GPS: 49.98822 2.73615*

The short circular **WALK Number 3** can be taken from here. Distance: 0.75 miles. Duration: 20 mins. See page 321

All the burials here, except three, are of Devons killed on 1 July, including the ill-fated **Captain Martin** (buried in a grave with two other Devon Privates). Another Devons' officer who had a premonition of death and who was proved right is also buried here. He is the poet **Lt William Noel Hodgson, MC** (won at Loos), Bombing (grenade) Officer of the 9th Battalion. In his last poem entitled *Before Action*, and published (not written as is commonly believed) two days before the attack, the final line of the final verse reads, 'Help me to die, O Lord.' Hodgson, son of the Bishop of St Edmunsbury, had been educated at Durham School and Christ College, Oxford. A brilliant scholar (with a First in Classical Moderation), he was also a fine athlete. This popular all-rounder (known as 'Smiler') had, as well as writing poetry, produced some accomplished prose, published under the pseudonym of Edward Melbourne. He, and as many of the 160 Devons that died that day as he could gather in, were buried by the Chaplain to the 8th and 9th Devons, the Reverend Eric. C. Crosse. 'Nearly all the casualties were just by the magpie's nest', Crosse wrote later to a fellow officer. 'I buried all I could collect in our front line trench.' Crosse survived to serve with the 7th Division on the Asiago Plateau from August to November 1918 and wrote an account of its actions there ('The Defeat of Austria as seen by the 7th Division'). He then went on to Marlborough College.

Today a **stone Memorial** outside the Cemetery entrance gate proclaims: 'The Devonshires held this trench, the Devonshires hold it still'. This is a modern version of

Memorial and entrance to Devonshire CWGC Cemetery

Headstone of Lt Hodgson

Headstone of Capt
Martin with two other
men of the Devons

the wooden sign, bearing the same legend, which stood on the same site for many years. The stone was unveiled on the seventieth anniversary of the battle on 1 July 1986 by the Duke of Kent, Col in Chief of the Devonshire and Dorset Regiment and President of the CWGC.

Return to the D938 and continue right towards Péronne. Stop at the small cemetery on the left.

• Gordon CWGC Cemetery/20.3 miles/5 minutes/Map K47/GPS: 49.98755 2.73843/OP

This small Cemetery contains six officers (2nd Lieutenants) and ninety-three men of 7th Division and 2nd Gordon Highlanders, all killed on 1 July and buried in their own support trench in a double semi-circle around the Cross of Sacrifice. There are also three artillerymen killed on 9 July buried in the Cemetery. Stand in the gateway to the Cemetery. To a first approximation a line over the left-hand back corner leads directly to Dantzig Alley Cemetery and a line over the right-hand back corner leads to Montauban. It was within this arc that the biggest advance along the whole front of 1 July 1916 was made. A night visit to this Cemetery can be very atmospheric. The height of the hedge

Gordon CWGC Cemetery, Mametz

is such, that by standing close to it and looking over the top, one has the impression of standing in a trench.

Continue on the D938 past a junction on the left with the D254 to the next crossroads with the C3. Turn left downhill on the C3 and stop at the cemetery on the left. On the left as you drive is La Guerre Wood, through which a light railway ran from left to right coming from Mansel Copse and continuing through Trônes Wood. There is now a good parking area by the Cemetery.

• Carnoy Mil CWGC Cemetery/21.4 miles/10 minutes/Map N7/GPS: 49.98221 2.75494

The Cemetery, which contains 837 burials, was begun on 15 August 1915 by 2nd KOSBs and 2nd KOYLIs. In it is buried **Capt W. P. Nevill** of the 8th East Surreys who, when on leave shortly before the Somme offensive, bought footballs for each of his four platoons. He offered a prize for the first football to be kicked into a German trench during his

Left: *Entrance to Carnoy Mil CWGC Cemetery*

Below: *Private Tribute to Capt Nevill, Visitors' Book, Carnoy Mil CWGC Cemetery*

company's assault on Montauban on 1 July. One football was inscribed 'The Great European Cup. The Final, East Surreys v Bavarians. Kick off at Zero'. Nevill (an Old Boy of Dover College) kicked off, but did not survive to award his prize. Two of the footballs were retrieved - one is in the National Army Museum and the other was in the The Surrey Infantry Museum at Clandon Park National Trust property which unfortunately burnt down in April 2015. Near Nevill's grave (on which there are always many private tributes) are three unusual headstones. On the first are two 2nd Lieutenants, on the second are two Lieutenants and on the third two Captains. They are all East Surreys killed on 1 July 1916. Also buried here is a Chaplain, the **Rev Charles Plummer** attached to 61st Infantry Brigade, and one of the family of four Newfoundlanders called Ayre (qv) to be killed on 1 July. He is **Captain B. P. Ayre**, who was serving with the Norfolk Regiment. Also buried here is **Lt Colonel F.E.P. Curzon**, age 57, 9 September 1916, who commanded the 6th Battalion RIR.

Turn round, return to the D938 and turn left towards Maricourt. Continue, passing a cemetery on the left.

This is Péronne Road (GPS: 49.97814 2.78203.) It was begun by fighting and medical units in 1916 and used for a year. It commemorates almost 1,000 men.

Continue to the crossroads with the D197.

[N.B.] By continuing some half a mile to a wood on the right and a small frame of trees on the left, amongst the trees the somewhat neglected obelisk **Memorial to the 224th RI (GPS: 49.97685 2.80153)** may be seen. The Regiment, raised in Paris and Normandy in August 1914, was part of the French 53rd Division. They took part in the Retreat from Mons, fought on the Chemin Des Dames and moved to Maricourt on 19 October. On 17 December they took part on the assault on nearby Hardecourt. Leading the attack was **Lt Robert Brodu**. Brodu and 2 other officers and 58 men were killed, 263 wounded, many seriously, in the unsuccessful action. Brodu is buried in the French National Cemetery, Albert (see page 142).

*Memorial to 224th
RI & Lt Brodu, Maricourt*

Turn left onto the D197.

You are now travelling in the direction of the attack of 30th Division, the extreme right hand British division and the only one to take and hold all its objectives by mid-day (see Holts' Map). Montauban was taken by 16th and 17th Manchesters of the Division and their memorial in the village is visited earlier in this itinerary. However, after Montauban fell to the Germans in March 1918, it was 7th Buffs and 11th Royal Fusiliers of 18th Division that recaptured the village on 25 August. This road marks the boundary between the French and British Forces.

Continue to the Memorial on the right.

Franco-British Memorial, Maricourt/23 miles/Map N1a/GPS: 49.98753 2.79093

On 7 November 2010, at the initiative of the Somme Remembrance Association, a Franco-British Memorial was put up recording the joint advance on 1 July 1916 of the 17th Bn King's Liverpool Regt, led by **Lt Col Bryan Fairfax**, and the 3rd Bn of the French 153rd RI, commanded by **Cdt Lepetit**. The front line crossed the road at right angles here and they advanced side by side across no man's land in the second wave of the attack as an act of friendship and co-operation. Informative details and a trench map section are shown on the Memorial.

Continue towards Montauban.

After the 1916 battles it was discovered that the much-loved Madonna of Montauban-de-Picardie had disappeared from the ruined church. It was not until April 1986 that the Mayor of Montauban, M. Froment, received a letter from a Miss Valerie Ives from Netherby in Yorkshire which explained her disappearance. The Madonna – or rather the bust that was all that remained of her – had been taken to England by a British Officer who gave it to a friend. She kept it

Memorial to Franco-British Advance, 1 July 1916, Maricourt

in her library, mounted on a plinth with the inscription, 'Montauban Madonna – Battle of the Somme' and on her death it was inherited by Miss Ives who decided it should be returned to its rightful home. She brought the bust back to Montauban in November 1986 when it was restored to its place in the rebuilt church.

Continue on to the crossroads with the D64 and turn right.

The first wood on the left is Bernafay Wood, which was taken on 4 July. Then, after a gap of some 600m, the next wood is Trônes Wood (Bois des Troncs) and as the road bends left, there is a memorial on the left at the edge of the wood.

Stop. Be careful to park off the road.

• 18th Division Memorial/25 miles/5 minutes/Map K41/GPS: 50.00664 2.8041

The first British soldiers to gain a foothold in the wood (broadly attacking from across the open ground to the right of the road) were 30th Division on 8 July, but it was finally cleared by 6th Northants, 7th Royal West Kents and 12th Middlesex of 18th Division on 14 July on the first day of Part III of the Somme Battle. Col Francis Maxwell (who won his VC in South Africa, then commanded 12th Middlesex, went on to command 27th Brigade and was killed on 21 September 1917 in the Ypres Salient) wrote home two days later,

> "To talk of a 'wood' is to talk rot. It was the most dreadful tangle of dense trees and undergrowth imaginable, with deep yawning trenches criss-crossing about it; every tree broken off at top or bottom and branches cut away, so that the floor of the wood was almost an impenetrable tangle of timber, trenches, undergrowth,

etc., blown to pieces by British and German heavy guns for a week. Never was anything so perfectly dreadful to look at … particularly with its gruesome addition of corpses and wounded men – many lying there for days and days. Our doctor found one today who had had no food or water for five days … but so dense is the tangle that even if you find a wounded man … then leave him, you have lost him, simply because you can't find your way back to him."

Recaptured by the Germans in March 1918, it was again taken by 18th Division on 27 August 1918. At one time a plain wooden cross commemorated the men of 8th Berks, 11th Essex and 7th Royal West Kents who fell in the 1918 fighting. Now only the stone obelisk Divisional Memorial remains, with the same simple words as at Thiépval, 'This is My Command, that ye love one another'. The Memorial was erected before the shattered wood had regrown.

18th Division Memorial, Trônes Wood

Continue along the D64 to the junction with the small Hardecourt au Bois road to the right.

Extra Visit to Maltkorn Farm (Map K42, GPS: 50.00210 2.81333) & Private Memorials to Boucher, Lapage and Capitaine Cochin (Map K48, GPS: 49.99405 2.82008)
Round trip: 2.4 miles. Approximate time: 20 minutes/OP

Turn right in direction of Hardecourt and continue to a memorial cross on the left.

Maltkorn Farm Calvary

This Calvary marks the site of **Maltkorn Duclercq Farm** (sometimes known as Maltz Horn Farm), destroyed in the battles which took place here between 1 July and 9 August 1916. The farm made a salient in the German lines and it actually fell to 89th and 90th Brigades of 30th Division on 30 July as they advanced towards Faffemont (or Falfemont) Farm (Map L6 area). Falfemont was taken by the Norfolks on 5 September 1916 during an attack by 5 Div along the line of the light railway below Ginchy. Standing by this cross the sharp-eyed can see the top of

Memorial to Boucher & Lapage, 153rd RI, Hardecourt

Pozières wireless mast to the left of Trônes Wood on the skyline. To the left of Trônes Wood is Bernafay Wood, at the left hand edge of which is Montauban Church.

Continue towards the next junction, before which on the right, up a track, is a Memorial stone to Marcel Boucher 'et son camarade' Roméo Lapage of the 153rd Infantry Regiment who were killed here on 28 July 1916. At the junction is a **Private Memorial to Capitaine Augustin Cochin** of the 4th Battalion, Chasseurs who was killed here in a brave action on 8 July 1916. The decorative cross is made from shells, machine-gun belt chains and incorporates the image of a soldier being carried aloft by angels.

Return to the D64 and continue on the main itinerary
Continue. To the right of the road as you drive is the area where an exceptional VC was won.

Memorial to Capt Cochin, Hardecourt

• SOA Capt Noel Godfrey Chavasse VC & BAR, MC/Map K43

On 9 August 1916, Capt Chavasse, the dedicated Medical Officer of the 1/10th King's Liverpool Regt:

"… attended to the wounded all day under heavy fire, frequently in view of the enemy, and during the night he searched for wounded in front of the enemy's lines. Next day he took a stretcher-bearer and under heavy shell fire carried an urgent case 500 yards into safety, being wounded himself on the return journey. The same night, with 20 volunteers, he rescued three wounded men from a shell-hole 36 yards from the enemy's trenches, buried the bodies of two officers and collected many identity discs. Altogether he saved the lives of some 20 wounded men, besides the ordinary cases which passed through his hands."

Chavasse was to carry out a similar act of repeated heroism, which earned him a bar to his VC (he was **the only double VC winner to gain both his awards in World War I**), at Wieltje in the Ypres Salient, but finally died of wounds on 4 August 1917 and is buried in Brandhoek New Military Cemetery in Belgium. There is also a Memorial to him in the village.

Continue and stop at the next cemetery on the left.

• Guillemont Road CWGC Cemetery/25.4 miles/20 minutes/Map K44/OP/ GPS: 50.01047 2.81579

Although Trônes Wood was taken on 14 July, continuous and furious fighting went on for the area of this road until September. Lost again in March 1918, it was retaken by 18th and 38th (Welsh) Divisions on 29 August.

The Cemetery contains over 2,200 burials, including the grave of **Lt Raymond Asquith**, of the 3rd Grenadier Guards, elder son of the British Prime Minister Herbert Henry Asquith, who managed to see his son on a visit to the front line on 7 September 1916. Also present was Raymond's brother, Herbert, a Captain in the Royal Artillery. Raymond was shot in the chest on the 15th, in Part 4 of the Somme Battle, leading his company into the attack. He died soon after in a nearby dressing station. Raymond was

Entrance to Guillemont Road CWGC Cemetery

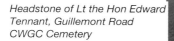

Headstone of Lt the Hon Edward Tennant, Guillemont Road CWGC Cemetery

said to be one of the most promising men of his generation. He was a barrister and had been President of the Union at Oxford, won the Craven, Derby and Ireland Scholarships, a First in Greats and a Fellowship at All Souls. A. A. Milne called him 'the most brilliant man I have ever met', Winston Churchill referred to him as 'my brilliant hero-friend', John Buchan said, 'he moved among us like a being of another world'. When he heard of his son's death, the Prime Minister wrote, 'Whatever pride I had in the past, and whatever hope I had for the future, by much the largest part of both was vested in him. Now all that is gone'.

Buried in the same row is **Lt the Hon Edward Tennant**, of the 4th Grenadiers. 'Bim' was a talented poet, author of poems such as *Worple Flit, Home Thoughts from Laventie* , and *The Mad Soldier* . This popular young officer (1 July 1916 was his 19th birthday and he was killed, by a sniper, on 22 September) would have admired Raymond Asquith, who, although considerably older (at 37) was part of the same social set. Their generation was known as 'The Coterie', and they were the children of the esoteric group of witty, privileged members of a few select families known as 'The Souls'. They were even related by the second marriage of Raymond's father to Margot Tennant, Bim's aunt. His mother, Pamela Glenconner, wrote *A Memoir* to her beloved son, which was published in 1919. In the row behind is the grave of **Lt Col John Collier Stormonth Darling** of the Cameronians, killed on 1 November 1916 while he was commanding the 9th HLI, age 38.

Walk to the seat in the back wall of the cemetery.

Some 300m straight ahead, away from the road is a shallow valley, once a major German trench line. The single track Albert to Péronne railway ran just behind that, from left to right, and the wood on the skyline is Delville Wood. At the left-hand end of Delville Wood it should be possible to spot Longueval church. Also in the valley is the Private Memorial to 2nd Lt Marsden-Smedley (Map K30). The wall that surrounds the Memorial can be seen, provided the crops in the field are not too high, in the middle distance just to the right of a line to the water tower at the edge of Delville Wood.

Return to your car and continue towards the village of Guillemont to a grassy path to the left. This is the best access route to the Marsden-Smedley memorial.

Private Memorial to 2nd Lt G.F. Marsdon-Smedley (with inset detail). Behind is Guillemont Road Cemetery

Extra Visit to the Private Memorial of 2nd Lt George Futvoye Marsden-Smedley/Map K30/GPS:50.01548 2.81653. Round trip: 0.8 miles. Approximate time: 20 minutes

Turn left down the narrow track (which can be muddy when wet) and continue bearing to the left. Continue to the memorial on the left which lies on the edge of what was the old railway line.

George Marsden-Smedley was educated at Harrow where he became an outstanding athlete. Instead of taking up his place at Trinity College, Cambridge, George joined the Rifle Brigade on leaving school in 1915. During his short period at the front, George often wrote to his family. He described leaving Southampton for France on 16 July, arriving at his battalion (the 3rd) which was then in reserve (somewhere near Albert). He discussed the Eton-Harrow Cricket Match, demanded a supply of mouth organs for his men and chocolates from Fortnum & Mason for himself. He talked of getting 'The Boche fearfully alarmed', of the Hun being pounded by our bombardment and on the day before he was killed, knowing the big attack that was being planned would take place on the morrow, promised his mother 'a better letter... possibly in three days time'. On 18 August the 19-year-old Subaltern led his platoon on an attack on Guillemont Station some 300 yards from the memorial towards the east. Between here and the station the major German second line defences ran roughly north to south. He single-handedly charged a machine gun post which was holding up the company but after shooting one of the Germans was himself shot. He fell on the German parapet, which was on the site of the present memorial. His body was never found and he is commemorated on the Thiépval Memorial. The Memorial was erected by his parents but fell into disrepair. When the family read our description (in an earlier edition of this guidebook) of the Memorial as being 'neglected' they decided to renovate the memorial, the surrounding brick wall and the wrought iron gate. This they did with the help of the WFA. The Memorial bears the inscription 'Lovely and pleasant in life, in death serene and unafraid, most blessed in remembrance'. A small plaque to the left of the gate says that for further information contact John Smedley Ltd, Lee Mills, Matlock DEA 5AG the old family business. The Memorial was re-dedicated on 19 July 1997 in a moving ceremony attended by some 30 family members, including the instigator, George's nephew Christopher Marsden-Smedley, who lost two cousins in the Second World War.

Return to the main road and pick up Itinerary Two

Continue into the village of Guillemont and stop at the church with a memorial in front of it.

16th (Irish) Division
Memorial, Guillemont

• 16th Irish Division Memorial/25.8 miles/5 minutes/Map K32/GPS: 50.01282 2.82443

The struggle for the village was a long and bitter one. As early as 30 July, elements of the 2nd Royal Scots Fusiliers got into the area but were forced out. Another assault on 8 August had some success, but it was not until 3 September that the village was cleared by 20th Light Division, supported by a brigade of 16th Division.

On 3 September 2009 a **Plaque** was inaugurated on the church behind the Memorial to **three VC winners**, two of whom were of the 16th (Irish) Division (**Pte Thomas Hughes & Lt John Vincent Holland**), the third was **Sgt David Jones** of the 12th Kings Liverpool Regt.

The German author **Ernst Junger**, born at Heidelberg in 1895, ran away from home at the age of 17 to serve with the French Foreign Legion. When the war broke out he returned home and joined the German Army. His war memories were published under the title *Orages d'Acier* ('Steel Storms') and in them is an entire chapter on Guillemont. Junger always seemed to be in the thick of things, and was wounded fourteen times during the war. On 22 September 1918 he won Germany's highest award for gallantry, the *Pour le Mérite*. Only thirteen other Lieutenants won this coveted decoration during the entire war. On 23 August 1916, he wrote that, as his unit was being transported by lorry, 'Jokes flashed around, accompanied by general bursts of laughter from one vehicle to another'. But as they approached nearer the front a German intelligence officer told them of 'of a new and harder world ... of monotonous days spent huddling in the trenches to escape shellfire, uninterrupted attacks, fields covered with corpses ... expressionless faces ... a macabre impression.' The nervous laughter ceased.

Junger fought again in the Wehrmacht in WW2. He had an ambivalent attitude towards Nazism, sometimes seeming to embrace, sometimes to oppose, its ideology. He went on to win many

Plaque to three VCs,
Guillemont Church

Memorial to 20th (Light) Division, Guillemont

*Memorial to Capt Fockedy,
265th RI, Guillemot*

awards for his literary and international personal achievements (such as the Peace Medal at Verdun in 1979). He died on 17 February 1998 at the age of 102 in Wiflingen, Germany, where he had been in retirement for the past 50 years.

Continue to the crossroads with the D20. Turn right onto the D20, signed to Combles.
Continue through the village and stop at the memorial on the right.

• French Capt Fockedy/265th Infantry Regiment Memorial/26.2/5 miles/5 minutes/Map K33a/GPS: 50.01414 2.83197

This obelisk Memorial commemorates the action of **Capitaine Hippolyte Marie Joseph Fockedy** and soldiers of the 265th Infantry Regiment of XI Corps who fell on 28 August 1914. It was erected by Old Comrades and *Souvenir Français* .

Continue to the crossroads with the D20E.

• 20th Light Division Memorial/27.2 miles/5 minutes/Map K33/GPS: 50.01444 2.83434

This Memorial, unveiled on 25 April 1995, replaced the old, leaning and crumbling memorial that was identical to the Division's Memorial in Langemarck in the Ypres Salient. The division took part in the capture of Guillemont.

Extra Visit to the 'Dickens Cross' Private Memorial, Map L3, GPS: 50.01876 2.85000 Round trip: 1.7 miles. Approximate time: 15 minutes
Continue on the D20 to a cart track to the left signed to the Dickens Cross.
About 400m up the track is a wooden cross to **Major Cedric Charles Dickens** (grandson of Charles Dickens) of the 1/13th (Kensington) London Regt, killed

---

near here on 9 September 1916 during the attack on Leuze Wood. The inscription reads, 'In loving memory of our darling Ceddy'. The cross originally stood in a small copse some distance up and to the left of the track. In it are the traces of trench lines. It was erected by his mother, Lady Dickens, and she planted the area with British flowering shrubs and small trees and, until the outbreak of World War II, made an annual pilgrimage to the cross. Attempts were made after the war to re-inter the body in a Commonwealth War Graves Commission Cemetery, but it could not be found. Dickens is therefore commemorated on the Thiépval Memorial. In September 1995 the cross was moved, with the family's consent, to its present location nearer to the road, in a complicated compensatory re-allocation of land after the building of the TGV railway line. The old wooden cross is now again surrounded by attractive shrubs and bushes. To the right of the D20 is Leuze Wood (known, of course, to Tommy as 'Lousy Wood'), the objective of the Kensington's attack.

Return to the junction with the D20E and rejoin the main itinerary.

Dickens Cross, Leuze Wood

Turn left on the D20E, in the direction of Ginchy. Continue into the village.

Following the general offensive in this area of 8 August 1916, 7th Division took the village of Ginchy on 3 September, only to lose it again the same day. It finally fell on 9 September to 49th Brigade of 16th Division.

Continue to the church, which is normally open. Stop and enter.

• Private Memorials to Major Dickens & Lt Irwin, Ginchy Church/28.0 miles/10 minutes/Map K17/18/GPS: 50.02389 2.83183

To the right of the altar is a brass Plaque with a French inscription which reads, 'To the glory of God and to the memory of Major Cedric Charles Dickens 1/13 Kensingtons the London Regt and of the million dead of the British Empire who fell in the Great War 1914-1918 and who, for the most part, rest in France. RIP.'

To the left of the altar is another brass plaque, with a Latin inscription which translates:

'Pray for the soul of Charles Patrick Michael Irwin, beloved son of Charles Trevor Irwin and Beatrix his wife and brother of Katharine Irwin of Oakley near Basingstoke of the 3rd Bn the RIF who was killed in the attack on Ginchy in France on 10 September 1916, in his 19th year, whose soul belongs to God. Amen.'

Plaque to Maj Dickens, Ginchy Church

Lt Irwin is buried in Delville Wood CWGC Cemetery.
Continue along the road to a memorial on the right, just before the power line.

• *Private Memorial to Lejoindre & Pfister/28.3 miles/5 minutes/Map K16/ GPS: 50.02902 2.82905*

An avenue of flowering shrubs leads to this neglected and sad French Memorial to *Médaille Militaire* and *Croix de Guerre* winners, Georges Lejoindre and Georges Pfister and their comrades of the 18th Régiment d'Infanterie fallen on the field of honour in the fighting for Flers and Ginchy on 26 September 1914.

Return to the village. Turn right at the crossroads signed to Longueval and then at the Y junction fork right to Longueval.

Straight ahead is the village of Longueval and Delville (Devil's) Wood with its prominent water tower. Across the field to the left is a small row of houses running down from the wood. Waterlot Farm stood at the left hand of that row. During the war it was a sugar refinery and a strongly defended German position. Once in British hands (it was finally taken on 17 July 1916) it was heavily bombarded by the Germans. Rebuilt after the war, it was demolished again in the early 1990s.

Continue to the South African Memorial area and park in the extensive car park by the Visitors' Centre.

Memorial to Lejoindre & Fister, Ginchy

Walk Number 4 can be taken from here. Distance 9.2 kms (approx. 6 miles). Duration: 2 hours. See page 322

• *Delville Wood: South African National Memorial, Museum, Memorial to Welsh VCs Cpl Davies & Pte Hill, Original Hornbeam Memorial, Information Centre/CWGC Cemetery/29.7 miles/50 minutes/ Map K 12/13/14/14a/14b/15/RWC/GPS: 50.02445 2.81270*

In 1916 the wood, known as Bois d'Elville, was a major German defensive feature in the German second line. On the left of the road is **Delville Wood Cemetery, Longueval**, which was made after the Armistice by concentrating ten or more cemeteries from the Somme battlefield. There are 5,493 burials and almost two-thirds, 3,590, are unknown. 151 graves are those of South Africans. One grave of note is that of **Sgt Albert Gill**, KRRC, who won a posthumous **VC** when rallying his platoon by standing up in full view of the enemy. Another is **Lt Charles Patrick Michael Irwin** of the 3rd Bn Royal Irish Fusiliers, attd 7th Bn, on Special Memorial A8, killed in action at Ginchy on 10 September age 19, who is commemorated on a plaque in Ginchy Church (qv). **Lt Niel Shaw Stewart** of D Coy, 3rd Bn the Rifle Bde, killed leading C Coy in the attack on Guillemont on 21 August 1916, age 22, and commemorated on a Plaque in Rancourt *Souvenir Français* Chapel (qv), is also buried here. The British Parliament decreed that private memorials could not be erected. However, overseas, this could only apply on land ceded or granted to the Commission, i.e. cemeteries or memorial sites. Thus one

Delville Wood CWGC Cemetery

way around the ruling for families wishing to erect a memorial to their lost one was to do so in a foreign church.

On the right of the road is Delville Wood itself, the South African National Memorial and the Museum built in 1985/86.

The Visitors' Centre was extended in 1994 when the whole complex was still run by dedicated curators Tom and Janet Fairgrieve. In September 2006 the Fairgrieves were replaced by South African curator Thapete Masanabo. Thapete's background is in business tourism and he has been working to make the Museum and Information Centre more accessible, pro-active and informative. Major ongoing renovations to the site took place in 2014/5. The Centre, which provides light snacks and has good toilet facilities, and Museum are **closed** on Mon and public holidays. **Open:** early April-Mid-Oct 1000-1730, rest of year 1000-16000. Tel: +(0)3 22 85 02 17. E-mail: info@delvillewood.com website: www.delvillewood.com As improvements are ongoing we recommend that you consult this site before your visit.

In July 2006 a new SA Coat of Arms was unveiled in the Museum with Plaques listing the casualties of the SA Native Labour Contingent and Cape Horse Artillery Transport Coys who are buried in Arques la Bataille Brit Cem and those who were killed in the tragic sinking of SAS *Mendi* on 21 February 1917 when 607 black troops, 9 white countrymen and 33 crew members were drowned off the Isle of Wight, ironically close to the mainland, and where the wreck still remains. The bravery of the dying soldiers is legendary and is the subject of a CWGC educational CDRom, *Let Us Die Like Brothers* (the words of their inspirational Minister, Isaac William Wauchope, as the ship went down). The *Mendi* was rammed in thick fog by the cargo ship *Darro*, whose master was later blamed for the accident and for not stopping to help. The story of the SA Native Labour Corps was the subject of a heart-rendingly moving exhibition in the Museum in 2015, featuring the names of all those killed on the *Mendi* and of all those killed in battle in Europe during the war. These names will be inscribed on Memorial Walls each side of the beautiful avenue leading to the Museum, in time for the 10 July 2016 Centenary commemorations, attended by the SA President.

On 6 Jul 2014 the re-interment, in a dignified tomb surmounted by a CWGC headstone, of the first S African Labour Corps soldier to land in France on 20 November 1916, **Pte Beleza Myengwa**, took place in the courtyard of the Memorial, attended by the Deputy President of S Africa. He died on the 27th. and was originally buried in Le Havre.

Monument to the last original tree, Delville Wood

The bitter struggle for Delville Wood

Bas Relief to SS Mendi sinking

Tomb of First SA Labour Corps Member to die in France

Memorial to Welsh VCs., Delville Wood

Castor and Pollux South African Memorial with Museum behind, Delville Wood

The battle for the wood was a complex one and is well told in the Museum and in booklets available there. The South African Brigade was attached to 9th Scottish Division and when the latter took Longueval village on 14 July in Part 3 of the Somme Battle, the Springboks were given the task of taking the wood. At dawn on 15 July the assault began with a fearsome artillery duel. By nightfall all four South African regiments were committed, the main direction of their attack being from the south-west – that is from the direction of the cemetery and Longueval village – and only the north-west corner of the wood remained in enemy hands. Waterlot Farm (GPS: 50.02022 2.81431), however, was still held by the Germans. Five days of hand-to-hand fighting followed. It rained every other day and enemy artillery fire reached rates exceeding 400 shells a minute. The landscape was a tangled mess of broken tree stumps, knotted undergrowth, huge shell holes and mud and water all overlaid with bodies of soldiers of both sides (many of whom still lie in the wood). Though the South Africans were told, and tried, to take the wood 'at all costs', they did not quite manage to do so, and when they were relieved by 26th Brigade on 20 July, only 143 men of the original 3,150 came out of the trenches. It was not until 25 August 1916 that 14th (Light) Division finally overcame all enemy resistance in the wood.

Lord Moran, later to become Churchill's doctor, but then serving with the 1st Bn the Royal Fusiliers in the trenches immediately south of Delville Wood during the battle, describes in his book *The Anatomy of Courage*, how his men attempted to help some of their fellows buried by shell fire:

"Shells were bursting all around and in the black smoke men were digging. Muffled appeals for help, very faint and distant, came out of the earth and maddened the men who dug harder than ever, and some throwing their spades away, burrowed feverishly with their hands like terriers. It was difficult to get the earth away from one place where they said someone was buried without piling it where others were digging also. We were getting in each other's way. We were afraid too of injuring those buried heads with the shovels and always through our minds went the thought that it might be too late. Then there was a terrific noise, everything vanished for a moment and when I could see, Dyson and the two men working beside him had disappeared. They were buried."

Following the Gulf War and Afghanistan there has been considerable debate about 'friendly fire'. The Royal Fusiliers had been under friendly fire during this incident.

In the 1918 battles the Germans over-ran the area on 24 March, and 38th (Welsh) Division retook the wood on 28 August.

The Memorial (unveiled by the widow of General Louis Botha on 10 October 1926) is topped by a **sculpture of Castor and Pollux** holding hands. Designed by Alfred Turner, it symbolised the unity of the English and Afrikaans speaking peoples of South Africa. A replica overlooks Pretoria from in front of the Government Buildings, designed, as was the Delville Wood Memorial, by Sir Herbert Baker ARA. It is a most beautiful Memorial, approached by a long avenue flanked by trees. Note that the shelters at each end of the Memorial entrance echo those in the Cemetery opposite.

Behind the arched Memorial is a Voortrekkers Cross, which replaces the traditional Cross of Sacrifice. The Stone of Remembrance in front of the Memorial is to South Africa's dead of World War II. **The Museum**, unveiled on 7 June 1984 by then Prime Minister P. Botha and built around the cross, is a replica of the Castle of Good Hope in Capetown. Its five bastions bear the names of other castles in Capetown. Just to the left inside is a magnificent coloured replica of the **H.P. Cart de Lafontaine (qv) CWGC Plaque**, specially made for this Museum. The Museum has delicately engraved glass windows round an inner courtyard and dramatic *bas reliefs* in bronze depicting the days of bitter fighting for the wood and the personalities involved. They were sculpted by Mike Edwards. Exhibits depict South Africa's World War I role in Delville Wood, the German South West and East African campaigns, her VCs, and the role of South Africa in other wars, notably World War II and Korea. The combined losses of these conflicts totals 25,000.

The rides in the wood have stone markers with the names of streets given during the war: Rotten Row, Bond Street, Regent Street, Princes Street, etc, and for Brigade HQ. One tree, a Hornbeam, remains from the terrible days of 1916. It is to the left and rear of the museum and in front of it is a Memorial stone unveiled by the South African Ambassador in 1988. To the left of it is a small Stone to the two Welsh **VCs, Cpl Joseph Davies**, 10th (Service) Battalion and **Pte Albert Hill**, both of the RWF, whose acts of conspicuous gallantry took place here on 20 July 1916. Davies survived until 1976 and Hill died in the USA in 1971.Their Plaque was unveiled by members of the Regiment in July 2001.

Continue towards Longueval. On the left is

•*Footballers' Memorial/28.2 miles/5 minutes/Map K15d/GPS: 50.02431 2.80901*

Unveiled on 21 October 2010 in an impressive ceremony, this Memorial (achieved with money raised by supporters, staff and footballers of the English and Welsh Football League Clubs) has now become a focal point for football fans visiting the Somme. It

commemorates the 17th & 23rd Bns, Middx Regt, known as 'The Footballers' Bns'. The first to join is reputed to be English centre-half, Frank Buckley, eventually reaching the rank of major. Although badly wounded he survived the war but never played football again. The Bn's most famous son, however, was the Tottenham player Walter Tull, the first black officer of the British Army (qv).

The story of the WW1 footballers is told in *'When the Whistle Blows'* by Andrew Riddoch and John Kemp.

Continue into Longueval on the D20 and stop at the crossroads.

[N.B.] In front of the church to the right is a well-preserved WW1 mortar.

To the left is the village Poilu War Memorial and on the adjacent corner is

*Inauguration of Memorial
to Middlesex Footballers
Bns, Longueval*

• *Pipers' Memorial/28.5 miles/5 minutes/Map K14c/GPS: 50.02615 2.80341*

The Memorial was proposed by members of the Somme Battlefield Pipe band, formed in 1989 under the Honorary Presidency of Ian C. Alexander of the War Research Society, to perpetuate the memory of the Pipers of various regiments who fought in WW1. Longueval was chosen for the site as it was captured by the 9th Scottish Division in July 1916 and through it many pipers marched. The project was supported by the Mayor, Jean Blondel. A world-wide fund was launched and Andy de Comyn, a Midlands-based sculptor, carved the 4-metre high white stone statue of a Piper, with black pipes, stepping over sandbags, on the base of a cairn. On the surrounding wall, constructed by a local builder, are the cap badges of each regiment who lost a Piper during the War, carved by the CWGC. Ian and his team worked indefatigably to raise the £35,000 needed to complete the project. The statue was unveiled on a sunny 20 July 2002 by Lt General Sir Peter Graham, KCB, CBE, late Colonel of the Gordon Highlanders, and Maj General Corran Purdon, CBE, MC, CPM, President of the RUR and London Irish Rifles Associations, at an impressive ceremony during which the pipe tune by George Stoddart, called Longueval, was played and the moving poem *The Piper* by Ron Venus was said.

THE PIPER

'Take my pipes', the Piper said
'And lay me down to sleep.
The sights I've seen have broke my heart
And caused my soul to weep'.
'Take my pipes', the Piper said
'And wrap me in my plaid.
The sights I've seen have made me cold
And all I feel is sad'.
'Take my pipes', the piper said
'And my heavy tartan kilt.
My friends have gone and left my side
Dragged down by mud and silt'.
'Take my pipes', the piper said
'And play them far away.
Their sound's too sweet to carry far
Upon this dreadful day'.
'But stay ...! Don't take my treasured pipes
I'll need them by my side
When I take up my Scottish lads
To the land on the other side.'

Pipe and drum bands had gathered from around the world - the Huntley & District from Aberdeen, the London Scottish and the London Irish, representatives from the Black Watch (with their Drum Major), the Highlanders and the Royal Scots, the Royal Corps of Signals, the Somme Battlefield Pipe Band, the President of the American Pipe Band Association,

Pipers' Memorial, Longueval

bands from Belgium, Germany and from Holland - to attend this special event. The colourful column, of 105 Pipers and over 75 Drummers, formed up at Delville Wood and marched along the road you have just driven to the rousing sound of the pipes and drums to the village. After the ceremony the massed bands played a poignant selection of tunes to the well over 1,000-strong enthralled audience in the tiny village square.

Turn right onto the D197 signed to Flers and the New Zealand Forces Memorial. At the Y junction 250m later fork left signed to the memorial and continue right.

• SOA/Wounding of Billy Congreve VC/Map K11

It was in this area that a most unusual VC was won by the son of a **VC** winner. **William La Touche Congreve** was born on 22 March 1891, the eldest son of Lt General Sir Walter Norris Congreve who won the VC during the Boer War battle of Colenso. Coincidentally, Lt the Hon Frederick Hugh Sherston Roberts also won the VC in the same action and he, too, was the VC son of a VC father – Earl Roberts. At the time of Billy's action his father was in command of XIII Corps on the Somme.

Billy Congreve, a popular and energetic Brigade-Major in the Rifle Brigade, had once before been recommended for the Victoria Cross for gallant action in the Battle for St Eloi in April 1916 and had been awarded the Distinguished Service Order. He already had the Military Cross for gallantry at Hooge in 1915. On 1 June 1916, Billy married Pamela Maude, daughter of the actor Cyril Maude and a great friend of Gilbert Talbot (after whom Talbot House in Poperinghe was named). After a brief honeymoon, Congreve returned to his regiment in time for the 1 July Somme Battle.

On 20 July an attack from the west was made by the 2nd Suffolks in an attempt to clear Delville Wood. Major Congreve who was based at Brigade HQ in the quarry on the Longueval – Montauban road, went forward to see what had happened to the leading Suffolk companies and was shot by a sniper. His body was taken to Corbie for burial (visited on Itinerary Three). His citation quoted 'Acts of Bravery: 6-20 July' during which 'by his personal example he inspired all those around him with confidence at critical periods of the operations'. On 1 November the young widow, who was pregnant with Billy's child, received on her husband's behalf, the VC, the DSO and the MC from King George V, the first officer to have won these three awards for gallantry. He was also awarded the Légion d'Honneur.

Continue past the calvary to the memorial and stop.

• New Zealand Memorial/29.4 miles/5 minutes/Map H26/GPS: 50.03928 2.80154

There is a CGS/H Signboard by the column. It marks the area from which the Division set out on the historic battle of Flers-Courcelette on 15 September 1916, Part 4 of the Somme Battle, when tanks were used for the first time, and together with the 14th and 41st Divisions entered Flers (2,400m away to the right at right-angles to your line of approach) behind 'a solitary tank'. The track behind the Memorial leads away to the right and into Flers and can be walked, following approximately the same route as the tanks did on 15 September 1916. The wood immediately behind you is Delville Wood. The New Zealand Memorial to the Missing on the Somme is in Caterpillar Valley Cemetery. The Division fought for twenty-three consecutive days on the Somme, advanced

New Zealand Memorial, Longueval

over 2 miles, captured 5 miles of the enemy front line and had 7,000 casualties. This Memorial was unveiled in October 1922 by Sir Francis Bell, the Leader of the Legislative Council in New Zealand.

Return to the Calvary. Turn right at the calvary junction and continue down the track to the D107 road.

Across the road, slightly left 650m away, is Caterpillar Valley Cemetery (qv).

Turn right and continue to the beginning of High Wood, known locally as Bois des Fourcaux. Park. There is a (probably muddy) track to the right along the side of the wood. Drive up it for 400m if you are brave. There is a memorial on the left.

• Cameron Highlanders & Black Watch Memorial/30.7 miles/10 minutes/ Map H25/GPS: 50.03881 2.78892

Following the failure of the cavalry at High Wood and subsequent ineffective attempts to nibble away the German strongholds such as High Wood, it was decided to try mining. 178th Tunnelling Coy placed 3,000lb of ammonal 25ft below and about 50ft behind the German front line and on 3 September 1916, 30 seconds after the mine was blown, the Black Watch charged and occupied the crater. They were driven out by German counter-attacks. Another charge of 3,000lb was placed close by the old crater and fired on 9 September. It blew into the first crater and both were occupied and held by the 1st Northants. When you face the Memorial, the craters, filled with water, are just behind it and to the right. The Memorial commemorates not only the Cameron Highlanders who fell here in September 1916, but all who fell throughout the war. The Black Watch inscription is on the back of the Memorial.

Return to the main road, turn right and drive 100m. Stop at the memorial on the right.

Cameron Highlanders and Black Watch Memorial

• 47th (London) Division Memorial/30.8 miles/5 minutes/Map H24/GPS: 50.03685 2.78593

The original wooden Memorial here was unveiled on 13 September 1923 by Lt General Sir George Gorringe and Maj General Sir William Thwaites commemorating the action of the Division on 15 September 1916. Its replacement stone 'porch' memorial was renovated in the 1980s from money raised by the Divisional Association, but in the mid 90s it was in such poor condition that it, too, was replaced by the current cross. It was the 47th Division that finally took High Wood and one of the assault formations was the 1st Battalion, Prince of Wales's Own Civil Service Rifles. They were told that they were to attack at 0550 hours on 15 September and that they would be supported by two tanks instead of having an artillery barrage. At zero hour the tanks had not arrived and the attack went in without them – and without artillery support – resulting in many casualties. The unit history records:

"Meanwhile the tanks had not shown up – though one of them later on, after nearly smashing up Battalion Headquarters, got stuck in a communication trench and materially interfered with the removal of the wounded. Its pilot got out and going into Battalion Headquarters asked the Commanding Officer where High Wood was. The CO's reply is not recorded. The other tank eventually got into action somewhere in front of D Company's objective and then caught fire."

Although High Wood was won by mid-day, only 150 men of the Battalion reached their objective.

Continue a further eighteen paces and stop on the right.

• 20th Battalion Royal Fusiliers Tree/30.8 miles/5 minutes/Map H23/GPS: 50.03695 2.78574
The oak tree at the edge of the wood was planted in memory of the battalion ('The Public Schools Battalion') who were killed here on 20 July 1916.

Continue a further 100m and stop on the right.

• Glasgow Highlanders' Cairn/31.1 miles/5 minutes/ Map H22/GPS: 50.03807 2.78355

Memorial to 47th (London) Division, High Wood

The cairn commemorates the unsuccessful attack of 9th (Glasgow Highlanders) Battalion, Highland Light Infantry of 15 July 1916. Privately erected by Alex Aiken, (he brought much of the material out in the boot of his car) whose book *Courage Past* deals with the attack, it was inaugurated in November 1972. One hundred and ninety two stones from near Culloden individually commemorate each man killed and form a cairn of 5ft 7in tall, the minimum recruiting height for the battalion. The square stone on top was a Glasgow paving stone. The Gaelic inscription reads, 'Just here, Children of the Gael went down shoulder to shoulder on 15 July 1916.'

Continue to the cemetery on the left and park.

Memorial Tree to Public Schools Bn, 20th R Fusiliers, High Wood.

Glasgow Highlanders Cairn, High Wood

• *London Cemetery & Extension/31.4 miles/15 minutes/Map H21/OP/*
GPS: 50.03880 2.78235

The original cemetery was begun in September 1916 by the burial of forty-seven men 'in a large shell hole' by 47th Division, and was later enlarged by the addition of other graves to make a total of 101. That area is immediately to the left of the main entrance, where there is also a **Memorial to seventy-eight NCOs** and men, the locations of whose graves are not known. The Cemetery was further extended after the Armistice and is the third largest on the Somme, containing over 3,330 graves of which more than 3,100 are unknown. There is also a World War II plot in the cemetery.

Death makes no political distinction, and just as Herbert Asquith, Liberal MP and Prime Minister, lost a son on the Somme (qv), so did Arthur Henderson, leader of the Labour Party at the time (and who was to win the Nobel Peace Prize in 1934). **Captain**

Entrance loggia, London CWGC Cem, High Wood

David Henderson of the Middlesex Regiment, attached to 19th London Battalion, was killed in High Wood on 15 September 1916, aged 27 and is buried here.

Go to the far end of the cemetery behind the main hedge and stand in the left-hand corner facing forward.

The key to the German positions on the British right flank was the high ground here of the Longueval-Bazentin-Pozières Ridge on which the woods and villages had been fortified. You are now standing in a German goal, with your goal posts the woods of Bazentin and Delville. Just beyond the left-hand edge of Bazentin-le-Grand Wood is the northern end of Caterpillar Valley and it was from there that the cavalry came forward in the attack of 14 July, heading for the goalkeeper. Very few made it to the net. To the extreme left and slightly behind you is Delville Wood. Now looking clockwise you can see: Longueval Church spire at the edge of Delville Wood; Caterpillar Valley Cemetery on the ridge; the unusual bulk of Montauban Church on the skyline; Bazentin-le-Grand Wood slightly right of straight ahead and to the right the wireless mast at Pozières Windmill. Looking straight ahead between the woods there is a valley some 300m away and it was there that the Cameron Highlanders formed up for the September attack on High Wood. To the left another, shallower, valley runs between you and Delville Wood towards High Wood and it was up that valley that the Deccan Horse charged in July.

Continue on the D6 to Martinpuich.

Just before the village **Martinpuich CWGC Cemetery** is signed to the left and in the local cemetery on the corner are five beautifully tended CWGC graves, one group of three (including **Able Seaman J. Wilkinson**, Drake Battalion, RND, age 21, 25 March 1918 'who was buried by the enemy in Martinpuich German Cemetery No 1 but whose grave is now lost') and two single graves.

Continue to the crossroads and turn right onto the D6E signed to le Sars. Stop at the gateway beyond the church in front of the Mairie/school.

• 47th Division/German Memorial/32.8 miles/5 minutes/Map H20/19/GPS: 50.04998 2.76453

The village was taken by the 15th (Scottish) Division on the afternoon of 15 September 1916. The 47th Division Memorial Arch (with battle honours) also comprises the covered loggia behind it and to the left. The school playground was presented to the village by Lt Gen Sir George Gorringe on Sunday 13 September 1925 when the 47th Div Memorial Gateway was unveiled. On the local Memorial behind the gateway is a German Memorial

Memorial Porch to 47th (London) Division, Martinpuich

Plaque to the 109th RIR. The site was beautifully renovated by the CWGC in 2014.

Return to the crossroads and go straight over. At the fish pond turn left signed to Bazentin. Stop just before the next fork to the right.

• Martinpuich Bunker/33.1miles/5 minutes/Map H17/GPS: 50.04689 2.75870

The large, well-preserved bunker is in the field to the right.

Turn round and return to the crossroads. Turn left on the D6 signed to Courcelette. Note the World War I pickets holding up the wire fences in this area. Cross the D929 and continue along the D107 about 500 yards to a small turning to the left.

Martinpuich bunker

[N.B.] By turning left here along Rue Chapitre and continuing to the Church in Courcelette, in the green opposite, beside the local *Poilu* Memorial, a brick Memorial to the **15th Bn Can Inf (48th Highlanders of Canada)** may be seen **(Map H9a, GPS: 50.05.888 2.74809)**. It commemorates an action of 18 September 1916 by the 3rd Can Inf Bde, consisting of 13th, 14th, 15th and 16th Bns of Canadian Infantry. The 15th Bn were tasked to take the first objective, the Front Line which ran some 400 yards, parallel to the Grande Rue, north of the church.

Memorial to 15th Bn, Can Inf (48th Highlanders), Courcelette

Continue to the cemetery on the right.

• Adanac Military CWGC Cemetery & Maple Leaf Gate/35.3 miles/10 minutes/Map H3/GPS: 50.07415 2.74349

The gate to this cemetery contains the Maple Leaf emblem, indicating that it is first and foremost a Canadian cemetery (its name is Canada backwards!) and indeed it contains 1,071 Canadian burials in its 3,172 graves (1,712 of which are unidentified). Two **Victoria Cross winners** lie here. One is **Piper James Cleland Richardson** of the 16th Bn, Manitoba Regiment, the Canadian Scottish (Richardson was born in Scotland). On 8 October 1916 Richardson's company was held up by very strong wire at Regina

Adanac Military CWGC Cemetery, Courcelette

Trench and came under intense fire about 500 yards south of here. Piper Richardson, who obtained permission to play the company 'over the top' strode up and down outside the wire playing his pipes, which so inspired the company that the wire was rushed and the position captured. Later the piper was detailed to take back a wounded comrade and some prisoners, but after proceeding some distance he insisted on turning back to recover his pipes which he had left behind. He was never seen again. Richardson's inspiring playing recalls other pipers who performed similar morale-raising acts: Piper Laidlaw at Loos (who also won the VC); and Lord Lovat's Piper, Bill Millin, who piped the Commandos onto the shores of Normandy at SWORD Beach on 6 June 1944. The other **VC is Sgt Samuel Forsyth** of the New Zealand Engineers, att, 2nd Bn, Auckland Regt who, on 24 August 1918, led attacks on three machine-gun positions in Loupart Wood (qv) and took the crews prisoner. He was later wounded attempting to get support from a tank that was then put out of action, so he led the tank crew and some of his own men in an attack which caused the enemy machine gun to retire and enabled the advance to continue. At this moment Forsyth was killed by a sniper.

Turn round, return to the crossroads, turn right onto the D929 and stop 100m later at the memorial on the right.

• Canadian Memorial, Courcelette/36.9 miles/5 minutes/Map H10/GPS: 50.05376 2.7521

The village of Courcelette is some 700 yds north west of this Memorial which commemorates the actions of the Canadian Corps from September to November 1916. It was the 2nd (Canadian) Division, formed in England in April 1915, that drove the Germans from this area on 15 September, aided by a tank called "Crème de Menthe" that evicted the enemy from a sugar factory nearby. This simple octagonal block of Canadian granite is the standard memorial erected on all sites where the Canadians performed with exceptional valour on the Western Front, after it was deemed that the winning design in a competition for a Canadian Memorial – the Vimy Ridge pylons – and the runner up – the Brooding Soldier at Vancouver Corner

Canadian Memorial, Courcelette

– were too expensive to duplicate. The area around the memorial was re-landscaped in 1985-6 following a severe winter in 1984 which damaged trees and shrubs. The Canadian assault was, broadly, towards you from the west along the line of the road. The Thiépval Memorial and the Pozières wireless mast can be seen from here.

> *Return to your car and continue to the Pozières wireless mast and park.*

There are two memorials here. The Tank Corps one is on the left of the road, the Australian one to the right of the road.

Heavy tank Mk IV

Gun-carrier tank Mk I

Medium A Whippet

Tank Memorial, Pozières. To the left the WWI tanks at each corner. The wireless mast to the right is a useful landmark

Heavy tank Mk V

• Tank Corps Memorial/37.8 miles/5 minutes/Map H16/GPS: 50.04472 2.73626

There is a CGS/H Signboard about tanks here. It was at the battle of Flers-Courcelette, Part 4 of the Somme offensive, that tanks went into action for the first time. This obelisk, with its four superb miniature tanks, is a memorial to the fallen of the Corps, and its fence is constructed from tank 6-pounder gun barrels and early driving chains. This point was one of several where the tanks mustered ready for the attack after assembling behind Trônes Wood on the night of 14 September.

Walk (carefully!) across the road.

• Australian Memorial, Pozières Windmill/RB/37.8 miles/5 minutes/ Map H15

The ruins of the old windmill can still be seen sticking out of the mound of earth. This was the high point of the Pozières Ridge, so bitterly and bloodily fought for by the Australians. Over the month of August when Haig, pushed by Joffre, was indulging in piecemeal attacks, it was the 1st, 2nd and 4th Australian divisions that hammered towards the high ground of the ridge along the Albert-Bapaume road (the one you are driving along). In forty-five days the Australians launched nineteen attacks and lost 23,000 officers and men.

Australia had immediately supported Britain when the war broke out and recruiting started on 10 August 1914. Forces were raised locally through the State Military HQ

Australian Memorial at the site of the Windmill, Pozières

and, thus, the Australian Imperial Forces (AIF) consisted almost entirely of Pals Battalions – albeit the geographical areas were much larger than in Britain. This local recruiting was followed after the war by local settling. The Australian Government had a number of programmes to help returned soldiers, including offering specially selected land areas to those prepared to settle them. These were administered by State Governments, supported by a Federal Grant of £625 per settler. One such soldier settlement area was around Stanthorpe, 104 miles south-west of Brisbane in south-east Queensland, and the intensity of their battle experience is reflected in the names of the new settlements that the Australian Pals founded – Pozières, Amiens, Bapaume … all joined by a railway line that had been opened in 1920 by the Prince of Wales. It had been a gruelling tour for the Prince, lasting 210 days, visiting over 200 towns and places and travelling 46,000 miles. One of his main aims

Water Tower, Pozières

was to 'mingle with war veterans.' Their boisterous obsession with touching the future Edward VIII left him 'black and blue'.

The site was bought by the Australian War Memorial Board. There are Information Boards beside the mill site whose inscription reads,

"The ruin of Pozières windmill which lies here was the centre of the struggle in this part of the Somme Battlefields in July and August 1916. It was captured on 4 August by the Australian troops who fell more thickly on this ridge than on any other battlefield of the war."

In fact, Australian casualties over the whole war were 215,000, which as a percentage of troops in the field, was the highest of any Allied force. Ten days after the Aussies left the Somme the tank made its debut. The Memorial was re-landscaped by the CWGC in 1986 and in 1993 a **Ross Bastiaan bronze Plaque**, sponsored by the Returned Services League, was unveiled by Lt Gen J. C. Grey, Chief of the General Staff.

It was behind the Windmill that **Australia's first VC winner of WW1** (gained at Courtney's Post in Gallipoli on 20 May 1915 as a Corporal) won the MC on 7 August 1916. He was perhaps Australia's most famous and best-loved soldier, **Albert Jacka** (qv) – obstreperous, outspoken to his superiors, non-conformist, popular and always ready to settle a dispute with his fists. Jacka led a platoon (known as 'Jacka's Mob') which was reduced by a fierce German attack to a mere seven men. These he launched at the 60 or so Germans opposing them and although two of the Australians were soon killed and every other man wounded (Jacka himself was hit seven times) he continued brandishing his revolver and personally killed at least twelve of the enemy. This brave action inspired his fellows, many in the process of being taken prisoner, to counter attack. Many believe that Jacka's action was worthy of a bar to his VC. C.E.W. Bean described it as 'the most dramatic and effective act of individual audacity in the history of the AIF.' Fearfully wounded and disfigured, Jacka was sent to the UK to convalesce but returned to his battalion in December, promoted to Lieutenant (he would never rise higher than Captain) in time to take part in the Bullecourt action (qv) where he won a Bar to his MC on 9 April '17.

It was also the scene of an incident on 5 August 1916 during which **Captain Percy Herbert Cherry** of the 26th AIF fired at a German officer who replied with a simultaneous shot. Cherry's helmet deflected the shot but he mortally wounded the German, who asked him to post the letters in his pocket. This he agreed to do. There is now a project by a group of local enthusiasts known as Le Digger-Cote (www.digger-pozieres.org/thediggercote160.html) to immortalise the scene in a sculpture as a memorial to all the heroic Australian actions that took place here, and funds are being raised. Cherry vies with Jacka for awards. He had the MC and was awarded the VC posthumously for his actions at Lagnicourt on 26 March 1917. He was killed by a shell the following day.

The **Pozières Remembrance Association**, instigated by Australian Barry Gracey, is dedicated to getting the outstanding efforts of the Australians at Pozières as much recognition as, say, Gallipoli and Villers Bretonneux. Their major project is a Memorial Park, hoped to be created in time for the Centenary, situated from the water tower to behind the Windmill and thence to the Courcelette Road. For details, see www.Pozieresremembered.com.au Barry is raising funds by the sale of bricks inscribed with your name (at $Aus 50 each) with the help of his Suzuki-sponsored van or via the website.

Continue downhill into Pozières.

The water tower on the right bears a mural of an ANZAC's head with sunburst, a poppy and the Victoria Cross emblem with the names of **VC winners Blackburn, Castleton, Clarke, Cook, Leak, O'Meara and Short**. Beside it is a stone **Memorial to Pilote-Aviateur Gustave Lemoine**, *Légion d'Honneur, Médaille Militaire*, holder of the world altitude record on 28 September 1933 (1,366m), who was killed in an accident at Pozières on 1 October 1934 in a Potez. The village entry sign has the figure of an ANZAC attached.

Turn left at the first turning after the water tower and stop at the memorial at the corner of the first turning left.

On the left is the welcoming **Butterworth Farm B & B**, run by Mayor Bernard Delattre and his wife, Marie. Tel: +(0)3 22 74 04 47. E-mail: contact@butterworth-cottage.com Website: www.butterworth-cottage.com B & B or self-catering. 4 en-suite rooms. Opposite is a Memorial.

• *Butterworth Memorial/38.2 miles/5 minutes/Map H17a/GPS: 50.04084 2.73102*

Instigated by M Delattre it is engraved to **George Sainton Kaye Butterworth**, 1885-1916, a talented composer. Son of Sir Alexander Butterworth, he studied at Eton and Trinity College before attending the Royal College of Music and worked with Cecil Sharp and Vaughan Williams, both of whom influenced him strongly. He was an active member of

Butterworth Memorial, Pozières

the English Dance and Folk Music Society. His best known works are his song cycle *The Shropshire Lad*, from A. E. Housman's poems, and the lyrical *Banks of Green Willow*, which both show his love of simple folk melodies and his sensitive scorings for strings. At the outbreak of War, Butterworth enlisted in the ranks of the Duke of Cornwall's Light Infantry and in November was posted to the 13th Battalion, the Durham Light Infantry as a 2nd Lieutenant. He served in the Armentières sector in early 1915 and was soon promoted to Lt. In July 1916 he was recommended (for the second time) for the MC and later for a third time on the night of his death. On 1 August the Brigade went up to the line for the fourth time in a month and it was at this stage that the trench that was officially named for him was dug between the British and German line. The Brigade made two attacks on 4 August, one a failure, the other successful. The second, led by Butterworth from the trench that bears his name, was a 'bombing' attack and 100yds were gained. During the attack Butterworth, 'a brilliant musician in times of war and an equally brilliant soldier in times of stress', according to his Brigadier, Page-Croft, was shot dead by a bullet through the head, a month after his 31st birthday. His hastily buried body was subsequently lost, and Butterworth is commemorated on the Thiépval Memorial (qv). It is a hauntingly beautiful experience to take a small tape recorder with a cassette of one of Butterworth's works, find his name on the Memorial, and quietly listen to the music under the awe-inspiring arches of Lutyen's massive creation.

A small ceremony is held at the Memorial on 5 August when members of the Butterworth family usually attend.

> **[N.B.]** The approximate area of **Butterworth Trench** may be found by continuing to a small crossroads **(GPS: 50.03674 2.74790)**. The end of the trench is located up a track to the left under a line of pylons. The actual site of the trench then goes to the left along cultivated **PRIVATE FARMLAND**. Butterworth was killed at the northern end.

Return to the main road and turn left. Continue. At the crossroads (signed right to Thiepval) turn left and continue to a track to the left signed to Sunken Road and 2nd Canadian Cemetery. Walk (or drive if it is very dry) up the track.

Maple Leaf insignia on gateway to 2nd Canadian CWGC Cemetery, Pozières

• *Sunken Road (Map K2, GPS: 50.03215 2.73155) & 2nd Canadian (Map K4, GPS: 50.03214 2.73009) CWGC Cemeteries/39.0 miles/10 minutes*

Continue to the cemetery on the right.

Sunken Road CWGC Cemetery was one of the last cemeteries to be finished, it contains 214 burials, 148 of them Canadians, 61 Australians and 5 UK.

Walk across the track.

2nd Canadian CWGC Cemetery was also one of the last cemeteries to be completed. It has a bronze Maple Leaf Canadian insignia on the entry gate and the 2nd (Eastern Ontario) Battalion used it from the beginning of September 1916 to mid-October.

Return to the main D929 road and turn left. Immediately on the left is a café.

• *Tommy Café du Souvenir/Dugouts/Museum/39.5 miles/15 minutes/Map H14/RWC/GPS: 50.03864 2.72505*

This used to be the Burma Star Staging Post Café run for many years by the redoubtable Madame Brihier. Completely refurbished with kitchen, enlarged **restaurant**, it is run by Dominique Zanardi. It offers snacks and light meals throughout the day (coaches must book in advance.). The café walls are covered in wartime photographs, posters etc and in the large group room is a list of the killed and missing Australians with photos and a fascinating museum with artefacts, more photos and equipment. In the garden is a recreated trench/dugout system, complete with uniformed models, many weapons and artefacts, British and German (from the superb collection of M Carreele Antoine de Mortemer) and sound effects (admission fee payable).

Open: 1000-1800 every day. Tel: +(0)3 22 74 82 84. E-mail: cafe@letommy.com

Recreated Dugout, Tommy Café, Pozières

• *End of Itinerary Two*

ITINERARY THREE

• **Itinerary Three** starts at Amiens Cathedral and heads east across the battlefields of 1918, via the Australian National Memorial at Villers Bretonneux. It continues east into the French sector of the 1916 fighting and then north behind the German second line to the Butte de Warlencourt and ends in Bapaume.

• **The Route: Amiens** – Cathedral, station area, French National Cemetery, St Acheul; Longueau railway; Longueau British CWGC Cemetery; Glisy Airport; the 'Nearest Point to Amiens'; first Tank Versus Tank Battle; Adelaide CWGC Cemetery; Villers Bretonneux – Museum, school, *Mairie*, marker stone, Australian National Memorial and Interpretation Centre ; Corbie – Church Congreve Plaque, Communal Cemetery & Extension, Colette Statue; Von Richthofen Crash Site; Australian 3rd Div Memorial; Beacon CWGC Cemetery; 58th (London) Div Memorial; Chipilly CWGC Cemetery; Bray – Côte 80 French National Cemetery, German Cemetery; P'tit Train Terminus, Froissy; Proyart – miniature Arc de Triomphe, German Cemetery; Col Rabier Private Memorial; Foucaucourt Local Cem; Estrées - Lt Col Puntous Memorial; Assevillers New CWGC Cemetery; Hem Farm CWGC Cemetery; 'HR' Private Memorial; Maurepas 1st RI Memorial; V. Hallard Private Memorial; Charles Dansette Private Memorial; Maurepas – French National Cemetery, Memorial; Combles – Communal Cemetery Extension, Guards Cemetery; Guards Memorial, Lesboeufs; Capt Meakin Private Memorial; Gueudecourt Newfoundland Memorial; AIF Grass Lane CWGC Cemetery; SOA Lt Col R. B. Bradford VC; German Memorial, Le Sars; Butte de Warlencourt, WFA & other Memorials; Warlencourt CWGC Cemetery; Bapaume.

• **Extra Visits** are suggested to: Marcelcave French National Cemetery; Vaire Com Cemetery; Capt Mond/Lt Martyn Private Memorial; Le Hamel Australian Memorial Park/RB Plaque; Heilly Station CWGC Cemetery, Private Memorial to L Cpl O'Neill;, Bray- French National Cemetery, Grove Town, Bray Military, Bray Vale and Bray Hill CWGC Cemeteries; Site of Carey's Force Action; Heath CWGC Cemetery; Ruined Village of Fay and Memorial Plaques; Vermandovillers - German Cemetery, RB Plaque Lt McCarthy VC, Capt Delcroix, Bourget & 158th RI, 1st Chass à Pied; Lihons - French National Cemetery, Polish Memorial, Murat Monument; Chaulnes – US & French Nurses, Ger 16th Bav Memorial; German Trenches, Bois de Wallieux; Fay – Ruined Village, Memorials to Capt Fontan, Abbé Champin & 41st RI 1940; French National Cemetery & Italian Memorial, Dompierre; Cléry - French National Cemetery/383rd RI Memorial; Gaston Chomet Private Memorial; Heumann/Mills/Torrance Private Memorial; 41st Div Memorial; Bull's Road CWGC Cemetery; French 17th/18th RIT Memorial; Achiet-le-Grand Comm Cem + Ext, Memorials to Pte C. Cox, VC and Lt Wainwright, RND, Loupart Wood.

[N.B.] The following sites are indicated:
Herleville – Plaque to Lt-Col Daly & 6th AIF; Logeast Wood - SOA T/Cdr Daniel Marcus Beak, VC; Courcelles le Comte – Mem to Pte Hugh McIver, VC, MM + Bar; Foucaucourt - French Cemetery; Herbécourt – Private Mem to Aspirant P. Maistrasse.

• **Planned duration**, without stops for refreshment or extra visits: **8 hours 45 minutes.**

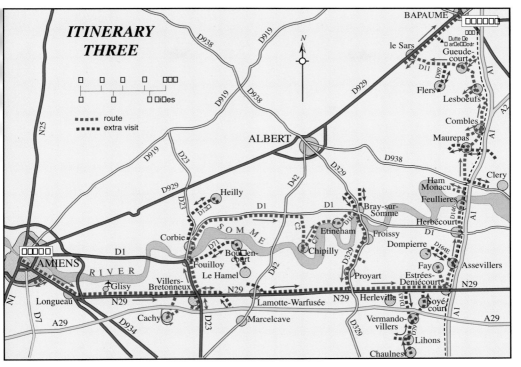

• **Total distance: 75.5 miles.**
**NOTE. This a long itinerary! You may want to split it into two and a convenient place
to break it would be before Assevillers New Brit Cem on page 245**

• *Amiens/ 0 miles/RWC/Map 1/6*

*Follow the brown signs **Parking Jacobin**, which is centrally placed and well signed from
main roads into the city, and park. **Set your milometer to Zero. Note that the time
spent in this walk is not included in the overall timing of the Itinerary.***

Walk following signs to the Cathedral. En route we advise visiting:

Amiens Métropole Tourist Office (GPS: 49.894579 2.301614).

This is in Place Notre Dame, The Cathedral Square. Tel: +(0)3 22 71 60 50 E-mail: ot@
amiens-metropole.com. Website: www.amiens-tourisme.com
Over the past few years the centre of Amiens has undergone a major 'facelift', with
many of the old façades, monuments and public buildings cleaned and renovated and
plenty of pleasant pedestrian shopping areas. It makes an ideal base for touring the
battlefield if you follow The Western Approach. This attractive city has just about every
category of Hotel and a variety of Restaurants in the Centre and in the suburbs and here
you can pick up helpful literature about these, restaurants and camping etc and local
events. See also the Tourist Information section at the end of the book.

Amiens Cathedral

Open daily: 1 April-30 Sept 0830-1815, 1 Oct-31 March 0830-1715. There is an entrance fee for guided visits. Autoguide in 3 languages €3.

On 28 August the Germans took Péronne and the citizens of Amiens trembled as the enemy fought their way towards the city, then occupied by Moroccan troops who were sent to take up defensive positions at Villers Bretonneux. A fierce fight was put up at Proyart, but the Germans counter-attacked and swept their way into Amiens on 31 August 1914, and, as recorded in a notice posted by the Mayor, M. Fiquet, seized twelve hostages from the town council, who, unlike German hostages taken in other towns, such as Senlis, were unharmed. They requisitioned half a million francs worth of supplies to sustain them on their drive towards Paris. Most of the force, after pulling down the French *tricolore* and hoisting the German flag on the town hall and raiding the safes in the savings bank, proceeded on their way *'nach Paris'*, but a garrison was installed with a town major on 9 September. A curfew was imposed, motor cars were requisitioned and 1,000 young men were sent into captivity. Following their defeat on the Marne, the Germans withdrew, and on 12 September the French Army, under General D'Amade, returned.

Although damaged by air attacks during the next $3^1/_2$ years, it was not until the German offensive of 1918 that the city again came under a major attack. From April to June it endured an almost continuous artillery bombardment, most citizens were evacuated and the Pope was asked by the Bishop to intercede with Kaiser Wilhelm to save the cathedral from the shelling. The Germans did not reach Amiens. They were stopped at Villers Bretonneux (see below). On 17 November 1918 a Mass of Thanksgiving was held here to celebrate the end of the war.

Designed by Robert de Luzarches, the Cathédrale de Notre Dame was begun in 1220 as a suitable resting place for the relic brought back from the Fourth Crusade by Walon of Sarton – the forehead and upper jaw of John the Baptist. It also houses relics of Saint Firmin, the first Bishop of Amiens. The cathedral is regarded as one of the finest and most harmonious examples of Gothic architecture and, at 142m long and 42m high, has the greatest volume. Ruskin called it 'the Bible of Amiens' as its stone façade and wooden choir stall contain so many carved pictures of Bible stories. Edward III attended mass in the cathedral on his way to the Battle of Crécy and Pte Frank Richards DCM, MM of the 2nd Bn, RWF, author of *Old Soldiers Never Die*, visited it in August 1914. Richards was 'very much taken up with the beautiful oil paintings and other objects of art inside. One old soldier who paid it a visit', he reported, however, 'said it would be a fine place to loot'. A huge restoration and cleaning project was started in 1994.

During World War I elaborate precautions were taken to protect the cathedral and its priceless art treasures – all portable items (including the stained glass, which was taken by firemen from Paris) being removed for safekeeping. The choir stalls were enclosed with reinforced concrete and sandbags (a precaution that was to be repeated in World War II), as was the principal façade. Although it received nine direct hits by bombs and some shells, none caused serious damage. During the Spring 1918 offensive, when the Germans reached Villers-Bretonneux and Amiens came under such fearsome bombardment that over 2,000 houses were hit and all the inhabitants fled, the British war correspondent Philip Gibbs described it under the moonlight, '… every pinnacle and bit of tracery shining like quicksilver, with magical beauty'.

It contains the standard **CWGC Memorial Plaque**, twenty-eight of which were designed for erection in cathedrals and important churches in Belgium and France by **Lt Col H.P. Cart de Lafontaine, FRIBA** and made by Hallward. The inscription was

Amiens Cathedral plaques: CWGC (left), US 6th Engineers, Carey's Force (right)

written by Rudyard Kipling. The Amiens Plaque was the first to be unveiled (by the Prince of Wales, then President of the CWGC) in July 1923. It is slightly different from the others, as it bears the Royal Coat of Arms alone and commemorates the war dead of Great Britain and Ireland who were killed in the diocese. The Plaques in other churches also bear the coats of arms of the Dominions. In Amiens there are separate **Plaques for Australia, Canada, Newfoundland, New Zealand, South Africa and the USA**. A replica of the Amiens Plaque is in the reception area of the CWGC headquarters in Maidenhead, and a similar Plaque is in Westminster Abbey. There is a **Private Memorial to Lt Raymond Asquith** (see Itinerary Two). There is also a **Plaque to General Debeney**, *'Vainqueur de la Bataille de Picardie'*, who liberated Montdidier on 8 August 1918.

Nearby are the ******Hotel Mercure Amiens Cathédrale**, 21/23 rue Flatters, Tel: +(0)3 22 80 60 60, e-mail: h7076@accor.com and the *****Ibis Styles Amiens Cathédrale**, 17-19 Place au Feurre, +(0)3 22 22 00 20, e-mail: h04780@accor-hotels.com. No restaurant but complimentary breakfast and tea/coffee.

Over the River Somme beyond the Cathedral is the picturesque old town of St Leu with some charming **Cafés and Restaurants**. Boats depart from the quay here for trips on the river, along which hospital barges plied from the battlefields, and the unique *Hortillonages* (see **Tourist Information**).

Return to your car, drive out of the car park and turn right along rue des Jacobins. Turn right following signs to SVCF Gare along rue des Otages to just short of the Station.

• *Amiens Station/Carlton-Belfort Hotel/0.5 miles/GPS:49.89054 2.30804*

The square in front of the station, now covered by a magnificent canopy, and with a car park underground, is the Place Alphonse Fiquet (named after the Mayor of Amiens in August 1914). The station and the 104m, twenty-six-floor-high tower opposite were both designed by August Perret. He gave his name to the Tower, which was once the tallest office building in the western hemisphere and still makes an excellent landmark. A residential block, the Tower is now surmounted by a 7metre high glass cube which is lit up at night, but is not yet open to visitors. The **Station Restaurant** was once renowned for its gourmet cuisine and the Prince of Wales lunched there after inaugurating the Thiépval Memorial on 31 July 1923. No stranger to Amiens, the young Grenadier Guards Officer had frequently dined in Amiens' popular restaurants when he had been in the Somme area during 1916. When the Prince himself could not get away, Raymond Asquith borrowed ... "Wales' excellent Daimler" and whipped off to Amiens where he "ate and drank a great deal of the best, slept in downy beds, bathed in hot perfumed water, and had a certain

The Carlton Hotel, Amiens.

amount of restrained fun with the very much once-occupied ladies of the town."

On the corner opposite the station is The ***Hotel Carlton**, Tel: +(0)3 22 97 72 22, e-mail: reservation@lecarlton.fr, excellent **Brasserie**) on the opposite left corner, once the famous Carlton-Belfort Hotel whose façade had altered little since 1918 until a change of ownership and a facelift in the late 1980s. Up to then a wartime sign, 'No Lorries Through Town' could still be discerned on the wall to the right of the main entrance on rue de Noyon. Apart from the wartime industrial activity which thrived in the city, its function as staff HQ's and its many temporary hospitals, Amiens was known chiefly as a place of relaxation for the Allied soldiers. Among **notables** who visited (and wrote about) the Carlton-Belfort were **Siegfried Sassoon, Edwin Campion Vaughan, Robert Graves, Cecil Lewis, and Mick Mannock**. Many famous war correspondents and artists were based at or visited Amiens, and other popular haunts were the Hôtel du Rhin (now no longer a hotel but the building may be seen by continuing down the rue de Noyon and turning left when you reach the Place René Goblet, with its World War II memorials to the Martyrs of Picardy and to General Leclerc). A regular patron of the Hôtel du Rhin in the days leading up to 'The Big Push' in 1916 was the cartoonist **Bruce Bairnsfather**, who was based at the administrative HQ at Montrelet as a lowly Staff Officer. The very name, he wrote, 'at once conveys visions to [one's] feverish mind of the gladdest nights that were then permissible'. **John Masefield**, commuting between Amiens and Albert while researching for his book on the Somme, 'dined on duck at the Rhin' at a dinner given by **Nevill Lytton** for the US Ambassador, Gen Bliss the US CGS and **Calvin Coolidge**, the future President.

Sir William Orpen, KBE, RA, describes, in his book *An Onlooker in France 1917-19*, how he dined at the Rhin with the Canadian **General Seely** and Prince Antoine de Bourbon, Seely's ADC. Orpen did a portrait of Seely while his friend, **Alfred Munnings**, who was official artist to the Canadian Cavalry Brigade, was painting an equestrian portrait of the prince. **Philip Gibbs** and other foreign correspondents found refuge there on the night when Amiens was under its greatest threat in April 1918. Bombs crashed around the hotel and the guests, who had voted whether to 'Stay or Go', stayed, but spent the night 'in the good cellars below the Hôtel du Rhin, full of wine casks and crates'. Outside raged 'a roaring furnace'. The Restaurant Godbert (62 Rue des Jacobins, but no longer a restaurant) was a favoured restaurant – 'The food was excellent and we all had money to burn', wrote **Dennis Wheatley**. But when he visited it on 1 April he found it rather like the *Marie Celeste*. It had closed suddenly when Amiens was being threatened and the Provost Marshal rounded up officers in all the main restaurants and ordered them back to their units at once. 'Every table in the big restaurant had been occupied and on all of them were plates with half-eaten courses. On some there were only hors d'oeuvres, on others pieces of omelette, fish, game, savouries and ice-cream that had melted. Beside the plates stood glasses mostly full or half-full of red or white wine.' Perhaps the Godbert's popularity had something to do with 'little Marguerite, [who]

Bairnsfather cartoon, 'A hopeless dawn. Just back off leave. Amiens is only 34 hours more in the train now. You know that because you can see the cathedral quite clearly.'

made eyes at all the pretty boys who craved for a kiss after the lousy trenches'. The poet, **Capt T. P. Cameron Wilson** of the Sherwood Foresters (commemorated on the Arras Memorial, qv), recalls the therapeutic effect of other waitresses with affection, including 'Yvonne, bringing sticky buns', in his delightful *Song of Amiens:*

> Lord! How we laughed in Amiens!
> For there were useless things to buy …
> And still we laughed in Amiens,
> As dead men laughed a week ago.
> What cared we if in Delville Wood
> The splintered trees saw hell below?
> We cared … We cared … But laughter runs
> The cleanest stream a man may know
> To rinse him from the taint of guns'.

Some encounters with the female population of Amiens were not so innocent. When most civilians evacuated in March 1918, a few enterprising girls remained. Wheatley found one such after his disappointment at the Godbert who had remained on duty

'Because I makes much money now there are few girls here'. It was not his first encounter with the oldest profession and he thoroughly recommended the dignified Madame Prudhomme's brothel. Such delights had been available in Amiens from the outbreak of war. **Private Frank Richards** had passed through the city on 13 August 1914 on his way to Mons. At that time **General French** was staying at the Hôtel Moderne (of which no trace remains) and Richards was billeted in a school, outside which was a fifty-deep queue of young ladies waiting to entertain the soldiers. Richards was 'sorry to leave' on 22 August. 'About the 16th August', he reports, he had 'attended a funeral of two of our airmen who had crashed; all the notabilities of the town were present.' This was the funeral of **Lt Perry and AM Parfitt**, who are buried in St Acheul Cemetery (see below). He also describes the bringing of Gen Grierson's body from the railway station to the Town Hall. He was Chief-of-Staff to General French. 'All sorts of stories were going around regarding his death. One was that he had been poisoned when eating his lunch on the train, but I believe now it was just heart failure from the strain and excitement. We took his body back to the railway station where a detachment of Cameron Highlanders took it down-country.' Lt-General Sir James Grierson, who was actually commander of II Corps, was buried in his home town of Glasgow.

The 64-year-old French Academician and novelist, **Pierre Loti** (the *nom de plume* of *Louis Marie Julien Viaud*), who had served with the French navy and who was put on the Reserve List in 1910, at the outbreak of war offered his services to General Galliéni as a liaison officer. On 2 October he recorded his 'first day of service as a liaison officer' in his diary and travelled through the early battlefields left by the Germans' rush for Paris. He lunched in Amiens before visiting GHQ at Doullens and returned there that night. He found the town criss-crossed with parades of soldiers, singing, holding flowers that the young girls had given them. He did not return to the area until 1917 (when he again visited Amiens) – after tireless negotiations with the Turks, the Belgians, in Alsace, in Salonika and many parts of the French line, during which work he kept up a prodigious writing output. This indefatigable patriot was eventually forced to retire, exhausted, at the age of 68 on 1 June 1918. Another famous French writer, **Jean Cocteau**, stayed at the Hôtel du Commerce (32 rue des Jacobins) while waiting to be posted to his hospital near Villers Bretonneux in June 1916 (qv). On the 25th of that month, the Fourth Army Commander took time off from his planning of the Big Push to attend the 167-strong annual Old Etonian Dinner in Amiens.

Return to your car. Continue. Turn right with the station on your left, onto the D1029 direction Longueau. Continue to the large school, Lycée Robert de Luzarches on the left and immediately turn right on the Boulevard de Pont Noyelles, which becomes Boulevard de Bapaume. Ignore the first sign to the left to the Cimetières de St Acheul and take the next left on Rue de Cottency. Continue to the cemetery and stop at the entrance on the left.

• French National Cemetery, St Acheul, Graves of Perry & Parfitt/ 2.0 miles/10 minutes/Map 1/7/GPS: 49.87799 2.31624

There is an Information Board (in French) just inside the entrance. In this French Cemetery, with its impressive memorial incorporating a sensitive sculpture of a mourning female figure, there are 2,739 French, 12 British, 10 Belgian and I Russian soldiers of World War I. The British plot, just inside the entrance and to the left, includes the graves of the first airmen to be killed on French soil – on 16 August 1914. They are **2nd Lt Evelyn W. Copland Perry**, RFC, age 23, the personal message on whose

Headstones of 2nd Lt E.W.C. Perry and Air Mech H.E. Parfitt, St Acheul French Cemetery

headstone reads, 'First on the roll of honour. All Glory to his name' and **Air Mechanic H. E. Parfitt**, age 21, the crew of a Royal Aircraft Factory BE8. Perry was the last of his Squadron (3 Sqn) to take off from Amiens airport at Glisy en route for Mons, when his machine stalled, plummeted to earth and burst into flames. Other contenders for 'first casualties' were Lt C. G. G. Bayly and 2nd Lt V. Waterfall of 5 Squadron RFC. They were killed on 22 August, six days later than Perry and Parfitt, but they were actually killed as a result of enemy action on a reconnaissance flight over Mons. They are buried in Tournai Communal Cemetery.

Return to the D1029 and turn right signed Longueau. Pass under a railway bridge, over a waterway which marks the junction of the Rivers Avre, Noye and Somme and then across a bridge over a large railway complex.

• Longueau/4 miles

This area became a major administrative centre, supplying the Somme battlefront and it was from it that railway engineers worked eastwards to repair the railways destroyed during the 1914 German advance and subsequent shelling.

Continue uphill on the D1029, passing the Hôtel de Ville of Longeau on the right, to a cemetery on the right by traffic lights at the junction of Rue des Alliés.

• *Longueau British CWGC Cemetery/4.9 miles/5 minutes/Map 1/8a/GPS: 49.86969 2.35986*

Unusually, the register box is incorporated at the bottom of the Cross of Sacrifice in this small Cemetery. It was begun in April 1918 when the British line was re-established before Amiens and used by fighting units and field ambulances until the following August. Plot IV was made after the Armistice by concentrating thirty-six graves from other cemeteries and the surrounding battlefield. Three US, one French and thirty-nine German graves have been removed. Now there are 68 soldiers, and airmen from the UK, 66 from Canada, 65 from Australia, 3 from the West Indies including 1 unidentified, and 14 unknown. Two graves were moved here as late as 1934.

Continue straight through a series of roundabouts (don't turn right following Autoroute signs) and follow signs to Villers Bretonneux/Péronne on the D1029.

You will pass near the group of hotels which includes the ******Novotel Hotel, ***Campanile and several other hotels** at this point (see **Tourist Information**).

Continue on the D1029 to the airfield on the left.

• *Glisy Airport/6.0 miles/Map 1/8/GPS: 49.86830 2.391212*

The area was used by the RFC/RAF as an airfield from the first days of the war and is currently both a commercial and club field. In the early 1980s a new bar complex was built and a Memorial to the **Red Baron** (originally destined to be erected at his crash site (qv) but rejected by local authorities) which used to stand in the old bar, went missing and is now thought to be in the hands of an Amiens collector. During the fighting of March 1918, **General Sir John Monash**, who commanded the Australian 3rd Division that played such a large part in the fighting up ahead at Villers Bretonneux, had his HQ in this vicinity. **Maurice Baring**, in *Flying Corps HQ, 1914-1918*, describes arriving at Amiens by train on 12 August where he was greeted with the scornful statement, *'Ah! les aviateurs, ils n'ont pas besoin d'aller à la guerre pour se faire casser la gueule ceux-là.'* ('Oh! airmen – that lot don't need to go to war to break their necks.'). 'After lunch' he went to the 'Aerodrome' and arranged supplies of 'water carts, … pegs for the aeroplanes, … a certain consignment of B.B. Oil', and then 'slept on our valises on the grass on the Aerodrome.' On the morning of the 13th, the first three squadrons of the RFC's total complement of four squadrons arrived, **Harvey-Kelly** (see also Vert Galand on page 61) being the first to land in his BE2A. They had taken off from a field above the White Cliffs of Dover, on the road to St Margaret's Bay. Today a Memorial stands at the entrance to that field, with the inscription, 'The Royal Flying Corps contingent of the 1914 British Expeditionary Force, consisting of Nos 2, 3, 4 and 5 Squadrons flew from this field to Amiens between 13 and 15 August 1914.' In the afternoon **Prince Murat** (qv) reported as their Liaison Officer and on 14 August **Sir John French** arrived to look at the squadrons. The airfield was also used during World War II.

To commemorate the WW1 Centenary, an important airshow was held here in 2014.

Continue (noting that the road runs due east), crossing the railway twice in the next 5 miles.

Note the tall column of the Australian Memorial which becomes more and more clearly visible to the left along this road.

Continue downhill past a wood on the right to a small crossroads with the D523. Turn right and stop as near to the crossing as practical.

• *The Nearest Point to Amiens/10.8 miles/5 minutes/OP/GPS: 49.86974 2.49029*

The German attack on 21 March 1918 forced the British and French armies into a hurried retreat, troops pouring towards you on their way back to Amiens. Up ahead of you on the crest is the village of Villers Bretonneux and it was not until 28 March that the German advance (which had begun some 50km away at St Quentin) was stopped 3km east of the village – i.e. the other side to where you are now – mainly due to the efforts of the 1st Cavalry Division. Short of troops, and with Amiens in great danger, Haig looked 100km north to Flanders and ordered down the Australians. Thirty-six hours after the German onslaught began again at dawn on 4 April it seemed as if Villers Bretonneux would be taken, but Lt Col H. Goddard commanding the 9th (Australian) Brigade, newly based in the town, ordered the 36th Battalion forward in a bayonet charge. The advancing Germans broke and withdrew and, before they could attack again, one of their aerial heroes, the 'Red Baron' (qv) was killed.

By 10 April, Haig knew the situation was critical and he begged Foch to take over some portion – any portion – of the front held by British and Commonwealth forces, stretched to the point of exhaustion. Foch agreed to move up a large French force towards Amiens. The next day (12 April), still waiting for them to arrive, a worried Haig issued his famous 'Order of the Day':

"To all Ranks of the British Forces in France. Three weeks ago today the Enemy began his terrific attacks against us on a 50 mile front …. Many amongst us are tired …. There is no other course open to us but to fight it out! Every position must be held to the last man: there must be no retirement. With our backs to the wall, and believing in the justice of our cause, each one of us must fight to the end…."

In the dawn mist of 24 April the German 4th (Guards) Division and the 228th Division, supported by thirteen tanks, tried again. It was to be one of the first actions in which the Germans had used tanks and **the first action in which tank fought tank**.

This time the enemy got into and through the village, despite the determined resistance by 2nd West Yorkshire Regiment at the railway station, so that by 2000 hours that evening the front line ran at right angles to the D1029 along the D523 (where you now are) across your front to your left and right. It was the nearest point to Amiens that the Germans reached. That evening at 2200 hours the Australian 13th Brigade counter-attacked in the area on the right but was caught in fierce fire by German machine guns of 4th (Guards) Division set up in the wood to your right – Abbey Wood.

In a remarkable action which won him the **VC, Lt C. W. K. Sadlier** led a small party into the wood and destroyed six machine-gun positions, thus allowing the attack to continue. An hour later the Australian 15th Brigade, in the light of flames from the burning château in the village, attacked in a pincer movement through the area beyond the railway line to your left. After the war Sadlier played an important role in the Returned Services League.

Continue on the D523 towards Cachy.
In springtime the banks and woods here are carpeted with celandine and cowslips.
Immediately before the motorway bridge turn sharp left towards Villers Bretonneux. Continue and pull in and stop just before the de-restriction 70 sign on the right with Villers Bretonneux church on the skyline ahead.

• First Tank versus Tank Battle Monument, Cachy/12.2 miles/10 minutes/ Map 1/14/GPS: 49.86060 2.49667

Stop here before visiting the memorial to read the following account and to see where the action took place.

The historic tank versus tank action took place in the fields to your left and to your right on the slope up towards Villers Bretonneux on the morning of 24 April 1918. At 0345 hours German artillery began an HE and gas shell barrage on British positions in the town and on the feature on which the Australian National Memorial now sits. The attack began at 0600 hours and, led by thirteen A7V tanks, the Germans inflicted heavy casualties on the East Lancashires of 8th Division in the area around the railway station. By 0930 four A7Vs were making their way across the fields towards where you now are. Earlier that morning three British Mark IV tanks, lagered in the wood through which you drove from the D1029, were ordered to move to this area forward of Cachy. They too were moving this way at about 0930. Commanding one of the British tanks was **Lt Frank Mitchell** and in his book, *Tank Warfare*, he told what happened:

> "Opening a loophole I looked out. There, some three hundred yards away, a round squat-looking monster was advancing, behind it came waves of infantry, and farther away to the left and right crawled two more of these armed tortoises …. So we had met our rivals at last. Suddenly a hurricane of hail pattered against our steel wall, filling the interior with myriads of sparks and flying splinters … the Jerry tank had treated us to a broadside of armour-piercing bullets … then came our first casualty … the rear Lewis gunner was wounded in both legs by an armour-piercing bullet which tore through our steel plate … the roar of our engine, the nerve-wracking rat-tat-tat of our machine guns blazing at the Bosche infantry and the thunderous boom of the 6 pounders all bottled up in that narrow space filled our ears with tumult while the fumes of petrol and cordite half stifled us."

Mitchell's tank attempted two shots at one of the A7Vs. Both hit but seemed ineffective, then the gunner tried again 'with great deliberation and hit for the third time. Through a loophole I saw the tank heel over to one side then a door opened and out ran the crew. We had knocked the monster out.'

When the war was over, Mitchell, tongue in cheek, recalling that the tanks were called 'landships', and that naval crews are entitled to prize money for sinking enemy ships, applied for prize money for himself and his crew for having knocked out an enemy 'landship'. The War Office descended into a puzzled silence and then turned the application down.

Before the day was over seven of the new British Whippet tanks charged into the German infantry and the advance stopped. The Germans, however, were now poised on the high ground. If Amiens were to be saved they had to be moved.

Just after dawn on 25 April the two attacking Australian brigades met on the other side of the town, taking almost 1,000 prisoners. It was ANZAC Day and Amiens was safe. After the action the

Tank versus Tank Memorial, Cachy

Australians recovered one of two German tanks that had broken down and shipped it to Brisbane as a souvenir. The village was almost obliterated by the fighting and so great was the destruction that a sign was put up in the ruins proclaiming, 'This was Villers-Bretonneux'.

Walk to the bottom of the hill – it is dangerous to park by the Memorial.

On the left is the small **Memorial to the Tank Action** with a caption in three languages, English, French and German, stating that 'Here on 24 April 1918 the first ever tank battle took place between German and British armour.'

Return to your car, turn round, return to the D1029, turn right and continue to the CWGC Cemetery on the left.

• *Adelaide Cemetery/14 miles/10 minutes/Map 1/13a/ABT3/GPS: 49.87024 2.49791*

Note: 'Australian Battlefield Tour (ABT) Point 3' – from Villers Bretonneux a numbered 'Australian' tour may be followed using a route described in a commemorative pack issued by the Office of Australian War Graves and available at Villers Bretonneux Museum.

The cemetery, which has the most delightful and varied array of plants, was started in early June 1918 and used by 2nd and 3rd Australian Divisions. By the Armistice it contained ninety graves and then 864 other graves were concentrated here. There are now over 500 Australians, 365 soldiers and airmen from the UK, including **Lt Col S. G. Latham, DSO, MC and Bar**, age 46, killed on 24 April while commanding the 2nd Battalion the Northampton Regiment, and 22 Canadians. The 113th Australian Infantry Brigade, the 49th, 50th, 51st and 52nd Australian Infantry Battalions and the 22nd DLI all at one time erected wooden crosses here to commemorate their dead in the actions of Villers Bretonneux. In Plot III, Row M, Grave 13 is a most unusual headstone. It records the fact that 'The remains of an Unknown Soldier lay in this grave for 75 years. On 2 November 1993 they were exhumed and now rest in the Tomb of the **Unknown Australian Soldier** at the Australian War Memorial in Canberra.'

Continue, again crossing the railway, and 800m later there is on the left a

Original grave of the Australian Unknown Soldier, Adelaide CWGC Cem

• *Memorial to the Villers Bretonneux Déportés of WW2/14.6 miles/GPS: 49.87059 2.51192.*

It is in front of the **Site of the Villers Bretonneux Château** whose flames lit up the attack of the Australian 15th Brigade on the night of 24 April. After the War it was used as the HQ of the Australian Graves Registration Unit. Local opinion has it that after the war the owner of the château collected a considerable sum of money in reparations and decided to spend it elsewhere. When Henry Williamson returned to the Somme in 1929, he met in an estaminet in Albert the 'son of a millionaire, who had made his "pile" since the war by buying for "cash down" the sites of shattered buildings, and rebuilding with the generous reparation grants later on'. The speculator himself then owned over fifty houses, shops, and three motor cars.

The ruins of the château were demolished in November 2004 as they were deemed to be dangerous. A housing estate has now been built on the site.

Continue some 300m to the crossroads with the D23 signed left to the Australian Villers Bretonneux Memorial. Turn right along the rue Maurice Seigneurgens. Turn right at the first crossroads along rue Driot to the next crossroads. Go straight over. The road is now called rue Victoria. Stop at the school on the left.

• Villers Bretonneux School & Franco-Australian Museum/15.4 miles/20 minutes/WC/Map 1/15/16/ABT1/GPS: 49.86625 2.51722

A Plaque on the school wall records that the building was 'the gift of the children of Victoria, Australia, to the children of Villers Bretonneux as a proof of their love and good will towards France.' 1,200 of their fathers, uncles and brothers gave their lives in the recapture of the village on 24 April 1918. Inside the school is a permanent exhibition of photographs of Australia. The Memorial obelisk in front of the school records the story of the school building project, from the visit by the President of the Australian Council on 25 April 1921, to its inauguration on 25 May 1927. The left wing of the school is marked 'Salle Victoria'. This hall is panelled in wood, surmounted by individually illuminated carvings of Australian fauna by Australian artist J.E.F. Grant. Large photographs of Australian scenes, donated in 2003, hang above. A Plaque by the entrance records the dedication of the Museum – which is on the top floor – and which

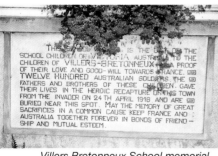

Villers Bretonneux School memorial plaque on the wall

Above - *Bronze model of A7V Tank in the Museum*

Interior of Villers Bretonneux Museum

Entrance to the Franco-Australian Museum, Villers Bretonneux

was founded by Marcel Pillon in 1975. It was then taken over by the Franco-Australian Association and completely refurbished. It was then run for them by the late M Jean-Pierre Thierry, for many years the Research Officer at the Historial, until his death in 2007 and has a centre of documentation, with a 35-seat video room showing Australian documentaries in English or French and a small book stall. The collection now includes some superb photographs, personal items, ephemera, artefacts, a model of a German A7V tank, (the type which took part in the Tank v Tank battle (qv), was later excavated near the village and transported to Wellington). Only 20 tanks of the A7V, with a crew of 18-20 people and a 57mm Maxim gun and 6 machine guns, were made in 1916. The model was made in 2004 by Franco-Aus Assoc Members Etienne Denys and Bernard Vaquez. Here too is the flag used to drape the coffin of the Australian Unknown Soldier during rehearsals for the ceremony of removing it to Australia. The family of kangaroos once housed in the Town Hall have taken up residence at the entrance here. Further improvements have been made throughout the Museum (re-opened in January 2015). Open: Nov-Feb: Mon-Sat 0930-1630; March-Oct: Mon-Sat 0930-1730. **Tel:** +(0)3 22 96 80 79. E-mail: neuf.fr. www.museeaustralien.com Closed: Sun and French public holidays. Annual closing: last week Dec-first week Jan. Entrance fee payable.

Return to the crossroads and turn left on rue de Melbourne. Stop at the large Ton Hall on the right in Place Charles de Gaulle.

• *Villers Bretonneux Town Hall/RB/15.6 miles/5 minutes/GPS: 49.86831 2.51755*

The main château in the centre of the town was also destroyed and it has been replaced by the Town Hall and memorial garden on the right. In front of it is a **Ross Bastiaan bronze tablet** unveiled on 30 August 1993 by the Governor General of Australia, the Hon Bill Hayden. Inside the Town Hall is a room devoted to the various connections between the village and Australia – Villers Bretonneux is twinned with Robinvale in Australia and there are still many joint activities.

Robinvale was named after **Lt Robin Cuttle** from Ultima, Victoria, Australia. In 1914 Robin volunteered but was inexplicably rejected. Not to be deterred he went to England and applied to join the RFC. Again he was rejected - because of his size: he was 6ft 8ins tall. So he joined the RFA in July 1916 and served as a Lieutenant throughout the Somme battles. Whilst attached to the 9th Scots Guards at the Butte de Warlencourt in November 1916 he was awarded the MC when he assisted in capturing many German guns. In 1917 he reapplied to join the RFC and by early 1918 was flying over France with C flight of 49th Squadron as an observer. Whilst returning from a reconnaissance and bombing mission on 9 May 1918 his plane was shot down. His body was never found and in 1923 members of his family came to France to try and find where he was buried. With the help of members of his squadron and local people they found bomb pieces similar to those carried by Robin's plane and aircraft wreckage by a crater at Caix near Villers Bretonneux. Back in Australia in October 1924 the expanding railway reached Ultima and a name was needed for the new station. Robin's mother, Margaret, hung a sign over the station which said 'Robin Vale' ('farewell Robin' in Latin). The mother's tribute to her dead son was eventually accepted as the name for the new township which, after initial hardships, prospered. In 1977 Alan Wood the local MP visited Villers Bretonneux and the links between the two townships were formed.

Cuttle is commemorated on the Arras Flying Services Memorial (qv).

To the left of the car park is the beautifully maintained local War Memorial with a stone

Memorial to the Australians in front and a sunburst gate.

Return to the crossroads with the D1029 and turn right. Continue to the turning to the D23.

[NOTE. This is the start point for Itinerary Five, the American, Canadian and French actions of 1918. See page 289]

Drive to the parking area by the local cemetery on the right and pull in as near as possible to the small entrance at the far end.

• *Villers Bretonneux Local Cemetery Allied Graves (GPS: 49.87051 2.52085), Demarcation Stone 16.1 miles/10 minutes/ Map 1/18/GPS: 49.87059 2.52598*

Just inside the wall is a CWGC plot containing 6 graves from 1918, 4 of them Australian.

Walk to the marker some 300m along the road.

After the war the Touring Clubs of France and Belgium, supported by the Ypres League, erected 118 official demarcation stones (for a long time it was generally thought that there were 240 stones but detailed research by **Rik Scherpenberg** defined the number as 118 with a private stone added at Confrecourt later making 119) along a line agreed by Maréchal Pétain's General Staff to be the limit of the German advance along the Western Front. 'Here the Invader was brought to a standstill 1918', is the inscription. Four still remain in the Somme area. The authors, knowing that the Germans had actually penetrated as far as 'OP1' on the far side of the village, asked the local *Souvenir Français* organisation why the stone had not been placed there. 'They were there for less than 24 hours', was the reply. Local historians now wish to move the stone to what they consider to be the correct site.

The Villers Bretonneux Demarcation Stone.

Extra Visit to the French National Cemetery at Marcelcave (Map 1/19, GPS: 49.86053 2.55919) Round trip: 3.8 miles. Approximate time: 20 minutes

Continue on the D1029(N29) to a right turn, signed to Cimetière Nationale de Marcelcave on the C203. Turn right and right again and stop at the cemetery on the left.

Marcelcave, 'Les Buttes', Cemetery, in the area where **Jean Cocteau** served, was created in 1916 after the 1 July Somme Battles. It contains 1,610 burials, many concentrated from other smaller cemeteries in 1922 and 1936. It was completely re-landscaped in 1980. Like John Masefield, Jean Cocteau, who had been exempted from military service in 1910 because of his poor health, volunteered for the Red Cross in 1914. Like Masefield, Cocteau continued his writing and other artistic activities during the war, notably writing *Thomas l'Imposteur* about the French

Marines, from his experiences at Nieuport and Coxyde in Flanders. He moved to the Somme in June 1916 and joined Evacuation Hospital No 13 at Marcelcave on 28 June in time for the 1 July Offensive. It was one of the most important French hospitals on the front and a great rail connection. From 28 June to 11 September 27,211 wounded passed through it, of which 4,170 were retained for further treatment, 829 of whom died – hence the formation of the cemetery. During his stay at the hospital, Cocteau wrote regularly to his mother, describing the hospital as *'le district des plaintes'*. He comments on the number of aeroplanes (*'Brouillard épais tissé par mille avions'* – thick fog, interlaced with 1,000 aeroplanes) and takes many photographs on Kodak film. On 16 July he is distressed by the death of Josselin de Rohan, *'mort tout près de nous'* (killed very close to us) on 14 July. Rohan was the son of the Dowager Duchess of Rohan and brother of Marie Murat. On 27 July Cocteau left the Somme to travel to Italy and to continue work on such diverse projects as the ballet Parade and the revue Le Mot. At Christmas time that year he recalled the horrors he had seen and described, in his poem No 1 1916, a 'war crèche' where the baby Jesus is all alone because the Three Kings were fighting, Mary was working at a hospital, Joseph guarded a road, the ox had been eaten, the donkey carried a machine gun, the Star was a signal and all the shepherds were dead and buried.

French National Cemetery, Marcelcave

At the high tide of the German offensive of 1918 Marcelcave ended up some 300 yards behind German lines.

Return to the marker stone and pick up the main itinerary.

Return to the crossroads and turn right on the D23 signed to the Australian Memorial which was widened in 2014 to take the increasing volume of traffic on ANZAC Day. Stop by the Memorial.

• Australian National Memorial, Interpretative Centre & Fouilloy CWGC Military Cemetery Villers Bretonneux/RB/17.3 miles/35 minutes/ Map 1/11/12/OP/ABT4/GPS: 49.88613 2.50819

NOTE. In April 2007 the Australian Government (qv) announced that they were providing $2.8 million to commence plans for a major Interpretative Centre near the Memorial. Further funding will become available as the project progresses. This was reinforced in 2014 by Prime Minister Tony Abbott who confirmed that the Centre, built behind the Memorial and named after Gen Sir John Monash, would open on Anzac Day 2018. Designed by Cox Architecture, it will provide a leading-edge integrated multimedia experience and tell the story of the extraordinary efforts of the 290,000 Australians who served on the Western Front with distinction. It will offer an evocative and educational experience for visitors of all nationalities and will honour Australian service and sacrifice in France and Belgium during the First World War.

Outside the Cemetery are CGS/H Signboards. When the beautiful old avenue of hornbeam trees that led up to the Memorial was thought to have outgrown its position it was replaced with 'France Fontaine', a denser and more compact variety of hornbeam.   It was an extraordinary coincidence that the two Australian brigades which encircled Villers Bretonneux should meet in the early hours of 25 April 1918 because three years earlier on that morning, then a Sunday, the Australian Imperial Forces had landed at Gallipoli. What happened on that terrible day lives on in the nation's memory, and every year young Australians make their way down to the Gallipoli Peninsula to commemorate what came to be known as ANZAC Day (see *Major and Mrs Holts Battlefield Guide to Gallipoli*). This site, of such emotional importance to Australia, is fast rivalling Gallipoli as the destination of choice to celebrate ANZAC Day by travelling Australians, many of them

Australian National Memorial & Fouilloy CWGC Cemetery, Villers Bretonneux.

young back-packers and some 6,000 visitors are expected for 2018 (and until the end of the 1980s Australian veterans regularly visited the village at this time).

Here is the Australian National Memorial which commemorates 10,797 Australians who gave their lives on the Somme and other sectors of the Western Front and have no known grave. The Cemetery, known as Fouilloy Cemetery, has 1,085 UK, 770 Australian, 263 Canadian, 4 South Africans and 2 New Zealand burials. There are some memorable private inscriptions on the Australian graves, which merit careful reading, e.g. **Pte C.J. Bruton**, 34th AIF, age 22, 31 March 1918 [II.C.5/7], 'He died an Australian hero, the greatest death of all'; **Pte A.L. Flower**, 5th AIF, 29 July 1918 [III.B.6.], 'Also **Trooper J.H. Flower**, wounded at Gallipoli, buried at sea 05.5.1915'. In VI.AB.20 lies **Jean Brillant, VC, MC**, 22nd Bn French-Canadian, age 22, 10 August 1918. His headstone,

engraved in French, records that he volunteered in Quebec and 'Fell gloriously on the soil of his ancestors. Good blood never lies.' His wonderful citation is in the Cemetery Report. There is a hospital named after Brillant in Quebec. Within the left-hand hedge at the edge of the lawn before the main Memorial, there is a **Ross Bastiaan bronze Plaque**, unveiled on 30 August 1993 by the Governor General of Australia. From this point the heights on the left can be seen, with the tall chimney of the Colette brickworks near which the Red Baron was shot down.

Unveiled by King George VI on 22 July 1938, the impressive main **Memorial**, designed by Sir Edwin Lutyens, consists of a wall carrying the names of the missing and a 100ft-high central tower which can be climbed with due caution. If the gate to the tower is locked the key may be obtained from the *Gendarmerie* on the D1029 at Villers Bretonneux, though during

Headstone of Jean Brillant, VC

the 100th Anniversary years this policy may change. If you intend to go up, allow an extra 20 minutes. The memorial was designed by Sir Edwin Lutyens and, due to delays occasioned by lack of funds, it was the last of the Dominion memorials to be inaugurated. The original plan for the Memorial had included a 90ft-high archway, but this was omitted, presumably for financial reasons. It bears the scars of World War II bullets (deliberately retained as an historical reminder) and the top of the tower was struck by lightning on 2 June 1978 and had to be extensively renovated. By facing directly away from the memorial, the cathedral and the Perret Tower in Amiens can be seen on a clear day. How near the Germans came! The war correspondent **Philip Gibbs** described how,

"The Germans came as near to Amiens as Villers-Bretonneux on the low hills outside. Their guns had smashed the railway station of Longueau, which to Amiens is like Clapham Junction to Waterloo. Across the road was a tangle of telephone wires, shot down from their posts. For one night nothing – or next to nothing – barred the way, and Amiens could have been entered by a few armoured cars. Only small groups of tired men, the remnants of strong battalions, were able to stand on their feet, and hardly that."

Later he reported:

"Foch said 'I guarantee Amiens'. French cavalry, hard pressed, had come up the northern part of our line. I saw them riding by, squadron after squadron, their horses wet with sweat. To some I shouted out *'Vivent les Poilus'* emotionally, but they turned and gave me ugly looks. They were cursing the English, I was told afterwards, for the German break-through. *'Ces sacrés Anglais!'* Why couldn't they hold their lines?"

Gibbs acknowledges that:

"Amiens was saved by the counterattacks of the Australians, and especially by the brilliant surprise attack at night on Villers-Bretonneux under the generalship of Monash."

In one of the strange coincidences of war, Gibbs was relieved to bump, quite accidentally, into his 'kid' brother Arthur who had become lost from his unit and was bringing up his field guns towards Amiens. 'I had never expected to see him alive again, but there he was looking as fresh as if he had just had a holiday in Brighton.'

Continue on the D23 to Fouilloy. Turn right at the T junction with the church onto the D1 and follow signs to Péronne and 'Toutes Directions' towards Corbie. After some 200m there is a sign to the D71 to the right.

Extra Visit to the Private Memorial to Capt Mond & Lt Martyn (Map Side 1/20a, GPS: 49.91158 2.57892), Australian Memorial Park (Map 1/24a, GPS: 49.89977 2.58161), Memorials at Le Hamel/ RB (Map 1/24b, GPS: 49.90005 2.56875). Round trip: 11.00 miles. Approximate time: I hour 15 minutes

Turn right, signed Hamelet on the D71 and continue to the centre of the village.
This is **ABT5**. Some 60 new British Mark V tanks and 4 re-supply tanks of the 5th Tank Brigade assembled here on 3 July 1918 and at 1030 moved south-east to their start points for the battle of le Hamel due to begin at 0310 the following morning, the attack to a first approximation being in your direction of travel. As an entirely Australian idea proposed by Monash, and executed solely under

Australian auspices, the success of the operation was a major boost to Australian self-belief. Having trained the infantry and tanks together and making maximum use of artillery and aircraft, the Australians saw Monash's plan as a blueprint for all future allied success. The action was over in under 100 minutes. Hamel was taken and 2,000 Germans were killed or captured while Australian casualties were some 1,400.

Continue towards Vaire.

In **Vaire Communal Cemetery (GPS: 49.91320 2.54291)** are four Australian soldiers of 8 August 1918 buried together.

Note that the 'Red Baron Chimney' may now be seen at 11 o' clock on the horizon to the left.

Continue to Vaire and turn right towards le Hamel on the D71.

It was to the right of this road at Pear Trench that **Private Harry Dalziel**, a Lewis Gunner of the 15th AIF, won the **VC**, capturing a German machine gun and killing two. He was twice wounded in the action but survived until 1965.

Continue through le Hamel to the T junction by the local War Memorial and turn left. Follow the road to the left signed to Bouzencourt on the C7. Continue to the memorial on the left (4.9 miles).

The Memorial is just before the village and surrounded by a small, well-tended garden. The French inscription translates, "To the memory of **Capt Francis Mond, RFA and RAF, age and Lt Edgar Martyn RAF** of 57th Squadron who fell gloriously in this area battling against three German aeroplanes on 15 May 1918. *Per ardua ad astra.*" They were flying their DH4 after attacking ammunition dumps at Bapaume

and were brought down at 1250 by Lt Johannes Janzen of Jasta 6, whose Fokker DR.I had been shot down on 9 May by 209 Squadron but survived. Janzen scored 13 victories before he was brought down again during a dogfight on 9 June 1918 with a SPAD during which he shot off his own propeller. He lived until the 1980s.

The dogfight which brought down Mond and Martyn was witnessed by 31st Aust Bn and one of their officers, Lt A.H. Hill, MC, went out under fire, extricated and identified their bodies. He then had them sent down to Bn HQ by river and their personal effects were sent on to Mond's family. Strangely, the bodies which had been escorted down the river, then seemed to disappear. An extensive search was undertaken by the Australians, by 57 Squadron and the CWGC prompted by Mond's Mother, who wrote to every officer and NCO who might have any information, and

Memorial to Capt Mond & Lt Martin RAF, Bouzencourt

visited over thirty cemeteries, keeping in touch throughout with Martyn's wife. Her efforts bore fruit in 1922 when she became convinced that two named graves in Doullens Communal Cemetery Extension No. 2 (qv) actually contained the bodies of her son and of Martyn. One grave was exhumed, watched by Mrs Mond and the father of the man named therein, Capt J.V. Aspinall. The body was indeed found to contain Mond so the adjoining grave was opened and contained Martyn, not the named Lt P.V. de la Cour, whose grave turned out to be the next one. Capt Aspinall is now commemorated on the Arras Memorial.

In 1919 Mond's father Emile had bought the land here where his son's plane had crashed and erected the monument you see today and surrounded it with chains supported by stone pillars, within which enclosure he planted trees, shrubs and flowers. The family continued to visit regularly, the last recorded visit being by Mond's sister in 1951. As the family then became untraceable the Commune of Hamel adopted it and they maintain it still. During WW2 the Cross of Lorraine and letter V were scratched on the stone, probably by the Resistance.

Edgar Martyn was a Canadian and came to Europe with the 19th Bn Can Inf before being commissioned into the RFC as a Lt Observer on 12 February 1918.

On the heights beyond the Memorial can be seen the tall chimney of the brickworks in the area where the **Baron von Richthofen** came down.

Continue to the bottom of the road to turn and return to le Hamel. On entering the village turn left uphill following the sign to Monument Australien, and left again.

There is a barrier and a sign with the park's **opening hours:** 0900-1800 1 April-31 Oct and 0900-1600 1 Nov-31 March. **Contact** the Mayor on +(0)3 22 96 88 06.

Continue to the large parking area on the right.

The Australian Corps Memorial Park, ABT16/OP/GPS: 49.89977 2.58161

The land for this Memorial was acquired by the Australians on the 80th anniversary of the Battle of le Hamel. Following its 2008 renovation and redesign it is now a dignified, informative and pleasantly landscaped area.

Stand in the open shelter and look over the Valley of the Somme. At 1 o' clock is the CWGC Cemetery Dive Copse (qv). At 12 o'clock on the skyline is the Australian 3rd Division Memorial (the 3rd and 4th Divisions defended this area during the battle of Amiens in 1918), at 10 o' clock is the chimney of the Richthofen crash site brickworks, at 9 o' clock are the twin towers of Corbie church, from which broad direction the Australian attack came.

On 4 July 1918 this was a German position known as the Wolfsberg and was on the final objective line for the assault. Apart from being a great success, a novel aspect of the attack was that the Australians were re-supplied by parachute. The choice of 4 July for the attack had been influenced by the hoped for participation of the recently arrived American 131st and 132nd Regiments, but Pershing ruled this out, though four companies did take part incurring 100 casualties. It was from these positions that the Australians set out on 8 August in the Allied offensive that marked the beginning of the end for the Kaiser, a day that Ludendorff called *Der Schwarze Tag* (The Black Day).

A path then leads towards the main Memorial and recreated trenches, from which the Australian Memorial at Villers Bretonneux may be seen to the right. Along it are Information Panels with maps, photos and individual stories about the campaign and the **VCs** and MoHs of:

1. Pte Henry (Harry) Dalziel (qv). Driver Dalziel's **VC** was gazetted on 17 August 1918 and was for his action as a Lewis gunner, who after silencing the enemy guns in one direction, dashed at gun fire from another direction. There, using his revolver, he killed or captured the entire crew and gun, despite being severely wounded in the hand, finally capturing the final objective. He was wounded again, in the head, and had inspired his comrades and saved many lives. The action took place at Pear Trench (qv).

2. Lance Cpl Thomas (Jack) Axford, MM, 22 years old, was awarded his **VC** (gazetted on 17 August 1918) for his action in clearing Vaire and Hamel Woods of German defenders. Single-handedly he entered a German trench and took the machine gunners in it, killing 10 and taking 6 prisoners.

3. Cpl Thomas Pope, who served with Coy E of 131st Inf, 33rd US Inf div, the first soldier to be awarded the **Medal of Honour** in WW1. It was for his action at le Hamel on 4 July 1918 when going alone he rushed a machine gun nest, killed several of the crew by bayonet and held off others until reinforcements arrived and captured them.

The Memorial. The shiny black tiles on the original 1998 Memorial started to drop off shortly after it was inaugurated and in 2006 it was in such a bad state of repair that plans were made to demolish and rebuild it. In March 2007 the Australian Government announced that they were allocating $7.9 million towards a 'facelift' for the Memorial. It was re-inaugurated on 8 November 2008. The new Memorial, maintained by the CWGC, is constructed as three blocks of curved granite set in a semi-circle with the Australian Forces sunburst badge in the centre block. It bears a quotation from the speech of French PM Georges Clemenceau of 7 July 1918, "... I have seen the Australians, I have looked in their faces. I know that these men will fight alongside us again until the cause for which we are all fighting is safe for us and our children."

Further repairs were required in 2014/5.

Australian National Memorial, le Hamel

Beyond the Memorial is a section of original trenches. On the horizon beyond them the distinctive spire of La Motte Church, on the N29 some 2 miles away, may be seen.

Remnants of Australian trenchlines, behind the Memorial.

Early in August the Australian 1st Division moved down to the Somme from Ypres and continued the chase to the east. Commanding the 3rd Brigade was **Brigadier Gordon Bennett**, the youngest Brigadier in the Australian Army, who would later be immersed in controversy over his conduct following the fall of Singapore in WW2.

Return towards le Hamel.

On descending towards the village the top of the Australian National Memorial at Villers Bretonneux may be seen straight ahead.

Turn left and then right and stop by the church on the left.

In front of the church is a **Ross Bastiaan commemorative Bronze Plaque (GPS: 49.90005 2.56875)** about the Battle of le Hamel, sponsored by Hugh and Marcus Bastiaan, John and Hazelle Laffin and Carbone-Lorraine Aust. On a wall to the right of the Church is a **May/June 1945 Plaque with an anchor to the Senegalese** of the 4th Col Inf Div (c.f .similar Plaque in Itinerary 5 at Mailly Raineval) who had a medical facility nearby. This is rue du General Monash.

Return to the D23, turn right and rejoin Itinerary Three.

Ross Bastiaan Plaque, le Hamel

Plaque to 4th Col Inf Div, le Hamel

Continue into Corbie, crossing the River Somme en route and follow signs to Centre Ville passing the picturesque, fairy castle-like Hôtel de Ville and war memorial on the left.

Corbie. The Château was built in 1863 and bought by the town in 1923. The *Hotel de Ville* and surrounds have recently been restored and landscaped into a pleasant park.

After 100m park in the Place de la République **(GPS: 49.90854 22.51219)**.

Note. On Friday there is a market in the square (now also beautifully landscaped) so it will not be possible to park here. To the left is the splendid *'Porte d'Honneur'* to the Abbey. The key to the church is held in the **Tourist Office** on the corner. Its opening hours vary according to the season, but it is usually closed on Sundays - other than in July and August - and often on Monday mornings. It shuts for lunch from 1200-1430. Over the road is the excellent restaurant **La Table d'Agathe** with superb regional dishes. Closed Sunday night and Monday and the first two weeks in July. Tel: + (0)3 22 96 96 27.

Walk along rue Charles de Gaulle to the church.

Just before it is the restaurant **Le Fauquet's** (closed Sun and Mon evening). **Tel:** +(0)3 22 48 41 17. Good choice of menus, fast service if required.

Continue towards the Church, passing the school. This is called *'Rose de Picardie'. Continue to the Church.*

• *Congreve Plaque, Corbie Church/19.7 miles/10 minutes/Map 1/10/GPS: 49.90878 2.51026*

Corbie has a fascinating history. It was attacked by the Normans in 896AD, in 1415 Henry V, desperately seeking a Somme crossing, was attacked here by a small force of French Knights, in 1475 the town was taken and burnt by Louis X1, in 1636 it was taken by the Spanish who were chased out by Louis XIII and Richelieu, and it was badly damaged in the French Revolution. In the distinctive twelfth-century church of Saint-Etiennes, whose architecture shows the transition between Roman and Gothic styles, is a Plaque, designed by Sir Edwin Lutyens, to **'Billy' Congreve VC** (qv).

Return to the Place de la République.

Across the square at No 8 is the delightful **'Maison d'Hôte' Le Macassar** (see also **Tourist Information** below). Five sumptuous rooms/suites furnished in period (from 'Colonial' through *'Art Nouveau'* and *'Art Deco'*) style but with state of the art plumbing in a superb private residence which was extensively renovated in the 1920s and '30s. Hosts Miguel and Ian encourage guests (but no young children please – some of the antiques are too precious) to makes themselves at home in the glorious public rooms and courtyard. Tel: +(0) 3 22 48 40 04. E-mail: bookings@lemacassar.com Website: www.lemacassar.com

From the Square take the D1 signed to Péronne, continue past the Hospice de Corbie on the left. Turn right following the green CWGC sign. Park at the cemetery.

• *Corbie Communal Cemetery & Extension/20.4 miles/10 minutes/ Map 1/20/GPS: 49.91528 2.52037*

Just at the top of the steps leading to the cemetery, a headstone is inscribed, '**Major W. La Touche Congreve, VC, DSO, MC**, Rifle Brigade. 20 July 1916. *Légion d'Honneur*. In remembrance of my beloved husband and in glorious expectation.'

Congreve, affectionately known as 'Billy', was the VC winner son of a VC winner father, Lt Gen Sir Walter Congreve VC, CB, MVO (who was commanding XIII Corps on the Somme at the time of his son's death). A conspicuously brave, and immensely popular officer, Billy Congreve kept a forthright diary until 17 January 1916, (which has been edited by Terry Norman as *Armageddon Road*). He was killed on 20 July 1916

Roses de Picardie
School, Corbie.

A LA MÉMOIRE GLORIEUSE
DU COMMANDANT
WILLIAM LA TOUCHE CONGREVE
DU RIFLE BRIGADE, DE L'ARMÉE BRITANNIQUE.
CHEVALIER DE LA LÉGION D'HONNEUR,
DÉCORÉ DE LA VICTORIA CROSS DU
DISTINGUISHED SERVICE ORDER ET
DE LA MILITARY CROSS.

HOMME SANS PEUR, SOLDAT VAILLANT,
IL TOMBA AU CHAMP D'HONNEUR LE 20
JUILLET 1916 À LONGUEVALLE, SOMME
A L'ÂGE DE 25 ANS A L'AURORE D'UNE
BRILLANTE CARRIÈRE, AIMÉ DE TOUS.

Il repose à Corbie

Memorial Plaque
to Maj William La
Touche Congreve,
in Corbie Church

Corbie Comm Cem
with headstone of
'Billy' Congreve,
VC, DSO, MC

at Longueval by a sniper (qv). He had been married on 1 June 1916 to Pamela Maude. Her poignant message on her husband's headstone refers to the fact that she was pregnant. She christened their daughter Gloria. A fellow officer had described Billy as 'absolutely glorious'.

On the headstone of **Lt F.C. Sangster** of the R Warwicks the personal message is on a bronze Plaque. Through the archway is the grave of CWGC worker, **George Hill**, 1946.

Return to the Hospice junction, turn right and continue to the female statue at the Y junction.

• Colette Statue/20. 8 miles/GPS: 49.91668 2.51662

The statue, known as 'Colette' (after the young citizen of Corbie who founded the Clarisse Religious Order), was unveiled in the presence of the Bishop of Amiens and the Curé of Corbie to commemorate citizens of the town who were killed in World War I. Colette managed to found seventeen monasteries in her life-time, during the difficult times of the Hundred Years' War.

Statue of Colette, Corbie

Extra Visit to Heilly Station CWGC Cemetery & Private Memorial to L Cpl O'Neill/Map 1/22/23/GPS: 49.94080 2.54203

Round trip: 4.8 miles. Approximate time: 25 minutes

Take the left fork on the D23 and after approximately 0.8 miles, fork right on the D120 signed Méricourt l'Abbé. After 1.5 miles (driving parallel to the R Somme and railway to the left) turn right following green CWGC signs at a crossroads. (Heilly 'Station' is signed to the left).

The railway ran through here from Amiens to the front and Heilly was the site of one of the Casualty Clearing Stations to which ambulance trains were due to run after the battle of 1 July 1916. As you turn right, the station house can be seen on the C11 to the left. This is a particularly lovely cemetery – in a quiet, rural setting, with beautiful flowers and shrubs – and unusual, partly due to the vastly greater number of casualties that arrived at the CCS than were anticipated. Men had to be buried two or three to a grave – a rare occurrence in a British cemetery. There was not, therefore, room to engrave the men's regimental badges, and so many of them are incorporated into the colonnaded brick wall on the right as you enter. There is also a Private Memorial erected by his comrades to **L Cpl J. P. O'Neill** of 13th NSW battalion, AIF, who was killed on 6 January 1917 when a grenade accidentally exploded. He had been recommended for a Military Medal.

It was to this CCS that Henry Williamson's fictional hero Phillip Maddison was brought and there is a totally realistic description of Maddison's wounding after going over the top at Ovillers, his crawling painfully back to find basic treatment at the First Aid Post, then being wheeled on a stretcher to the Advanced Dressing Station at Albert, being encouraged by an RC Padre, given an injection and then lifted into a Ford ambulance and driven to Heilly. There he 'was carried into a hut for officers', laid on a rubber sheet and covered with a blanket, fed tea, bread and butter and jam and given 'the latest number of *The Bystander'*. This was the magazine which carried the popular cartoons of Bruce Bairnsfather, known as *Fragments from France* and which featured 'Old Bill' (see page 93).

Return to the Colette statue and continue with the main itinerary.

Heilly Station CWGC Cemetery, showing Private Memorial to L/Cpl O'Neill

Keep to the right on the D1 signed to Péronne and Bray, passing on the right a picnic site (Pointe de Vue de Sainte Colette) with tables and benches and a superb view over the River Somme. Continue to the brickworks on the left with a tall chimney.

• *Von Richthofen Crash Site, Vaux-sur-Somme/22.5 miles/5 minutes/Map 1/21/GPS: 49.93248 2.54136*

The chimney, now crumbling somewhat at the top, is visible for miles around and makes a good reference point. The precise cause and location of the Baron's crash is still open to some debate, but many qualified experts place it in the vicinity of the brickworks.

The 'Red Baron', Baron Manfred von Richthofen, was credited with eighty kills. His squadron, Jasta II, was known as the 'Flying Circus' because of the bright colours of their planes. Richthofen's own Fokker triplane DR-1 425/17 was vermillion. They were based at Cappy, just south of the River Somme and south east of Bray. On Sunday 21 April 1918 the squadron went up at mid-morning, after Richthofen had posed for a photograph for a mechanic, despite the superstition held by many pilots that being photographed just before a mission meant that one would not return. The Baron did not. After an active dog fight with British RE 8s and Camels led by Capt A. Roy Brown, a Canadian with eleven kills, von Richthofen crashed near this spot, coming down from your right. Brown claimed the victory. So did Australian Lewis gunners of 14th Artillery Brigade near Vaux. Subsequent research gives credence to the Australian claim. Even the angle at which the fatal bullet entered the Baron's chest – from below, not above (as Brown was flying) – points to a hit from the ground. What is indisputable is that Richthofen's apparel and possessions and his red tri-plane were soon stripped, as by a plague of locusts, by souvenir hunters. Many items found their way to Australia and several have since been donated to the Australian War Memorial. Von Richthofen was buried in Bertangles (Map 1/5, Western Approach) on 22 April, with ceremony, by the Australians. In 1925 his remains were re-interred in Fricourt German Cemetery (Map J34) and from there were transferred to his family home in Schweidnitz, in eastern Germany. Contemporary accounts claim that only the skull had been removed and P. J. Carisella, American author of a book on the Baron's death, states that he unearthed the rest of the skeleton in Bertangles in 1969 and that he presented it to the German Military

The brickworks near where Manfred von Richthofen (the 'Red Baron') was shot down

Air Attaché in Paris.

In the Kent Battle of Britain Museum, Hawkinge, www.kbobm.org there is an excellent von Richtofen display, including a replica of his triplane (made for the film *Flying Boys*) and a realistic maquette showing the area of the brickworks.

Continue. Park by the memorial on the left.

• *Australian 3rd Division Memorial/24.3 miles/5 minutes/Map 1/23a/* *GPS: 49.93605 2.57959*

The obelisk is similar to the 1st Division Memorial at Pozières (Itinerary One). It lists the battle honours of the Division, including The Windmill (Pozières), Bray and Proyart (both the latter are seen on this Itinerary). It stands pretty well on the final line the Germans reached by August 1918 which ran roughly north to south across the road here. The Division, raised in Australia, was formed on Salisbury Plain in July 1916 and reached Flanders under General Monash in December that year and the Somme in March 1918. The Memorial overlooks the ground across the other side of the Somme where four Australian Divisions (2, 3, 4 and 5) attacked roughly parallel to your direction of travel in the early morning fog of 8 August 1918. This side of the Somme were the British 18th and 58th Divisions. It was a remarkable assault, with fine co-operation between infantry, cavalry, tanks and aircraft. Determined efforts had been made to keep preparations for the attack secret and it was launched without a preliminary bombardment.

The British front (the Fourth Army – III Corps under Butler where you are now, to the south, the Australian Corps under Monash and then the Canadian Corps under Currie) stretched about 23km south from around Albert which is over to your north front. The unsuspecting German Second Army of six weak divisions, without a single tank, were suddenly confronted by 360 heavy tanks, 96 Whippet light tanks, 1,900 aeroplanes (against 365) and accompanying bombardment from 2,650 guns and a total force of 16 divisions. In his book, *Wings of War*, **Rudolf Stark**, serving with *Jagdstaffel 35*, tells how he flew over the front of 8 August, and how the sky was full of aircraft:

> "There are fights in the upper air. There are fights in the lower air. The numerical superiority of the enemy gives him the advantage, so it does not matter where we fight …. But the ground swarms with men in brown. They crouch in every shell hole and run forward along every hollow. Grey squat things roll through their midst – tanks. Here, there, everywhere."

Except at the extremities, an advance of more than 8km was achieved everywhere. Although the Germans recovered quickly, and the attack lost its momentum after the first day, for Ludendorff, the German Commander, it was the final straw that broke the back of his determination to win.

In Germany more than 1.5 million workers were on strike, the spreading influenza epidemic was weakening his armies, the civilian population was starving and Ludendorff was suffering from nervous exhaustion. Although the gains by the Allies on 8 August did not compare to the territorial conquests of the Germans in their March Offensive, the *'Kaiserschlacht'*, the shock of 8 August loosened the Germans' grasp upon the initiative and it passed to Foch.

Around the Memorial are Information Panels, detailing the Division's casualties on

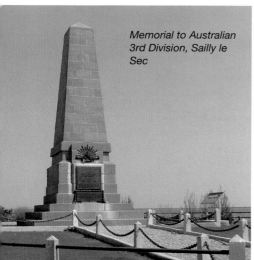

Memorial to Australian 3rd Division, Sailly le Sec

the Western Front – 6,200 killed, 24,000 wounded, etc. By looking across the Somme River towards the high ground the Australian Memorial at le Hamel can be seen and the church on the horizon straight ahead is La Motte Warfusée to the right of the windmills.

Continue on the D1, passing on the right a sign to **CWGC Dive Copse Cemetery (Map 1/23b, GPS: 49.92902 2.60492)**. This was begun during the 1916 battles and is the cemetery that can be seen from the Australian Memorial at Le Hamel.

Continue to the next cemetery on the right.

• *Beacon CWGC Cemetery/26.0 miles/5 minutes/Map 1/23c/GPS: 49.93700 2.61650*

The Cemetery report here records that the

> "... first fighting in this part of the Somme took place on 26/27 March 1918 when the Third Army withdrew to a line between Albert and Sailly-le-Sec. This line was held until 4 August when it was advanced nearly to Sailly-Laurette and on 8 August, the first day of 'The Battle of Amiens', Sailly-Laurette and the road to Morlancourt were disengaged."

Burials began here as the Third Army withdrew before the German onslaught of March 1918. Others were made by the 18th Div Burial Officer on 15 August. The cemetery was then greatly increased after the Armistice by the concentration of 600 graves from the battlefields and small cemeteries around. There are many almost unbearably poignant personal messages on the headstones here and some proud parental statements in the Cemetery Report of sons' academic and career achievements. The Cemetery was designed by Sir Edwin Lutyens and named after a brick beacon on the ridge. There are some 570 UK burials and 190 Australian. At 9 o'clock the Golden Madonna at Albert may be seen and to her right on the high ground the Thiepval Memorial.

Continue over the crossroads with the D42 and turn right at the next crossroads onto the C2, signed to Chipilly and Cerisy. We probably need to point out here that road numbers on the ground do not always match the numbers given on maps!

This road runs down towards the Somme at Chipilly where a spur (roughly a direct extension of this road) juts south into a bend of the river. On 8 August 1918 the Allied assault south of the Somme made advances of 8km or more in the day, but at Chipilly

Beacon CWGC Cemetery

village and on the spur the Germans made a stand. 58th (London) Division supported by 131st Infantry Regiment of the 33rd (American) Division made a joint assault here at 1730 hours on 9 August. The Americans lined up parallel to, and 50m to the right of, this road, having had to march in double-time for 7km to reach the start-line. In the following action, supported by the 4th (Australian) Division attacking the village from south of the river, both Chipilly and the spur were captured – the latter, it is said, by a six-man Australian patrol. **Corporal Jake Allex** of 33rd Division won the **Congressional Medal of Honour** for single-handedly destroying a German machine-gun post, killing five of the enemy and taking fifteen prisoners. Allex survived the war and died in 1959. In 2006 a short documentary film called 'Corporal Jake' was made about his action.

Continue downhill on the C306 to the church road junction in Chipilly.

• *58th (London) Division Memorial/29.0 miles/5 minutes/Map 1/26/GPS: 49.90889 2.64946*

There is a CRP Signboard beside the Memorial. This striking Memorial, sculpted by Henri-Désiré Gauque, 1858-1927, a well-known French sculptor who excelled at animal figures, is of a soldier saying goodbye to his dying horse and is reminiscent of the famous Mantania painting *Farewell Old Man*. Unusually it commemorates not only 58th Division, but also the French, Canadian and Australian action of 8 August. The Americans were not mentioned, presumably because on 8 August they were in reserve. When the Australians came to enter the village from the south they found that the Germans had blown both bridges across the river. With typical Aussie ingenuity they took the girders from the longer bridge and balanced them on the piers of the shorter to restore the crossing.

Memorial to 58th London Division, Chipilly

[N.B.] Cérisy-Gailly Mil CWGC Cemetery (GPS: 49.90424 2.63174). By turning right downhill at the crossroads and continuing over the bridge towards Cérisy, (with picturesque views to each side over the Somme and its tranquil pools - paradise for fishermen) this Cemetery may be reached. Continue through Cérisy village, following signs to Cérisy-Gailly French National Cemetery, with a British Communal Plot attached and to Cérisy-Gailly Mil Cem. This is beyond the Brit Com Plot and to the left.

In it (in D13) is buried **Squadron Commander John ('Jack') Petre**, RFC, 13 April 1918. Before his accidental death (for details see *Elsie & Mairi Go to War* by Diane Atkinson) this distinguished pilot was due to marry Mairi Chisholm, one of the famous "Two at Pervyse".

Entrance to Cérisy-Gailly CWGC Cemetery

Turn left past the church and continue uphill on the C7, signed to Etinehem and almost immediately there is the local cemetery on the right with good parking.

• Chipilly Communal Cemetery & Extension/29.1 miles/5 minutes/Map 1/28a/GPS: 49.91066 2.64999

In the Cemetery are a number of British and French military graves from July 1916. The plot was started in August 1915 and used until March 1916. It contains fifty-five UK burials (including **Rifleman E. F. Slade**, QVR, who was drowned whilst swimming in the Somme, 12 August 1915) and four French. The Extension was used between March 1916 and February 1917 and contains 31 graves. The Cemetery has extensive views over the Somme Valley from the back wall.

Continue.

The route that you are following (which has some delightful bucolic views over the Somme Pools) is that fought along by the American 131st Infantry from 9 to 19 August 1918. Keep to the left of the river and drive to Etinehem village. This was taken by the Americans and Australians on 13 August.

Chipilly Communal & Extension Cemetery

At the junction with the V2 take the C2 signed to Albert along Rue du Moulin. Continue following signs to the French National Cemetery.

French National Cemetery, La Côte 80 (Hill 80)

• *French National Cemetery, 'La Côte 80' (Hill 80)/32.3 miles/10 minutes/ Map M6/GPS: 49.93810 2.69095*

As has happened with most of the French cemeteries on the Somme, this is now landscaped *'à l'Anglaise'*, with flower beds in front of the rows of graves. This is a concentration cemetery, which contains 955 French burials and 49 British, as well as the tomb of **Abbé Thibaut, Chaplain to the 1st Infantry Regiment**. He was a *Chevalier de la Légion d'Honneur*, and was mortally wounded in the assault on Frégicourt on 26 September 1916 (a night attack near Combles). He died at Maricourt the following day. The monument, erected by the officers, NCOs and men of the Régiment de Cambrai, bears a Plaque with the Abbé's portrait. To the right and left of it are two rows of Australians from August 1918. The other CWGC graves, of mixed nationality and units, are near the flagpole in the centre and are from 1916. Like many French cemeteries, Hill 80 was the site of a military hospital. Serving there in 1916 was the French humanist writer, man of letters and other arts, and Member of the *Académie Française*, **Georges Duhamel**. Duhamel, born in Paris in 1884, studied medicine before being drawn into a literary and artistic life. However, when war broke out, he joined the 110th Regiment of Line as a medic. His experiences are described in *Vie des Martyrs (1917)* and *Civilisation* (which won the Prix Goncourt in 1918). In the latter he describes the area around Hill 80: the churned up mud made by 2,200 horses being taken daily to drink from the Somme, the tented city marked by vivid red crosses, the circle formed by 30 balloons, the continual puffs of smoke from lines of artillery fire. His adjutant warns him,

"You will see passing here more wounded than you have hairs on your head, and more blood flowing than there is water in the canal. All those who fall between Combles and Bouchavesnes are sent here."

Continue to the D1 crossroads and turn right towards Bray. On entering the town go downhill to the German Cemetery (Cimetière Militaire Allemand/Deutscher Soldatenfriedhof) on the left and park near the boules pitch. Climb the steps to the cemetery.

• *Bray German Cemetery/33.4 miles/10 minutes/ Map M7/GPS: 49.94005 2.71319*

Enclosed by a hedge are the 1,079 graves and 43 bodies in a mass grave. A new stone monument surmounted by a black cross bears the names of the missing. There are no flowers in this stark, sad cemetery, with its black crosses which bear four names. There are only three German cemeteries in the triangle formed by the D1029 Amiens-Albert-Bapaume road, the N336 Amiens-Villers Bretonneux-Asservillers road and the A1 Bapaume-Asservillers motorway. In the same triangle there are some eighty British CWGC Cemeteries.

Continue to the church in the town.

German Cemetery, Bray

• *Bray/33.6 miles/RWC*

Bray was the 1916 junction of Rawlinson's Fourth Army to the north (the side of the river you are now on) and Fayolle's Sixth Army to the south. An important administrative centre and railhead, it suffered badly from the attentions of German aeroplanes. In the March 1918 assault it was easily taken by the Germans on 26 March, due to a mix-up in Fifth Army orders. On the night of 23 August, 40th Battalion of 3rd (Australian) Division attacked along the river and recaptured it. Among the units simultaneously attacking along the road from Etinehem was the 15th (London) Regiment, otherwise known as the 1st Civil Service Rifles. It was commanded by Lt Col Rowland Feilding, DSO, whose book *War Letters to A Wife*, published in 1929, is one of the most telling personal accounts of the war. Bray was adopted by the town of Eastbourne after the war.

There are **Commemorative Plaques** in the nave of the church to **Gen Girodon, Cdt XII DI**, and to **'*Prétres Soldats'*** [soldier priests] killed in the Bray area.

Extra Visit to Grove Town and the Bray group of cemeteries/Map M8, 9, 10, 11 Round trip: 4.9 miles. Approximate time: 25 minutes

This is the **French National Cemetery of Bray-Sur-Somme (GPS: 49.94198 2.71737)** in a plot at the rear of the local cemetery, completely renovated in 1990.

It contains 1,044 French soldiers, of which 102 are in a mass grave, and one British soldier. Before it, on a well-kept garden and lawn, is a fine *Poilu* Memorial.

Continue, and take the second road to the right, following the green CWGC sign. Continue to the cemetery, signed to the left.

This is **Bray Military Cemetery (GPS: 49.94721 2.71968)**, begun in April 1916 by fighting units and Field Ambulances. In September 1916, the front line having been pushed further east, it was used by XIV Corps main Dressing Station and in 1917, 5th, 38th and 48th CCS came forward and used it. In May 1918 the village and cemetery fell into enemy hands but were retaken by 40th Australian Bn on 24 August and used again. The Allied counter attack that opened the 'Hundred Days' began on 8 August 1918 in the area of the Australian 3rd Div Memorial that

Poilu outside French National Cemetery, Bray

you visited earlier and by 21 August had reached here but of course trench lines are not straight! After the Armistice there were more concentrations and it now contains 739 UK burials, including **Sgt M. Healy, DCM, MM and Bar and (the extremely rare) Albert Medal**, of the 2nd Royal Munster Rifles, 31 Australians, 13 Indians, 3 Canadians, 2 South Africans, 79 unknown and, unusually, 8 Egyptian labourers. Most unusually the Indian and Egyptian labourers have their own plot to the right of the War Stone.

On 1 March 1917 Sgt Healy,

"… with a total disregard for his own personal safety and solely prompted by the desire to save his comrades, rushed to pick up a live bomb which had been thrown by a Private and which struck the parapet and rolled back into the trench near Lt Roe and the Private. Sgt Healy, fearing the party could not escape in time, made a most gallant effort to seize and hurl the bomb from the trench. It exploded, however, and mortally wounded him. This was the last of Sgt Healy's many acts of gallantry and devotion to duty."

Headstone of Sgt M Healy, DCM MM and Bar and Albert Medal, Bray Mil Cemetery

Healy died the following day of his wounds, age 25.

Turn round, return to the main road and turn right on the D329. Continue approximately 300 yards to a junction of 3 roads.

Each road leads to a Cemetery and after each one return to this spot to proceed to the next by following the signs (or GPS).

1. Grove Town; 2. Bray Vale; 3. Bray Hill.

1. Take the left fork. The road is tarmacked but pot-holed and narrow. Your sat-nav may be a bit confused at this point but keep straight on to the T junction, turn left and left again.

This remote cemetery needs determination to find but is well worth the effort as it is little visited.

Grove Town Cemetery (GPS: 49.96439 2.68542). This was designed by Sir Edward Lutyens. Among the interesting burials here is that of **Maj Edmund Rochfort Street, DSO**, 2nd Battalion the Sherwood Foresters who died of wounds on 15 October 1916. Age 40, born in London, Ontario, he was gazetted in 1898 as a Lieutenant in the Hampshire Regiment, served in India and the South African campaign, resigned 1906, gazetted Capt in the Sherwood Foresters October 1914. Also buried here is **Sgt Leslie Coulson** of the 2/2nd Londons (known as the 'Two and Twopennies'), 8 October 1916. This unusual war poet, a professional journalist before the war, and whose collected poems (including the bitter *Who Made the Law?*) were published by his father as *From an Outpost*, was wounded near Lesboeufs in the same attack that killed Maj C. C. Dickens (qv). His family chose the closing words of Manoah's elegy for his son Samson from Milton's *Samson Agonistes* – '... nothing but well and fair, and what may quiet us in a death so noble'.

An unusual rank on a headstone here is that of **Shoeing Smith Ernest Arthur Smither** of the 21st (E of I) Lancers, 25 March 1917, age 30. Also buried here is **Sgt Henry ('Harry') Cook**, 12th Bn Yorks Regt, 9 January 1917, age 23. He played football for Middlesborough FC from 1913-1915.

The register records the fact that in September 1916 the 34th and 2/2nd Londons established a clearing station here (called locally '*demi-lieue*') to deal with casualties from the Somme battlefields. It was moved in April and except for a few burials in August and September 1918 the cemetery was closed. It contains 1,366 burials from the UK, 14 Australians, 11 Newfoundlanders, 1 New Zealander, 1 French and,

Sgt Leslie Coulson, poet, buried in Grove Town CWGC Cemetery

originally, 34 German prisoners who were removed in 1923. It was here, at 20th Inf Bde HQ, that Capt Martin's 'plasticine' model (qv) of the ground threatened by the crucifix machine gun overlooking Mansel Copse was displayed.

Return.

2. This is **Bray Vale British Cemetery (GPS: 49.95501 2.70768)**, attractively landscaped on two levels. It was begun in August 1918 and enlarged after the Armistice by the concentration of isolated graves. It contains 256 UK, 17 Australian, 3 Newfoundland, 1 Canadian and two unknown burials. On the lower level there are many burials unknown by name, but identified by Regiment, from 1 July to October 1916. Two burials of particular interest are '**A Drummer of the Great War**. South Lancashire Regt' and **Maj G.**

Headstone of Sgt Leslie Coulson, Grove Town CWGC Cemetery

A. Gaffikin, RIR, killed on 1 July 1916, age 30 who has a quotation from Leigh Hunt's *Abou Ben Adhem* on his headstone, 'Write me as one that love[d] his fellow men'. This, and the following cemetery, were designed by A.J.S. Hutton.

Bray Vale British Cemetery

In the late evening sun the beautiful stone wall seems to glow with a yellow light. *Return.*

3. This is **Bray Hill British Cemetery (GPS: 49.95918 2.71702)**. This tiny Cemetery was made by 58th (London) Division on 31 August 1918 as they advanced from Corbie. It originally contained forty-one graves and after the Armistice sixty-three graves were concentrated here. The two German graves were later removed. It now has 102 UK (65 of the London Regt) and 2 Australian burials. *Return to the crossroads in Bray and rejoin Itinerary Three.*

Turn right onto the D329 direction A1/Montdidier and Proyart. Some 300m later cross the River Somme. Continue through Froissy and turn left into the car park at the large sign to the P'tit Train Museum.

• P'tit Train/Railway Museum, Froissy-Dompierre/35.1 miles/15 minutes (but allow at least an hour if you take a train ride)/ Map 1/34/GPS: 49.92271 2.72889

The Picardy Association for the Upkeep of Old Vehicles (APPEVA) has lovingly restored 7km of this 1914-18 narrow gauge (60cm) 'portable' Decauville track. The system was invented around 1880 by the industrialist Paul Decauville and adopted in 1888 by the French artillery to move guns and ammunition. Verdun, Toul, Epinal and Belfort all had a network connecting their forts to the main Citadel. The Froissy-Cappy line, of which this was a part, was capable of moving 1,500 tons of ammunition per day. Dompierre, at the other end of this stretch of the line, was captured by French Colonial troops on 1 July 1916. Life in and around the trenches at Dompierre in 1914 is described in detail in the letters of Captain F Belmont of the Chasseurs Alpins in *'A Crusader of France'* published in 1917. He was killed in December 1915.

The present rail route was laid down for use by local industry and the tunnel constructed after the war. Rides can be taken on genuine World War I rolling stock (made for eight horses or forty men) pulled either by a World War I steam locomotive or a Maginot line diesel engine. The zig-zag climb up a steep incline, the haul up the 3km-long ramp, the journey through the 300m-long tunnel – all add to the excitement. 2006 was the P'tit Train's 35th Anniversary. It is twinned with the Leighton Buzzard Railway.

The Museum has been extended and sophisticated and the entrance to the station is beside it. There is CGS/H Information Board here. Opening hours vary through the season but basically it is closed (other than for reserved groups from April to October) from end September to end May. Then it is open on Sundays in May, June and September and for the rest of the week in July and August. There are special 'Steam Gala' days. The fare includes entrance to the Railway Museum, which has the most

WW1 steam P'tit Train, Froissy-Dompierre

comprehensive collection of 60cm railway material. **Tel:** +(0)3 22 83 11 89 for details of special steam days. E-mail: appeva@club-internet.fr www.appeva.perso.neuf.fr (with a wonderful video) **Opening times** and timetables are somewhat complicated, but basically the trains run from May-September. Please consult the website for details.

Continue on the D329 signed to Proyart.

The road from here to its junction beyond Proyart with the D1029 Amiens-Assevillers road, some 5km ahead, runs across the front of the Australian Division's attack (from your right) of early August 1918. Following the dramatic success of the first day's advance of some 10km on 8 August from the start line some 12km to your right, the next 2km – to where you now are – took almost two weeks. On 23 August the 1st (Australian) Division under General Glasgow attacked right to left across this road and in what is known as the Battle of Proyart, the Aussies captured the village of Chuignes (some 2.5km to your left ie. east), a 14in German naval gun and 2,000 prisoners.

Continue to a small junction and turn left following signs to the German Cemetery.

• German Cemetery, Proyart/36 miles/5 minutes/Map 1/28/GPS: 49.89382 2.71142

This is the third of the Cemeteries in the Amiens-Bapaume-Assevillers triangle (the others being Bray and Fricourt) and contains 4,643 burials. Stark black crosses, mostly with four names, bear the name, rank and date of death when known. They are interspersed with Jewish headstones. Most of the burials are from 1918. Unusually there does not appear to be a mass grave.

The infantry start line for the 1st Div 23 August attack was just beyond the back of the cemetery. To their immediate north was the Australian 3rd Division.

German Cemetery, Proyart

Return to the D329, continue and stop at the magnificent Memorial on the right.

• *Proyart Miniature Arc de Triomphe Memorial/36.7 miles/10 minutes/ Map 1/27/GPS: 49.88870 2.70522*

This Memorial, almost incongruously impressive for such a small, rural village, is a replica of the Arc de Triomphe in Paris. Under the arch stands a Poilu, with the triumphant cry, '*On les a*' inscribed at his feet. The great French rallying cry at Verdun was '*On les aura*' (we'll get 'em). Proyart's Poilu says, 'We've got 'em!' Beautifully executed *bas relief* sculptures flank each side of the arch, a miniature cannon stands on the lawn in front of it and the gateposts are surmounted by bronze *Poilus'* helmets and carry the emblem of the *Légion d'Honneur*. Altogether it is one of the most photogenic memorials on the Somme. It was 'offered in memory of M & Mme François Normand, *sa Marraine de Guerre* [soldier's lady benefactor] from the town of Cognac and the heroic French and Allied Defenders'.

Continue on the D329 to the crossroads with the D1029.

'Arc de Triomphe'
Memorial, Proyart and
detail of the bas relief

Extra Visit to Site of Carey's Force Action (Map 1/25, GPS: 49.87606 2.57877) and Heath CWGC Cemetery (Map 1/25a, GPS: 49.87297 2.67269). Round trip: 12.6 miles. Approximate time: 30 minutes

Turn right at the crossroads and enter the village of Lamotte Warfusée.

It has the most splendid fretwork-effect *Art Deco* church spire, renovated in 2013. The church was designed by prize-winning Paris architect Godefroy Tessière with stained glass windows by Jacques Gruber. It was consecrated on 12 July 1931. Many devastated Somme villages were aided after the war by towns and villages in Normandy whose regiments had fought in the area – e.g. the 329th that liberated Lamotte came from le Havre, which paid for books for the new library in the village in 1919. Among their fund-raising efforts was a concert by 'The Band of HM Royal Garnisson [sic] Artillery'.

The 'fretwork' Art Deco spire of Lamotte-Warfusée church

At the traffic lights by the small church on the right, turn right on the D42 and after 100m turn left on the D122 signed to Fouilloy. Drive 500m to the first Z bend and stop.

In March 1918 the German advance towards Amiens was so rapid that, fearful for the safety of the city, General Gough decided to occupy an old French defensive position, 'The Amiens Defence Line', which had been constructed in 1915. It was 8 miles long and ran across the St Quentin-Amiens road immediately west of this village. On the night of 25/26 March an ad hoc force about 3,000 strong was gathered to occupy the position under the command of Major General C. G. S. Carey and it became known as **'Carey's Force'**. Among the patchwork of small units involved were two companies of American 6th Regiment Engineers from the US 3rd Division, totalling some 500 men who had been building bridges at Péronne. They were the first American soldiers to fight in a full-scale battle since their own Civil War in the 1860s, and they have a memorial plaque in Amiens Cathedral (qv). The very first American casualties in the war were three soldiers killed on 3 November 1917 in Lorraine and they have a memorial in Bathelemont. Here the Americans occupied the line from the road to the wood about 1 mile to your right (north) and came into action on the night of 27 March against German patrols in the town. You are standing on their front line positions. They resisted German attacks on 29 and 30 March and stayed in the line until relieved on 3 April. The Prime Minister, Lloyd George, referred disparagingly to the rapid withdrawal of Gough's 5th Army and gave undue importance to the action of Carey's Force by saying that 'it closed the gap to Amiens for about 6 days' and that it had been formed on the initiative of General Carey. In fact it, and other similar forces, had been formed by the much-maligned Gough – Carey's Force had been created while Carey himself was on leave in England.

Turn round and return to the D1029. Turn left and continue to the CWGC Cemetery on the right.

This is **Heath CWGC Cemetery**, so named from the wide expanse of country on which it stands. Designed by Sir Reginald Blomfield, it has an attractive, somewhat pagoda-shaped shelter with a tree-lined avenue behind it. Not made until after the Armistice, this British and Commonwealth

Headstone of Pte R.M. Beatham, VC, Heath CWGC Cemetery

cemetery (particularly beautiful in early autumn) stands on the site of a French military cemetery, started in August 1914, that contained 431 French and 1,063 German graves which were all removed. After the war, 1,813 bodies were buried

The pollarded avenue of trees, Heath CWGC Cemetery.

here from the Bray-Harbonnières battlefields and it now contains 958 Australian soldiers and airmen, 839 UK, 9 Canadian, 6 New Zealand, 2 South African, 369 unknown and 24 Australian and 19 UK Special Memorials. Among the large Australian contingent, lie **Pte Robert Matthew Beatham, VC** of 8th Bn Aust Inf, killed 11 August 1918, age 24 and **Lt Alfred Edward Gaby, VC** of 28th Bn Aust Inf, killed the same day, age 26. Beatham attacked four German machine guns, killing ten and capturing ten men and was killed while bombing a further machine gun. Gaby captured four machine guns and fifty prisoners at Villers Bretonneux on 8 August.

Continue to the crossroads with the D329 and rejoin Itinerary Three.

Turn left onto the D1029, direction Péronne, and continue downhill on the D1029 to a bend in the road at the bottom. Stop at the memorial on the left.

Monument to Col Rabier and the
55th Inf Bde, Foucaucourt.

Plaque to Lt Col C.W.D. Daly, DSO, and 6th Bn AIF, Herleville

• Colonel Rabier Private Memorial/Foucaucourt Local Cem/39.0 miles/5 minutes/Map 1/28b/GPS: 49.87436 2.73746

This Monument is to Col Rabier, Commandant of the 55th Infantry Brigade. According to the inscription, which is a message from General Castelnau of the Second Army, the Colonel led, with the greatest energy, the 24 September 1914 attack on Foucaucourt-Herleville. He died gloriously at the head of his brigade.

Continue to the turning to the right on the D143e.

[N.B.] This leads to Herleville (1km), where there is a bronze Plaque below the local war memorial outside the church, (Map 1/49), to **'Lieutenant-Colonel C.W.D. Daly, DSO** and 413 officers and men of the 6th AIF' killed in France 1916-1918 (**GPS: 49.86476 2.74983**). It was funded and presented by a former member of the 6th Battalion, The Royal Melbourne Regiment, Ron Austin, in 1992, and is the highlight of his annual pilgrimage. Ron publishes military books through his company Slouch Hat Publications. The village and the woods to the north were captured after very heavy fighting on 23 August 1918 and in the woods **Lieutenant W.D. Joynt** of 8th AIF won the **VC** and **Lieutenant Norm Tutt** was awarded a bar to his **MC**, won at Gallipoli as a CSM. The 6th Battalion had fought through Gallipoli, the Somme in 1916, Flanders in 1917 and back again to the Somme in 1918. Few original members survived. In the churchyard are buried Pte P. Wiggins, SWB, 7 Oct 1915 and Pte W. Farrell, Leinster Regt, 16 Oct 1915.

Continue to the local cemetery further on to the right.

[N.B.] **Foucaucourt Local Cemetery (Map 1/28a, GPS: 49.87424 2.76278).** In it is a **CWGC Plot** of eight graves, all of 1918, at the rear - including that of **2nd Lieutenant Attwater MGC**, 22 March 1918, age 29, with the personal message 'Until we meet. Your little son Mervyn'. Ernest Attwater is commemorated on the Arundel War Memorial. French military graves include **Gustave Lemoine** who was killed in Paris in the *Garde Mobile* in 1871 *'Triste destin de la Guerre'* (Sad fate of war), **Daniel Delavenne**, 8 August 1916 and **Noel Viguane Garin**, killed in Indo-China in 1945.

Continue to the crossroads with the D143.

Extra Visit to Vermandovillers - the German Cemetery (Map 1/30, GPS: 49.85607 2.78176), Memorials to Capt Delcroix and 1st Chasseurs à Pied, to P.V. Bourget, 1st & 31st BCP & 158th RI (GPS: 49.85014 2.78360), RB to McCarthy VC (Map 1/30b,GPS: 49.85067 2.78438) at Vermandovillers; Polish Memorial & Murat Monument (GPS: 49.82818 2.77053 and French Cemetery at Lihons (Map 1/29, GPS: 49.82786 2.74790); French and US Nurses (GPS: 49.81492 2.80534), Poilu Memorial (GPS: 49.81887 2.80056), German Memorial (GPS: 49.81939 2.80739), Chaulnes (Map 1/46/47) and German trenches at Soyécourt (Map 1/31, GPS: 49.86729 2.79138). Round trip: 10.6 miles. Approximate time: 60 minutes.

Turn right on the D143, direction Vermandovillers/Soyécourt. Continue over the motorway and stop immediately at the cemetery on the left.

This vast **German Cemetery** at **Vermandovillers** is the largest of any nationality on the Somme with 9,400 graves and 13,200 buried in fourteen mass graves. In one of the latter is buried the German expressionist, poet and short-story writer, **Alfred Lichtenstein**. A Prussian Jew, son of a factory owner, he satirised the life of the bourgeoisie in Berlin. After obtaining a law degree, Lichtenstein entered his year's obligatory military service in October 1913 and was caught up in the Great War at its outbreak. Serving with the 2nd Bavarian Infantry Regt, which was immediately called to the front, Lichtenstein died of wounds at Vermandovillers on 24 September 1914, after being hit by a sniper. He was 25 years old. Despite his early death, Lichtenstein wrote several powerful war poems, the most enduring being *Die Schlacht bei Saarburg* ('The Battle of Saarburg') written only days before his death. It describes in vivid detail the horrors of being under machine-gun and artillery fire and in it he, like Alan Seeger and many other war poets, anticipated his own death:

I brace myself in the greyness
And face death.

Also buried in Vermandovillers is **Reinhard Johannes Sorge**, the young, brilliant German Expressionist playwright. Sorge, whose works all contained a strong religious theme, was born in 1892, and by 1914 had decided to become a priest. But in October 1915 he had been called up into the 56th Infantry Regt and was serving in Belgium. On 20 July 1916 he was mortally wounded by a grenade at Ablaincourt. His innovative and influential play, *Der Bettler* ('The Beggar') was produced to enormous acclaim by the famous producer Max Reinhardt on 22 December 1917. After the war Reinhardt worked with Marlene Dietrich.

Among the black crosses, with white, almost fluorescent names, are some magnificent willow trees.

German Cemetery, Vermandovillers

Continue into the village of Vermandovillers and at the crossroads turn left towards the church.

This is *Place du Souvenir*. Beside the Place sign is a brass Plaque on a stand to **Pierre Victoire Bourguet** (erected by his sons on 6 September 2000) and to the **158th RI** with a sketch map showing the site of their action at Boyau du Duc on 6 September 1916. To the right of the church is a large cross with a calvary. The inscription translates, 'In this place **Capt Jean Delcroix**, Commander of the 14th Coy of the **327th RI**, *Chevalier de la Légion d'Honneur*, fell gloriously for France on 6 September 1916 at the head of the brave soldiers that he commanded.' This memorial was recently moved here from a field outside the village.

Beside it is a small stone Monument in memory of 11 officers, 24 NCOs and 133 corporals and chasseurs of the **1st Bn, Chasseurs à Pied** who fell from 17 August to 23 December 1916 in the battles of Soyécourt, Vermandovillers, Deniécourt and Ablaincourt. The Memorial goes on to describe how on 6 Sept 1916 the 1st Bn of Chasseurs, after a rapid advance of 1,500m, fought a hard battle at Vermandovillers which cost them 8 officers, 10 NCOs and 58 chasseurs killed. They took 200 prisoners, six 240 mm guns and in the face of violent counter-attacks held this ground in front of the cemetery until relieved on 11 September 1916. On the side of the Monument is a Plaque with a photo to **Chasseur François Lamy**, 6 September 1916.

On the wall of the *Mairie* of Vermandovillers (just round the corner from the church) is a non-standard **Ross Bastiaan bronze commemorative Plaque** at the top of which is the emblem of the **Victoria Cross.** It is in tribute to **Lieutenant Lawrence McCarthy, VC**, whose only child, Lawrence, was engaged to Ross Bastiaan's mother before he was killed on Bouganville in 1944. She later married and when Ross was born the Australian veteran VC treated him like a grandson, filling his young mind with stories of the Great War and of Australian achievement in it. He was undoubtedly the inspiration for the wonderful series of commemorative plaques that Ross has raised wherever Australians served with

Memorial to Captain Delcroix, 327th RI Vermandovillers

distinction in two World Wars. This one was raised at Ross's sole expense. The Plaque describes how on 23 August 1918 McCarthy showed singular bravery and initiative in single-handedly capturing 460m of German trenches, 5 machine guns and over 50 prisoners at the nearby Bois à Fame.

Turn round and turn left at the crossroads. At the next junction, turn right onto the D79, signed Rosières and Lihons.

The French Front Line of 1 July ran between Vermandovillers and Lihons, at the southern extremity of the line.

Continue to the local cemetery on the left on the outskirts of Lihons.

Turn left immediately past the cemetery up a small but well-surfaced road and follow it round as it bends to the left. Stop at the green metal gates in a laurel hedge on the right, just before the road ends. On the right is

A **Polish Memorial Stone** to those who served Louis XV, in 1870, 14-18, 39-45, in Indo-Chine etc. It was erected by the 5th Regt of Cuirassiers of the Oise in memory of the Regiment's action in which Prince Murat took part.

Up a path in a grove beyond is the **Private Memorial and grave of Maréchal de Logis Prince Louis Murat**. According to the inscription, he was Louis Marie-Michel Joachim Napoléon, born at Rocquencourt on 8 September 1896, volunteer, Maréchal de Logis (this equates, perhaps, to a British quartermaster, a non-commissioned rank, whose functions were to find billets) of the 5th Regt of Cuirassiers à Pied, son of Prince Murat of Pontecorvo, grandson of Joachim Murat (Napoléon's brother-in-law), grand-nephew of Napoléon 1, died for France on 21 August 1916. 'Like them, he served his fatherland'. Further inscriptions record how his father, Napoléon, Prince of Pontecorvo, and his mother, Marie Cécile Ney, erected this memorial to their son, 'because of his faith and his gentleness God chose him for a sacrifice and clothed him with His glory. Although he was the youngest of all, his youth was nowhere apparent in his actions'. Princes Charles and Paul Murat, in memory of their brother Prince Louis, restored the monument in 1961 and gave the site to the commune of Lihons. The local council accepted the responsibility of maintaining the tomb and the surrounding grove – hence the tarmacadam road and the immaculate garden surrounding the Monument. Below the magnificent monument, surmounted by an exuberant Imperial eagle, is Murat's tomb. Extensive researches in France, the

Ross Bastiaan Plaque to Lt McCarthy VC, Vermandovillers

Polish Memorial, Lihons

UK, the USA and Canada with the Murat family and the International Napoleonic Society have not established the relationship between Prince Louis and the 'Prince Murat' and his cousin mentioned by Maurice Baring at Glisy Airport. Unfortunately Baring gives no fore-names, so the complicated Murat family tree by Prince Lucien, which shows no fewer than nine contemporary Prince Murats, does not help!

Return to the main road and turn left following signs to the French National Cemetery.

The Lihons French National Cemetery, which was started in 1915 and completely renovated in 1988 and again in 2013, contains 6,581 French and six British graves. There are 1,638 bodies in the four mass graves, in No 1 of which is thought to be the American poet, **Alan Seeger** (see Itinerary Four). On 5 July 2006 a Plaque to Alan Seeger, organised by the Chaulnes Committee of French Commemoration, was inaugurated at the cemetery by Matthew Dever, US Embassy 1st Secretary in the presence of the Sous-Prefet of l'Aisne and a contingent of Legionnaires. The Plaque is outside the Cemetery and bears a quotation from Alan Seeger's poem, *Bellenglise*.

Memorial to Prince Murat, Lihons

Oh should I fall tomorrow, lay me here
That o'er my tomb, with each reviving year
Wood flowers may blossom and the wood doves croon,
And lovers by that unrecorded place
Passing, may pause, and cling a little space
Close-bosomed at the rising of the moon.

Turn round, return to Lihons and bear right following signs to Chaulnes on the D337.

Chaulnes was a heavily-fortified German defensive position, held by them despite many courageous French attempts to retake it, from 29 September 1914 onwards.

Here fought, in January 1915 as Commander of 9th Coy, 3rd Battalion of

Plaque to Poet, Alan
Seeger, Lihons

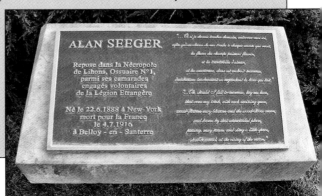

Reserve infantry Regiment 272, one of the most innovative German Expressionist poets of the Great War, **August Stramm**, e.g.

War Grave
Sticks imploring crossing arms
Writing timids pale unkown
Flowers cheek
Dusts shy.
Flickers
Tear
Glare
Oblivion.

Drinking fountain Memorial to American and French Nurses, Chaulnes

He was killed on the Russian front later in the year.

On entering the town continue through on rue Roger Salengro down to the crossroads and stop on the right.

On the opposite corner of rue Ernest Boitel on the wall is an exuberantly painted *bas relief* figure of a nurse with a sick child round a drinking fountain. It is in memory of the collaboration of the **American Red Cross and the** *Union des Femmes de France and Croix Rouge Française* working in Chaulnes, 1917-1919.

Turn round and drive back up to the road, turning second right into a large open square and green. Drive to the church on the right.

Opposite is the dramatic **Local War Memorial**, erected in 1920, which incorporates two standard memorial designs by Jules Déchin – 'Victorious France' and 'Dying Poilu'.

Continue and turn right along rue de la Sablonnière on the D45 signed to Lille and follow the road to a large grey stone on the left.

This is a rare **German Memorial to the 16th Bavarian Infantry Regiment**, moved here from a German cemetery (and indeed originally there were important memorials in most German cemeteries) by young German volunteers in 1992. In it was found a bottle containing a list of German soldiers (now in the *Historial*). Adolph Hitler joined up with the 16th Bavarian Reserve Infantry Regiment in 1914.

Local War Memorial, Chaulnes

Return to Lihons and continue on the D79 through Vermandovillers to Soyécourt. In the centre of the village, by the Crucifix, turn left to the church.

The inscription on the Local War Memorial before the church (selected from a catalogue of designs and known as 'Writing History'), commemorates the contribution to its erection in 1925 by Chatellerault near Poitiers, by the Channel Island of Jersey, by families of those who fell in the area and by public conscription. A contingent of **The Royal Jersey Militia** (known as 'The Jersey Pals') served in France with the Royal Irish Rifles at Loos, on the Somme (at Guillemont and Ginchy for instance) and at Cambrai. In 1918 they served with the Hampshire Regiment in Flanders. The contingent's losses were very high and their Roll of Honour lists 862 men.

Memorial to 16th Bavarian Inf Res Regt, Chaulnes

Drive north downhill past the church on rue de Wallieux. At the bottom of the hill turn up the track to the left, just before house No 5 on the right.

In the tip of the copse (Keman Copse) to the right are well-preserved German

Local War Memorial, Soyécourt with inscription commemorating the contribution to its cost by, among others, Jersey

80th Anniversary Sculpture by Ernest Pignon, Bois de Wallieux

Dugout entrance, Bois de Wallieux

trenches. These trenches at the **Bois de Wallieux** have been acquired by the CGS/H and have been sympathetically preserved. At the entrance are **CGS/H Signboards** and a fenced-off trail leads through the tranquil and evocative wooded area, with profuse wild violets in springtime. Wooden bridges pass over the trench lines and craters to preserve them from erosion by too many feet passing through them. Along the circular route are contemporary photographs on stands and you will notice at least two obvious entrances to underground works. The path leads to a crater in which there appear to be some fractured tree stumps. This is the metal sculpture by **Ernest Pignon**, commissioned by the State (with the support of the CGS) to mark the 80th Anniversary of the Armistice of 11 November 1918.

Continue to the D1029 (N29), turn right and rejoin the main itinerary.

Continue to the crossroads at Estrées Deniécourt.
There are signs pointing to the left to Fay on the D164 and then to the right to Bois de Wallieux (Soyécourt).

Extra Visit to Fay (Map 1/27a, 27b, GPS: 49.88550 2.80757 & 49.88685 2.80417) Round trip: 2 miles. Approximate time: 20 minutes.

Turn left on the D164 following the sign with a poppy to the church in Place du Souvenir Français. Stop.

Ruins of Fay village

To the right of the door is a **Plaque to Officiers of the Gendarmerie and Capitaine Fontan**, Fay 18 December 1914 and to the left to **Abbé Ernest Champin, Sous-Lieutenant of the 329th**, Fay 4 July 1916 and above a small Plaque to the **41st RI** who had a bitter engagement against the enemy here on 7 June 1940.

Continue following the poppy sign to the edge of the village along a rough track to the enclosed site on the left.

This is the original site of Fay, the only destroyed French WW1 village not to have been rebuilt on its original site. Around the landscaped site are **CGS/H Signboards** showing pictures of the '*Ancienne village de Fay*', left in its ruined state and rebuilt where you now see the houses and church.

Return to the crossroads with the D1029 and rejoin Itinerary Three.

Continue on the D1029 into Estrées Deniécourt. Stop at the Mairie on the right and walk across the road to the memorial on the corner to the left.

• Lt Col Puntous Memorial, Estrées/43 miles/5 minutes/Map 1/32/GPS: 49.87519 2.82237

The front line of 1 July was some 2km to your rear (towards Amiens). One of the factors contributing to French success in the Somme offensive was their use of small units in independent actions, moving according to circumstance and terrain rather than in line with a pre-ordained pattern. The action here was typical. The French 329th Infantry Regiment advanced up the road as you have done, led by their commanding officer, **Lt Col Puntous**, who was killed, together with a number of his officers, NCOs and soldiers, on 4 July 1916. The inscription describes the *'Chevalier sans peur et sans reproche'* (a phrase originally used to describe Pierre de Terrail, Seigneur de Bayard, an illustrious French officer of the fifteenth/sixteenth centuries) who took Estrées with an irresistible élan.

The village was heavily defended by the enemy who counter-attacked with violence. The brave Colonel resisted all these assaults except that from the left and the Regiment was overcome. The next day it regrouped under Lt Col Albert who, in a memorable bayonet charge, ejected the enemy from the village. The Michelin Guide reports that:

"The village had to be captured house by house. On the evening of July 4, after three days of fighting, the Germans held only the eastern part of the village. For the next twenty days about 200 of them hung on desperately to it, holding back the assailants with machine-guns posted in the cellars, which fired through the narrow vent-holes. To overcome this resistance, which prevented all advance north or south, it was necessary to sacrifice these houses, and for six consecutive hours 9-in, 11-in, and 15-in shells pounded this small area. Only fifteen survivors were found in the ruined foundations; the rest of the German garrisons had been wiped out. This terrible struggle utterly destroyed the village."

The Memorial was erected by the *Anciens Combattants* of the 329th RI of Le Havre on 5 June 1933. Today it is beautifully maintained by *Souvenir Français*.

Continue to the roundabout. Turn left signed to Assevillers and continue on the D146 to the crossroads in the village. Follow the green CWGC sign to the right on the D146E signed to Péronne. Stop at the cemetery on the left just short of the TGV railway line.

*Memorial to Lt Col
Puntous, C 329th
IR, Estrées*

• *Assevillers New British Cemetery/45.2 miles/5 minutes/ Map 1/33a/GPS: 49.89648 2.84254*

The Cemetery was one of the later ones to be completed on the Somme and was not finished until the late 1930s. It contains 777 burials and now overlooks the motorway and the TGV railway line. The village was taken by the French on the third day of July in the Somme Battle, re-taken by the Germans on 25 March 1918 following the withdrawal of the British XIX Corps and recaptured at the end of August. Just before the Cemetery is an obvious British stone plinth which now bears a local calvary.

Turn round and return to the crossroads in Assevillers.

Assevillers New Brit CWGC Cemetery

Extra Visit to the French National Cemetery & Italian Memorial at Dompierre-Becquincourt/Map 1/33/GPS: 49.90538 2.80142 Round trip: 4.4 miles. Approximate time: 15 minutes

Go straight over and then take the D164E left to Fay/Cappy and fork right at the T junction signed to Becquincourt and immediately left. Follow signs to Dompierre-Becquincourt. Turn left past the small chapel and pharmacie and left on rue de Péronne. Continue through the village to the Poilu memorial. Turn right on the D71 signed to Chuignes. The cemetery is on the left.

The Cemetery was built in 1920 for the casualties from the Somme Battles of 1914-18, concentrating burials from local civilian cemeteries in the region and later exhumations from the battlefield. It contains 7,032 World War I burials, of which 1,671 are in four mass graves.

To the right of the entrance past the usual information board, is an unusual and elaborate **Memorial from the Italian residents of Dompierre** (stone masons who came to help with the reconstruction) to their French comrades who died for the Fatherland. To the left of the entrance are some beautiful, cone, or shell-shaped fir trees. Also in Dompierre is the terminus (which does not have a station building like

Froissy) of the Froissy-Dompierre Decauville railway (see above). The Swiss writer **Blaise Cendrars**, born in 1887, was a francophile who, after travelling in Russia and the USA, took part in the literary life of Paris and wrote some highly influential avant-garde poems. When the war broke out he joined the French Foreign Legion and fought in Champagne and on the Somme. On 26 September 1915, he lost an arm, but his wartime memories were not published until 1946, as *'la main coupée'*. The book describes his 1915 experiences in the Dompierre-Frise-Feuillières-Curlu

Italian Memorial, French National Cemetery Dompierre-Becquincourt

area. He describes a night patrol to Curlu to make contact with the next Regiment in the line. It was not until after the war that he realized, to his chagrin, that among its officers was the 'genial master of Cubism, **Georges Braque**', a friend whose hand he would 'dearly have liked to have shaken'.
Return to the D146 and rejoin Itinerary Three

Turn right and continue on the D146 through Herbécourt.
This village, in the German second line, had been taken the day before Assevillers in July 1916 and its history in 1918 was a similar story.

[N.B.] Near the *Salle des Fêtes* (**GPS: 49.92223 2.84120**) is a beautifully maintained **Private Memorial** by the crossroads of the D1/D146 to **Aspirant Pierre Maistrasse**, age 19, 29 July 1916 with a *bas relief* of his head on an obelisk.

Continue on the D146 signed to Feuillières going downhill into the Valley of the Somme, crossing the river and its fragmented pools and eel farms in the picturesque village of Feuillières.
The village is a paradise for fishermen getting away from it all in their weekend cabins and has an immaculate local WW1 Memorial.
Cross the lock on the Somme Canal, over the Somme bridge and after some 400m turn left on the D146E following CWGC signs to Hem-Monacu. Continue through the village to the cemetery.

Memorial to Aspirant Maistrasse, Herbécourt.

• Hem Farm Military Cemetery/50.5 miles/10 minutes/Map N6/GPS: 49.95368 2.83157

The 5th (Australian) Division crossed the Somme here by hastily constructed bridges during their advance on Péronne of 30 August 1918. The Cemetery contains 138 of their dead, 88 South Africans, 4 Canadians and 1,563 British. There are two **VC** holders buried here - **2nd Lt George Edward Cates** of the 2nd Rifle Brigade, was killed on 9 March 1917 while deepening a captured German trench, when his spade struck a grenade. When it started to burn he put his foot on it and it immediately exploded. By sacrificing his own life he saved those of his companions in the trench. Cates, who was an Assistant Scoutmaster with Wimbledon YMCA, is also commemorated on the Rifle Brigade Memorial in Winchester Cathedral. It is thought that some 17 known Scouts were awarded the VC during the First World War. On 1 September 1918, during the attack on Mont St Quentin, **Pte Robert Mactier** of the 23rd (Victoria) AIF:

"… rushed out of [his] trench, closed with and killed the machine-gun crew of eight men and threw the gun over the parapet. He then moved to another strong-point and captured six men. He disposed of a third machine-gun, but in tackling a fourth was killed. This action enabled the battalion to capture Mont St Quentin a few hours later."

Return to the D146. Turn left and continue to the crossroads with the D938.

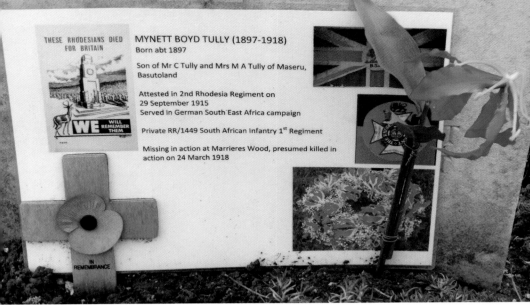

THESE RHODESIANS DIED FOR BRITAIN

WE WILL REMEMBER THEM

MYNETT BOYD TULLY (1897-1918)
Born abt 1897

Son of Mr C Tully and Mrs M A Tully of Maseru, Basutoland

Attested in 2nd Rhodesia Regiment on 29 September 1915
Served in German South East Africa campaign

Private RR/1449 South African Infantry 1st Regiment

Missing in action at Marrieres Wood, presumed killed in action on 24 March 1918

IN REMEMBRANCE

Personal Tribute at Headstone of Pte M.B. Tully, 1st Regt SA Inf, Hem Farm Mil CWGC Cemetery

---

> ### *Extra Visit to the French National Cemetery (Map O2, & 363rd Infantry Regiment Memorial (Map O3), Cléry (GPS: 49.96293 2.85914) Round trip: 1.4 miles. Approximate time: 15 minutes*
>
> *Turn right onto the D938 and go over the motorway. Turn left towards the cemetery and stop at the memorial at the entrance.*
>
> The Memorial commemorates the feats of the 363rd Regiment between 7 August and 2 September 1916.
>
> *Continue up a bumpy track to the cemetery.*
>
> The Cemetery contains 2,332 burials, of which 1,129 are in two mass graves and is a concentration of graves from the old front line in this area. At the entrance to the Cemetery are large boards showing maps of all the French cemeteries in the area and of the Somme Battlefield, with photographs.
>
> *Return to the crossroads and rejoin the main itinerary.*

Memorial to French 363rd RI, Cléry

French National Cemetery, Cléry

Continue over the crossroads for 100m.

• 'HR' Memorial/52.1 miles/5 minutes/Map 01/GPS: 49.96334 2.85006

On the left-hand bank of a narrow road junction is a small Memorial, with the inscription 'HR, 12 August 1916'. [In 2015 there was a chair placed by the Memorial.] It bears a *Souvenir Français* roundel, but all firm information about the subject appeared to have been lost. Volunteers from the memorialgenweb.org have done a great deal of research to discover who 'HR' was, and an entry posted by 'Anne' in June 2013 suggests that it might be 31 years old Henri Joseph Rayssiguier who was killed at Cléry on April 12th/13th 1916. The 170th Infantry Regiment was fighting in the Cléry area and lost 54 men on the 13th, so further research is underway to name each one. In order for the dates to match (i.e. August and April), mistakes must have been made in the records. We have already been through that research process with John Kipling which led to our biography '*My Boy Jack*'. We will leave this 'HR' work to 'Anne'!

Continue on the D146 to Maurepas. Stop at the cemetery at the fork on the outskirts of the village.

Private Memorial to 'HR', Cléry

• French National Cemetery, Maurepas/53.7 miles/5 minutes/Map L8/ GPS: 49.98789 2.85270

This Cemetery was formed in 1921 from two temporary cemeteries at Maurepas and at Suzanne, about 12km away. Besides two mass graves which contain 1,588 bodies, there are another 2,070 French, 19 Russian and a Rumanian burial. The first cross seen on entering the Cemetery is that of Sgt Leclerc. It was his namesake General who liberated Amiens in 1944.

Extra Visit to the Edouard Naudier Private Memorial (Map O4, GPS: 49.98165 2.87363). Round trip: 3.4 miles. Approximate time: 10 minutes.

Turn right onto the road past the cemetery to Leforest on the C5. Continue through Le Forest on the D146E, under the TGV line and the motorway, turn sharp right and continue on a narrowing (and often muddy) road for half a mile to the monument on the left, opposite a junction to the right.

The inscription on the broken column Monument reads, 'Our beloved son, **Edouard Naudier**, tax collector, died for France at Hospital Farm. 1890-1916. Eternal regrets of all the family'. The Ferme de l'Hôpital is the farm on the rise to the left of the Monument. *Return to the French Cemetery and rejoin the main itinerary.*

Private Memorial to E. Naudier, Ferme de l'Hôpital left rear

Continue to the T junction at the square in Maurepas.

Extra Visit to the Gaston Chomet Private Memorial (Map K49, GPS: 49.98569 2.82991). Round trip: 1.4 miles. Approximate time: 5 minutes

Turn left on the D146B on Rue Général Frère. Keep to the right of the church and follow signs to Hardecourt au Bois on the D146E. As the road begins to rise, the memorial is on the top of a bank to the left and is often very overgrown.

The stone Monument is to French soldier **Gaston Chomet** of the 160th RI, killed at Maurepas on 30 July 1916. It was restored by the Albert branch of the *Souvenir Français* (whose rondel is missing) but already has a chipped corner on the inscription panel.

Return to the square in Maurepas and rejoin the main itinerary.

Turn right and immediately left.

There is a **CGS/H Signboard** here which describes how the reconstruction of the village, completely destroyed during the battle, was funded by the Pouret family whose son was killed in action here on 30 July 1916.

Private Memorial to Gaston Chomet, Maurepas

Continue to the small memorial to the left in the square.

• *1st RI Memorial, Maurepas/54.1 miles/5 minutes/Map L7/ GPS: 49.99134 2.8472*

This commemorates the fallen of the 1st (Cambrai) Infantry Regiment who, together with the Zouaves, entered Maurepas on 12 August 1916, taking the areas around the church and cemetery. The village had been strongly fortified by the Germans and it was not until 24 August that, with British help, it was wholly cleared, by which time it was totally destroyed. The inscription reads, 'To our comrades of the 1st RI who fell in 1916 for the deliverance of Maurepas'.

Memorial to 9th Zouaves, Maurepas

Memorial to French 1st Inf Regt, Maurepas

Continue round the square, to the Poilu memorial on the left.

Beside it on the ground is a **Memorial to the 9th Regt Zouaves**, July-20 Aug 1916 with their crest (in need of a little care). (**GPS: 49.99059 2.84713**). They fought at Souchez, at Verdun and later at the Aisne.

Turn left again on the D146 direction Combles. Continue some 1.5 miles to a junction to the right with the D146A. Stop by the memorial on the bank.

• *V. Hallard Private Memorial/55.5 miles/5 minutes/Map 4b/GPS: 50.00214 2.86727*

The inscription translates, 'Here lies our beloved son Victor Hallard, known as Tredez, 110th Régt de Tirailleurs who died gloriously 12 September 1916 at the age of 28 years'. It was once cared for by *Souvenir Français*.

Continue into Combles on the D146 to the crossroads with the D20. Turn right signed to Rancourt and stop at the large memorial on the right just before the High Speed Train line.

Private Memorial to Victor Hallard, Maurepas

• *Charles Dansette Private Memorial/56.4 miles/10 minutes/Map L4a/ GPS: 50.00716 2.87490*

The inscription on this important-looking Memorial reads:

"Beneath this cross, erected to his memory, lies 2nd Lt Charles Dansette, born at Armentières and who fell gloriously for his country on 25 September 1916 at the age of 22 years. This élite officer who had always distinguished himself since the beginning of the campaign by his energy and his indomitable courage fell gloriously on 25 September 1916 leading his assault section against a German trench, which was brilliantly taken. "

There is also a quotation from Victor Hugo, 'Those who piously die for their fatherland have the right that the crowd should come to their tomb and pray.' On another side is a citation dated 18 April 1915, 'On 5 April 1915 during the attack on German trenches in the Pareid Wood proof was shown of an ardour and an enthusiasm which was a fine example for his men'.

Return to the crossroads. Turn right following the CWGC signs and stop at the cemetery on the left.

Private Memorial to Charles Dansette, Combles

• Combles Communal Cemetery Extension/56.9 miles/5 minutes/Map L4/GPS: 50.01059 2.87212

This Cemetery was begun by the French in October 1916, the first British burials being in December 1916 and enlarged after the Armistice. It contains 1,041 UK, 5 Canadian, 1 South African and 13 special memorials.

Turn round, return to the junction, turn right and follow the road down and round into the village to the imposing Hôtel de Ville with its splendid memorial and the CWGC sign pointing left to the Guards Cemetery.

• Combles/57.4 miles/RWC

During their two and a half years of occupation, the Germans had turned Combles into a formidable redoubt in their third line of defence. Much of the strength of the position was due to the extensive catacombs and tunnels beneath the church and under Lamotte Château which stood opposite. (For many years there was talk of opening up these works to the public, but as yet nothing has transpired.) The German writer, Ernst Junger, remembers Combles with dread.

Entrance to Combles Comm Cem

He described the daily hour-long bombardment between 0900 and 1000 of a 'demented violence', when 'the ground shook and the sky seemed a giant's boiling cauldron'. Worst of all, however, was the stench:

'There floated above the ruins … a thick odour of corpses, for the shelling was so violent that nobody could look after the dead. One literally had death in one's nostrils … this heavy, sickly smoke wasn't only nauseating, mixed with the acrid vapour of explosives it inspired an almost visionary exaltation, which only the close presence of death could produce.'

The town held out as the Allied assaults of September 1916 inched their way past on either side. In a set piece attack on 25 September by the British in the north and the French in the south, the 56th (London) Division and the French 73rd and 110th Infantry Regiments cleared the town by the following morning, taking 1,200 prisoners. During 1917 when the British took over the front line down to the Somme, Combles became an important military railway centre and, to conceal the movement of men and material, long lines of high canvas screens were erected alongside the roads leading to the town. **Sir William Orpen RA**, who was sent to France in April 1917 as an official war artist, drew the screens in a picture called *The Great Camouflage, Combles*, now in the Imperial War Museum, London.

In the German advance of 1918 Combles fell on 24 March, despite stubborn resistance by the South African Brigade and then, when the tide again turned, it was retaken by 18th Division on 29 August.

The town was adopted by Portsmouth.

Turn left and keep to the left of the church. Continue straight on to the cemetery on the right.

• Guards CWGC Cemetery, Combles/57.8 miles/10 minutes/Map L5/GPS: 50.00586 2.86025

The Cemetery was begun by the Guards Division in September 1916 and at the Armistice contained a hundred graves, nineteen of which were Foot Guards. There are now 150 burials, including **Gunner Squire Lawrence Taylor**, RHA, service number 111111, killed on 28 February 1917, aged 25. Taylor was with the famous 'L' Battery, which at Néry during the retreat from Mons in 1914 won three VCs. Also of 'L' battery, but after Mons, is Major Guy Horsman, MC, age 25, 28 February 1917, who served throughout the Gallipoli campaign. Oddly he is not listed in the Cemetery Report. **Second Lieutenant L.L. Paterson** of the Post Office Rifles, age 24, 1 September 1918, has the inscription, 'His men wrote a rough cross "In memory of a very brave British officer"'. He had enlisted in Winnipeg as a private soldier. Seven Coldstream Guardsmen lie in a row, all killed on 11 December 1916.

Extra Visit to Private Memorial/Graves to Heumann, Mills & Torrance (Map L6, GPS - at roadside: 50.00260 2.848152). Round trip: .8 mile. Approximate time: 10 minutes

Continue to a farm on the right, where the metalled road peters out.

This is Faffemont (sometimes seen as Falfemont) Farm, although the original farm building was on the site of what is now a copse beyond and on a rise to the right of the present building.

Continue left on a track past the farm to the first pylon on the left. Stop.

The flat stone Memorial (**GPS: 50.00395 2.84430**) is on **private land in the middle of a cultivated field** and is now virtually impossible to visit. If the crops should allow it, **one must ask the farmer** (who calls the pylon *'la Tour Eiffel'*) **for permission to visit it**. The Memorial is some 450m up the slope to the right, on a line between the pylon and the small copse and is completely invisible when there are tall crops. It is in theory maintained by the Commonwealth War Graves Commission and is the grave of **Capt R. ('Dick') Heumann, Sgt Major B. Mills and Sgt A. W. Torrance** of the 1/2nd Londons, killed here on 10 September 1916 during their battalion's attack on a German trench known as Leuzenake at the southern edge of Leuze Wood (just over half a mile due north of here). They were originally buried in a shell hole. Their burials are listed under CWGC Rancourt. After the war, Capt Dick Heumann's family (who had French connections) bought the land and the families of all three men erected the flat headstone, then with

an elaborate surround, and left money for its maintenance. At the time, permission was granted to maintain a path to the site but sadly this is not the case at the moment. Capt Heumann was commissioned in the Regiment in 1908 and fought with it in France from January 1915, being MiD in June 1916. Sgt Mills was also a regular soldier who had already had awarded his Volunteer Long Service Medal. Sgt Torrance was an enlisted man.

Turn round and rejoin the main itinerary.

Return to Combles Town Hall. Turn left, continue 100m and turn right onto the D74, signed to Morval, then keep left on Rue de Morval and continue to Morval.

Private Memorial to Capt 'Dick' Heumann, Sgt B. Mills & Sgt A.W. Torrance, Faffemont Farm. The wreath is inscribed with a quote from Woodbine Willie's poem, 'His Mate'

It was the capture of this village and Lesboeufs 2km ahead, both on high ground north of Combles, on 25 September 1918 that ensured the success of the assault on the Combles German redoubt on that same day. The road you are on runs directly across the front of the attacking Fourth Army (they came from your left) among whose troops were Guards, New Zealanders and Birmingham Pals (15th and 16th Battalion, the Royal Warwickshire Regiment). One of the Pals afterwards recalled the euphoria of victory on the morning of 26 September:

"One of our fellows passed by, wounded and drunk. He had been having a rummage round a dugout. Said he had found bottles of beer and by his description, enough to keep the Army going. When he said he had had the lot before coming back we understood. He sold me a trench dagger and a pair of excellent field glasses for 11 Francs. He seemed very satisfied and so was I."

To the left *en route* is **Morval British CWGC Cemetery**, (Map L2, **GPS: 50.03182 2.86985**) designed by Sir Reginald Blomfield, which contains burials from 26 August-6 September 1918. Its register is in the Guards Cemetery. Morval was captured by the 5th Division on 25 September 1916 and remained in Allied hands until 24 March 1918 and the German Advance. It was regained by the 38th (Welsh) Division after fierce fighting on 1 September 1918.

Continue through Morval to the T junction in Lesboeufs signed left on the C5 to Ginchy and the Guards Cemetery. Follow the signs and stop at the cemetery on the right.

• *Guards Cemetery, Lesboeufs/62.7 miles/5 minutes/Map I4/GPS: 50.0376 2.85324*

This large Cemetery contains 2,827 UK burials, including 2nd Grenadiers from the 25 September attack, 202 Australian, 11 New Zealand, 4 Newfoundland, 1 Canadian and 88 Special Memorials. At the Armistice, there were forty graves and most of the burials are concentrations from the surrounding battlefield, made after the war.

Continue to the obelisk on the right.

• *Captain Meakin Private Memorial/62.9 miles/5 minutes/Map L1/GPS: 50.03544 2.84937*

This sadly neglected tall column is to **Capt Herbert Percy Meakin** of the 3rd Coldstream Guards, attached to the Guards Trench Mortar Battery, killed near this spot on 25 September 1916. It is not a grave, and Capt Meakin is commemorated on the Thiépval Memorial.

Continue to the memorial cross on the right.

*Sadly neglected obelisk to Capt Meakin,
3rd Coldstream Guards, Lesboeufs*

Grenadiers on Parade, Guards CWGC Cemetery, Lesboeufs

• Guards Memorial, Lesboeufs/63.3 miles/5 minutes/Map K19/GPS: 50.03160 2.84251

The Memorial stands immediately to the south of the German 1916 third line. The Guards Division was formed in September 1915 and was made up from four Grenadier battalions, three Coldstream, two Irish, two Scots and one Welsh. The Memorial commemorates the action of 25 September 1916 when the division, in concert with 6th Division, captured Lesboeufs. On the back is an inscription which states that this memorial replaces the wooden cross erected close to this site immediately after the battle of September 1916. During their three weeks holding the sector they sustained over 7,000 casualties. Ginchy Church can be seen straight ahead.

Return to the village.

The village of Lesboeufs was the scene of a remarkable stand by twelve machine guns of 63rd Machine Gun Battalion during the German 1918 Offensive, but it fell on 24 March. It was recaptured by 10th South Wales Borderers on 29 August.

Guards Memorial, Lesboeufs

Turn left past the church and fork left on the D74 signed to Gueudecourt.

The next 7km of this road, up to where it meets the Albert-Bapaume D929 at le Sars, runs effectively 1,000m to the left of and parallel to the 1916 final line reached by the British. The 1916 Somme offensive, coming from your left, finished in November.

Enter Gueudecourt and in the centre of the village turn right on the D574 Rue du Caribou signed to Beaulencourt. Continue to the Caribou memorial on the right.

• Newfoundland Caribou Memorial, Gueudecourt/66.6 miles/10 minutes/ Map 12/OP/GPS: 50.06512 2.85366

Five Caribou Memorials were erected by Newfoundland after the war and they became the responsibility of the Canadian Government when Newfoundland joined Canada in 1949. This memorial stands just in front of the British line of 17 November 1916 (and there are some preserved trench lines within the memorial confines) therefore it is probably the nearest point to Bapaume reached throughout the entire 1916 offensive. Even closer towards Bapaume, probably 50 yards on from the memorial, was the German line known as Stormy Trench. Although the village from which you have come was taken on 26 September, this area was not secured until 12 October – by the

Newfoundlanders. The advance stopped here and British and German forces (the latter straight ahead of you) faced each other until February 1917 when the Germans withdrew to the Hindenburg line.

By using the *Holts' Battle Map* and binoculars you can orientate from the road outside the Caribou by looking up the road to Gueudecourt church which is at 12 o'clock. To the left on the horizon at 11 o'clock is

Newfoundland Caribou, Gueudecourt

AIF (Grass Lane) CWGC Cemetery, Flers

Delville Wood, at just past 12 o'clock is High Wood, and at 1 o'clock is the wireless mast at Pozières. At 1.30 is the Thiépval Memorial and at 2 o'clock is the Butte de Warlencourt.

Turn round and return to Gueudecourt crossroads, then turn right on the D74 (once known as Cheese Road), signed to le Sars. After some 700m follow a CWGC sign to the left. Park and walk up the track to the cemetery.

• AIF (Australian Imperial Forces) Grass Lane Cemetery, Flers/ 67.7 miles/15 minutes/Map H11/GPS: 50.05988 2.83109

Australian medical units that had established themselves in nearby caves began the Cemetery in November 1916 alongside a track known as Grass Lane. After the Armistice it was enlarged and now contains the graves of some 2,800 British soldiers, sailors and marines and approximately 400 Australians, 80 New Zealanders, 70 Canadians, 25 South Africans, 160 French and 3 German prisoners. A measure of the dreadful intensity of the fighting in the area is that two-thirds of the British burials are unknown. One that is known is that of **Sergeant Harold Jackson** of the East Yorkshires, who won the **VC** for individual actions in May 1918, four months before he was killed.

Return to the D74, turn left and continue to the crossroads with the D197.

Extra Visit to the 41st Division Memorial (Map H12, 50.04977 2.82147), Bull's Road CWGC Cemetery (Map H13, GPS: 50.04917 2.82831), 48th Middx (Footballers') Mem (Map H12a, GPS: 50.04785 2.82151) & French 17th/18th RIT Memorial (Map H27, GPS: 50.04403 2.8190). Round trip: 8.2 miles. Approximate time: 25 minutes

Turn left onto the D197 and drive into Flers. Stop at the memorial on the left.
This is the **41st Div Memorial**, an evocative bronze figure of a fully equipped Tommy which was immortalised by being the illustration on the cover of Rose Coombs' pioneering work *Before Endeavours Fade*. An identical Memorial to the

Royal Fusiliers stands in Holborn. (The village *Poilu* memorial nearby makes an interesting contrast in styles.) The Tommy is facing the direction in which his Division attacked on 15 September 1916 in Part 4 of the Somme Offensive.

It employed a new secret weapon – the tank. The Official History described how a tank helped to liberate Flers – 'firing as it went, the tank lurched up the main street followed by parties of cheering infantry'. It was commanded by **Lt Arnold** who won the MC and his **Gunner, Glaister** received the MM. The war correspondent **Philip Gibbs** described the action:

"On that morning of September 15th, 1916, the front-line troops got out of their trenches laughing and cheering, and shouting again because the tanks had gone ahead, and were scaring the Germans dreadfully while they moved over the enemy's trenches

Memorial to 41st Division, Flers

and poured out fire on every side. One of them called 'Crème de Menthe' had great adventures that day, capturing hundreds of prisoners, and treading down machine-gun posts, and striking terror into the enemy. A message came back: 'Crème de Menthe is walking down the High Street of Flers with the British army cheering behind.'"

The small crested china tank popular with collectors is thought by some to represent Crème de Menthe. Sadly, the shock effect of the tanks did not last long.

"There were too few of them,' Gibbs maintained, 'and the secret was let out before they were produced in large numbers."

Turn left following the CWGC sign up the small road to the cemetery.
Bull's Road Cemetery contains 485 UK, 148 Australian, 120 New Zealand, 2 unknown and 15 Special Memorials.
Return to the D197. Turn left, continue through the village to the church on the left. Beside it is
Memorial to Men of the Clacton Orient Football Club who served with the 17th ('Footballers') Bn, 48th Middlesex Regt. This handsome Memorial, funded by Leighton Orient FC supporters, players and RBL in memory of the men of **Clacton Orient** (as it was known), bears a football on the base to the left and a pair of football boots to the right. It was inaugurated on 21 July 2011 by Supporters' Club Chairman, David

*Memorial to Clacton Orient
(17th Bn Middx Regt), Flers*

Dodd, ex-player Peter Kitchen and the *Maire* of Flers. It is inscribed with the logos of Leyton Orient FC and the Memorial Fund. In March 2015 Leyton Orient announced that their players and staff would wear special Centenary Memorial shirts as a tribute to the 41 Club's ex-players who served in the war. Three died on the Somme: Coy Sgt-Maj Richard McFadden (buried in Couin New Brit Cem) and Privates William Jonas (on the Thiepval Memorial) and George Scott, buried in St Souplet Brit Cem.

Continue to the junction with the C5 to the left and stop at the memorial on the bank to the left.

This **Memorial to the French 17th and 18th Infantry Regiments** of 82nd Territorial Division commemorates the Battle of Flers, Ginchy and Lesboeufs of 26 September 1914 and has a red, white and blue *Souvenir Français* Plaque.

Return to the D197/D74 junction at Gueudecourt to rejoin the main itinerary.

Memorial to 17th & 18th RI Bns, 82nd Territorial Div, Flers

Continue over the crossroads towards le Sars. As the road bends right and then left in l'Abbaye d'Eaucourt just before the D929 in this area is the site of a Victoria Cross action.

• Site of Action of Lt Col R. Boys Bradford VC/Map H6/approx GPS: 50.06650 2.79493

On 1 October 1916, here at l'Abbaye d'Eaucourt, **Lt Col (later Brig Gen) Roland Boys Bradford** of the 9th Bn, the Durham Light Infantry, when a battalion suffered very severe casualties and lost its commander, took command of it in addition to his own. By his fearless energy under fire of all descriptions and skilful leadership of both battalions, he succeeded in rallying the attack and capturing and defending the objective, an action which won him the **Victoria Cross**. Brig Gen Bradford was killed on 30 November 1917 at Cambrai and is buried at Hermies British CWGC Cemetery. His brother, **Lt Commander George Nicholson Bradford RN**, also won the **Victoria Cross** in April 1918, but was killed in the action of storming the Mole at Zeebrugge which won him the award and is buried in Blankenberge Town Cemetery.

Continue to the crossroads with the D929 at le Sars. Turn left. Continue to the last building in the village on the left and turn up a small track to the left by a Calvary. Walk about 80m to the overgrown memorial behind the farm buildings to the left.

• German 111th RIR Memorial, Le Sars/70.3 miles/10 minutes/Map H5/ GPS: 50.06820 2.77817

This little-visited Memorial is one of the most important German monuments still remaining on the Somme battlefield. It is in the form of a large, sadly crumbling, stone, with fading inscription. A Teutonic cross can still be discerned on it and the words, '*RIR 111. Einen Toten* [our dead]' and on the other side the battle honours of Fricourt, Mametz,

Montauban and la Boisselle. The memorial is illustrated in the original Michelin Guide to the Somme which describes it as standing in a ruined German cemetery.

Turn round and continue along the D929, direction Bapaume.

Le Sars, which was completely devastated during the war, formed part of the German third line in 1916 and was not taken until 7 October when 23rd Division captured it attacking from your left. They attempted to continue right towards Bapaume but 1km further on were stopped by a formidable line of German defences on the Warlencourt Ridge, the last height before the town. Its central position was a solitary 50ft-high mound of chalk, said to be an ancient burial ground, known as the Meakin, on Hill 122, which equated to the British as Mort Homme in the Verdun sector did to the French.

Continue through the village, past the local cemetery on the right.

It bears a CWGC *Tombes de Guerre* sign and in it lies **Sgt R. Hinds**, 1 September 1944.

As the road goes downhill out of the village, turn right onto the narrow road that leads to the Butte, which is signed. Keep to the left and park at the foot of the mound.

Memorial to German 111th RIR, le Sars

• *Butte de Warlencourt/71.5 miles/15 minutes/Map H7/GPS: 50.07629 2.79501*

The site is owned by the **WFA** and at the foot, which is fenced about, is a bronze sign whose French inscription reads, 'This site is sacred, respect it. Passers-by you are entering this site at your own responsibility. British soldiers fell in 1916 in the Battle of the Somme and still lie here'. On a tree by the parking area is a Plaque to the 8th Bn, Post Office Rifles, 7-9 October '16, 47th London Div. A danger warning is repeated in English and says that the Butte is the property of the WFA. There are duckboard steps up to the summit and wooden railings. It can be very slippery if wet.

This position was the very tip of the British advance in 1916. The attack that began just 10.5km back down the road at Tara-Usna on 1 July had gained an average of 77 metres a day to settle here on 17 November. The daily casualty rate averaged over 3,000. That is forty men for every metre of the advance – one man for every inch. Some of the fiercest fighting took place on and around the Butte. Riddled with tunnels, bristling with mortars and machine guns and guarded by waves of barbed wire, it stood firmly in command of the road to Bapaume. It was never taken and held by the British in 1916. Some reports say that it changed hands seventeen times, but it was not until 25 February 1917 during the German withdrawal that it was finally taken by the 151st Brigade.

In April that year the 6th and 8th Durhams placed individual battalion crosses on top of the hill to commemorate an action there on 5 November 1916 and after a protest by the brigade Commander, who said that it had been a brigade action, they were quickly joined by a large cross for 151st Brigade. Not to be outdone, the 9th Durhams added their own battalion cross. All four crosses were brought back to England after the war, the Brigade cross to Durham cathedral, where it rests today in the DLI Chapel in the south transept. A wooden cross was also placed on top of the Butte to commemorate the German defenders and two further crosses were erected at the base of the mound in memory of the South African 3rd and 6th Battalions. Later, in July 1917, King George V and General Byng visited the Butte. For many years after the war an ornate *Souvenir Français* cross, like the hilt of a sword, and a wooden cross to commemorate the German actions in the area, sat on the mound. They were replaced by an important WFA bronze Plaque which was inaugurated on 30 June 1990, when much of the dense vegetation was removed to return the Butte nearer to its 1914-18 appearance. Ten years later it had all grown up again and the site has proved very problematical to maintain. However a major restoration project for the Centenary was undertaken in 2013 led by Dundee-

Plaque to 8th Bn (Post Office Rifles) 47th London Division, Butte de Warlencourt

WFA Memorial on Summit

Path to Summit of Butte de Warlencourt

based Bob Paterson, WFA European Officer, with donations from Dundee companies.

Continue on the D929 to a "small road" to the left. (You will return to this road if you wish to take the Extra Visit.) Continue past a sign that marks the Front Line of 20 November 1916 to the cemetery on the right.

• *Warlencourt British CWGC Cemetery/72 miles/5 minutes/Map H8/GPS: 50.08079 2.79911*

This Cemetery was not established until the end of 1919 when it was made by concentrating burials from the le Sars-Warlencourt battlefield. An idea of how many small burial plots there were may be gained from the fact that the largest single number of graves moved from one plot was seventeen, and there are over 3,000 burials in the cemetery. Here is buried **Sgt Donald Brown**, 2nd Bn Otago Inf Regt, age 26, who was awarded the **VC** for attacking a machine-gun single-handedly in High Wood on 15 Sept 1916. He was killed on 1 October that year.

Continue to the Centre of Bapaume, (but to take the following Extra Visit, turn round after the Cemetery and return to the "small road" to the right).

Extra Visit to Memorials to Lt Cdr Oswald Wainwright, Hawke Bn, RND, Loupart Wood (Map E2/GPS: 50.09841 2.78910)/Private Christopher Cox, VC (Map E2a/GPS:50.11531 2.78248), Achiet-le-Grand Comm Cem (Map 2b/GPS: 50.11545 2.78232). One way trip: 6 miles. Approximate time: 40 minutes

Turn right on the narrow unsigned road (with a 10ton restriction). Keep straight on over several crossings to a house at the edge of a wood (this is Loupart Wood, GPS: 50.09402 2.793322). Drive left round the house on a rough but usable track (in dry weather). The Memorial is some 300 yards into the wood on the left of the pot-holed track.

The Memorial was unveiled on 4 June 2005 to Allée [Pathway] Paymaster **Lt Cdr Oswald Johnston Wainwright of Hawke Bn, RND**. The stone Memorial bears a Plaque with the Hawke Bn insignia and the French inscription translates 'Disappeared on this spot 25 August 1918. Passer-by Remember!' At the colourful ceremony to unveil the Memorial were four generations of the Wainwright family, three resplendent in Naval Uniform, including Ltd Cdr Michael Wainwright, RNR, grandson of Oswald Wainwright, who instigated the Memorial. He unveiled it with André Coilliot, of Arras *Souvenir Français*, in the presence of many local standard bearers and local dignitaries. Oswald Wainwright had joined the Royal Navy as a young man and served on several ships around the world. When war broke out he joined the RND. Twice wounded in previous engagements, he led an attack through Loupart Wood and was killed charging a German machine-gun post, as were some 20 of his men (some of whom are buried in Bucquoy Cemetery). Wainwright was among those whose bodies were not found (although a colleague had

Three generations of Wainwrights: Oswald's grandson, great grandson and great, great grandson, at the inauguration of the Memorial

managed to retrieve three silver coins from the body which were on show at an exhibition on the day of the unveiling) and he is commemorated on the Vis-en-Artois Memorial.

Continue on the track through the wood until it emerges at a small T junction (the Wainwright Memorial is signed back into the wood at this juncture). Turn left.

In the wood are the remains of important concrete bunkers. Please note that the Wood and the small roads that you will be driving along now are private property and should be driven with discretion. On no account is it permitted to enter the wood which has traps inside. The whole area was a German WW2 airfield and many areas of concrete hard standing still remain.

Continue following the small private road until it meets the D29. Turn left and very shortly right on a narrow unsigned road through the old airfield. Continue to a small crossroads and a memorial against a barn wall on the left.

Memorial to Christopher Cox, VC, Achiet-le Grand

On 17 March 2007 (the 90th Anniversary of the Liberation of Achiet-le-Grand by the 7th Bedfords) a **Memorial**, built with reclaimed Victorian wire cut Bedford bricks by Paul Roberts and Joseph King-Johnson, was unveiled here to **Pte Christopher Cox, VC** by his son, Ian Cox. Cox was born on Christmas Day 1889 in King's Langley and worked as a farm labourer until he enlisted in the 7th Beds in September 1914. He served as a stretcher bearer during the operation on Achiet-le-Grand in March 1915. Cox went from shell hole to shell hole, heedless of fire, treating the wounded from his own and a neighbouring battalion and bringing them in. Cox survived the war and returned to Kings Langley where he was buried after his death in August 1959. The Memorial was initiated by then-SRA Vice-President, Philippe Drouin, who located the exact site of Cox's act of gallantry, and erected with assistance from the Kings Langley Council who also erected a Plaque to Cox in All Saints Church, Kings Langley. It was a moving and colourful inauguration ceremony with members of the Cox family, of the Somme Remembrance Association, *Souvenir Français*, local dignitaries and standard bearers and a contingent of the 2nd Bn Anglia Regt, whose Colour Sgt Rob Parry read the poignant roll of Honour of the Bedfords who died in the Battle for Achiet-le-Grand.

Continue. Fork right and continue into Achiet-le-Grand over the old railway line.

Continue to the T junction and turn left and left again on the D7 signed to Achiet-le-Petit, over the railway line and immediately right.

[N.B.] At this point by taking the D32 north to Courcelles-le-Comte a **Memorial to Pte Hugh McIver, Mc, MM + Bar, 2nd Bn R Scots (Lothian Regt) age 28**, may be reached (**GPS: 50.16420 2.77406**). It is by the *Mairie*, close to the Church.

On 23 August 1918 McIver, a Company Runner, under heavy fire killed 6 of the enemy in their machine-gun post, capturing 20 prisoners and 2 machine-guns. Later he won the MM + Bar, only to be killed in action on 2 September. He is buried in Vraucourt Copse Cemetery (qv).

The inauguration of the Memorial on 23 August 2008, instigated by the Somme Remembrance Association, was a splendid occasion, attended by many family members, Regimental representatives, local dignitaries, the RBL and the Somme Pipe Band.

Inauguration of Memorial to Pte H. McIver, VC, Courcelles-le-Comte, with local Maire & Philippe Drouin

Fork left on the rue de l'Egalité and go straight over the crossing following green CWGC signs to

Achiet-le-Grand Comm Cemetery and Extension, GPS: 50.13612 2.77603.

The village was occupied by the 7th Bedfords on 17 March 1917 and lost on 25 March 1918 after a defence by the 1st/6th Manchesters until recaptured on 23 August 1918. During its period of Allied occupation 45th and 49th CCS operated here and the Communal Cemetery and its Extension was extensively used by Commonwealth medical units. The local station was an Allied railhead. In March and April 1918 the Germans used the Cemetery Extension after which it was again used by the Allies in August 1918. After the Armistice the present Plots III and IV of the Extension were made when 645 graves were concentrated here from the surrounding battlefields. Now there are only 4 WW1 graves in the Communal Cemetery and 1,424 in the Extension, 200 of which are Unknown. Special Memorials record the names of those who were buried in other cemeteries and whose bodies were then lost. There are 42 German graves. There is an extraordinary range of nationalities and regiments. Some of the headstones

New type Headstone of Pte A. Mitchell, Achiet-le-Grand Com Extension`

have been replaced with a new type of engraving which highlights the regimental or national insignia. The Extension was designed by Sir Edwin Lutyens. It is a most pleasing design with pagodas which are covered in wisteria in season and daffodils that blaze in the spring.

[N.B.] By continuing approximately one mile along the D7 one reaches **Logeast Wood** (Map E2c, **GPS: 50.13909 2.76128**). Here another **VC** was won on 21/25 Aug and 4 September 1918 by **T/Commander (later Major-General) Daniel Marcus William Beak** of Drake Bn, RND. The Naval Division had been part of a south-easterly two Corps attack on entrenched German positions on the Achiet-le-Grand to Bucquoy Spur (see *Holts' Somme Battle Map*). The attack began in thick mist just after midnight on 20 August with the help of some tanks, and the Division, passing Logeast Wood, reached the objective of the Achiet-Arras railway line, though the Drake Battalion was held up on the outskirts of Achiet-le-Grand. German counter-attacks forced local withdrawals but Commander Beak stabilised the line. He led his men to the capture of 4 enemy positions under heavy enemy fire. Four days later, although dazed by a shell fire, he reorganised the entire brigade under heavy fire and again led his men to their objective. Accompanied only by a runner he broke up a machine-gun nest, bring in about 10 prisoners. Following the disbandment of the RND Beak joined the Army serving in France and becoming GOC Malta in 1942. He died in May 1967 and was buried in Brookwood Cemetery. During his distinguished service career he won 12 awards, including the DSO and the MC and Bar. His medals were sold at Spinks for a then world record price of £155,000 in November 2003. In October 2006 a Plaque was erected to Beak on the balustrade surrounding the Borough War Memorial in Cheltenham instigated by *This England* magazine, Cheltenham Borough Council and Cheltenham YMCA (of which Beak was once Secretary).

Now follow signs to Bapaume and pick up the main Itinerary.

• *Bapaume/75.4 miles/5 minutes/RWC/GPS: 50.10352 2.84998*

Bapaume has had a chequered history, having been burnt or razed over thirteen times. It was the Allied objective on 1 July 1916 and had been occupied by the Germans as they pushed westwards in 1914 and held by them until 17 March 1917 when they retreated to the Hindenburg Line. It was then occupied by the Australian 2nd Division who found the German fires still burning. According to the Michelin Guide:

> "As they [the Germans] left they destroyed trenches, devastated the entire district, set death traps everywhere, stretched chains connected with mines across the roads and paths and set fire to shelters .... Not a house was spared."

A delayed-action bomb even exploded on 25 March, killing two members of the French Parliament, **Deputies Albert Tailliandier and Raoul Briquet**. There is a **Memorial** to them in *Art Deco* style to the left of the Town Hall entrance. Beside it are two **Australian Plaques**, one to members of the AIF killed in that explosion and the other with the names of the 19 men believed to have been lost in it and the cemeteries or memorials where they are buried or commemorated. They were inaugurated on 26 March 2011. The Australian 'Government's Overseas Privately Constructed Memorials Restoration Programme' contributed $Aus 1,420 to the cost of the Plaques.

The French journalist Serge Basset wrote, 'It is a town to cry over. Pillage preceded fire in each house. A stench of burning and of corpses, envelopes this assassinated and violated town.' This systematic destruction, followed by further devastation in 1918, left the town totally destroyed. The Germans returned during the March Offensive of 1918 until ejected by the New Zealand Division, together with Welsh troops, on 29 August. The Town Hall, in the main square, Place Faidherbe, was rebuilt between 1931 and 1935.

In it are several memorials, frescoes and paintings which commemorate the 1914-18 War. In the square is the statue which gives it its name – to **Gen Faidherbe**. This is a replica of the statue, sculpted by the Parisian Jules Dechin that was inaugurated in 1891. Luckily he kept the model for it as on 29 September 1916 the statue was hit by shellfire. The Germans took it for its scrap value, leaving the base. Dechin made the new statue, which was unveiled on 18 August 1929, placing it on the original base which still bears the scars of war.

Bapaume was 'adopted' by Sheffield after the war. It boasts a completely modernised hotel, with gourmet restaurant – **La Paix**, 11 Avénue Abel Guidet, Tel: +(0)3 21 07 11 03. It belongs to the same group as the **Royal Picardie** in Albert and **Le Prieuré** in Rancourt. There are also several smaller restaurants which are handy for lunch breaks – but do not leave it much after 1300 hours or you might find that the chef has gone home (presumably for lunch!). See also Tourist Information.

• *End of Itinerary Three*

Memorial to Deputies Tailliandier & Briquet and Plaques to Australian casualties, Bapaume Mairie

ITINERARY FOUR

- **Itinerary Four** starts at Exit 13 from the E15/A1 Motorway, direction Péronne, at Asseillers and heads east to Péronne, over the Canal du Nord, through Rancourt to Bapaume.
- **The Route:** Asseillers; Belloy and the Alan Seeger Memorials; the French National Cemetery, Villers Carbonnel; the British and Indian CWGC Cemetery, La Chapelette; Péronne – the *Historial*, the town hall; Mont St Quentin, 2nd Australian Div Memorial/Remembrance Trail; Bouchavesnes-Bergen – Private Memorials to French soldier Fuméry and French Aspirant Calle and the 106th Infantry Regiment Memorial, Marshal Foch Statue; Rancourt – German Cemetery, CWGC Military Cemetery, the French National Cemetery, the *Souvenir Français* Chapel; Sailly-Saillisel British CWGC Cemetery; the French Memorials, le Transloy; the German Cemetery and Memorial, Villers au Flos; Bapaume.
- **Extra Visits** are suggested to: Biaches – Memorials in Biaches local cemetery, French Colonial Memorial/ 2nd Lt Brocheriou; Remains of German Cemetery, Flaucourt; French National Cemetery; Ecoust St Mein HAC Cemetery; Bullecourt – Letaille 1917 Australian Museum, Slouch Hat Memorial, Digger's Park Memorial, Memorial to Missing.
- **[N.B.]** The following sites are indicated: Vaucourt Copse CWGC Cem, Grave of Pte McIver, MC, MM + Bar; Nr Bullecourt – Memorial to 15th Bn Can Highlanders.
- **Planned duration**, without stops for refreshment or Extra Visits: **3.0 hours.**
- **Total distance: 28.8 miles.**

• *Péronne-Asseillers Motorway Exit 13/0 miles/*
GPS: 49.89605 2.84506/RWC

There is a motorway complex nearby with petrol station, shop, tourist information, cafeteria and fast food outlets. The ***Ibis Styles Hotel**, Tel: + (0)3 22 85 78 30, e-mail: h0560@accor.com makes an ideal and comfortable starting base for touring the battlefield if using the Eastern Approach.

*From the motorway exit, **SET YOUR MILEOMETER TO ZERO**. Immediately turn left onto the D1029 and then left towards Belloy-en-Santerre on the D79. Take the second left into the village and stop in the square outside the church/Mairie.*

• *Belloy – Alan Seeger Memorials/0.9 miles/10 minutes/*
Map 1/35/GPS: 49.88269 2.85593

This powerfully fortified village was taken by the French on 4 July (American Independence Day) 1916, their advance having been faster and deeper than the British to the north. The famous French Foreign Legion was ordered to carry the position at bayonet point at 0600 hours. The Michelin Company produced a series of small battlefield guidebooks from 1919 as a memorial to their employees who were killed in the war, and the Legion's charge is described in the Michelin Somme Guide thus:

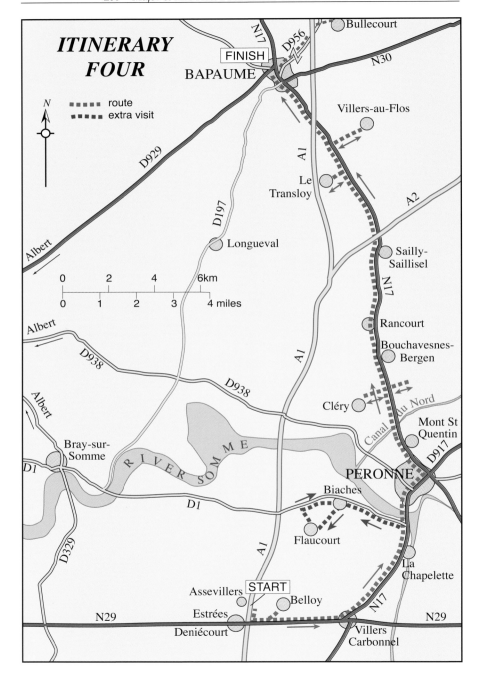

"Deployed in battle formation, they charged across a flat meadow 900 yards broad. When 300 yards from their objective, machine-guns hidden in the path from Estrées to Belloy were suddenly unmasked and a deadly fire mowed down the French ranks. The 9th and 11th Companies sustained particularly heavy losses, all the officers falling. One of these companies reached the objective under the command of the mess corporal. Belloy was captured and 750 Germans were taken prisoners."

Among those to be mowed down was the talented and promising young American poet, **Alan Seeger**, who had been living in France when war was declared and who immediately volunteered. He served with the Legion in the Reims and Aisne sectors throughout 1915 and in the spring of 1916 wrote the prophetic poem *Rendezvous*, that was to guarantee his immortality. Its opening lines are:

I have a rendezvous with Death
At some disputed barricade ....

After the war, his grieving parents paid for a **Memorial Bell** to be placed in the belfry of the rebuilt church of Belloy. Its peal represented his voice, still singing over the land he grew to love. In 1940 the church was again badly damaged but a new bell continues to sing out in his name. The village children are taught some lines of their *'poète américain'*

and there is a **Plaque** to him on the *Mairie*/school, opposite the church and an Information Board with English translation on the reverse.

Seeger was posthumously awarded the *Croix de Guerre and the Médaille Militaire*. He is thought to be buried in the French National Cemetery at Lihons (see Itinerary Three) where a Plaque was unveiled to him in 2006. Alan Seeger is the uncle of the folk

Plaque to poet, Alan Seeger, Belloy

Alan Seeger Information Board, Belloy

name of their son carved on it.

singer Pete Seeger. The village war Memorial also bears the name of 'Alain' Seeger and honours the **French Foreign Legion**, July 1916. On the rear of the Memorial the fierce defence of Belloy by the 117th RI in May / June 1940 is commemorated. The road is called Rue de Catalogne, and the 'Men from Barcelona' are also commemorated in the church.

Return to the D1029, turn left direction Péronne and continue to just short of the junction with the N17. Stop at the French cemetery on the left.

• French National Cemetery/Chinese Graves, Villers Carbonnel/4 miles/10 minutes/Map 1/3/GPS: 49.87638 2.89326

The Cemetery contains 2,285 burials, of which 1,295 are in two mass graves. Fifty-nine men are named in Ossuary 1 and thirty-five in Ossuary 2. Inside the Cemetery is the local World War I Memorial. Muslim headstones and Latin crosses are often back to back. In 1941 eighteen French bodies from World War II were exhumed and reburied here. In the adjoining local cemetery there is a plot hidden in trees at the back containing three **Chinese CWGC graves** from October 1918. The concrete frames of the graves are inscribed 'Concession à perpétuité'. Normally French graves have a limited concessionary period and signs offering graves for reburials are often seen in French cemeteries. It is pleasing to know that the remains of these obscure Chinese labourers, who came so far to give their lives, will always be preserved here, although not always in pristine condition.

Turn left on the N17, direction Péronne and the Historial and stop at the British cemetery some 3 miles further on to the right.

French National Cemetery, Villers Carbonnel

Chinese Headstone, French National Cemetery, Villers Carbonnel

• *La Chapelette British & Indian CWGC Cemetery/6.8 miles/5 minutes/Map 1/37/GPS: 49.90564 2.92997*

One of the later Cemeteries to be completed (it was still listed in the 1929 version of *Silent Cities* as one of the cemeteries which 'for various reasons … have not yet been constructed') it contains approximately 250 British, Australian and 'Christian Indian' graves from 1917 and 1918 and a plot of some 325 Indian Labour Corps from the same period on the left. This stretch of road for about 500 yards each side of the Cemetery runs immediately parallel and alongside what the French called 'Raoul Trench'.

Over the road the Campanile Hotel has now become the 2 star **Fasthotel Relais** and is completely renovated. Good initial reviews. Tel: +(0)3 22 84 22 22. E-mail: peronne@directfasthotel.com

Continue to the traffic lights at the junction with the D1, just before the River Somme.

La Chapelette British & Indian CWGC Cemetery, with the River Somme beyond

---

Extra Visit to Biaches (Map I38/38a/39, GPS: 49.92493 2.90806) Local Cemetery, French Colonial Memorial & Tomb of 2nd Lt Brocheriou (GPS: 49.91758 2.89703); Wartime German Cemetery, Flaucourt (GPS: 49.91202 2.86716) & French National Cemetery at Biaches (GPS: 49.92760 2.88712).
Round trip: 9.1 miles. Approximate time: 50 minutes

Turn left and continue to Biaches.

Biaches was occupied by the Germans on 28 August 1914. During the 1916 Somme Offensive, the French advance on Biaches was so rapid that they took the village on 10 July 1916 after an intense and bitter struggle for a strongly fortified position known as the Herbécourt Redoubt, which was taken, when, according to the Michelin Guide, 'a Captain and eight men, with "extraordinary daring" crept up to and entered the redoubt. The garrison, which still numbered 112 men and 2 officers, lost their presence of mind and surrendered without offering any resistance.' Several strong counter-attacks followed, on 15 and 17 July and the Germans temporarily regained the village, only to be driven out again on the 19th. The loss of the village, the last defence along this road before Péronne, was a great blow to the Germans, hence their bitter fight for it. The French remained in the sector until January 1917, when it was taken over by the British 48th (S Midlands) Division, which included battalions of the Royal Warwickshire Regiment. It was a bitterly cold winter, with snow and hard frosts and very intense fighting took place with the enemy. The 7th Battalion occupied part of Biaches, the village green being in No Man's Land, but a pump in the centre was apparently used by both sides. The Germans retreated from the village to the Hindenburg Line in March 1917, leaving it in complete ruins. The Warwicks then moved on and entered Péronne (see page 31). They made a strong impression on the village and in January 1922 Leamington Spa held a public meeting (typical of many such gatherings throughout Britain) to vote that because of the 7th Warwicks' connection with Biaches (and as Leamington was famous for its health-giving water and the village pump had provided the Warwicks with water in their hour of need) the town should 'adopt' the devastated village. Members of the British League of Help had already visited the damaged areas and they reported, with the help of photographs, the rubble and the appalling plight of the inhabitants (who had numbered 446 before the war and who were now reduced to 229, living in huts). By August £331 5s 10d had been raised. £200 was spent on fruit trees, £50 on garden and farm seeds and the rest on 'Communal Equipment', which included public weighing machines, fences and gates for the rebuilt cemetery. In June 1930, the Mayor of Leamington, Dr R. F. Berry, and the Town Clerk, Mr Leo Rawlinson, joined a large group of British local government officials who first visited Paris, where they were greeted by the President of the Republic in the Elysée Palace and hosted to a grand dinner in the *Hôtel de Ville*. They then moved on to Amiens by train and thence by road to the various villages that they had 'adopted'. At Biaches, Dr Berry and Mr Rawlinson inspected the gifts bought with the money raised by the citizens of Leamington and presented a fine illuminated address (which still hangs proudly in the *Mairie*) to mark the visit. A marble Plaque (now in the Mairie awaiting a suitable base around the green), stating 'Don de Lamington [sic] Spa', was attached to the weighing machine, now dismantled, and the school children were granted a day's holiday. Many other Somme villages benefited in equally practical ways. Montauban's water supply and lighting system were supplied with funds from Maidstone, for example.

In the village turn left on the rue de Barleux at the edge of the green in front of the Mairie. Continue to the left of the Mairie and fork right then continue to the cemetery on the right.

Biaches Local Cemetery. On the right-hand gatepost is a **marble sign reading 'Don de Lamington** [sic]**-Spa'** (see details of the 'adoption' above) and on the left a sign reading Tombes de Guerre. In the cemetery is a well-maintained memorial to 33 Cuirassiers of the 9th Regiment, who fell on 24 September 1914 at la Maisonnette. Next to it is another mass grave to 12 *Chasseurs Alpins* of 7th Battalion who died at la Maisonnette on 28 August 1914.

French 7th Battalion Chasseurs Alpins and 9th Regiment graves, Biaches Local Cemetery

Continue to the junction and go right again. As the un-made, narrow road descends through a small copse, stop opposite a yellow sign in the bank, on the right at the top of some steps, which directs you to the memorial.

The French Colonial Memorial set in a glade, commemorates the Colonial Forces who in 1916 fought in this sector and who died here.

Behind the Memorial is the grave, marked by a white cross, of **2nd Lt Marcel Brocheriou**, of the 22nd RI of Lille, *Croix de Guerre, Chevalier de la Légion d'Honneur*, killed on 6 August 1916. (In contrast to the good state of maintenance of this Memorial, that to the 56th Battalion Chasseurs à Pied, which was in the nearby hamlet of la Maisonnette, was demolished in 1994 by the farmer on whose ground it stood and no trace of it now remains.)

Continue along the road to the outskirts of Flaucourt.

In a field to the right is a brick shelter with the clear plaque, 'Zur Ehre der Fur Kaiser ond [sic] Reich Gefallen Sohne Deutschlands' ('To the sons of Germany fallen for Kaiser and for State').

Originally this was a **German Cemetery** and until the mid-1970s metal name plaques were still in place on the remains of wooden crosses in a semi-circle round the shelter. This rare German memorial has withstood the fate of many other wartime German monuments that were often destroyed by resentful civilians

returning to their destroyed villages after the war or dismantled by farmers whose ploughing they impeded.

Continue to the crossroads and turn right. Continue through the village, noticing the remarkable painted Poilu by the Mairie on the right and at the junction with the D1 turn right. Continue to the French cemetery on the right.

Biaches French National Cemetery contains 1,362 graves, of which 322 are in two mass graves. It was completely renovated in 1974.

Continue and return to the N17 and rejoin Itinerary Four.

Biaches French National Cemetery

Continue, passing on the right a small road, signed to Flamicourt (Bvd des Anglais). It was here on 12 October 1924 the first rebuilt bridge across the River was opened. It was funded by Blackburn under the British League of Help and was named **Blackburn Bridge**.

Continue into Péronne, crossing the Canal du Nord and the Somme and follow signs to the town centre. Turn left at the signs to the Historial and park in front of it if you are stopping.

• *Péronne/8.7 miles (GPS: 49.92885 2.93245) For details of Péronne and the Historial, see Eastern Approach, page 30*

Note: the Péronne Tourist Office is to the immediate right on the square as you face the entrance to the *Historial*, at 16 Place André Audinot, Tél : + (0)3 22 84 42 38. E-mail:

accueil@hautesomme-tourisme.com, www.hautessomme.tourisme.com

Beside the *Historial* (which is fully described on page ??) is a hall marked 'Salle Mac Orlan'. It was named in honour of **Pierre Dumarchey**, born in Péronne on 26 February 1882. Dumarchey was educated at Orleans, then moved to Paris to artistic and literary life. He became friendly with Picasso and the fellow *avant-garde* poet (also playwright and critic) Wilhelm de Kostrowitzky, whose *nom de plume* was Guillaume Apollinaire. (Apollinaire served with the infantry in Champagne, was badly wounded in March 1916 and gassed, and died on 9 November 1918 of influenza in Paris.) Like Apollinaire, Dumarchey took *a nom de plume* – 'Mac Orlan'. After considerable travels he joined the French Foreign Legion – before the war broke out – and served on the Somme. In 1916 Mac Orlan was wounded at Cléry. One of his most famous war-time works was the poem *Chanson de la Route de Bapaume* ('*Song of the Bapaume Road*'). Like Charles Sorley's *All the Hills and Vales Around*, the poem hides a bitter message behind an apparently jolly marching song rhythm. After the war Mac Orlan wrote novels, one of which, *Quai des Brumes* ('*Quay of Mists*'), was made into a popular film.

Return to main road, turn left, passing the town hall on the left on Roo de Kanga! Continue following signs to A26 Bapaume and turn left on to the D1017, direction Bapaume/A26/ Arras/Calais. Continue to Mont St Quentin. Stop at the memorial on the left.

• *Australian 2nd Division Memorial/RB/10.6 miles/10 minutes/Map 1/40a/GPS: 49.94757 2.93273*

This fine figure of an Australian 'Digger' with bronze *bas relief* plaques of Australians in action on each side of the base, is post-World War II. The original 1925 Memorial portrayed a Digger bayoneting a German eagle and was objected to and destroyed by the occupying German soldiers in 1940. There is a model of it in the *Historial* (qv). The French and Australian flags fly to each side of the statue. Behind the Memorial is a **Ross Bastiaan bronze *bas relief* Plaque** unveiled by Senator John Faulkner, Australian Minister for Veterans' Affairs, on 3 September 1993. Around the base of the statue are informative Plaques telling of the progress of the battle. It is Point Number 2 on the Remembrance Trail (see below).

Mont St Quentin, on the right, 390ft high at its apogée, protected the northern approaches to Péronne. Here the Germans sited their heavy artillery and built strong entrenchments protected by thick barbed wire and *chevaux-de-frise*. The hill was riddled with underground galleries and huge, well-furnished shelters. Before their retreat to the Hindenburg Line in March 1917, the Germans mined these defence works and blocked the entrances to the underground tunnels, setting light to the wooden props and causing a fire that rumbled on for several days. They re-occupied the area in their March 1918 Offensive, and remained there until the night of 30 August when they were attacked by the Australian 2nd Division 'bombers' who then held the ground despite three fierce counter-attacks by the Prussian Guard the following day. Monash had achieved surprise by building several bridges over the Somme (the Australian's start line ran roughly parallel to this road on the other side of the river which is in the valley beyond the statue – Point Number 3 on the Remembrance Trail gives a good overview) and using them to move his main force against the Hill rather than Péronne itself. As the troops were tired they were issued with rum to lift their spirits and at 0500 hours on 31 August the 17th and 20th Battalions of the 2nd Division charged directly at the hill 'yelling like a lot of bushrangers'. Péronne itself was taken on 2 September, the Australians winning four more VCs and suffering some 3,000 casualties in all.

Detail of Digger's face

Detail of Bas Relief

Memorial to Australian 2nd Division, Mont St Quentin

Australian Mont St Quentin Remembrance Trail Point No 5, Embedded Shell

Australian Mont St Quentin Remembrance Trail Point No 1, Old Church

In April 2015 an **Australian Remembrance Trail** was inaugurated around the village. It was researched and installed by the Historial with Australian funding. See the *Historial* entry on page 30 for details of the Australian Salle which gives a good background to this trail. There are **6 Stopping Points**, marked with flat stones (easy to miss if you are unaware of their presence) each with a theme, maps, quotations and photographs: **Point No 1.** Near the old church (49.94748 2.93465) with a map to locate the battle and details of the other points. **Point No 2.** Around the Australian 2nd Div Digger Memorial. Theme: 'Memory and Loss'. **Point No 3**. View Point over Péronne and site of Elsa Trench (in field directly below). Theme 'Determination'. **Point No 4**.
Bouchavesne Crest by Crucifix. Theme: 'Determination'. **Point No 5**. Shows a shell still embedded in the wall of the ruined village, then heavily fortified. Theme: 'Destruction'. **Point No 6**. German trench line in the wood (better visibility when leaves are off trees.) Theme: 'Courage'.

Three Australian **VCs** won in this area on 1 September 1918 were: **Pte Robert Mactier**, 23rd (Victoria) Bn, AIF, (buried in Hem Farm Cemetery (qv), Map N6, Itinerary Three); **Sgt Albert David Lowerson**, 21st (Victoria) Bn, AIF, (who survived until 1945); **Lt Edgar Thomas Towner, MC**, 2nd Bn, Aust MGC (who survived until 1972).

Continue, crossing the Canal du Nord, some 2 miles and turn left on the D149 towards Cléry. Continue to the cross on the right at the end of a copse once known as 'Road Wood'.

• Memorial to Gustave Fuméry & 132nd Infantry Regiment/13.3 miles/5 minutes/Map 1/40c/GPS: 49.96944 2.90398

This Cross, maintained by *Souvenir Français*, commemorates Gustave Fuméry, aged 20, and 150 comrades of the French 132nd RI, killed here on 4 October 1916 and buried the same day.

Turn round and return to the D1017. Cross the main road to the rough track straight ahead and drive or walk, depending on the state of the track (it can be muddy), to the memorial ahead.

Memorial to Gustave Fuméry

• Memorial to Aspirant Louis Calle, 106th Infantry Regiment/14.1 miles/ 10 minutes/Map 1/40b/GPS (at end of track): 49.97382 2.91951

This Cross commemorates Officer Cadet Louis Philippe Calle of the 106th RI who, 'ardent and brave' fell near Bouchavesnes (up ahead) carrying out a perilous mission with remarkable courage and sang-froid for which he volunteered, on 25 September 1915. The inscription on the stone is so worn that Louis Philippe's surname could be Galle. The Bouchavesnes war dead are also commemorated on the monument, several families obviously losing two or, in the case of the Melotte family, three members.
Return to the D1017, turn right and continue downhill to the impressive monument on the left.

Memorial to Officer Cadet
Louis Calle

• Marshal Foch Memorial, Bouchavesnes-Bergen/14.8 miles/5 minutes/Map 1/40d/ GPS: 49.98394 2.91577

Bouchavesnes marks the furthest limit of the French advance during the Battle of the Somme. On 12 September 1916, Messimy, the former Minister of War, in command of the Light Infantry Brigade, finally took the village. After the war, a francophile Norwegian industrialist called Wallem Haackon asked Marshal Foch what in his opinion was for the French the most significant battle of the Somme offensive. Without hesitation, Foch named Bouchavesnes. Thus it was that Haackon financed the fine statue of Foch here and the village added the name of Bergen, Haackon's birthplace, to its own. The Monument commemorates the taking of Bouchavesnes by French forces on 12 September 1916 and by British forces on 1 September 1918, Marshal Foch then being Commandant in Chief of the Allied Armies. A Plaque at the local school with Haackon's picture commemorates the gift.

Continue on the D1017 to Rancourt. At the edge of the village follow the signs left towards Combles and the German Cemetery and stop.

General Foch Statue, Bouchavesnes-Bergen

• German Cemetery, Rancourt/15.8 miles/10 minutes/Map 1/41/GPS: 49.99717 2.90550

This Cemetery contains 11,422 burials, of which 7,492 lie in a mass grave. The crosses here are of grey stone, unlike the other Somme German cemeteries which have black metal crosses. It was in this area on 11 March 1917 that the German air ace Werner Voss, flying with Jasta 2, claimed the 14th of his 44 victories.

Return to the D1017, turn left and continue to the British Cemetery to the left. Park.

• Rancourt Military CWGC Cemetery/16.3 miles/5 minutes/Map 1/42/ GPS: 49.99796 2.91056

This small cemetery (ninety-two graves) reflects the fact that the village was taken by the 47th (London) Division – fifty-seven of the graves are of the Division – on 1 September 1918. It was begun by units of the Guards Division in winter 1916.

Cross the road to the chapel and cemetery.

• Souvenir Français Chapel, Museum & Welcome Centre/16.3 miles/15 minutes/Map 1/43

There is a CGS/H Signboard beside the Chapel which was raised as a result of private initiative by the distinguished local du Bos family as a memorial to their son, Lt Jean du Bos, *Chevalier de la Légion d'Honneur* and *Croix de Guerre*, age 26, killed on 25 September 1916, and to his comrades of the 94th RI. The maintenance of the Monument was undertaken by *Souvenir Français* in 1937. There is a Memorial to Jean on the floor as one

German Cemetery, Rancourt

Rancourt Mil CWGC Cemetery

French National Cemetery, Rancourt

Souvenir Français Chapel & Museum, Rancourt

*Stained glass window in the Rancourt
Chapel to the Somme Battles*

enters and behind is a photograph of the young man, and a short history of his action. Above the archway of the entrance is an inscription describing how his mother had the idea of erecting the Memorial Chapel and how his father devoted the last years of his life to realising her dream. The Chapel contains many Memorials and plaques which make fascinating reading. One reads (in translation):

> "To the memory of **Josselin de Rohan-Chabot, Duke of Rohan**, Member of Parliament for the Morbihan, Capt in the 4th Bn of Chasseurs à Pied, *Chevalier de la Légion d'Honneur*, decorated with the *Croix de Guerre* and the Medal of China, *Mort pour la France* 13 July 1916 at Hardécourt-au-Bois. A marvellous soldier, loved by all for his profound disregard of danger, his knightly courage, his beautiful qualities as leader of men, a cavalry officer who transferred to the 4th Bn the Chasseurs à Pied, decorated with the *Légion of Honour* for his magnificent conduct during the first attacks on Verdun when he was wounded. He had only just returned to the front when he was mortally hit on 13 July, a few metres from the German trenches, where he was carrying out an extremely perilous recce for an operation that he was asked to lead."

The body of the Duke (among his ancestors was one of Louis XIII's most famous generals) was returned to the family château at Josselin in the Morbihan and buried in the crypt of the chapel. His death was mourned by his friend, Jean Cocteau (see Itinerary Three). The Count and Countess Rohan-Chabot of the same family were present at the inauguration of the Airborne Forces cross in Ranville CWGC Cemetery in September 1944. To the left of the doorway in the left wall are two British plaques. One is to **Lt Niel Shaw Stewart** of the Rifle Brigade who was killed leading 'C' company in the attack on Guillemont on 21 August, age 22. He is buried in Delville Wood CWGC Cemetery. The other is to **Lt Alan Humphrey Cheetham**, of the 2nd Bn, Duke of Wellingtons, age 20 who was killed at Sailly-Saillisel on the night of 15th/16th December 1916. He is commemorated on the Thiépval Memorial.

Adjoining the **Chapel** is a small **Museum**, now renovated and with interesting exhibits added to the original items as diverse as the medical instruments that were presented by the Brooklyn Post No 2 Jewish War Vets of the US on 4 July 1918, to a model of the 'Long Max' gun from Laon and models of World War II rocket launching pads in the district. It is maintained by guardian, M J-P Desain who also runs the **Welcome Centre**, approached through a door on the opposite side of the Chapel. It has a small Information Centre, souvenir shop and WC. Tel: +(0)3 22 85 04 47. E-mail: memorial-rancourt@neuf.fr. **Open** every day.

Walk into the adjoining cemetery.

• *French National Cemetery, Rancourt/16.3 miles/10 minutes/Map 1/44*

This is the largest French Military Cemetery on the Somme, with 8,566 burials, of which 3,240 are in four ossuaries. It is a concentration cemetery from all the surrounding battlefields and testifies to the sacrifice of the French from September to November 1916 in the region. It ranks in emotional importance as a focal point of remembrance to the French as do the Thiépval Memorial and Tyne Cot Cemetery in the Ypres Salient to the British. Because of the closeness of the three different nationality cemeteries here, joint Anglo-French-German ceremonies are held on important anniversaries. It also affords an opportunity to compare and contrast the different styles of remembrance of the three nationalities.

Continue into the village.

The 2 star Logis de France **Hôtel Prieuré** , part of the same group as the **Royal Picardie** at Albert and **La Paix** at Bapaume, is on the right, **Tel:** +(0)3 22 85 04 43. E-mail: contact@ hotel-le-prieure.fr It has a *'restaurant gastronomique'*.

Continue on the D1017 to the British cemetery to the left on the outskirts of Sailly-Saillisel and park. Traffic moves very quickly on this road and it is very difficult to stop.

• *Sailly-Saillisel British Cemetery/17.8 miles/5 minutes/Map 1/44a/GPS: 50.01966 2.91007*

Sailly-Saillisel was the scene of desperate fighting on 28 August 1914, when the French Reserves were trying to stop the German rush 'nach Paris'. The consequences were terrible for the French – see le Transloy below.

The village was captured by the French in 1916 and remained in Allied hands until the German Offensive of March 1918, when it fell on the 24th. It was retaken by the 18th and 38th (Welsh) Division on 1 September 1918. The Cemetery records 559 UK, 12 Australian, 7 Newfoundland and 185 unknown burials and 8 Special Memorials. It was made after the Armistice by the concentration of small graveyards, including 'Charing Cross' and 'Aldershot'. After the war the London connection was continued. Marylebone paid for the *'Salle des Fêtes'* in the rebuilt village.

Continue on the D1017/917 to le Transloy and turn left at the T junction with the D19, following signs to the French 'Monument aux 800 Morts'. Drive to the French Poilu in the village, keeping to the right.

• *War Memorial, Le Transloy/21.8 miles/5 minutes/GPS: 50.05766 2.88889*

This commemorates victims from the Franco-Prussian War of 1870-1 and cites the Order of the Day of 24 September 1920 which awards the village with the *Croix de Guerre* for suffering complete destruction in the bombardments, and for always showing dignity and courage in its afflictions under enemy domination. Of the long list of towns and villages thus honoured, many are on the Somme and nearby battlefields, notably Albert, Amiens, Arras, Assevillers, Authuille, Aveluy, Bapaume, Beaucourt, Beaumont-Hamel, Bouchavesnes, Bray, Chipilly, Combles, Contalmaison, Corbie, Courcelette, Dompierre, Doullens, Feuillières, Flaucourt, Flers, Fouilloy, Fricourt, Ginchy, Guillemont, Heilly, Hem-Monacu, Lihons, Mailly-Maillet, Mametz, Maricourt, Montauban, Mont St Quentin, Ovillers, Péronne, Pozières, Proyart, Sailly-Saillisel, Suzanne, Thiépval, Vermandovillers and Villers Bretonneux.

The ridge upon which le Transloy sits was the target of a series of attacks during October 1916 which were opened by 56th Division of XIV Corps on 7 October. Heavy rain turned the fields into liquid mud and the Corps Commander, Lord Cavan, questioned whether the continuous effort was worth the loss in men. French forces were attacking alongside to the south and the British efforts may have been part of the C-in-C's 'co-operation policy'. In any event, the ridge was not taken.

Continue right of the Memorial to the cemetery on the left at the far edge of the village and drive into the car park.

• *Monument to 800 Dead of 28 August 1914/22.2 miles/15 minutes/Map I3/ GPS: 50.05440 2.88160*

There are several Memorials inside the gate beside the local *cimetière communal*. On the wall to the left are individual Plaques and photographs and there are two major Monuments – one a tall column to the 800 *braves* who fell on 28 August and 26 September

Individual plaques to two of the '800 morts', le Transloy Cemetery

ICI REPOSE
LÉON JULES CHAZETTE
Mort pour la France
à la bataille de Rocquigny
le 28 Août 1914
REGRETTÉ DE TOUS LES SIENS

Memorial Column, Le Transloy

À LA MÉMOIRE DE MON MARI
EUGÈNE JAMOT
Tué à l'ennemi à Bapeaume
le 28 Août 1914
Regretté de toute sa famille
et de ses amis

1914, erected by their families (with a Plaque on the back saying that the names of the missing are held in the archives in the Mairie), the other, a marble wall carrying the names of the missing 792 soldiers 'Morts Pour la France' at le Transloy on 28 August and 26 September 1914 who rest here. Another stone on a mass grave commemorates ten officers who fell on those same dates and there are individual graves to 2nd Lt Emil Rabache of the 338th RI from Limoges, 28 August 1914 age 23, *Croix de Guerre*, 2nd Lt Reservist Alfred Grouzillard, 28 June 1879-28 August 1914, *Chevalier de la Légion d'Honneur*; a cross to Capt Anatole Thepernier, 26th RIT, 26 September 1914 and the tomb of sixteen other named NCOs and soldiers of 26 September.

These reminders of this massive slaughter are extremely moving. Even locally, the full facts are little known today. The story is, however, fully documented in a detailed study of the tragic episode called *28 August 1914. Les Combats de le Transloy, Rocquigny, Sailly-Saillisel*, by Maurice Pasquet, grandson of one of the participants, who had been brought up on stories of the massacre told by his widowed grandmother. He uses regimental histories, diaries and personal accounts by survivors to piece together what happened. The story starts at Mons. The British formed the left-hand end of the French line. On 23 August 1914 they briefly held Von Kluck's right wing at Mons and began a three-day withdrawal to le Cateau. Gen Joffre, seeing that his left wing was now exposed, rallied forces to fill the gap left by the British and on 24/25 August, untried French reservists of the 61st and 62nd Divisions were rushed to Arras by train. Their orders were to extend the British line to the west. Meanwhile the British made a brief stand at le Cateau on 26 August and then began their long retreat to the Marne. Von Kluck declined to follow the British, and sent Von Linsingen's 2nd Army Corps west to Cambrai (where they arrived in the area of Marcoing, which would feature in the

1917 battle) on 26/27 August. The French, now unable to contact the retreating BEF, sat astride Bapaume – the 61st Div to the west, the 62nd Div to the east.

At this point the subsequent actions can be more easily followed by referring to the Michelin map 236, folds 26 and 27.

On 27 August 1914 the German forces, spearheaded by the 49th and 149th Infantry Regiments, headed south-west, roughly along the line of the A2-E19 motorway from Cambrai and reached Sailly-Saillisel (where the motorway crosses the N17). En route they had flank engagements with the French 62nd Inf Div who were in the area between the A2-E19 and A1-E15 motorways south-east of Bapaume. Thus the Germans were south of the French divisions. That night there was fighting at Sailly-Saillisel and Von Kluck, anxious to maintain his advance, yet keen to isolate the French, ordered that the 49th and 149th should manoeuvre to prevent the French from crossing the Somme (which they were vainly and tardily attempting to do in order to block the Germans in their rush 'nach Paris'). The following morning, in thick fog, the two German regiments moved north along the line of the N17 at le Transloy and hit the flank of the unsuspecting 338th Regt of 123rd Bde of 62nd Div coming, in marching formation, from the north-east in what they thought was pursuit of the Germans. The 338th Regt suffered heavy casualties from the encounter – all its officers were killed or wounded – and the accompanying 278th Regiment, despite attempting to march around the Germans to the north, was also cut down. By 1000 hours the French were falling back to Arras, leaving behind some 1,200 prisoners and a battlefield littered with materiel – much of which the Germans collected. Von Kluck, however, was not pleased with what would seem to be an overwhelming victory. His orders for the 28th had been 'to cross the Somme between Corbie and Nesle'. The French, despite their horrendous casualties, had delayed the Germans by as much as the British had done at Mons and le Cateau.

At the end of the day on 28 August, the normally peaceful fields around le Transloy looked like a vision from the Apocalypse, much as the battlefield of Waterloo had looked on the night of 15 June 1815. It had been a scorchingly hot day and the wounded suffered on the battlefield, lying amongst their dead comrades. There are varied reports of the victors' treatment of the victims. In some places the Germans gave water, basic first aid and an attempt at some shelter from the sun. In others the wounded were put out of their misery – and not for humane reasons. The shocked inhabitants of the village rallied. Farmers brought up their vehicles and carts to move the wounded to improvised hospitals. In the absence of any professional medical help, the women and girls became caring nurses. The next day motor ambulances arrived from Arras and the evacuation of the wounded was completed by nightfall. 'Après les blessés, les morts', was the villagers' priority. Their wounded in safe hands, on the third day after the battle they set out to pick up the dead who lay on the plain between Rocquigny, Sailly-Saillisel and Morval. Again with their farm carts and vehicles, they brought the bodies, by now in an advanced state of decomposition because of the heat, to the small cemetery at le Transloy and gently searched for identification. Organized by the Curé, M. Blasart, wallets, identification discs and papers, photographs of loved ones, personal possessions – all were lovingly tied up in knotted handkerchiefs and labelled with a name. Then a huge ditch, 10 metres long and 4 metres wide was dug and the bodies were reverently laid, side by side 'comme à la parade'. Ten officers were buried in a nearby mass grave.

The inhabitants were soon evacuated, and when they were allowed to return in 1919 to find their village – and the cemetery – completely destroyed, the mayor, M. Malet, received a flood of letters from relatives of the dead, wanting to know details of their burial. By 1920, the villagers had found the site of the mass grave and the first landscaping took place, so that on 5 September 1920 relatives and dignitaries were able to join in a ceremony of commemoration. A subscription was raised for a suitable monument and on 25 September 1921 it was inaugurated. From then on a ceremony was held annually on the 3rd Sunday of September and in 1927 marble panels, inscribed with the names of the 800 '*braves*', was unveiled.

When the Germans finally pushed their line well south towards the Somme they used the relatively high ground of the cemetery (then quite small) as a formidable defensive position, building a near semi-circle of trenches and multiple lines of barbed wire around it to a radius of 250 yards.

Return to the D917 and turn left. Continue to the junction with the D11 in Beaulencourt. Turn right signed to Villers au Flos and continue to the village crossroads and then turn left, following signs along a small meandering road, to the German Cemetery. It is approached down a long brick path.

• German Cemetery & XIV Reserve Korps Memorial, Villers au Flos/24.7 miles/10 minutes/Map 1/45/GPS: 50.08273 2.90193

The Cemetery contains 2,449 burials under black crosses, but with only two, rather than the usual four, men marked on each. Most of the burials are of July 1916. At the back of the cemetery is a high stone memorial tower to the XIV Reserve Korps, 1914-18 which was originally in the cemetery at Bapaume. The X1Vth held this area during the 1916 battles (see the Holts' map).

Return to the junction with the D917, turn right and continue the Itinerary by following signs into Bapaume Centre.

• Bapaume/28.8 miles

End of Itinerary Four
OR

Extra Visit to H.A.C. Cemetery, Ecoust-St Mein (Map 1/51, GPS: 50.17186 2.90506); Bullecourt and the Australian/British 1917 Actions: Museum (Map 1/46, GPS: 50.19181 2.92723), Slouch Hat & Tank Crew Memorials (Map 1/47, GPS: 50.19292 2.92963), Digger Memorial Park (Map 1/48, GPS: 50.19477 2.93833), Memorial to the Missing (Map 1/49, GPS: 50.19528 2.94388)
Round trip: 17 miles. Approximate time: 80 minutes.
From Bapaume take the D956 signed to Douai and continue towards St Ecoust St Mein and stop at the cemetery on the left.
H.A.C Cemetery, Ecoust-St Mein (Map 1/51)
The village and enemy positions around it were captured by the 4th & 7th Australian Divisions on 2 April 1917. The Cemetery was begun by 7th Division after the battle when 27 members of the Honourable Artillery Company who fell (with one exception) on 31 March or 1 April were buried in what is now Plot I, Row A. After the German counter-attack near Lagnicourt on 15 April, 12 Australian Gunners were buried in the same row. Rows B, C and part of D were made in August and September 1918 when the ground was recaptured by the 3rd

Division. After the Armistice graves were added from the battlefields of Ecoust and Bullecourt and other small burial grounds, including French, German and Russian casualties. Now there are nearly 2,000 WW1 casualties (over half of which are unidentified (and one is emotionally hit by seeing row after row of 'Known Unto God' burials here) and there are Special Memorials to 17 UK, 14 Australian and 34 UK soldiers whose graves were destroyed by shellfire.

Here are buried: **Maj Francis Fitzgerald ('Ferdy') Waldron** (qv), 60th Sqn RFC, age 29, 3 July 1916, only son of Brig-Gen F. Waldron, CB, RH, RFA and **Capt Auberon Thomas ('Bron') Herbert,** 8th Baron Lucas and 11th Baron Dingwall, 22nd Sqn RFC, 3 November 1916. He is also listed in the Cemetery Report as 'Capt Auberon Thomas Herbert Lucas, "Alias", 3 November 1916' and additionally '5th Baron. SEE HERBERT, the true family name'. Maurice Baring (qv) wrote a poem entitled *In Memoriam, A.H. (Auberon Herbert, Captain Lord Lucas, RFC killed November 3 1916).* 'Bron' Lucas was one of the great personalities of his time. An Oxford (Balliol) rowing 'Blue' he went to cover the S. African war as *Times* correspondent where he lost a leg. This did not deter him from hunting and shooting on his return. He entered Parliament and rose to the position of President of the Board of Agriculture in 1914. When war broke out he joined the Hampshire Yeomanry and despite being vastly over-age (39) managed to join the RFC, serving in Egypt with 13 Sqn where he was M.I.D. In October 1916 he was given command of 22 Sqn, stationed at Bertangles (qv) where Maurice Baring (first Henderson's and later Trenchard's Private Secretary) visited him. On 3 November he was at first posted as missing but later was reported to have been shot in the neck but able to land his machine. He died shortly after and was buried 'near Bapaume'. His grave was then lost and not rediscovered until the Allied advance to Victory in autumn 1918.

Also buried here is **Rifleman John Woodhouse**, KRRC who was 'Shot at Dawn' on 4 October 1917 for desertion, and the poet, **Capt Arthur Graeme West**. This unconventional war poet, despite defective eyesight, joined the 16th Public Schools Battalion of the Middlesex Regiment as a private in February 1915. He was killed by a sniper on 3 April 1917 in his trench near Barastre, to the east of Bapaume. In August 1916 he had been commissioned in the 6th Bn, the Oxs and Bucks. Educated at Blundells School and Balliol College, Oxford, he was an admirer of Bertrand Russell and veered towards atheism. His poems reflect his non-conformity to the usual patriotic and resigned public school attitude. *'God! How I Hate You, You Young Cheerful Men!'*, he wrote in early 1916.

AN EXCEPTIONAL CEREMONY

It was here on Tuesday 23 April 2013 that the Re-interment of four soldiers of the Honourable Artillery Company took place. Their remains had been discovered by a local farmer in a nearby field in 2009. Two of the four were identified as **Lt John Harold Pritchard** (by a silver identity bracelet) and **Pte Christopher Douglas Elphick** (by a signet ring bearing his initials). Because a large number of family members of both men had been found and attended the ceremony, it attracted much press attention by the British and French media which greatly added to the poignancy of the day.

We have chosen to feature this ceremony at unusual length for one of our guidebooks as it epitomised the caring, superbly accurate, highly professional and quietly efficient work of the Commonwealth War Graves Commission (see

Burial party approaching the grave

Entry of Lt Pritchard's coffin bearing his sword,
Ecoust St Mein CWGC Cemetery

Lowering the coffin

The Pritchard Family singing

Prince Michael of Kent receives the folded flag

The HAC
delegation

also page 325), who unobtrusively prepared the graves area and backed up the immaculate and reverential burial party in the perfectly maintained Cemetery: of the Joint Casualty and Compassionate Centre (see also page 328) who deal with the newly found remains, identification and liaison with any family members; of the HAC, who buried four of their own, who died 96 years ago, with pride, gentle precision and compassion and, finally, of the MOD Press Service who bring the event to the attention of the public so that they are aware of the work of the afore-mentioned organisations.

The service was conducted by the Rev Mark Speeks CF and the Rev David Reindorp CF (Retd) with participation by Prince Michael of Kent, Royal Hon Col; Lt Col Howard Wilkinson and RSM WO1 Andy Campbell of the HAC and family members. Unusually, but movingly, the service was completed by four members of the Pritchard family singing Tennyson's *Crossing the Bar*, the song that Lt Pritchard sang to his mother before he finally left for the front.

A unique element of the burial was that on the coffin of Lt Pritchard was his sword. It was lost when he was killed and somehow found its way into the hands of an American collector, Mark Cain, who generously returned it to the family. It is visible in our picture which, with the others, tell the story of the re-burial.

[N.B.] By driving some 1.5 km to the south east **Vraucourt Copse CWGC Cemetery (GPS: 50.15907 2.91534)** may be reached. In it is buried **Pte Hugh McIver, MC, MM + Bar** (qv).

As part of the Hindenberg Line the Germans had built a small salient of barbed wire and trenches around Bullecourt which projected forward towards you. As you enter the village the forward edge of the salient stretched across the road to about 500 yards each side and then bent back away from you. Fighting therefore went on from three directions.

Continue on the D956 into Bullecourt. Turn left signed Musée Militaire and immediately stop on the right at No. 1bis rue d'Arras.

Bullecourt 1917 Museum of Jean and Denise Letaille.

For many years the highlight of a visit to Bullecourt was to go to the Private Museum of Monsieur Letaille where one was assured of a warm welcome from Jean and his wife Denise. This extraordinary couple had worked tirelessly in ensuring that the Battle of Bullecourt and its many Australian and British casualties would never be forgotten, being instrumental in the erection of the various memorials and trails that visitors can now enjoy in the area. The work of the former Mayor and his wife was recognised by the award of the Medal of Australia.

Their wonderful collection, housed in a barn in their courtyard, was built up over the years from objects found in the surrounding countryside and donations from many contributors. It contained many personal possessions (including some of Sergeant Jack White, whose remains were found near Bullecourt and reburied in October 1995 (qv)) and fascinating accounts, e.g. of Captain Albert Jacka, who won his VC (the first to be awarded to a Commonwealth soldier) as a Lance-Corporal in May 1915 at Courtney's Post in Gallipoli. There were collections of entrenching tools, ammunition boxes, weapons etc.

After Denise's death, Jean's health declined and he came to an arrangement with the Australian Government to donate his collection to them and in return they would house and care for it in the modern Museum you are now about to visit. He died in tragic circumstances on 10 March 2012, a month before the official opening. The couple are strongly featured and honoured in the Museum which bears their name.

There is a WC, access for the disabled and a small books stall. **Open:** Mon-Sun 1400-1800. Entrance fee payable. Audio-guide in French and English. Tel: + (0)3 21 55 33 20. E-mail: musee-bullecourt1917@orange.fr

Turn round, return to the main road, turn left and stop near the Town Hall. Opposite is

The Slouch Hat Memorial (Map 1/47), a felt Digger's hat which has been bronzed, in *'Square du Souvenir Français'*. The brick base bears the badges of the 1st, 2nd, 4th

Display in Australian Letaille Museum, Bullecourt

'Slouch Hat' Memorial, Bullecourt.

Detail of the Slouch Hat

Memorial to Heavy Bde, Machine Gun Corps, Bullecourt

and 5th AIF, the 58th (London) Division, the 62nd (W Riding) Division and the 7th Division.

The first attempt to seize Bullecourt began on 11 April in driving snow when two brigades of the 4th Australian Division, supposedly led by twelve tanks, set out to take the village and its neighbour, Riencourt. Unfortunately the tanks failed – nine had direct hits and the others had mechanical problems. To compound the difficulties the artillery support was insufficient, due to ammunition shortage and lack of information about the movements of the forward troops – some 17th Lancers coming up to support came under 'friendly fire'. Despite valiant and determined efforts by the Australians they were unable to consolidate the small gains that they had made and fell back in confusion, though for a brief period they had held one small part of the Hindenburg Line without a supporting barrage. One observer called the 11th "a day of unrelieved disaster": Australian losses were some 3,000.

To the right of this Memorial is a **Memorial to the Tank Crews of D Bn HBMGC** who were engaged at Bullecourt on 3 May 1917. It was erected by *Souvenir Français*, Arras, in April 2010. Below it is part of the track of tank No 586 of L. Clarkson, destroyed near the village of Riencourt. Above is a plan of the 4 points of the **Australian Battlefield Track** around the village.

Continue and fork right on the rue des Australiens following the green CWGC sign to the Australian Memorial on the right.

Digger's Memorial Park (Map 1/48). To the left is a bench with the Plaque SEGPA Marquion 1997 and there is a **Ross Bastiaan bronze Plaque**. The fine bronze statue is sacred to the memory of 10,000 members of the AIF who were killed and wounded in the two battles of Bullecourt, April, May 1917 and to the Australian dead and their comrades in arms who lie here forever in the soil of France. It was dedicated on ANZAC Day 1992, the 75th Anniversary. On the reverse the sculptor Peter Corlett explains how he has depicted 'the characteristics for which the

Australians are known – sturdy, arcadian, audacious, resolute' and that the uniform is authentic.

The second attempt to take Bullecourt began on 3 May and formed part of an overall assault on a front of some 15 miles by 14 divisions, with the town at the right flank. Although the attack had been carefully rehearsed it was, like the first attempt, too complicated. Supporting artillery reduced Bullecourt to ruins and the Australian 2nd Division led off the attack (this time without tanks) later being joined by the 1st and 5th Divisions. The 5th Brigade on the right failed to make any impression, while to its left the 6th Brigade made gains that it resolutely held against fierce counter-attacks by the German 27th Wurttemberg Division. Eventually, on 17 May, the last remnants of Bullecourt fell, a progressive achievement involving troops and tanks of the British 7th, 58th and 62nd Divisions. The Australians lost 7,000 men during the fighting and won two **VCs: Corporal G.J. Howell** (who survived until 1964) and **Lieutenant R.V. Moon** (who survived until 1986).

Digger Memorial, Bullecourt

Memorial to 2,423 Missing Australians, Bullecourt

Continue up the road to the monument in the bank on the left.

Memorial to 2,423 Australians, missing with no known grave (Map 1/49). This cross, with the words 'Remember' was erected in 1982. It is on the Second German Line, on 'Diagonal Road'. On the side of the base are small personal plaques.

Bunny Hug and Starfish and a trench railway ran roughly north to south. This is Point 4 on the Australian Track (qv).

Return to the Town Hall, park and, if desired, follow the other points on the recommended route by foot. Return to Bapaume.

Six Crossroads Point 4 on the Australian Track, Bullecourt

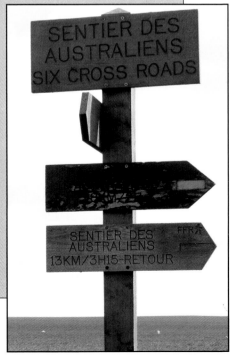

[N.B.] Some 2 miles further north from Bullecourt on the D956 there is a Memorial to the **15th Bn Canadian Highlanders (GPS: 50.218854 2.953521)**. It was unveiled in April 2010 and commemorates an attack by the 15th on the village and the high ground behind the Memorial of 1 September 1918.

End of Itinerary Four and Extra Visit

ITINERARY FIVE

THE AMERICAN, CANADIAN AND FRENCH SECTORS
MARCH-AUGUST 1918
THE BATTLEFIELD TOUR

It is recommended that this tour be taken from Villers Bretonneux - see page 210.
• **The Route:** the tour begins at Villers Bretonneux and continues to Montdidier via Crucifix Corner and Démuin CWGC Cemeteries, past the Canadian Cavalry/Flowerdew VC/Queen's Own Oxfordshire Hussars Mem, the French 31st Corps Mem, the Capt Aviator Aubry and *Poilu* Mems at Moreuil, Morisel German Cemetery, Sauvillers Mongival 4DIC Mem, British WW2 Graves, Machine-Gunner Mem and 87th RI Plaque, Grivesnes Mon to 325th& 125th RIs 1918, Cantigny American Memorials and US 1st Division Monument. Alternative endings to the tour are then given, either direct to Villers Bretonneux or via the French 19th Division Memorial.
[N.B.] The following site is indicated: Toronto CWGC Cemetery.
* **Planned duration**, without stops for refreshment or Extra Visits: **8 hours.**
* **Total distance: 23.70 miles**
> Drive to the crossroads with the D1029/D23 **(GPS: 49.87104 2.51798)**.
> *SET YOUR MILEOMETER TO ZERO*

During this itinerary it is broadly accurate to say that the German attacks during the Kaiser's Offensive came from your left. During the 100 Days the Allied attack came from your right. It is a glorious drive in fine weather, with rolling vistas of ever-changing hills and valleys.
> *Take the D23 south, signed to the A29 motorway, cross it and immediately afterwards turn sharp right onto a small road and drive back parallel to the D23 to the Cemetery on the left.*

• *Crucifix Corner CWGC Cemetery/1.4 miles/10 minutes/Map 3/1/GPS: 49.85359 2.52403*

As the Itinerary 5 Map shows, the German Kaiser's Battle advance was stopped just west of the area of the cemetery and it was from there on the 8th August 1918 that the allied 100 Days offensive began with what is generally known as the 'Battle of Amiens.' Broadly speaking the Australians (5th Div) were north of the motorway here and the Canadian Corps (2nd Div) south. The Cemetery was begun by the Canadians in August 1918, the original plot containing some 90 graves and a large number of French burials. After the Armistice it was enlarged, when it included American and German burials which have been removed, as were many of the French. There are now over 650 burials, including 159 Unknown UK, 236 Australians and 70 Canadians. On the left is a French plot of 142 graves, including several Colonial troops and 6 Russians. In front of it is a Memorial *'Aux Héros morts pour la défense de Villers Bretonneux, 24, 25 Avril 1918'*, erected

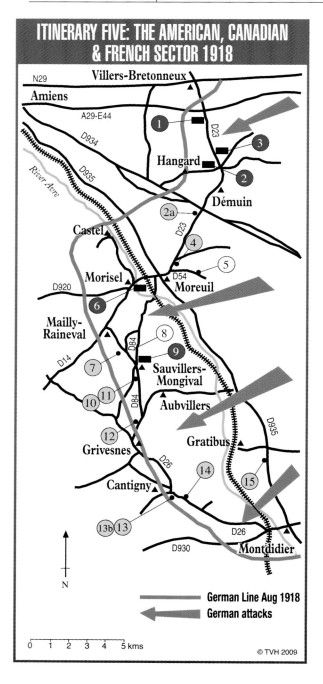

ITINERARY FIVE: THE AMERICAN, CANADIAN & FRENCH SECTOR 1918

Legend for Itinerary Five

1. Crucifix Corner CWGC Cemetery
2. Démuin CWGC Cemetery
2a. Canadian Mem to Moreuil & Rifle Woods
3. Toronto CWGC Cemetery
4. French 31st Army Corps Mem
5. Mem to Capt Aviator Aubry, Moreuil,
6. Morisel Ger Cem
7. Mem to 4 DIC, 1940, Mailly Raineval
8. Mem to 29th CAP
9. RAF WW2 Graves, Sauvillers-Mongival Local Cem
10. Sauvillers-Mongival MG Poilu Mem
11. French 87th RI Mem Sauvillers-Mongival church
12. French 125th/325th RI Mem 1918, Grivesnes
13. American Mon & Maj McCormick Mem, Cantigny
13b. US 28th Inf Statue
14. 'Big Red One' Mon, near Cantigny
15. Mon to the 'Beau Dix- Neuf', D935 near Montdidier

Crucifix Corner CWGC Cemetery.

by the inhabitants. The Cemetery, designed by Sir Edwin Lutyens, stands out as an oasis of peace and beauty against its somewhat unprepossessing surroundings. The ruined Crucifix which gave it its name stood for many years by the entrance but has now disappeared.

Continue to the cemetery on the right.

• Demuin Brit CWGC Cemetery/3.2 miles/5 minutes/Map 3/2/GPS: 49.82629 2.53530

The village of Demuin was taken by the Germans on 29 March and changed hands several times in 1918 until it was finally recaptured by the 58th Canadian Battalion in August, when the cemetery was made by the 3rd Canadian Battalion. Enclosed by a beautiful flint wall, this tiny Cemetery contains 43 burials. All the graves, other than 2 Unknowns and **Lt L Mc. Sinclair** of the Canadian Engineers, died 18 August, are from 8 August 1918, the first day of the battle.

In this area the French forces of Gen Debeney's Army initially took over from the British, the two forces often co-operating at tactical level with British tanks aiding French Infantry. German attacks, coming from your left, continued until August but these were not advances, these were savage struggles for the small villages and hilltops between here and Montdidier.

Démuin CWGC Cemetery.

[N.B.] To the left is signed **Toronto CWGC Cemetery, GPS: 49.83723 2.53658.**

The Cemetery was begun by the 3rd Can Bn (Toronto Regiment) in August 1918, and used by other Canadian units for the burial of their dead in that month.

It contains 97 Commonwealth burials of the First World War, 22 of which are unidentified, and four German graves.

Continue on the D23, under the A1 motorway to the junction with the D934 and immediately beyond it a slip road to the right - drive up it.

• Canadian Cavalry Bde Memorial to the Battles of Rifle and Moreuil Woods & Lt Flowerdew, VC and the Queen's Own Oxfordshire Hussars/ 5.2 miles/10 minutes/Map 3/2a/ GPS: 49.80479 2.51861

Designed by WO1 Gordon Crossley, Curator and Archivist of the Fort Garry Horse Museum in Winnipeg, with Col Dave Atwell, CO of the Fort Garry Horse and Maj Mike McNorgan of the RCD, the **Monument** was inaugurated on 9 June 2004 in the presence of a large Canadian delegation and local dignitaries. The polished grey granite, three-sided obelisk, made by a Villers Bretonneux stonemason bears on one side the story of the Canadian Cavalry Brigade's exploits in the area, on another that of **Lt Gordon Muriel Flowerdew's VC** and his citation (qv), and on a third side a map showing the area of the battles of Rifle Wood (also known as Dodo Wood and Bois de Hourges) and Moreuil Wood. Beneath the descriptive, illustrated panels, which were made in Canada, are maple leaves, traced from the leaf brought back by Gord Crossley from Vimy Ridge in 2003. The Oxfordshire Yeomanry Trust, hearing of the plans for the Monument, asked if they could place a Plaque on it to commemorate the men of the Queen's Own Oxfordshire

Memorial to Canadian Cavalry Bde.

Hussars. One of the maple leaves was removed to make room for a black **Plaque** listing the roll of honour of the 20 Hussars who lost their lives in the 1 April 1918 battle. It

was inaugurated by Col Timothy May, President of the Trust with a delegation of 5 (QOOH) Signal Sqn and Peter Maasz, the nephew of **Pte Clarence Maasz** who is mentioned on the Plaque. The erection of the Memorials was supported by the Luce/Maple Leaf Association, a group of local historians based beside the River Luce which runs from Amiens and roughly follows the Canadian line of advance of August 1918.

At the northwest corner of Moreuil Wood (the wood ahead before the town of the same name) Gen Jack Seely (whose grandson Brough Scott attended the inauguration of the Memorial) Commanding the Canadian Cavalry Brigade, set up his HQ during the attack on the wood (see below) on 30 March 1918. Local farmer M. Brunel, who owns the land, found the remains of **Pte John Willoughby**, Lord Strathcona's Horse, in 1986. He erected a small Cross in Willoughby's memory in June 2004 on his private land, accessible only by a dirt road. Willoughby was reinterred in Terlincthun Brit Cem, Wimille.

Plaque to Lt
Flowerdew VC.

Rifle Wood is the group of trees immediately to the west of the Memorial and on 1 April, two days after the Battle of Moreuil Wood (see below) the Canadians – the Fort Garry Horse, Lord Strathcona's Horse and the Royal Canadian Dragoons – followed by the British King's Own Hussars, the Queen's Own Oxfordshire Hussars and the 20th Hussars, launched an unmounted attack that took the wood. The attack came towards you along the line of the D934 that you can see running west to east.

Continue to the large memorial to the left at the junction with the D28 and continue past it to the slip road to the parking area.

• Memorial to French 31st Army Corps/7.5 miles/10 minutes/Map 3/4/ GPS: 49.77975 2.50143

This impressive Memorial displays the date 8 August 1918 and lists the 64th and 65th Infantry Divisions, the 108th RAL and the 31st Aviation. The land on which it was erected was the gift of Monsieur le Comte de Rouge in 1926 and it was raised by contributions from the officers and men of the Corps, commanded by Gen Toulorge. The legend translates, 'Here pm 8 August the Corps broke the German lines, chased the enemy as far as Houdroy where, on 7 November, the German plenipotentiaries negotiated the Armistice'. A Plaque on the wall below the obelisk notes that the Monument was destroyed by 'the soldiers of Hitler' in 1940 and rebuilt by *Souvenir Français* in 1955.

The wood to your right and front is Moreuil Wood. The road down which you have just driven was bitterly contested ground, with features and high ground changing hands, sometimes several times in a day. On 26 March two French divisions brought up by lorry from the south (i.e. they came towards you) were driven back to Moreuil, the town ahead, by the fierceness of the German attack. Another division, the 163rd, arrived

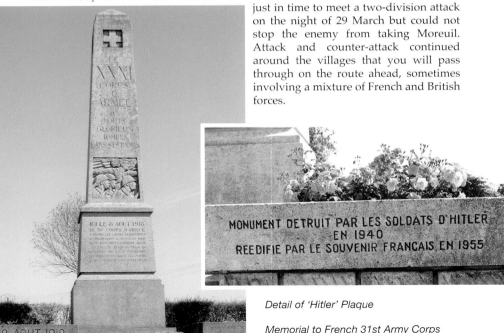

just in time to meet a two-division attack on the night of 29 March but could not stop the enemy from taking Moreuil. Attack and counter-attack continued around the villages that you will pass through on the route ahead, sometimes involving a mixture of French and British forces.

Detail of 'Hitler' Plaque

Memorial to French 31st Army Corps Moreuil Wood

On 8 August, the first day of the Allied Picardy counter-offensive, 66th Division of General Toulorge's 31st Corps retook Moreuil. Other divisions listed on the Memorial, the 37th and the 42nd, cleared the areas to the east up the D28 towards Mezières. The front line in this area in August was on the other side of the River Avre which you will shortly cross. It was the start of the 'Hundred Days' that led to final victory.

However the 30th March battle that the Canadians call the Battle of Moreuil Wood was centred in this area. The Germans had taken the village of Moreuil on the night of the 29th and their attacks towards and through the wood came from the east down the line of the road, the D28 from Mezières, that passes the Memorial. The ground here and towards Rifle Wood is relatively high and if lost might separate the British and French forces. Should the Germans gain control of it a major break-through might follow. Just to the west of the wood in the area of the village of Castel (see Map 3) was Brig Seely's Canadian Cavalry Brigade and after consultation with the French and with the support of the British 3rd Cavalry Brigade, Seely galloped his Brigade into action. The Royal Canadian Dragoons heading the charge suffered heavy casualties and Seely re-inforced them with Lord Strathcona's Horse, impressing upon the leading ("C") squadron commander, **Lt G.M. Flowerdew (qv)**, the urgency of the situation. Flowerdew charged the enemy, his troopers killing many with the sword and, despite losing some 70% of his force, stayed the German advance, an achievement for which he was awarded the **VC**. Sadly he died from his wounds the next day and is buried at Namps-au-Val British Cemetery, some 17 miles due west of here. His headstone lists his rank as "Captain" and the story goes that he was promoted to Captain by Brigadier Seely, on the day he died. His military records refer to him as Lieutenant" throughout. Flowerdew was born in Norfollk and later moved to Canada. In Flowerdew's squadron was **Lt F.M. Harvey, VC**, who had won his award almost exactly one year to the day earlier at Guyencourt south of Pontavert on the River Aisne. Harvey survived the war and went on to become a Brigadier.

General John Edward Bernard Seely, 1st Baron Mottistone, CB, CMG, DSO, TD, PC, JP, DL, was born on 31 May 1868 and died on 7 November 1947. He served as both a Conservative and a Liberal MP and became Secretary of State for War in 1912 before having to resign due to the 'Curragh Incident'. Jack Seely was a great friend of Winston Churchill and the only Cabinet Minister to survive the four years of the war. Renowned for his dashing Cavalry charge here he was also famous for his long partnership (until 1941) with his horse, Warrior, who became a great favorite with the troops. They served together from 11 August 1914 through Mons, Ypres, the Somme, Cambrai and Passchendaele, Warrior surviving several severe injuries and near-misses. After the war Warrior returned to the Seely family home on the Isle of Wight until his death at the age of 33 in April 1941. In 1934 Seely wrote, *My Horse, Warrior,* which was illustrated by Sir Alfred Munnings (recently republished). Munnings also painted a stirring picture of *Flowerdew's Charge*. Warrior's fame was renewed with the stage version and Spielburg film of Michael Murpurgo's book, *War Horse*. In September 2014 Warrior, dubbed 'the horse the Germans could not kill', was posthumously awarded an honorary PDSA Dickin Medal (the animal equivalent of the VC). It also honoured all animals who were killed in WW1.

Continue to the outskirts of Moreuil and take the sharp turn to the left at 7.7 miles signed (visible once you have turned!) to le Plessier Rozainvillers on the D54.

Continue approx 1 mile to the far end of a wood that straddles the road.

From this point the French 31st Army Corps Monument can be seen on the horizon.

Immediately up a track to the left is

Refurbished memorial to Capt Aviator Aubry, le Plessier Rozainvillers.

• Memorial to Capitaine Aviateur Aubry/8.8 miles/5 minutes/Map 3/5/ GPS: 49.77173 2.50883

The Capitaine, of C43 Squadron, CAP, was killed here 'gloriously' on 26 March 1915. For many years the small Monument fell into ever greater disrepair but in 2005 it was beautifully restored by the Town of Moreuil with new green railings, a gravel surround and repainted inscription. Many such private memorials were erected soon after the war by comrades or grieving parents. As time goes by these connections are severed and maintenance now depends on organisations such as *Souvenir Français* and local councils and historical circles.

In response to our appeal locally, the following information was supplied by researcher, J.P. le Palec: Jules Louis Aubry was born in 1874 at Feuquières, son of *Général de Brigade* Aubry and was a graduate of the *Ecole Militaire* of St Cyr. Attached to 1st Aviation Group he obtained Military Pilot License No 175. On the day of his crash he was giving a visiting Artillery Officer a ride as he made an aerial reconnaissance. Aubry was mortally wounded in the head and died in ambulance No 3 from Hargicourt. His passenger 'ejected' (presumably jumped because parachutes were not issued by any belligerents until later in the war) and received only light injuries. Aubry was awarded the *Croix de Guerre* and other decorations.

Turn round, return to the main road and turn left on rue du 8 Aôut 1918. Continue into the main square of Moreuil and stop in front of the Town Hall.

Moreuil War Memorial.

• Moreuil Town Memorial/9.6 miles/10 minutes/GPS: 49.77201 2.48320

When the Kaiser's Battle opened on 21 March 1918, two trains carried over 2,000 people from the area back to Amiens but over 100 refused to go. French accounts tell that the town was totally destroyed with more than 1,000 buildings being left beyond repair.

By the Town Hall is the exuberant *Art Deco* Church, reconstruction of which began in 1929, with stained glass windows by Rinuy and Hébert Stevens and to its left is the splendid white stone **Local Memorial** with a *Poilu* in *bas relief*. The legend describes, from a Communiqué of 8 August 1918, the retaking of Moreuil on that day, when the French troops attacking with great bravery crossed the River Avre, and despite enemy resistance over ran their defences. The Monument was inaugurated on 12 October 1924 by Gen Mollet, Minister of War. The sculptor was Albert Roze. Around the Monument the names of Moreuil's dead from the 1870, 1914-1918 and 1939-1945 Wars are listed.

Follow the signs to Ailly to the left on the D920, signed to A16, crossing the River Avre. Continue to a cemetery on the left.

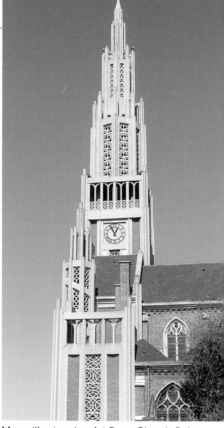

Moreuil's stunning Art Deco Church Spire

• German Cemetery, Morisel/10.6 miles/10 minutes/Map 3/6/GPS: 49.76820 2.47060

This forlorn cemetery with a large black cross in the centre contains 2,640 burials of 1918. In the front row are soldiers from the great battle to liberate Moreuil on 8 August, originally taken by the Germans on 4 April- to the left Kurt Zehm and to the right Gustave Röller. In the top right hand corner is a mass grave.

Continue and immediately turn left signed Mailly-Raineval on the D14 to the local cemetery on the right just before the village sign.

• Memorial to 4th DIC/11.9 miles/5 minutes/Map 3/7/GPS: 49.74871 2.45183

On the local Cemetery wall by the gate is a metal Anchor Plaque to the 4th Colonial Infantry Division in Memory of May/June 1940.

German Cemetery, Morisel

Memorial to 4th DIC, 1940, Mailly-Raineval Local Cemetery

This matches the Anchor Plaque in the village of Le Hamel (qv). The Division was part of the French 1st Army Corps which briefly held up the German advance through the Somme in 1940.

Continue and turn next left on the D14E signed to Sauvillers-Mongival. Continue through Mailly-Raineval, past the Town Hall and continue, direction Sauvillers, to a stone memorial on a crest opposite a row of trees.

• Memorial to 29th Bn CAP/13.7 miles/5 minutes/Map 3/8/GPS: 49.73406 2.46488

The Memorial commemorates **Volunteer Sous-Lieutenant Jean de Séganville, Sergeant René Antoine and Léon Hochet** of the 29th Bn Chasseurs à Pied.

The men commemorated here of the 29th CAP, part of 36 Corps, died on 4 April 1918 when the Germans, attacking from the east, (i.e. from behind the Memorial), took a large stretch of the French line including Mailly-Raineval, Morisel and as far north as Castel.

Continue towards the village of Sauvillers Mongival to the cemetery on the left with a green CWGC Tombes de Guerre sign.

Memorial to 29th Bn CAP, Mailly-Raineval

Machine-gunner Poilu Memorial, Sauvillers-Mongival

• Sauvillers Mongival Local Cemetery with British Graves/14.3 miles/5 minutes/Map 3/9/GPS: 49.72843 2.47060

In the Cemetery are the graves of a Lancaster crash of 15 April 1943 of **Sergeants Buxton, McLean and Hancock, Sqn Ldr Jerrard Latimer, DFC and Lt Gerard Muttrie RNVR** of *HMS Daedalus*. Latimer, of 106 Sqn, is thought to have had 6 victories to his credit when he was killed. Muttrie was serving with the Sqn. Three members of the crew survived, one of whom, **Flt Lt Leslie Broderick**, took part in the March 1944 mass (about 80 airmen) escape from Stalag Luft III Sagan prisoner of war camp, but was recaptured. The Gestapo, apparently on Hitler's orders, executed 50 of those who were recaptured but three made it home. Broderick survived. The escape was the basis of the film, *'The Great Escape'.*
Continue into the village of Sauvillers-Mongival.
The village was retaken from the Germans on 23 July, together with Mailly-Raineval, through which you have recently passed, and Aubvillers, a village about 2kms ahead. It was a considerable success for the French who took over 1,800 prisoners and some 300 machine guns.
Turn left signed Grivesnes and stop immediately by the church in Sauvillers-Mongival.

• Sauvillers-Mongival Memorials/14.5 miles/10 minutes/Map 3/10/11/ GPS: 49.72843 2.47060

On the right is the local War Memorial, a statue of a determined machine-gunner *Poilu*. On the church wall behind is a **Plaque**, erected in 1959, to the **Men of the 87th RI** who fell in July 1918 in the liberation of the village.
Continue to the right fork to Grivesnes on the D84. Fork right and continue to the large memorial on the right with fir trees behind.

• Monument to 125th and 325th RI/17.5 miles/5 minutes/Map 3/12/GPS: 49.69674 2.46941

This impressive Monument commemorates the 325th and 125th Infantry Regiments actions of May 1918. The 125th had fought on the Marne, at Verdun, on the Aisne and here at Grivesnes, where despite coming under 'friendly fire', a bayonet charge carried the German lines and earned a commendation from General Debeney Commanding the French 1st Army. Information on the 325th is difficult to come by. It seems that the regiments were raised from the same home depot and that the 325th may well have consisted of reservists from the 125th.

Enter Grivesnes.
German attacks began here from the direction of Malpart to the east (i.e. your left) on 30 March, five unsuccessful assaults being made on that day alone. The next day the 1st Division of Prussian Guards took the town, apart from the Château where the Commanding Officer of the 350th RI defending the town held out with a few men. Writing a message asking for help and ending it with the words, 'I am in the castle and shall hold

Monument to French 125th and 325th Infantry Regiments 1918

until death', he sent a cyclist off to seek help. Extraordinarily the man got through the German lines, support arrived including two armoured cars and, after house to house fighting, the town was cleared. Further attacks followed by the Guards on 1, 3 and 5 April but stubborn resistance by the 67th RI and 25th Chasseurs held the line.

Continue through the village and onto the D26 on rue de 31 mars 1918.
Continue to Cantigny and stop by the church.

• *American Memorials, Cantigny/20.3 miles/20 minutes/ Map 3/13/GPS: 49.66338 2.49129*

For many years, in the garage at No 19 rue Aignon, was the small Museum, now defunct, run by the-then Mayor, Monsieur Lefever, who, born just after the end of the Great War, was taken prisoner during the '39-'45 War. He remembers seeing Hitler pass through the village and the fearful bombardment as the Americans liberated the village.

In front of the church is a *Conseil Régional de Picardie* **signboard** describing the Monument opposite, with a picture of the unveiling. It describes how on 28 May 1918 (when the Germans were re-occupying the Chemin des Dames and retaking Soissons) the Americans launched their first large-scale operation on the Western Front to free this village. Under the French X Corps of Gen Maire Eugène Debeney's 1st Army the 28th Inf Regt of the American 1st Division (in WW2 to be affectionately known as 'The Big Red 1') were told that the village (which had twice been unsuccessfully attacked by the French) had to be retaken at all costs. The 28th had been chosen as the assault force largely on the reputation of its commander, **Col Hanson E. Ely**, said to be 'as hard boiled as a picnic egg'.

The assault was carefully prepared and was launched at 0645, backed by 37mm guns, Stokes mortars, flamethrowers and French tanks. The Americans, easily recognised by their distinctive uniforms, attacked against heavy machine-gun and artillery fire. They took 225 prisoners (including 5 officers), 16 machine guns, 2 mortars and 500 rifles. The village had been evacuated, save for an ancient lady who insisted on remaining. The Germans responded with intensity after losing 600 dead and 400 wounded, shelling the village for 72 relentless hours. But the 1st Division, (later to adopt the motto, 'No mission too difficult, no sacrifice too great: duty first'), did not concede one inch. The victory was psychologically important as it was the first assault on French soil by a wholly American Army and demonstrated that the Americans could fight just as well as the other Allies - something about which some British and French Commanders had had doubts. Back in the USA the resolute response by the 26th Yankee Division to the German attack at Seicheprey in the St Mihiel Salient on 20 April 1918 had already been promoted as the 'First American Victory'.

Now, the Americans under their new General, Robert Bullard (who later led the 1st Army) whose HQ was at Mesnil St Firmin, barely 3.5 miles south-west of Cantigny, were warned of the coming task on 15 May. This launched the Division's staff (including one **Lieutenant-Colonel George Catlett Marshall** who was to play such a major role in the next war and its aftermath) into two weeks of planning. On 23 May the 28th moved into a back area to begin rehearsals for the attack. The ground had been chosen for its similarity to that at Cantigny and trenches had been dug to match aerial pictures taken of the German lines.

After the war **Col Robert McCormick**, who lived in Wheaton, Illinois, near Chicago, and who had commanded the 1st Bn, 5th Field Artillery Regt of the 28th, renamed his estate 'Cantigny' and had as its gates replicas of those at Cantigny Château in honour

American Memorial,
Cantigny.

Inauguration of Doughboy Memorial, Cantigny, with
serving members of the US 1st Div & 'Pershing's
Doughboys'

of the battle. McCormick, owner and publisher of
the *Chicago Tribune* newspaper, died in 1955 and
left his estate to become a Museum and Park for
the people of Illinois – see www.cantigny.org. The
1st Division Foundation has its HQ there and there
are plans for a new Museum at Cantigny in France
when funds can be raised.

Opposite is the **American Monument** and as
you walk across the road towards it you are moving
directly towards the advancing Doughboys of 1918.
The Monument was designed by Arthur Loomis
Harmon and inaugurated on 9 August 1937. It
commemorates the 199 men killed and the 867
wounded and gassed here. The elegant white stone
shaft is surrounded by a beautifully tended park.
At the entrance is an **American Battle Monuments
Commission Plaque** describing the Cantigny
operation. The street behind the park is rue 1ière
Division USA.

Memorial to Maj R. McCormick,
Cantigny

To mark the 90th Anniversary of the Battle on 28 May 2008, the 1st Div Cantigny Foundation erected a fine bronze **Statue of a 'Doughboy'** (a 'Black Lion', so-called after the insignia of the 28th Infantry Regiment). It was inaugurated in an impressive ceremony attended by Gen John B. Craddock, Supreme Allied Commander Europe, Brig-Gen (Retd) David L. Grange, President and CEO The McCormick Foundation and senior representatives (civil and military) of the American, French and German nations. The $111,000 statue was sculpted by Stephen Spears, son of a US Air Force Colonel, who also sculpted the three US Naval Figures for the US Navy Memorial at UTAH Beach and the 'Leadership' Tribute Statue to Lt 'Dick' Winters of Easy Coy at Brécourt. We were privileged to have been invited to all three events.

Beyond the Doughboy on the green is a Bronze Memorial **Plaque to Maj R. McCormick**.

Continue down the hill to the memorial up the bank on the left.

• US 1st Division Memorial, near Cantigny/21 miles/5 minutes/Map 3/14/GPS: 49.65925 2.50144

This handsome column surmounted by an eagle (sculpted by Jo Davidson) has Plaques around bearing the names of the Missing in Action and the message of 10 November 1918 from the Commander in Chief acknowledging the Division's esprit. Its famous red numeral on a brown tabard was not adopted as shoulder insignia until after the Armistice. The Memorial is identical to those at St Juvin in the Meuse-Argonne, Vignelles in the St Mihiel Salient and Mons in Belgium.

The Division had come into the Cantigny area some 6 weeks before the battle and suffered greatly from German shellfire and gas attacks, though in its counter-artillery fire it was said that the Division despatched over 10,000 shells every 24 hours onto the German lines. However, the Americans found the gas attacks particularly troubling and some 60 years later Sgt George Krahnert of the 26th Inf remembered his encounter with mustard gas: 'I went out into this field one morning to do you know what and I made the mistake of using some grass to clean up. Christ did it burn. My rear end still looks like it's petrified! As for the other part of my body, well I fathered eight children after the war so it couldn't have bothered me permanently. I never did report it as a

Monument to the US 1st Division (the Big Red 1), Cantigny.

wound - just kept bathing with GI soap.' (*Make the Kaiser Dance, Henry Berry*.)

Continue downhill towards Fontaine sous Montdidier.

The German 9th Division occupied the village on the morning of 28 March. An immediate counter-attack by the French 132nd RI recaptured the village and fighting in the area around Montdidier surged backwards and forwards over the coming months until the Allied Offensive of 8 August.

Continue into Montdidier on the D26, then D930. Follow signs for Centre Ville and park opposite the Town Hall, next to which is the **Tourist Office***, Place Gen de Gaulle.*

Montdidier (23.7 miles) (GPS: 49.64682 2.56765)

This makes the ideal lunch break after the tour which takes a morning to complete. The **Tourist Office** has lists of restaurants and hotels. Montdidier was the birthplace of **Antoine Augustin Parmentier**, the pharmacist who introduced the potato at the court of Louis XVI which led to its ongoing popularity. His statue is to be seen at the top of the street. The bicentennial of his death was celebrated on 1 April 2013 in the town.

The town was completely razed during the battles of March-August 1918 and was rebuilt in the 20s and 30s in *Art Deco* style and was under German occupation during the '39-'45 War.

Statue of Parmentier, Montdidier

On 27 March 1918 the German advance was so rapid (20 miles in 6 days) that the defence of Montdidier was abandoned and the enemy entered the town at 1830 hours. The Germans remained in the town until Gen Debeney's great offensive of 8 August when the 3rd Div of 9 Corps crossed the Avre, and finally on the night of 9 August the Germans evacuated Montdidier in great confusion. The French had entire possession of the town by noon on the 10th.

• *End of Itinerary Five*

OR

Return to Villers Bretonneux by returning to the bottom of the hill and following signs to Amiens on the D935. Continue past the airfield on the right to the monument on the left.

Monument to the 'Beau Dix-Neuf' *(Map 3/16)/GPS: 49.67835 2.55866*

This colourful Monument bears the insignia of a trumpet and has an inscription in Latin, detailing the actions of the 19th Division from 1854 in the Battle of the Alma in the Crimea, through the Great War to 1945. In WW1 the Division was in action from August 1914 until the Armistice, fighting mainly in the Meuse, Marne and Verdun areas. We have not discovered why the memorial is where it is. Can anyone help?

Continue on the D935 to Moreuil and thence back to Villers Bretonneux.

Monument to 'Le Beau Dix-Neuf'
– the French 19th Division.

ITINERARY SIX

THE KAISER'S OFFENSIVE
21 MARCH-25 APRIL 1918
St Quentin to Villers Carbonnel/
**Nearest Point to Amiens

Please Note. Inevitably when so much happened in the same areas over a period of four years, there will be overlap between itineraries. We have managed to avoid 99% of such inconveniences, but here the reader will need to exercise a certain amount of mental agility because, although the beginning of this tour travels the battlefield in the same direction that the Germans did (i.e. from St Quentin) as far as Villers Carbonnel, at the latter it joins with part of Itinerary Three which is coming from the opposite direction (i.e. from Amiens)! However we do of course continue this Kaiser's Offensive tour in the direction of the German advance up to the Nearest Point that they reached towards Amiens.

   ** We list the complete tour, but navigation from Villers Carbonnel onwards is by GPS supported by map references, plus references to the pages in Itinerary Three where the relevant background and historical information can be found.

   The German attack took place along a broad front east to west. Here we concentrate on the axis of the D1029, St Quentin-Villers Bretonneux road which heads directly towards Amiens. We begin at the German start line and follow their rapid advance to the point where it was stopped.

• **Itinerary Six** starts at St Quentin and from there moves to the German jump-off trenches and Memorials at Fayet, past the Enghien Redoubt and Manchester Hill. It returns to St Quentin and then follows the retreat of a typical British infantry battalion to the Somme at Pargny and there traces the details of an action which led to the winning of a VC. The tour ends at Villers Carbonnel French Cemetery just over the Somme towards Amiens.

•**The Route:** ((St Quentin – Centre, (but see **Note** below)) French National Cemetery; Fayet – German Jump-off Trenches, Memorial Water Tank, Town Memorials; Enghien Redoubt; Francilly-Selency – 2nd Manchesters & French Memorials, Manchester Hill; St Quentin German Cemetery; Pargny – Site of Maj Roberts' VC, Bridge, Brit Mil CWGC Cemetery; Bethencourt German Cemetery; Villers Carbonnel National Cemetery; thence, using GPS, map and page references to the Nearest Point to Amiens.

•**Extra Visit:** St Quentin Northern Cemetery.

• **[N.B.]** The following sites are indicated: 1944 Memorial to Fusillés; Vraignes 1944 Memorial; Memorial to racing drivers, Bouriat Quinot and Trintignant.

• **Planned duration**, without stops for refreshments: **3.5 hours.**

• **Total distance: 43.2 miles.**

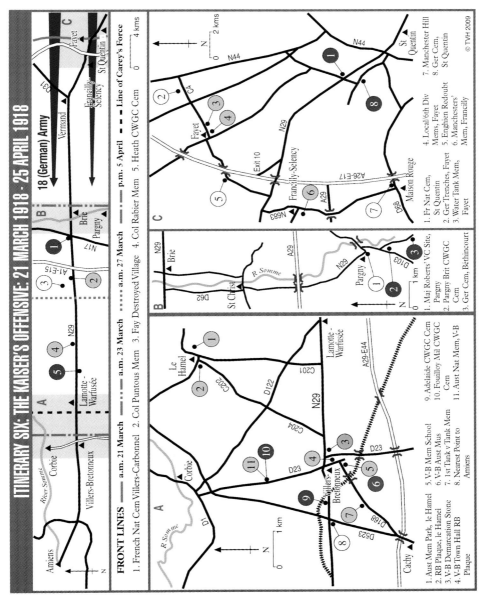

NOTE: The map references to ITMap 6 throughout this Itinerary refer to the In-text Map 6A/B & C above as this section does not appear on the main Holts' Battle Map, to which all other itineraries make reference.

• *St Quentin*

Note: It must be said that St Quentin town centre is extremely difficult to negotiate and to park in. Therefore the main Itinerary starts at the French National Cemetery on the outskirts. If you nevertheless wish to visit this interesting town first, it is described between ((...))

*((Follow signs to **Centre Ville** and then 'i' for Tourist information to the*
Tourist Office 3 Rue Emile Zola, 02100. Tel: + (0) 3 23 67 05 00. www.saint-quentin-tourisme.fr

There you can pick up a town plan and leaflets about restaurants, hotels and other attractions. They also produce an interesting booklet in English *Saint Quentin and The Great War*, which lists the sites in the city with connections to the Great War. The most important '14-18 Memorial is found by crossing the ornate bridge over the St Quentin Canal, built between 1927 and 1929, to the Place aux Monuments aux Morts/Square de *Souvenir Français*. It was designed by Paul Bigot in the shape of a triumphal portico whose ten pillars bear the names of the missing. At either end two *bas-reliefs* designed by Landowski and Bouchard recall the heroic defence of the town which was for many years the frontier between the French and Austrians. On the right the siege of 1557 and on the left the siege of 1870 are represented whilst in the centre the Great War struggles of the city are vividly depicted.

At first occupied by the British (who had their HQ in the Grammar School, Place du Lycée Henri Martin, which was used as a hospital for the wounded from Le Cateau, the town was also the HQ of the RFC from 25 August 1914.) St Quentin was attacked by the Germans on 28 August 1914 and the next few days saw bitter combat in the outskirts as the French 1st Army Corps counter-attacked. They were rebuffed, however, and from September 1914 to February 1917 the town was under German occupation. On 15 February the Kaiser visited St Quentin as part of his grand inspection of the German lines to celebrate his fifty-sixth birthday. Many bronze memorials from the Franco-Prussian War were demolished and sent to Germany for melting down to make munitions.

On 28 February the civilians were evacuated as the town became one of the most important bastions of the German Hindenburg Line. It was then systematically pillaged and heavily bombarded. From its ruins the German offensive of 21 March was launched. It was finally retaken on 1-2 October 1918 by the French when it was almost completely destroyed. Capt H.A. Taylor in his wonderful 1928 book, *Goodbye to the Battlefields*, revisited the city and remembered that in 1917 and 1918, 'In those days distance lent enchantment. For all its broken roofs and riddled gables, the city was fair to the eyes of the trench-bound soldier. When, ultimately, in the autumn we came this way again, and St Quentin fell, the city was a sorry picture of ruin and desolation, and one wondered how many decades must elapse before it could recover its former neatness. On my last visit to St Quentin I was astonished at the progress that had been made. There are streets and boulevards in which one might walk observantly without guessing that war had devastated this city so recently... On the whole the rebuilding of St Quentin has been done tastefully.'

After the war St Quentin was adopted by Lyon and the long reconstruction began. Many of the main buildings were rebuilt in the popular *Art Deco* style (notably the main post office in rue Vesoul) and today it is an elegant and interesting town.

The famous Basilica received its first damage on 1 July 1916 when some of the precious SGWs were blown in by the explosion of a munitions train in St Quentin station. German wounded from the Somme battle were treated here until it was deemed too dangerous as more windows collapsed. On 4 April 1917 the French Gen Humbert ordered French troops to try to avoid the Basilica when shelling the city hut on 17 August it caught fire and the vaulting caved in. After the war there was a notice in the Basilica, 'Visitors, do not forget that before they left the city in October 1918 the Germans drilled ninety holes for explosives in the pillars and structural elements of the Basilica. This was clearly intended to blow up the building, which would have been completely destroyed if the French had not arrived twenty-four hours earlier than expected by the enemy'. In 1941 the Germans ordered the holes to be filled in.

It was not until October 1956 that the rebuilt Basilica was inaugurated and the belfry was not completed until 1976. Today guided tours can he arranged from the **Tourist Office** (qv).))

Exit from the A26 motorway at the St Quentin on Exit No 10. Continue direction St Quentin on the D1029 to the second roundabout **(GPS: 49.85900 3.24729)**. *Turn left and then immediately right and stop in the small parking area for the French Military Cemetery.* **Set your mileometer to zero.**

• *Nécropole Nationale de St Quentin/0 miles/10 minutes/ITMap 6C/l/* GPS: 49.85528 3.26215

This vast French Cemetery contains 4,947 WW1 French burials, 1,319 of which are in two ossuaries, plus two Rumanians and 117 Russians. There are also 207 French burials from the 39-'45 War. It was started in 1923 with burials from the 1914-1918 Aisne battlefield. It was enlarged in 1934-5 with exhumations from cemeteries around St Quentin and the Aisne. In 1954 the WW2 burials were brought in from the Aisne. At the entrance there are **Information Panels**, one describing the Battle of Guise, 1914 which took place some 15 miles east of here.

Return to the roundabout and continue towards St Quentin to the next roundabout. Turn left, signed Cambrai on the D1044. Continue over one or more roundabouts and traffic lights to a T junction signed left to Cambrai (GPS: 49.85756 3.27826).

Entrance to the French Nécropole Nationale, St Quentin with Croix de Guerre emblem on the gate.

CWGC headstones of Rfm Hughes & Pte Hand, St Quentin Nord Cemetery. Behind is the 1870 Monument

Extra Visit to St Quentin Northern Cemetery (GPS: 49.85795 3.28975)
Round trip: 2 miles. Approx time: 25 minutes.
Turn right signed Centre Ville and at the next roundabout turn left signed Cimetiere
Saint Jean on the Rue Georges Pompidou. Continue to the cemetery on the right.

In the huge **St Quentin Northern Cemetery** in the St Jean Quarter are the graves of **Rifleman J. Hughes**, 2nd RIR, age 20 and **Pte Thomas Hands**, 1st King's Own R Lancasters, age 21. (Consult the Cemetery Guardian for the exact site.) Both were shot by the Germans on 8 March 1915 when they were captured wearing civilian clothes and thus automatically deemed to be spies and subject to the death penalty. Their story is similar to that of Robert Digby and his companions, also sheltered by local people and shot when discovered in Le Catelet. The formers' case is well-documented from minutes of the St Quentin Town Council, copies of which are held in the *Historial*. They reached St Quentin during the Retreat at the end of August and couldn't get out before the Germans arrived to occupy the town. They were looked after by townspeople but were eventually arrested, Rifleman Hands after he was imprudent enough to go out after the 1900 curfew, and Hughes after being denounced. They were tried by a military tribunal on 11 February 1915 when their attitude was described as 'dignified'. Their death sentence was declared the very day of their execution, 8 March. Hughes asked to see Madame Preux who had sheltered him and who treated him like one of her children. This was refused. They were taken to the barracks and shot by a firing party of six. The Germans refused them burial in the newly-created St Martin German Cemetery (qv) where other Allied soldiers were buried. 'You can put Frenchmen in our cemetery', said Lt Hauss of the German Command, 'but not Englishmen. They are scum'. They were therefore buried in the St Jean Cemetery and their graves were soon covered in flowers by the local people. Gustave Preux, the weaver who had hidden Hughes, was condemned to fifteen years of forced labour in Germany and returned after the war his health broken. At the same time eleven British soldiers and the miller who had taken them to hospital were shot in nearby Guise. On 14 April a letter arrived at the *Mairie* saying that the Commandant of the 2nd Army was punishing the town of St Quentin with a fine of 50,000 francs because two Englishmen had recently been found in the town and because after their execution insulting notices to the Command were still being posted around the town. Count Bernstorff, the Commandant, also posted a notice around the town proclaiming the execution of the two English soldiers.

Return to the National Cemetery and pick up the main itinerary.

Go left signed to Cambrai on the D1044.

[N.B.] At 2.4 miles on the left is a well-maintained **WW2 Memorial (GPS: 49.87231 3.27073)** to twenty-seven patriots killed by the Nazis on 8 April 1944, with a Plaque to commemorate the 50th Anniversary. It stands upon the line of a German communication trench called 'Major Alley' that ran at right angle across the road here.

Memorial to 27 WW2 Patriots

Continue to a left turn signed to Fayet on the C4. Turn left and continue towards power lines on the top of the plateau. Stop below them. You have now reached the area of the German front line trench with the fighting line about 300 yards ahead and in front of that is No Man's Land.

• German Trenches, Fayet/2.9 miles/20 minutes/ITMap 6C/2/GPS: 49.87364 3.26526

The German jump-off trench lines here in the wood to the right ran almost due south for about 2,000 yards and at this point were barely 200-300 yards from the British trenches. The attack was made in the direction you are driving. The British force between here and the northern edge of St Quentin (the cathedral should be visible to your left) was the 2nd/8th Worcesters, part of 182nd Brigade of 61st Division of the 5th Army. These were Forward Zone positions. The battalion put two companies forward, A and B, each covering a front of about a mile with their company HQs in Fayet village (B Coy) and 1,500 yards south of it (A Coy). D Company was nominated as a counter-attack force and centred on Fayet village, while C Company and battalion HQ occupied a central redoubt about a mile behind the lines, i.e. in front of you.

The *Regimental History* described the defences as 'for the most part merely shallow ditches not more than waist deep. Neither labour nor materials had been available to improve the defences. There was but scanty wire protection save around the actual defensive posts.'

What happened here is described now in selected extracts from the *Regimental History*. On the night of 20 March a raiding party went into the German trenches. 'The raiders brought back prisoners from three different German regiments. Those prisoners stated that the German army would attack the next day. The Corps Commander decided to put into force the pre-arranged dispositions for meeting an attack. The order to man the battle stations reached HQ 61st Division at 0435 and at that very minute all along the line the German artillery opened fire... For several hours the platoons of the 2nd/8th Worcesters endured the bombardment. The mist, torn only by the blaze of the shell bursts and then thickened by their smoke, hid everything from the eyes of the crouching sentries. Gas shells added their fumes to those of the high explosives and the survivors groped in the trenches, half-blinded by their gas masks. On every side parties of the enemy's infantry came looming through the mist... instead of advancing in regular waves they worked in groups. The forward posts were overwhelmed one by one.'

All of the Worcesters' companies were decimated, small bands of survivors struggling hack to battalion HQ: 'A ring of small defensive posts connected by a trench... from 1020 attack after attack beat against the defences. The enemy closed in from every side... two-thirds of the defenders had been killed or wounded... ammunition ran out... the German infantry charged in with the bayonet and the remnants of the defenders were compelled to surrender.' It was 1730 hours. What the gallant Worcesters did not know was that Holnon, the village a mile or more behind them, had been taken and passed by the enemy seven hours earlier. Altogether the battalion lost nineteen officers and 560 men on that day, almost exactly the same total as the Tyneside Scottish lost at La Boisselle on the first day of the Somme.

To your right about 100 yards away across the fields, is an arc of wood. In that wood signs of original German jump-off trenches still remain and, crops permitting - be very careful not to damage anything that may be growing - it is possible to walk to them across the field. You can therefore stand exactly where the Kaiser's Battle began.

Continue.

In about 300 yards you cross over the British front line Landerneau trench area and at the roundabout is the site where the Duguesclin Redoubt was established around a mine crater (du Guesclin was a Breton knight in the 100 Years War).

Continue over the roundabout on the C4 into the village of Fayet.

It is a *'Village Fleuri'* and if you visit it during the spring or summer you will be overwhelmed by the colourful glory of the flowers throughout the village.

Continue to a ruined archway on the right and stop on the left at an ornate structure at the corner of the Chemin Vert.

The Oxford Water Tank, with its ornate façade, Fayet.

• Water Tank, Fayet/3.6 miles/5 minutes/ ITMap 6C/3/GPS: 49.86912 3.25150

The elaborately carved structure contains a water tank, donated to Fayet by the town of Oxford after the war. The ruined archway over the road is all that remains of the Ecole Apostolique. Alongside and roughly parallel to the road you have just taken was the Duguesclin Alley communication trench leading forward to the Redoubt.

Continue to the T Junction, turn left and immediately stop at the beautifully tended memorial park beside the Mairie.

• Fayet Memorials/3.7 miles/10 minutes/ ITMap 6C/4/GPS: 49.86804 3.25086

In the centre is the main village obelisk Memorial. To the left are Memorials to the fighting of 28 August-16 September 1914 and to the trench warfare along the Hindenburg Line from March 1917-March 1918. It celebrates the retaking of Fayet on 30 September 1918 by the 46th and 47th French Divisions and the 6th English [sic] Division. The 6th held the area just north of the village and were relieved by the French 47th on the night of the 29th having moved up from the area of Manchester Hill to where the route continues. On the right is a Memorial to the evacuation of the villagers to Marpent on 15th February 1917 and Noyon on 22nd, the total destruction of the village by fire or mines in March 1917 and the felling of all trees from April 1916-March 1917.

Turn round and go downhill past the church then turn left at the bottom of the hill on the rue Quentin de la Tour signed Francilly on the C3. Immediately after the road crosses the motorway there is what appears to be a

Memorial to 46th and 47th French Divs and 6th 'English' Div's recapture of Fayet, with Church behind.

rectangular wooded area about 100 yards off the road to your right with a track leading to it. Stop and walk to the redoubt.

• Enghien Redoubt/4.5 miles/10 minutes/ITMap 6C/5/GPS: 49.86627 3.23613

The area enclosed by trees is in the precise form and position in the the centre of a British redoubt called Enghien (presumably based upon an earlier French fortification, since Enghien was the name of the Marshal of France who gave Vauban his opportunity to become France's greatest fortifications exponent). The northern boundary of 2nd/Bth Worcesters was the road along which you are driving. One thousand yards due south of here was Ellis Redoubt where the Worcesters had battalion HQ. Redoubts were meant to be mutually supporting and the ground between them covered by machine-gun fire. The mist prevented that. This redoubt was held by the 2nd/4th Oxs and Bucks,

Site of the Enghien Redoubt.

who, with a few Worcester stragglers, survived until 1630 on 21 March.

Continue to the T junction and turn right, then take the next left signed to Francilly-Selency on the 0683 and continue to the church on the right and the memorials in front of it.

• 2nd & 16th Manchesters/Manchester Hill & French Memorials, Francilly-Selency/5. 6 miles/5 minutes/ITMap 6C/6/GPS: 49.85604 3.22530

Headed 'Manchester Hill', the British Memorial commemorates the actions of the 2nd Manchesters on 2 April 1917 and the 16th Bn on 21 March 1918. It was erected by the King's Regt on 30 June 1998. Beside it are the village WW1 Memorial and Memorials to the Battle of 18-19 January 1871 (during the Franco-Prussian War) and to Lionel Lefèvre, 1902-1974 and *Cdr de la Légion d'Honneur* Joseph Loiseau, chief of the Aisne Resistance, deported by the Nazis in 1943 to Camp Dora, the V2 Weapons site near Nordhausen - there is a museum there today.

Continue through the village and over the motorway to the T junction and turn left on the D68 towards St Quentin into Maison Rouge. Stop just beyond the last house on the left beside which is a gateway.

• Manchester Hill/7.2 miles/5 minutes/ITMap 6C/7/GPS: 49.84103 3.22708

To the right of the gate is all that remains of the scene of the heroic defence of the Redoubt at Manchester Hill on 21 March 1918 – a small wooded mound known to the Germans as *Margarine Hohe*. Today it is fenced around and the traces of the concrete and steel artillery post on top are hard to find - and **remember it is on private ground**. Behind the mound are the remains of the quarry (Brown Quarry) that existed in 1918. In his

The gateway to the remains of 'Manchester Hill'.

Memorial at Francilly-Selency to
Manchester Hill and to the 2nd and
16th Manchesters.

1934 book, *The March Retreat*, Gen Sir Hubert Gough wrote, 'The defence of Manchester Hill in the Forward Zone is another instance of the heroic behaviour of our troops. This hill - opposite St Quentin on the front of the 30th Division - was held by the 16th Manchester Regiment, under Lt Col Elstob. On taking over the defence of this position, he had already impressed on his battalion that "There is only one degree of resistance and that is to the last round, and to the last man". This injunction was heroically carried out to the letter. At about 11 a.m. Col Elstob reported to his brigade that the Germans were swarming round his redoubt. At about 2 p.m. he said that most of his men were killed or wounded, that he himself was wounded, that they were all nearly dead-beat, that the Germans had got into the redoubt, and hand-to-hand fighting was going on. He was still quite cheery. At 3.30 p.m. he answered a call on the telephone and said that very few were left and the end was nearly come. After that, communication ceased. Wounded three times, using his revolver, throwing bombs himself, and firing a rifle, he was last seen on the fire-step, and when called on to surrender by Germans within thirty yards, replied "Never!" upon which he was shot dead.'

For this act of heroism, **Lt-Col Wilfrith Elstob** was awarded the **VC**. His name is recorded on the Pozières Memorial (qv).

From just behind the hill a major British trench line named successively Havre, Island and North ran to some 200 yards behind the Enghien Redoubt.

Continue under the motorway, on the D68, keeping left at the water tower at Faubourg St-Martin (during which time you cross over the British front line, No-Mans-Land and into the German lines) *and continue downhill towards the Cathedral. At the bottom turn sharp left signed Vermand and continue straight onto a tree-lined avenue to the German Cemetery on the left.* Between the sharp left turn and the cemetery you crossed over the thick defences of the Hindenburg Line from German lines into No Man's Land.

• *St Quentin German Cemetery/10. 1 miles/10 minutes/ITMap 6C/8/GPS: 49.84874 3.26265*

Over 6,000 named burials marked by small black crosses, some irregularly placed, with up to four soldiers in a grave, are gathered here, originally known as St Martin, many from the 1918 Offensive. They are interspersed with Jewish Stars of David which bear the legend 'With the help of God' in Hebrew. The cemetery was actually inaugurated by the Kaiser on 18 October 1915 and there is a record of the cordial meeting he had - in perfect French - with the *Maire* of St Quentin to discuss the setting up of the cemetery. Inside the entrance on the left-hand border of the cemetery is an impressive Memorial in the classical style carrying the names of almost 2,000 missing with no known grave. The Kaiser was particularly concerned with the siting of the Monument so that it would receive the best possible light. A short flight of steps was flanked by two larger-than-life Graeco-Roman soldiers by the Berlin academician Wilhelm Wandschneider which were pejoratively described locally in 1917 as 'gross idols of an abject Munich-style of art'. The statues are, however, of a very high artistic quality and because of their bronze content very valuable. Fearing that they would become the targets of art collectors or vandals, the *Deutsche Kriegsgräberfürsorge* took them to their local headquarters at Chaulnes where they were renovated and were re-instated on the 90th Anniversary in 2008. The steps lead to a central panel with laurel wreath and sword, headed by the words *'Resquiescat in pace'* - Rest in peace.

The Memorial, with restored statues, German Cemetery, St Quentin.

Turn right opposite the cemetery on rue A. Parmentier and continue to the T junction. Turn left, still on rue A. Parmentier. Continue to a crossroads and turn right on rue C. Naudin. Turn left at the roundabout with the French Cemetery on the right, direction Amiens all the D1029. Continue through Holnon.

In the village on the right is the delightful **Pot d'Etain restaurant/hotel** (Tel: + (0) 3 23 0934 34. E-mail: info@lepotdetain.fr Website: www.lepotdetain.ir).

Continue through Vermand and past Poeuilly to the junction with the small road to the right to Vraignes.

[N.B.] Just before the junction is a well-maintained **Monument to the '10 Victims of the barbarous Nazis, 29 August 1944' (GPS: 49.87852 3.07389)** from the Commune of Vraignes.

Memorial to 10 Victims of WW2, nr Vraignes

As you make your way towards Amiens following the line of the retreat, two literary personal accounts will considerably add to your understanding of what it was like to have taken part in this momentous and often terrifying event. First there is **Col Rowland Feilding's** moving *Letters to a Wife*. In 1918 this sensitive and popular Regimental officer was commanding the 1st Civil Service Rifles. His account of the Battalion's withdrawal from Ronssoy to Bray is dramatic and realistic, describing the casualties, the pitiful refugees who fled before the armies and his own wounding and treatment. Second, there is **Sir Herbert Read's** *In Retreat*, published in 1925. Read was a Captain in the Yorkshire Regiment, and served with distinction, winning the DSO and the MC. *In Retreat* is both coolly factual and vivid. It describes men as 'dazed', 'haggard'; the fighting as 'bloody', 'hellish', 'ghastly'. We share the light relief of his battle-weary group when a forager brings (no questions asked about its provenance) 'French bread, butter, honey and hot, milky coffee in a champagne bottle! We cried out with wonder: we almost wept. We shared the precious stuff out, eating and drinking with inexpressible zest.' Of such contrasts are battles made.

Continue to the crossroads with the D937 (24 miles).

[N.B.] On the right is a fine **Memorial to two motor racing drivers, Guy Comte Bouriat Quint and Louis-Aimé Trintingant (GPS: 49.87731 2.97879)** who were killed in trials for the *Grand Prix de Picardie* on 20 May 1933. Trintingant's nephew, Jean-Louis, was a famous actor and movie star (he played a racing driver in *Un Homme et une Femme*, 1966) and his brother Maurice twice won the Monaco Grand Prix and the Le Mans 24 Hours race.

Memorial to racing drivers Bouriat Quint & Trintingant, Brie

Continue into Brie, passing a sign to Brie Brit Cemetery on the left. Immediately after crossing the Somme and the Canal du Nord (or Canal de la Somme - the two merge above Peronne) turn left on to the D62 and continue through St Christ-Briost and Cizancourt, under the A29 motorway and through Epénancourt.

As one drives from Brie to Pargny the line of the Canal de la Somme, with the River beyond it, is to the left. These waterways formed a barrier to the Germans' advance and for them an intact bridge was vital- hence the importance of the one at Pargny.

When the Allied counter-attack began on 8 August it started on a line roughly parallel to the road you are driving along about 20 miles to your right. By 7 September the advance had reached here, just behind the barrier of the River Somme in exact reverse of the German's situation in March.

Continue into Pargny village. As the road enters the village, it runs abruptly left; as the buildings begin. Pause.

• Site of Maj Roberts' VC, Pargny Village & Bridge/31.8 miles/15 minutes/ ITMap 6/B1 /GPS: 49.81475 2.94957

When the March German attack opened, the 1st Battalion of the Worcesters was at Moringhem six miles east of St Omer. Next morning they and the whole of 24th Brigade marched to St Omer and entrained at midday, reaching Amiens that night. After a short delay the train continued to Nesle some five miles south of here where the troops got out at 0230 hours on 23 March in darkness. The Worcesters marched north and took up positions on the west bank of the Somme (i.e. this side) covering Pargny. Their task was to hold the river line and to cover the retreat of the Fifth Army. Very early in the morning the route across the Somme, through the village, became congested with refugees and by 1400 hours battalions of the Fifth Army began to stream back, closely followed by the Germans. That evening, about 2000 hours, Germans began to cross the Somme by the bridge at Pargny, which had been incompletely blown. Maj (acting Lt-Col.) F. C. Roberts of the Battalion, seeing what was happening, gathered about forty-five men, where you now are, determined to drive the enemy back across the Somme. At 2100 hours **Maj Roberts'** party set off from here towards the bridge in an action that was to win him the **VC**.

Drive through the village, bearing left past the church, to the bridge and stop.

Here is the story in Maj Roberts' own words, 'We started off with fixed bayonets and magazines loaded. For the first hundred yards or so we went in two parties in single file on each side of the main road at the walk and as quietly as possible. The first sign I had of the enemy was some shouting from houses we were passing and then both machine-gun and rifle fire from windows and doors, with small parties dashing into the streets and clearing off in the direction of the bridge. Once this started we all went hell-for-leather up the street firing at anything we saw and using the bayonet in many cases. Every man screamed and cheered as hard as he could and, by the time we reached the church, the village was in an uproar - Bosches legging it hard for the bridge or else chucking their hands up. In the churchyard itself the hardest fighting took place - tombstones being used as if in a game of hide and seek. After clearing it we had a few moments rest and went smack through to the bridge where a crowd of Bosches were trying to scramble across. Some did and some did not. That more or less ended it - we actually captured six light machine guns, fifteen to twenty prisoners and killed about eighty. Our own losses were heavy.' Maj Roberts later became a Maj-Gen and on 25 June 2005 a Plaque in his honour was unveiled at St Lawrence College, Ramsgate, his old school.

Pargny Brit Mil CWGC Cemetery.

Turn round, return past the church and turn left to Nesle, still on the D62. Then follow signs to the right to Pargny Brit Cem on the D0103. When you stop at the cemetery on the left it is advisable to leave your hazard lights on.

• Pargny British Military CWGC Cemetery/33.2 miles/10 minutes/ITMap 6B/2/GPS: 49.80337 2.94440

The beautiful Cemetery, sloping up the hillside, was made after the Armistice by concentrations from the surrounding battlefields. Fragrant box shrubs shaped like pyramids line the central path that leads to the Cross. The majority of the men here are of the 61st (S Midland) and 8th Divisions whose resistance at the Somme crossings of 24 March materially helped to delay the German advance. There are sixty-one soldiers and airmen from the UK, six Canadians of the Motorised Machine Gun Service and Special Memorials on the left as one enters, to sixteen UK soldiers and two RAF officers, **Lt C.H. Roberts and 2nd Lt J.H. Davies**, 98 Sqn, RAF, 19 August 1918. Between their graves is a headstone describing how they were originally buried in Pertain Mil Cemetery which was destroyed in later battles.

Three quarters of the 619 burials are Unknown. Buried here is **Rfn Berry**, 2nd Bn Rifle Bde, 23 March 1918. A message in the Visitor's Book recorded that Berry won the MM for defending the Bridge at Pargny, but the decoration is not inscribed on his headstone.

Continue uphill and down to the crossroads with the D15. Turn left to Bethencourt. Enter the village and turn left before the bridge on the D62, signed to the German Cemetery. Continue to the cemetery on the left. It is by the exit sign of the village before the local cemetery and is not signed at that point. The entrance is up a path to the left.

• Bethencourt German Cemetery/35.7 miles/10 minutes/ITMap 6B/3/ GPS: 49.79761 2.96242

This is immaculately maintained although devoid of any colour. A fine beech hedge surrounds the Cemetery in which there are some great oak trees. In the centre is a large black cross around which are the small black crosses and two Jewish headstones that mark the 1,242 burials. The majority are from

Cross to Robert Westphal and Eugen Holtz, Béthencourt German Cemetery.

1916, but there are some from 1917 and others from the March attack of 1918.
The Canal runs beside and just over the road from the Cemetery.

Continue through Fontaine-les-Pargny back into Pargny. Return to the D1029 Amiens road by retracing your steps to Brie. Turn left and continue towards Amiens through Estrées and Mons (not to be confused with the Mons in Belgium!). Continue to the junction with the N17. Continue to the French cemetery on the right.

• French National Cemetery/Chinese Graves, Villers Carbonnel/43.2 miles/10 minutes/ITMap 6/1/GPS: 49.87638 2.89326. See Itinerary Four, page 265 for details.

THE KAISER'S OFFENSIVE TOUR IS COMPLETED VIA THE FOLLOWING SITES, WHOSE DETAILS ARE GIVEN IN ITINERARY THREE:
Heath Cemetery (page 235, Map 1/25a, GPS: 48.87297 2.67269); **Site of Carey's Force Action** (page 234, Map 1/25, GPS: 49.87606 2.57877); **Le Hamel: Australian Memorial Park, RB Plaque** (page 215, Map1/24a,b, GPS: 49.89977 2.58161); **Villers Bretonneux: Demarcation Stone** (page 210, Map 1/18, GPS: 49.87059 2.598), **Australian National Memorial, RB Plaque, Cemetery & Interpretation Centre** (page 211 Map 1/11/1, GPS: 49.88613 2.50819), Town Hall (page 209, GPS: 49.86832 2.1755); **School & Franco-Australian Museum** (page 208, Map 1/15/16, GPS: 49.86625 2.51722), **First Tank v Tank Battle** (page 206 Map 1/14, GPS: 49.86060 2.49667), **Nearest Point to Amiens** reached by the Germans (page 205, GPS: 49.86974 2.49029), **Adelaide Cemetery**/65.0 miles (page 207, Map 1/13a, GP: 49.87024 2.4791).

• End of Itinerary Six

The Bridge at Pargny.

Four 'Circular' Walks
on the Somme

It is clearly possible to walk much as one pleases around the battlefield but doing so without a plan can mean that sites of interest or relevance are missed. However, in suggesting walks that might be followed, there are factors that must be considered:

- Private land restrictions
- Dangerous roads. The French are not slow drivers.
- That one's parked transport can end up a long way away from where a walk finishes
- The distance that one might want to walk

Four Themes. Therefore, bearing the above in mind, we have suggested 4 'thematic' timed and measured walks which are circular, i.e. the **end** point is back at the **start** point, thus simplifying transport arrangements. They also use a minimum of potentially dangerous tarmac roads.

Maximise the Experience. A portable GPS device (or smart phone etc) will add to the experience as will a pair of binoculars, stout footwear and frequent reference to the **Holts' Somme Battlefield Map** which should accompany this guide book.

Note: The **Walking Time** given is exactly that – it does not include any time that you might stop *en route*.

Points *en route*. Each has a page reference, e.g. 'page xxx,' where more information can be found and also a map reference if it is shown on the **Holts' Map**, e.g.' 2-A-1' (Map 2, Grid A, Point No. 1). There is also a GPS reference.

The four themes are: –

    1. **Walk 1.** Thiepval - Leipzig Salient- Authuille. 1.5 hours

    2. **Walk 2.** Sunken Road – Malins - Redan Ridge - Hawthorn Crater. 35 minutes

    3. **Walk 3.** Mansel Copse (Devons) - Shrine Alley. 20 minutes

    4. **Walk 4.** Delville Wood - High Wood. 2 hours

Finally: We recommend that you take a picnic. Some of the Walks will take you away from available lunch stops and the Somme area is very beautiful … see Tourist Information page 339.

Somme Walk No 1 - Page 94
Thiepval - Leipzig Salient - Authuille - Thiepval

- **Start/Finish Point:** Thiepval Visitor Centre. GPS: 50.05122 2.68792
- **Distance:** 6.0 kms (approx. 3.7 miles).
  Walking Time: Approx 1 hour 30 mins
- **Number of Visits *en route:*** 9
- **This route** is over the area of the Leipzig Salient, fought for between July and September 1916. Details of sites *en route* are given at the **Page number** listed against each point.

Notes: **a.** Parts are muddy in wet weather. **b.** A portable GPS and binoculars will add greatly to grasping the importance of the high ground of the Salient. **c.** 'Holts'' refers to the location on the **Holts' Battlefield Map of the Somme**. **d.** The walk begins in German territory and moves towards the front line at the cross-tracks tip of the Leipzig Salient (Point 3).

1. **Start/Finish Point.**
   page 94 Holts' 2-G-44a

2. **Leipzig Chalk Pit.**
   GPS: 50.04430 2.68133

3. **Private Memorial.**
   page 99 Holts' 2–G–49.
   GPS: 50.04297 2.68015

4. **Dorset Memorial.**
   page 99
   GPS: 50.04121 2.68485

5. **Lonsdale CWGC Cemetery.**
   page 100 Holts' 2-G-49
   GPS: 50.04006 2.68248

6. **Authuille Memorials.**
   page 96 Holts' 2-G-42a
   GPS: 50.04305 2.66907

7. **Authuille CWGC Cemetery.**
   Holts' 2-G-42
   GPS: 50.04078 2.66635

8. **18th Div Memorial.**
   page 96   Holts' 2-G-44
   GPS: 50.05273 2.68561

9. **Carton de Wiart Memorial.**
   page 90 Holts' 2-G-44b
   GPS: 50.04430 2.68133

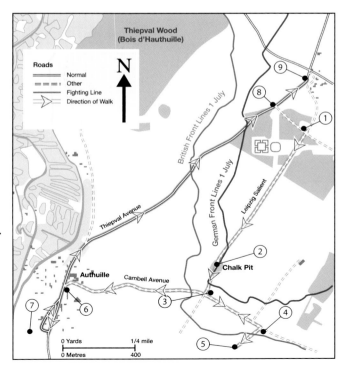

SUNKEN ROAD - MALINS - REDAN RIDGE - HAWTHORN CRATER

- **Start/Finish Point:** Argyll & Sutherland Highlanders Memorial. GPS: 50.08572 2.64853
- **Distance:** 2.75 kms (approx. 1.7 miles)
- **Walking Time:** Approx 35 mins
- **Number of Visits *en route*:** 9
- **This route** walks the Sunken Road featured in Malins' famous photo of the Lancashire Fusiliers just before the assault on 1 July, and then heads directly towards and over the German lines of 1 July 1916.

Notes: a. Parts can be VERY MUDDY in wet weather. **b.** 'Holts'' refers to the location on the **Holts' Battlefield Map of the Somme. c.** We suggest that the route is followed as indicated, because a visit to No. 9 is much more meaningful at the end, once the overall lie of the land has been seen.

1. **Start/Finish Point.**
   page 120 Holts' 2-G-4

2. **CWGC Redan Ridge No 2.**
   page 124 Holts' 2-G-5a
   GPS: 50.08892 2.65262

3. **German Front Line.**
   GPS: 50.0872 2.65311

4. **Track to Rue de Serre.**
   GPS: 50.08583 2.6557

5. **51st Highland Division Flagpole.**
   page 122 Holts' 2-G-8
   GPS: 50.08440 2.65613

6. **Stained Glass Beaumont Hamel Church.**
   page 123 Holts' 2-G-7
   GPS: 50.08379 2.65625

7. **German Front Line.**
   GPS: 50.08455 2.65150

8. **Hawthorn Crater.**
   page 121 Holts' 2-G-6
   GPS: 50.08295 2.65048

9. **CWGC Beaumont Hamel British.**
   page 121 Holts' 2-G-3
   GPS: 50.08589 2.64995

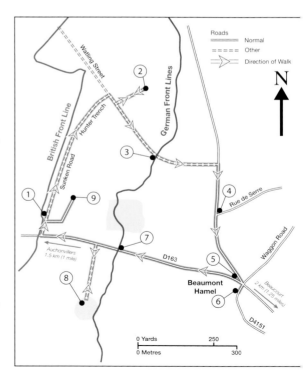

Mansel Copse - Shrine Alley - Mansel Copse

- **Start/Finish Point:** Devonshire CWGC Cemetery. GPS: 49.98830 2.73586
- **Distance** 1.3 kms (approx. 0.8 miles).
- **Walking Time:** Approx 20 minutes
- **Number of Visits *en route*:** 7
- **This route** is in the area attacked on 1 July 1916 by the 9th & 8th Devons and 2nd Gordon Highlanders. Details of sites *en route* are given at the Page number listed against each point.

Notes: **a.** Parts are muddy in wet weather. **b.** A portable GPS will add greatly in grasping how small an area the attack took place in. **c.** 'Holts'' refers to the location on the **Holts' Battlefield Map of the Somme**. **d.** The broad axis of the attack was along the D938 towards Mametz with the Devons below the road and the Gordons

1. **Start/Finish Point.**
   page 165 Holts' 2-K-46

2. **German front line trenches.**
   GPS: 49.99177 2.73490

3. **German second line trenches.**
   GPS: 49.99367 2.73479

4. **Shrine Alley Machine Gun.**
   page 162
   GPS: 49.99367 2.73374

5. **Railway Halt Machine Gun.**
   page 164
   GPS: 49.99285 2.73204

6. **German second line.**
   GPS: 49.99180 2.73314

7. **German front line.**
   GPS: 49.99140 2.73357

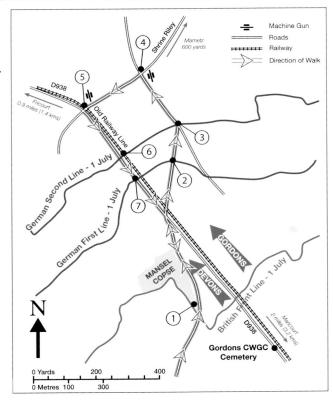

DELVILLE WOOD - HIGH WOOD - DELVILLE WOOD

- **Start/Finish Point:** Delville Wood Museum Car Park. GPS: 50.02467 2.81270/ Footballer's Memorial. GPS: 50.02428 2.80905
- **Distance:** 9.18 kms (approx. 6 miles).
  Walking Time: (excluding time at Delville) Approx 3 hours
- **Number of Visits *en route:* 9**
- **This route** is in the area fought over from 14 July 1916 until late in September. Details of sites *en route* are given at the Page number listed against each point.

Notes: **a.** Parts are muddy in wet weather. **b.** It is easy to spend over an hour visiting the Delville Museum, Visitor Centre, the Wood itself and the CWGC Cemetery. **c. 'Holts''** refers to the location on the **Holts' Battlefield Map of the Somme. d.** On some maps it is impossible to be precise about trench locations so we have used the term 'Fighting Lines' to describe the general positon of the front line trenches.

1. **Start/Finish Point.**
   page 177 Holts' 2-K-14/ 2-K-15a

2. **Pipers' Memorial.**
   page 182 Holts' 2 –K-14c
   GPS: 50.02615 2.80901

3. **New Zealand Memorial.**
   page 183 Holts' 2-H-26
   GPS: 50.03954 2.80151

4. **London CWGC Cemetery.**
   page 186 Holts' 2-H-21
   GPS: 50.03880 2.78235

5. **Glasgow Highlanders Cairn.**
   page 185 Holts' 2-H-22
   GPS: 50.03804 2.78358

6. **Public Schools Bn Tree.**
   page 185 Holts 2-H-23
   GPS: 50.03693 2.78576

7. **47th London Div Memorial.**
   page 185 Holts' 2-H-24

8. **Cameron Highlanders & Black Watch Memorial.**
   page 184 Holts' 2-H-35
   GPS: 50.03881 2.78894

9. **Bristol's Own Cross Memorial.**
   page 158 Holts' 2-K-29
   GPS: 50.02515 2.79718

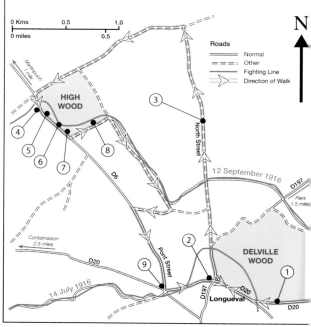

ALLIED AND GERMAN WARGRAVES & COMMEMORATIVE ASSOCIATIONS

AMERICAN BATTLE MONUMENTS COMMISSION (ABMC)

The Commission was established by Congress in March 1923 and has been responsible for commemorating members of the American Armed Forces where they have served overseas since 6 April 1917 (the date of the U.S. entry into WW1). Its task was to erect suitable memorials and cemeteries. It now administers 24 permanent burial grounds (in which there are 30,921 WW1 burials in 8 cemeteries of a total of 116,516 killed in the war), 21 separate Monuments and three 'Markers', as well as four Memorials in the USA.

Its first chairman was Gen John J. Pershing (qv) who served until his death in 1948 when he was succeeded by another WW1 veteran, Gen George G. Marshall. From 1959 to 1969 the Chairman was Gen Jacob L. Devers and he was followed by Gen Mark Clark until his death in 1984. From 1985 to 1991 Gen Andrew J. Goodpaster served, to be followed by Gen P.X. Kelley, Gen Frederick F. Woerner in 1994 and Gen P.X. Kelley again in 2001, followed by Gen Frederick M. Franks Jr. The current Chairman is Retired Air Force Gen. Merrill A. McPeak, who was chief of staff of the U.S. Air Force from 1990 to 1994. He was elected in June 2010.

After WW1 families were allowed by the War Department for the Dead to choose to have their loved ones repatriated (at Government expense) or to be buried near where they fell. In each of the beautifully landscaped WW1 cemeteries at Brookwood, Surrey; Flanders Field, Waregem; Somme, Bony; Aisne-Marne, Belleau; Oise-Aisne, Fère-en-Tardenois; Meuse-Argonne, Romagne; St Mihiel, Thiaucourt and Suresnes, near Paris, there is a non-denominational Chapel (although the atmosphere is predominantly Christian). The land for the cemeteries was given free of charge by the various host countries. The graves are surmounted by brilliant white marble crosses, interspersed by Stars of David for Jewish servicemen. There is no appropriate symbol for men and women of other denominations or for atheists and when the authors queried how a Star of David came to be placed on the grave of an Unknown in Flanders Field the Superintendent explained that the percentage of Jewish servicemen was known and the Unknowns were deemed to be Christian or Jewish in that same proportion. Unknown graves bear the legend, 'Here rests in honored glory an American soldier known but to God.' Identified graves bear the name, unit, date of death, (but not of birth), and the home State. Headstones of Medal of Honor winners bear a gold star and the wording is picked out in gold. The pristine grave markers are laid out in perfectly symmetrical lines on immaculately manicured emerald green grass. There are no flower beds in front of the rows but the graves areas are surrounded by beautiful shrubs and trees. Each cemetery contains a luxuriously-appointed Visitor's Room with a Superintendent's office where information about the burials may be obtained and in which there is always a Visitor's

324 • Major & Mrs Holt's Battlefield Guide to The Somme

Book, an example of the Purple Heart medal and photographs of the current President of the USA and of other American cemeteries. Most cemeteries contain Tablets of the Missing and features like marble battle maps, colourful mosaics and dramatic sculptures. Some of the best architects of the day were employed to design them.

The American flag flies proudly and is lowered when the cemetery closes (now a standard 1700 hours in each cemetery throughout the year, opening time 0900) when Taps (the American equivalent of the Last Post) is played. There are rest rooms and good parking. The overall impression is one of pride and glory, with gilded seals and mosaics much in evidence giving the feeling that no expense should be spared to honour the dead.

A progressive programme of installing carillons with pealing bells and a sequence of patriotic and wartime songs in ABMC Cemeteries is underway and is funded by the McCormick (qv) Tribune Foundation (www.rrmtf.org who donate the necessary funding to AmVets National Service Foundation www.amvets.org). The first carillon was installed in 1985 in the Manila Cemetery and the process in still continuing. Of the WW1 Cemeteries the Aisne-Oise, Meuse-Argonne, Oise-Aisne and Somme (Bony) already have their carillons.

As well as the Cemeteries, the ABMC maintain the impressive WW1 Memorials at Audenarde, Kemmel, Bellicourt, Cha[with circumflex]teau-Thierry, Cantigny, Sommepy, Montfaucon, Montsec and Brest (Naval).

There are also some 700 Private American Memorials in Europe which are presently being located and listed, often by the Superintendents in the nearest ABMC Cemetery. Many of them are in a neglected state but local authorities are being encouraged to help maintain them and there is now a non-profit-making charitable organisation, American War Memorials Overseas Inc, whose mission is to document, raise awareness of and care for these private memorials. **Contact**: Lil Pfluke (a long-time friend of the authors) 6 rue de Larienty 92210, St Cloud, France. Tel: 336 1173 1332. E-Mail: info@uswarmemorials.org website: uswarmemorials.org

Memorial Day programmes are held on different days near to the actual Memorial Day date at the end of May in each ABMC Cemetery. Then every grave is decorated with the flag of the United States and that of the host nation. There are speeches, usually including one from the appropriate American Ambassador, and the laying of wreaths with ceremonies that include military bands and units.

Memorial Day 2015, Somme American Cemetery, Bony

The nearest American Cemetery to the **Somme** is at **Bony** in which there are 1,844 named burials and 333 'mia'. **Tel:** +(0)3 23 66 87 20. E-mail: somme.cemetery@abmc-er.org. **Open:** 0900-1700.

Head Office: Courthouse Plaza II, Suite 500, 2300 Clarendon Boulevard, Arlington, VA22201, USA. Tel: + 703 696 6897. Fax: + 703 696 6666. Website: www.abmc.gov.

European Office: 68 rue du 19 janvier, 92380 Garches, France. Tel: + (0)1 47 01 19 76.

COMMONWEALTH WAR GRAVES COMMISSION
Summary Of The Commission's Work By Mr Colin Kerr, Director External Relations, With Particular Reference To The Somme Centenary

Part of the landscape of any of your tours will be the Commission's war cemeteries. Large or small, on open plains, or on high peaks, these cemeteries provide a form of reassurance that these men are not forgotten and that, by maintaining sites in a condition of quiet beauty, we somehow see our own values reflected back on us. The sheer scale of a Tyne Cot or a Bayeux can be, literally, shocking to the first time visitor, but any quick scan through the visitors' books will tell you that these sites still retain the power to move people.

Origins
Traditionally, the Commission has kept a very low profile (although this is changing); so, who or what is this organisation, recently described by Sir Max Hastings as a "national treasure"?

Prior to 1914, the military practice after a battle was to place all of the dead into a large pit. This was still the practice in 1914. However, a young officer in the Ambulance Corps, Fabian Ware, working in France in 1914, began to establish a more formal "graves registration unit" and, with Government support, a comprehensive process of recording and tracking was put in place, which continued until the end of the war. By 1917, the scale of the losses was such that an Imperial War Graves Commission was established by Royal Charter, with the Prince of Wales as the patron, managed by Ware.

In the aftermath of the war, cemeteries were constructed on land donated "in perpetuity" to Britain, with a "cross of sacrifice" and a "stone of remembrance" In some cases, bodies were exhumed and brought into more central locations. Headstones (of Portland stone) replaced the wooden crosses and families were given the option of adding personal lines at the bottom of each headstone. Major figures worked with the Commission, including Lutyens and Kipling. After impassioned national debate, important decisions were taken: there would be no repatriation of bodies and there would be no distinctions of rank: a general's headstone would be identical to a private's headstone. Of the 1 million dead of the Empire, some two thirds were identified, but the balance were not. Of that remaining one third, memorials would be erected, showing the names of the missing: these would include the massive memorials at Ypres (the Menin Gate), the Somme (Thiepval) and Arras, all designed by Lutyens. Of these men, the bodies of many were found, but could not be identified: they too were buried and Kipling created the phrase "a soldier of the Great War, known unto God". When the Menin Gate was opened by General Plumer in 1926, he declared that "they are not missing, they are here". The words were Kipling's. Churchill, in a speech to Parliament, talked of "periods as remote from our own as we ourselves are from the Tudors, when the graveyards in France shall remain an abiding and supreme memorial to the sacrifices made in the great cause".

This had been a *world* war. Beyond the western front, cemeteries and memorials were erected in Palestine, in Mesopotamia, in Macedonia, in Gallipoli, in Italy and in a host of far flung sites from China, to Kenya, to northern Russia, to the Falkland Islands. The Commission established itself in headquarters in London and was funded by the main countries of the Empire, proportionate to the losses (which were 80% British). The Commission hired skilled gardeners to bring a sense of tranquillity to the sites and skilled craftsmen to maintain the walls and the headstones. A couple of myths to dispel: the gardens were not designed by Gertrude Jeykll (although she participated in some initial thinking) and they were not supposed to be an "English country garden". The design guidance, drafted by Frederick Kenyon in 1918, talked only of ‚Äúa sheet of grass and occasional beds of flowers‚Äù.

Naval casualties were a different matter. Although a specifically naval cemetery was built at Scapa Flow, in the Orkneys, most men went down with their ships. Accordingly, three huge memorials were constructed at Portsmouth, Plymouth and Chatham, to record the names of the missing, most of which were lost at the Battle of Jutland. A further memorial was built at Tower Hill, in London, for the Merchant Navy seamen lost during the war (including the huge losses from the *Lusitania*).

In the UK, the situation was also different. Some 250,000 men from World War 1 are buried in the UK, mostly as a result of dying in hospitals, from their wounds (but also from the influenza epidemic). They will be found, mostly, in big city cemeteries, where the local Councils allocated space for the war dead to be buried. Go to any British town today, and you will see, in the main cemeteries, a section with a cross of sacrifice and the neat rows of headstones, with the high standards of maintenance and gardening which you would find in France. British people are generally unaware of what is on their doorstep.

So, the Commission settled down to complete its cemeteries and memorials and then to maintain them as millions of families made their pilgrimages to these resting places.

World War 2

The end of World War 2 brought a further aspect to the work of the Commission, with a further 700,000 casualties of that conflict. Some of the geography was similar (which is why you will find men from both wars in the cemeteries in France and Belgium), but new cemeteries had to be built in the Netherlands, in Germany, North Africa, Italy, Norway, Singapore and Burma. The other significant change was that the major losses of aircrew resulted in scattered graves literally all over the world and to a new memorial to missing aircrew at Runnymede, in England. The existing naval memorials in England were extended to record the names of the missing from this war.

In the 1960s, the Commission changed its name to the Commonwealth War Graves Commission.

The Commission today

100 years on, the Commission continues to go from strength to strength.

With Headquarters now in Maidenhead, England, the Commission comprises the Governments of the UK, Australia, Canada, India, New Zealand and South Africa. It runs its operations from offices in Leamington Spa (UK), Arras (France), Ypres (Northern Europe), Larnaca (Mediterranean) and Delhi (Africa, Asia, Pacific) with smaller offices in Rome, Malta, Cairo, Tel Aviv, Salonica and Gallipoli.

Every year, another 20 to 30 men are found, identified (frequently) and buried with full military honours.

The Arras office contains a headstone production unit, where 22,000 new headstones each year are shipped from the quarries (no longer Portland, but Italy and Bulgaria) and engraved on five machines using computerised images which link back to databases in England. Headstones - particularly in coastal areas - can deteriorate badly over the years. Every five years, the Commission grades every one of its headstones to ensure that, above all else, they are readable.

Details of all 1.7million casualties are stored on the Commission's database, which is accessible through the website **(cwgc.org),** where as long as you know the name, they will tell you where he is buried (or his name commemorated) and how to get there. They also keep records of foreign nationals (mainly German and French) who are buried in the Commission's cemeteries.

If you were to ask the Commission's staff for a view, they would ask you to think about three things:

* please don't forget the sites in the UK: just go to your local cemetery

* visitors will always go to the Menin Gate and to Thiepval, but please go a bit off the beaten track and visit the lesser known sites: they are every bit as beautiful and they all have their own stories to tell

* if you are going on holiday, see if there is a site near your destination: they are all over the world.

The Somme 1916 Battles
The Centenary of the Battle of the Somme brings some challenges for the CWGC. The sheer scale of the battle, compounded by the scale of the losses and by the challenges inherent in attempting to make any sort of objective conclusion on the campaign – all of these factors combine to provide unique challenges to CWGC.

Firstly, the scale. The battlefield is some 25 miles square and the Commission has more than 200 cemeteries. Most British people think of the Somme in terms of the overwhelming casualties of July 1 1916: however, the campaign went on for 141 days of very tough fighting. The first challenge for the Commission is in getting visitors to move beyond the iconic sites of July 1 – the Thiepval Memorial, the Ulster Tower, the Caribou at Beaumont Hamel and the Sheffield Park. Vast and beautiful cemeteries lie all over the Somme battlefield, but are far less visited than the July 1 sites. We hope that this excellent guidebook will attract visitors to Flers, Mametz, Lesboeufs, Longueval and a host of other very special locations.

Secondly, the emotional mindset. A visit to any CWGC site, large or small, is – for most people – a deeply moving experience. However, there are nuances. Visitors to the sites in Normandy, for example, cannot help but be moved by the fact that this was a *success:* without in any way diminishing the sense of loss. Somehow, there is less inclination to think in terms of lives wasted. The Somme, on the other hand, carries a profound sense of

Engraving headstones in the field

waste, almost as an inherent part of the national psyche. It is not for the Commission to argue the rights and wrongs of the Somme campaign, but any appraisal of the Somme must recognise that it stopped the German assault on Verdun and that it had a huge impact on the German Army (whose losses matched the British).

Thirdly, the Commonwealth countries. British people think of the Somme in terms of July 1, although the British elements of 4th Army were in action for some ten weeks. However, for the Commonwealth forces, their key dates are not July 1 (other than the Newfoundlanders), but are those dates on which their forces came into the line over the 141 days. So, for South Africans at Delville Wood, Canadians at Courcelette, Australians at Pozieres or New Zealanders at Longueval, the locations are different and the dates are different. The same point applies to the Welsh at Mametz.

Fourthly, on behalf of the MoD, the Commission maintains scores of Battle Exploit Memorials (BEMs) – some small, some very large – right across the Somme battlefield. For many people, these memorials will be the focus of their visit. The details are set out in the guidebook, but the Commission encourages visitors to the memorials to be sure and visit the nearby cemeteries.

Maintenance of the sites on the Somme is a major commitment for CWGC. We maintain the Thiepval Memorial and we appreciate deeply that large numbers of people still come to this profoundly special place. But we would also encourage visitors to go further in to the battlefield: use this excellent guide and visit the beautiful CWGC sites across the whole of the Somme – these men must not be overlooked.

Colin Kerr
Director External Affairs

Note: If you are visiting the Somme with the aim of finding a specific grave or memorial it is important to check the location before you leave. **Contact: Head Office**, 2 Marlow Road, Maidenhead, Berks, SL6 7DX, UK. Tel: +(0)1628 507200. Website: www.cwg.org (which includes the Debt of Honour Register). E-mail for enquiries: casualty.enq@cwgc.org.

The **Area Office in France** is at rue Angèle Richard, 62217 Beaurains (see Itinerary One), Tel: +(0)3 21 21 77 00 E-mail: france.area@cwgc.org.

There is an interesting and informative CWGC Newsletter: newsletter@cwgc.org that will also keep you up-to-date.

19-18 Project Manager: Andrew Stillman: E-mail: andrew.stillman@cwgc.org

Also be aware that there will be many commemorations for the Centenary of the Somme 1918 battles (See Itineraries 5 and 6).

JOINT CASUALTY & COMPASSIONATE CENTRE (JC&CC)

In April 2005 the Army, Navy and RAF amalgamated in the Joint Casualty & Compassionate Centre, part of the Service Personnel and Veterans' Agency, to deal with any remains of service personnel (principally from WW1 and WW2) where there was any likelihood of an identification. The agency replaced the MOD PS4(A)NWG Cas/Compassionate Cell. They liaise with local embassies and CWGC and use case files and other appropriate means in their research. Once an identification has been made they use the media to trace any family. The wishes of the family are then paramount as to the form of the burial (e.g. quiet or formal).

Contact: Sue Raftree, RAF Innsworth, GL3 1HW. Tel: +(0)1452 712 612 ext 6303. E-mail: dbs-jcccgroupmailbox@mod.uk Any news will be reported on the general MOD website.

One of the most famous and well-documented find was at St-Laurent-Blangy near Arras, when in January 2001, excavations began for a business site called Actiparc over

Iris Empress of India

Iris Pink Horizon

Blue Iris

Iris Flamenco

Yellow Rose

Paeony Karl Rosenfield

Oriental Poppy

Cerianthus Suber

*Selection of flowers in one of some 140 CWC Cemeteries (Adelaide)
on the Somme one day (21 May) out of 365.*

*Campanula Telham
Beauty*

Campanula Persicifolia

Delphinium Black Knight

*Delphinium Summer
Skies*

Dianthus

Polygonum Bi Sorta

London Pride

Osteospinum

the sector where, in 1917, five different British units were facing the Germans during the April offensive. Then human remains were discovered, notably a trench containing twenty-three soldiers, with badges of the Lincolnshire Regiment (the Grimsby Chums). Poignantly their arms appeared to be linked together. The CWGC at Beaurains were informed and working with the Arras Archaeological Service and a forensic scientist from MOD PS4 stringent efforts were made to further identify the men. Unfortunately, no identifications could be made and the soldiers were buried in nearby Point du Jour CWGC Cemetery in June 2002. (This cemetery still has space, as the French remains originally buried here in a significant plot were later removed.) A video for television was made of the incident called *Bodyhunt Search for the Unknown Soldier*.

In the case of remains found at Athie, near Arras, in June 2001 all five sets had 15th Bn Royal Scots insignia found with them. Two sets of remains also had identity discs and one set had a ring with the initials WG inscribed. The CWGC area office, by looking at its own 'Debt of Honour Register', was able to ascertain that the two identity discs belonged to soldiers who were still recorded as missing - Cpl William Gunn and Pte Archibald McMillan who were apparently both killed in action on 9 April, the first day of the Battle of Arras. It was also able to supply a list of missing soldiers from 15th Bn Royal Scots whose initials were WG. Research by MOD PS4 traced the family of Pte McMillan and on 20 June 2002 his 87-year-old son, Archie McMillan, his grand-daughter and great-grandson attended the re-interment in Point-du-Jour CWGC Cemetery. The Regiment buried their sons with full military honours on a grey and wet morning with a ceremony of tremendous dignity and tenderness. The authors were privileged to be present.

On 23 April 2013 four soldiers were reburied at Ecoust-St. Mein CWGC whose story can be read on page 282 and the account of the making of a new CWGC Cemetery at Fromelles in 2011, the first to be built for over half a century, is in our Western Front-North book.

SERVICE DES SÉPULTURES DE GUERRE

The French organisation for the maintenance of wargraves and memorials comes under the Ministry of *Anciens Combattants et Victimes de Guerre*. Details of the *Nécropoles Nationales* can be obtained from their head office at 37 rue de Bellechasse, 75007 Paris. Tel: +(0)1 48 76 11 35.

A law was passed on 29 December 1915 to give the rights to a free, and eternally maintained grave to every French or Allied soldier who was killed in the war. Another law was passed on 18 February 1916 to set up a service to deal with pensions, to give information to families and to cope with the thousands of burials of the enormous casualties that were being incurred. On 25 November 1918 a National Commission of Military Graves was set up which undertook to progressively make landscaped cemeteries, each with a flagpole (and it is marvellous to see the French *tricolore* proudly flying), and to mark each grave with a concrete cross or headstone (for Colonial forces, agnostics, Jewish burials etc). The marker bears the soldier's rank, name, regiment and date of death and the words, '*Mort Pour la France*'. As with the CWGC, there are differently shaped markers for each nationality. The Treaty of Versailles of 28 June 1919 specified that each signatory country should respect and maintain the graves of military foreigners on their land. On 27 January 1920 the Ministry of Pensions absorbed the *Service des Sépultures* and regional teams were set up. The immediate post-war task of identifying bodies and helping relatives to find their loved ones' burial sites is movingly depicted in Bernard Tavernier's award-winning 1989 film, *La Vie et Rien d'Autre* ('Life

French National Cemetery, Notre-Dame de Lorette,
showing Lantern Tower

Ayette Poilu Memorial,
'Singing in Victory'

and Nothing But'). On 31 July 1920 the cemeteries became 'national' and many small front-line cemeteries were concentrated into these larger national burial grounds. By the end of 1925, 960,000 reburials had been made and the bodies of 22,000 *Poilus* had been repatriated from Germany. Between 1926 and 1935 more than 122,000 French and German bodies were found, without graves, on the battlefields. On 11 July 1931 the treasury voted funds to embellish the cemeteries and the larger ones, like Notre Dame de Lorette (France's largest military cemetery with 20,058 graves and 20,000 in mass graves, on a 25 hectare site) were quickly completed.

Like the CWGC, the French decreed that there should be no distinction because of rank or status in the burials, following the Constitution's principal of equality. No 'sumptuous' decoration could be placed on the graves and only cut flowers. Unidentified bodies would be buried in mass graves (*ossuaires*) which should be surrounded by a wall and bear a memorial plaque. The erection of individual monuments was permitted by families and regiments. At first only 'sterile' material, like gravel, was allowed round the lines of graves and on the mass graves. But in 1950 lawns and polyanthus roses were permitted. It is very evident that this concept has been emphasized in the past few years and the somewhat stark appearance of the French cemeteries is now giving way to the more garden-like aspect of the British, with more flowering shrubs and sheltering trees. Maintenance is organized in sectors, with a technical service which has an annual budget. There is a box inside the entrance gate of most cemeteries, with the cemetery register and, a recent addition, a Visitors' Book. Other recent additions are explanatory boards just within the cemetery gates which describe the historical background of the Somme battles and show the national cemeteries in the area. The *Ministère des Anciens Combattants et Victimes de Guerre* publish an *Atlas des Nécropoles Nationales*, which is obtainable from the *Historial de la Grande Guerre* at Péronne. It describes the 265 national cemeteries in France, and divides them into sectors, each with a map. There are some twenty in the Somme battlefield area.

SOUVENIR FRANÇAIS

This association was founded in 1872, after the Franco-Prussian War and revived after World War I. Its aim is to keep alive the memory of those who died for France, to maintain their graves and memorials in good condition and to transmit the 'flame of memory' to future generations. Their Head Office is at 9 rue de Clichy, 75009 Paris. There are active local branches in Albert, Amiens and Arras. Signs of their attentive care can be seen on many of the local *'Poilu'* memorials, and on private memorials, French and British, in the area. Often their red, white and blue roundel insignia is attached when refurbishment has

The Souvenir Français Roundel

taken place. Representatives lay wreaths at many ceremonial and commemorative ceremonies.

Somme Branch: Contact Mme Lisette Quéyrat, 19 Rue de L'Eglise, 80131 Framerville-Raincourt. Tel: + (0)3 22 85 82 91.

VOLKSBUND DEUTSCHE KRIEGSGRÄBERFÜRSORGE (VDK)

In September 1919 Siegfriend Eulen, a former army officer, initiated what was to become the VDK of today. He believed that an organisation should be established to locate, mark and care for German war graves and that it should be a charity. He sought and obtained the support of like-minded people for his idea. Thus the beginnings of the VDK have an interesting parallel with the initiative taken by another individual, Fabian Ware, which was the formation of today's CWGC.

By the end of the 1919 Eulen's initiative had led to the creation of a working committee with the name *Volksbund Deutsche Kriegsgräberfürsorge* – The People's Association for War Graves – which, now having obtained political support, set out to estimate the size of the task. It took ten years to find out that almost one million German war dead would need to be commemorated in some 30 countries and that around half of those were in France. The 'five crosses' symbol used by the VDK is an interpretation of a photograph on the cover of the organisation's first publication of German graves in Poland. It appears on the ironwork gates of many cemeteries and the signs which directs one to the cemetery.

The VDK organises the *Volkstrauertag* – Memorial Day (a day of national mourning) – each November, which takes place locally and also centrally in the Bundestag.

The German War Graves Welfare Association's Head Office is at Werner-Hilperts Strasse 2, D-34117 Kassel, Germany. Website: www.volksbund.de The organisation is similar in function to the Commonwealth War Graves Commission in that it maintains

Sign to German Cemetery, Bray

the war cemeteries and memorials to the German War Dead from World War I onwards, and assists relatives in locating and, in many cases, visiting the graves.

The German cemeteries are not as standardly uniform as the British and French. The markers vary from flat tablets, to upstanding squat stone crosses, to black metallic crosses. Jewish soldiers are marked with a headstone, which bears the Star of David. The markers bear scant information, sometimes only a name, with occasionally a rank, regiment and date of death. Most cemeteries have a mass grave, the names of the unidentified missing soldiers probably buried therein being listed on bronze panels. Under the majority of markers two, four or even more soldiers will be buried. There are two reasons for this. It signifies 'comradeship in death' and also, on a practical note, the Germans were not allocated as much territory in which to bury their dead as were the Allies. In some German cemeteries there is a small memorial chapel, and often there will be some statuary – normally of bereaved parents or comrades. There will be a register in alphabetical order and sometimes a Visitors' Book to sign. Oak trees, symbolizing strength, are a frequent feature. There is a marked lack of flowers and colour in most German burial grounds. They are sad, sombre, mournful places – but then the death of a soldier is sad and mournful.

The maintenance of the German cemeteries in France is administered by the Service for the Care of German Cemeteries (SESMA), whose **regional office** is at rue de Nesle prolongée, 80320 Chaulnes, Tel: +(0)3 22 85 47 57. There are thirteen German cemeteries on the Somme Battlefield of 1916-18 including (number of burials in brackets): Sapignies (1,550); Achiet-le-Petit (1,314); Villers-au-Flos (2,491); Fricourt (17,026); Rancourt (11,422); Bray (1,122); Proyart (4,634); Morisel (2,642) and Vermandovillers (22,600). Individual leaflets are available for each of them, but all German War Cemeteries in France, Belgium, Luxembourg and Holland are described, with maps, in the *Atlas Deutscher Kriegsgräber*, available from the Head Office in Kassel.

There is also a WW2 Cemetery at Bourdon (off the A16 near Exit 21 near Amiens) containing 22,213 burials. Here on 21 September 2007 the remains of Lt Hans-Joachim Rimarski were re-interred. They had been found in the wreck of his Messerschmitt 109-4 by the Somme Aviation '39-'45 Association. The simple ceremony was attended by the authors in the presence of the German Defence Attaché from Paris but sadly, despite the identification and attempt to find them, no relatives. The small casket was buried to the left of the headstone bearing 21 year old Rimarski's name. The next burial will be central to the headstone, the third to the right and the two other names inscribed below Rimarski's. The young pilot of the 2nd 'Richthofen' Squadron was brought down by an American B-26 on 19 August 1943.

CONSEIL GENERAL DE LA SOMME/HISTORIAL /CIRCUIT DE SOUVENIR

The *Département de la Somme* is working with the Historial Museum at Péronne to preserve and promote battlefield sites in their area. Notable are the acquired sites of the preserved trenches at Soyécourt (Map 1/31), the Gibraltar bunker at Pozières (Map G48) and the site of the vanished village of Fay (Map 1/27a). Routes for a Circuit du Souvenir are marked by a stylised red poppy on a brown sign and there is a booklet and leaflet describing it. Descriptive signboards are progressively being placed at the entrance to sites of historic interest (signified by CGS/H - *Conseil Général de la Somme/Historial* throughout this book). They are at: Australian Memorial, Villers-Bretonneux; Australian Memorial, Mont St Quentin; Newfoundland Memorial, Beaumont-Hamel; New Zealand Memorial at Longueval; South African Memorial, Delville Wood; Ulster Tower; Thiepval Memorial; Lochnagar Crater, la Boisselle; Canadian intervention at crossroads of D23 Villers-Bretonneux-Moreuil; P'tit Train, Froissy; Lochnagar Crater; *Souvenir Français* Chapel, Rancourt; Tank Memorial, Pozières; Bazentin; Frise; Combles; Mametz (to the Welsh Memorial); Maricourt; Maurepas; Sailly-Laurette and four signboards that relate to Manfred von Richthofen, the 'Red Baron' – at Cappy, Vaux-sur-Somme (near the brickworks), Bertangles and Fricourt. Website: www.somme14-18.com. It must be pointed out, however, that many signboards are in very agricultural areas and prone to destruction by passing tractors!

ASSOCIATION PAYSAGES ET SITES DE MEMOIRE DE LA GRANDE GUERRE.

Founded in Paris in 2011 to undertake the enormous task of preparing an inventory and plan for UNESCO recognition of WW1 memorial sites on the Western Front. This involves 12 French Departments from Nord-Pas de Calais to the Haut Rhin, plus sites in Belgian Flanders and Wallonia, with a total of 45 major sites. A significant number of them are on the Somme battlefield. In 2015 the Association declared its aims to avoid the 'touristic Disneyfication' of the battlefield sites and to promote their moral value for humanity with the obligation of keeping alive the memory and the desire to learn.

Paysages et sites de mémoire de la Grande Guerre

The authors are proud to be *'Partenaires'* and totally support this aim.

Contact: Secretaire-général Serge Barcellini, Controleur Général des Armées. E-mail: paysagesetsitesdememoire@gmail.com Website: **FIRST WEBSITE CHANGED** - www.heritage-grandeguerre.fr www.paysages-et-sites-de-memoire.fr

THE DURAND GROUP
For Historical Research Into Subterranean Military Features
This 'fraternal association of individuals who have voluntarily undertaken to work together' comprises former and current military personnel and civilians with skills as historians, archaeologists, technicians, explosives and munitions experts, engineers,

archivists, surveyors, cartographers, mountain and cave rescuers, IT, film production and medics. In just a few years they have become a pre-eminent authority on what might be described as 'underground battlefields' using highly sophisticated and technological equipment and methods in a most responsible manner.

The work that triggered the later formation of the group was initially organised by Lt Colonel Phillip Robinson in the late 1980s at the behest of the Director of the Vimy Memorial Site. The Royal Engineers investigated the La Folie mining system, and found two armed mines, one of which, the Durand Mine (the abandoned *fougasse* mine which gave the group its name), contained 6,000 lb of ammonal and was located under a public area. Research also suggested a much larger charge at the end of a blocked tunnel close to the Broadmarsh crater.

In 1996, upon return from extended service abroad, Phillip Robinson organised a volunteer team to access the Broadmarsh mine. Fortuitously, it was thought to have been neutralised but further investigation of the Durand mine by Lt Col Mike Watkins, a serving officer of the Royal Logistic Corps and a leading EOD expert, indicated that it was fully viable and a potential threat. Working in arduous and dangerous conditions Mike Watkins disarmed it.

Following from this Mike Watkins and Phillip Robinson formed and constituted the Durand Group. Working in co-operation with Veterans Affairs Canada, the Group has since accessed about seven kilometres of tunnels under Vimy Ridge, disarmed two further sitting mine charges and undertaken archival and site studies aimed at identifying areas of potential risk to the public and site staff. In addition to two of the deep British fighting systems and a German system – which is still being investigated – they have also opened up nearly 500 metres of the former Goodman subway, revealing extensive and sometimes poignant graffiti inscribed by the Canadian soldiers as they waited to move into their assault positions.

Other work has included advice on underground features during construction of the Thiepval Visitor Centre (qv), assistance to the Pas de Calais and Arras archaeological authorities, continuing investigation of underground workings at Beaumont Hamel and recording and correlation of graffiti.

A professionally produced film of the early work of the Group is available through www.fougassefilms.co.uk in the form of a DVD, complete with multi-media resource pack. This vividly portrays the work of the Group, and the particular hazards, highlighted by the tragic dedath of Lt-Col Mike Watkins in 1998 when part of an excavation at Vimy collapsed upon him. He is commemorated on a Memorial Plaque placed by Veterans Affairs Canada near the entrance to the Grange subway at Vimy.

During projects the Group is usually based at a former farm near St Pol owned by one of the Members. They can be **contacted** through their website, www.durandgroup.org.uk which gives much information on their work. Reports and DVDs covering certain projects are also available. Additionally a charity has been established (with Lord Astor of Hever, grandson of Field Marshal Earl Haig, as Patron) to support research and investigation into military mining and promote knowledge of the Tunnellers. Donations to the 'Durand Charity (No. 1105311), which may be gift aided, are welcome.

THE FRIENDS OF LOCHNAGAR

Founded on 1 July 1978 this Association aims to preserve the Lochnagar Crater and the memory of the men who fell there in 1916. **Contact:** Founder and Chairman, Crater owner Richard Dunning, Little Down, Hog's Back, Seale, Surrey, GU10 1HD. E-mail: Richard.dunning@uwclub.net.

Nurses & VADs Memorial Seat, Lochnagar

Excellent magazine, *The New Chequers*, e-mail: chequers@friendsoflochnagar.co.uk
Website: http://www.lochnagarcrater.org/

THE ROYAL BRITISH LEGION (RBL)

The UK's foremost Association for the welfare of ex-servicemen, formed in 1921, through the energetic efforts of Earl Haig, received its Charter in 1925 and its 'Royal' prefix in 1971. Active Somme Branch. **Contact:** President Rod Bedford, Tel: +(0)3 22 76 29 60, e-mail:chairman@rblsome.org website: http://www.britishlegion.org.uk/branches/somme

Annual ceremonies at Thiepval on 1 July and 11 November, Annual Dinner 30 June. Newsletter - *The Somme Bugle*.

THE SOMME ASSOCIATION

Contact their base at the Somme Heritage Centre/Museum at 233 Bangor Road, Newtownards BT23 7PH, Co. Down, N. Ireland, Tel: +(0)28 9182 3202, website: www.Irishsoldier.org E-mail: shc@hotmail.co.uk The Association Director, Carol Walker, daughter of Ulster Tower stalwarts Teddy and Phoebe Colligan, is dedicated to co-ordinating research into Ireland's part in the First World War (e.g. of the 10th and 16th (Irish) and 36th (Ulster) Divisions). It has research and education programmes, sponsors publications, organises anniversary commemorations and battlefield tours. Much of their information comes from the records of the Ulster Patriotic Fund (an endowment fund for widows and families provided by well-to-do business men, one of whose projects was the building of the Ulster Tower) which is still under the Official Secrets Act. Their database lists every man who served in an Irish Regiment from 1914-1921 and can be searched by name/regiment/details of next of kin/place of commemoration etc. It also maintains the Ulster Tower and its Visitor Centre (qv).

SOMME REMEMBRANCE ASSOCIATION

Founded in July 2005, the aim of this Anglo-French Association is to preserve the memory of soldiers of WW1 on the Somme in collaboration with like-minded organisations and individuals and to co-ordinate commemorative events (such as the unveiling of Memorial to Pte Cox, VC (qv)). Several new plaques, commemorative benches and memorials are planned in the near future for the Centenary. For membership details see their website: www.somme-remembrance.com

Contact: President, Philippe Drouin, **Tel:** + (0)3 21 59 85 95. E-mail: philippe.dr@tiscali.fr 1 rue de Bapaume, 62121 Achiet-le-Grand. Treasurer, François Bergez.

GUILD OF BATTLEFIELD GUIDES

Launched on 28 November 2003 the Guild aims to provide a 'kite-mark' for Battlefield Guides in the form of a badge which the public can trust and which it will be deemed an honour to wear. Mission Statement: "To analyse, develop and raise the understanding and practice of battlefield guiding." The Guild is an inclusive organisation, not a regulatory body and aims to engender a 'Club' environment with a magazine and educational and social meetings. The popular and well respected founder Patron, Prof Richard Holmes, sadly died in 2011. The authors are Founding Hon Members.

Experienced Guild Guides are supporting STS in the Governments' Centenary scheme to conduct a teacher and two pupils from every State school to the WW1 battlefields.

The coveted and respected badge of an accredited Guide of the Guild of Battlefield Guides.

Contact: The Secretary, e-mail: secretary@gbg-international.com Website: www.gbginternational.com

ROSS BASTIAAN *BAS RELIEF* COMMEMORATIVE PLAQUES

The series of beautifully designed, durable, informative plaques that can be seen at sites on the Somme - at Bullecourt, Digger Memorial; Le Hamel, Town Hall; Mont St Quentin, by the Digger Memorial; Mouquet Farm, by roadside; Péronne, *Historial* entrance; Pozières, Windmill site and 1st Div Memorial; Vermandovillers Town Hall (non-standard, to McCarthy, VC); Villers Bretonneux Town Hall and at the Australian

Memorial – are the inspiration of Australian dentist, **Ross Bastiaan** (qv). At first Ross received no support (and initially little acknowledgement) from the Government in his dedicated work of designing, researching, creating, erecting and finding sponsors for these magnificent plaques which are gradually being placed around the world wherever Australian forces were engaged with distinction. They were first introduced in Gallipoli in 1990 where the authors first met Ross (recently vandalised and repaired by Ross) and 261 are now sited as far afield as Johannesburg and Damascus. Ross was properly recognised in Australia for his dedicated work and was appointed to be Deputy Chairman of the Council of the Australian War

Ross Bastiaan with his Plaque to Monitor M33, Portsmouth

Memorial by then Prime Minister, John Howard, whom he guided round the Gallipoli and Somme battlefields in 2000. His latest project was the erection a Plaque in Portsmouth on the 100th Anniversary of the Monitor 'M33' shelling Gallipoli on 6 August 1915. The ship has been restored on the outside but left untouched on the inside, and it is there that one of the most moving battle presentations that the authors have ever experienced has been set up. It is short, with minimum commentary plus a great deal of battle noise, and projected on the surrounding walls of the interior. The nearest other such presentation experienced by the authors is that at Guernica where 90% is in total darkness. **Website:** www.plaques.satlink.com.au

WESTERN FRONT ASSOCIATION (WFA)

Formed by John Giles in 1980 to further the interest in WW1 and to perpetuate the memory, courage and comradeship of all who fought in it. Two excellent publications, *Stand To* and *The Bulletin,* Chairman: Bob Paterson. **Contact:** Hon Sec Stephen Oram, Spindleberry, Marlow Road, Bourne End, Bucks, SL8 5NL. E-mail via the website: www.westernfrontassociation.com

PIPE BANDS

There are two Pipe Bands based in the Somme who attend many commemorative events, inaugurations of new memorials, gatherings of Pipe Bands, Celtic Nations etc, not only on the Somme but throughout France and abroad. They will both be particularly active during the Centenary years.

1. The Somme Battlefield Pipe Band. Founded in 1989 by Ian Alexander (pictured on the front cover), Hon Pipe Major, to promote the music and history of Scottish soldiers who fought in the region, '14-'18. Members wear the uniforms of Scottish Regiments who fought on the Somme. www.sommebattlefieldpipeband.com

2. The Samarobriva Pipes and Drums. Founded in Amiens in 2007 by Chairman Pascal Lebeau to unite people who are passionate about Celtic music and culture and to promote remembrance of WW1. Somme Director of Tourism François Bergez (a Breton by birth) is an enthusiastic member. The *Conseil Général de la Somme* has given the Band a subsidy for the Centennial period. (See page 148).

http://samarobriva-pipes-and-drums.blogspot.com www.unitedpipersforpeace.com/

TOURIST INFORMATION

It is the ironic and inevitable fate of a guide book that some information given in it will have become out of date by the time it is published. For instance, the reader may be surprised to see how many new Visitors' Centres and memorials have been erected on the Somme since the first edition of this book in 1996 and even more so since their first small guide book to the Somme 10 years earlier still. New roads and the ubiquitous roundabouts appear, road numbers change. The personnel mentioned in hotels, restaurants, museums and tourist offices retire or move. Opening hours for these establishments often change. The tourist information in this guide is, therefore, as the cliché goes, 'correct at the time of going to press' and we apologise in advance for any changes that may have occurred since. However to alleviate these dangers we give website details for such places so that checks can be made before traveling.

Our best advice, if you have obtained this book before you leave home, is to go through it carefully in conjunction with the accompanying *Major & Mrs Holt's Battle Map of the Somme*, marking the sites or itineraries that you intend to follow, then obtain the relevant tourist information and brochures from the addresses below:

French Tourist Office, French Tourist Office, Lincoln House, 300 High Holborn, London. Tel: 020 7061 6631 E-mail: info.uk@france.fr Website: www.france.fr

You can also contact local **tourist offices** for more detailed information on **accommodation, restaurants**, general local tourist information, holidays and calendar of events, including festivals – the serious student of the battlefields may well wish to avoid the latter as local hostelries will be full and roads congested.

Where to Stay & Where to Eat

Hotels and restaurants that are conveniently on the routes are mentioned as they occur in the Itineraries. In many cases the comments about them reflect the authors' subjective views for which they receive no financial benefit. For more comprehensive information see under '**Tourist Offices**' below.

THE SOMME PAST & PRESENT

A Brief History to the Outbreak of World War I

The Département of the Somme was created in 1790 when France was reorganized administratively. It incorporated the major part of the ancient Province of Picardy and its character remains 'Picard' to this day. The region has been inhabited and invaded by many different peoples. Recent advances in aerial archaeology show the distinct traces of Gallic fortified camps (*oppida*). Julius Caesar occupied the area in 57BC, overcoming the indigenous Belgic tribes. Evidence of the Roman (Gallo-Roman) era are found throughout the Département in the form of temples, baths, theatres and farmsteads. Christianity came to the area at about the end of the third century AD. The first Bishop of Amiens was Firmin, who was martyred for his faith in 287. Another famous Christian was Martin, the Roman soldier who divided his cloak and shared it with a naked beggar in Amiens, was converted, and died in 397 as Bishop of Tours.

The era of the *Pax Romana* was a relatively calm period, but at the end of the fourth century a series of invasions began. The Vikings, in the ninth and tenth centuries, were perhaps the most feared, until they were beaten by the Carolingian King Louis III at Sacourt-en-Vimeu. In the Middle Ages, abbeys and châteaux flourished under the feudal lords, resulting in local power struggles. Agriculture and the cloth industry expanded in the twelfth and thirteenth centuries. Towns grew up as trading developed, but the increasingly prosperous land continued to be fought over – by the rival counts of Amiens and Flanders and the kings of France. In 1185 the *'Comté'* (the land ruled by a count) was taken over by the Crown.

In 1297 the *Comté* of Ponthieu came under English domination, when Edward III married Eleanor of Castille, who had inherited it. In 1328 Edward staked his claim on the French throne, and the Hundred Years' War began. In 1329 Philip VI persuaded Edward (as Count of Ponthieu) to come and pay homage to him in Amiens Cathedral. But the following year Edward landed in Normandy and marched through the Somme, making a defensive stand at Crécy en Ponthieu. The English and Welsh longbows routed Philip's army and the flower of French knighthood was destroyed.

Henry V was the next English King to march through Picardy, in 1415. He encamped at Corbie, where he publically hanged one of his soldiers for stealing a golden vessel – an incident featured in Shakespeare's Henry V. Crossing the Somme at Ham, Henry led his weary army right across the area which was to be the setting for the 1 July 1916 battle, through Beaumont Hamel itself, on his way to Agincourt. It was another disaster for the French. *'Voulez-vous voir la France, allez à Londres'*, was the saying after Agincourt, for in London were the only remaining knights and lords of French extraction, who had come with the Norman invasion of Britain in 1066.

The Somme then passed to Anglo-Burgundian rule until 1477, when Louis XI retook the area.

The Spanish were the next invaders. They took Amiens in 1597, but it fell again to Henry IV of France after a siege of six months. In 1636 they took Corbie, which in its turn was retaken by Henry. In 1653 the Santerre (qv) was devastated by the Great Prince of Condé, allied with the Spanish, in the Civil War known as the *Fronde* (meaning 'wind of revolt'.)

Then a period of peace eventually ensued and gradually prosperity returned to the province once more, especially in agriculture and the cloth industry.

1870 saw the arrival of the Prussian Army in the Franco-Prussian War. Amiens was taken in 1870 after the Battle of Dury (south of Amiens). General Faidherbe had some limited successes with his army of the North – notably at Pont Noyelles near Querrieu (qv).

Forty-three years later came the outbreak of World War I. Amiens was again occupied, on 31 August 1914. Picardy was once more to become a battlefield and this time the devastation was so terrible that it was thought it would never be cultivated again.

The Aftermath of the Great War

After the war, the parts of the Somme most frequently and bitterly fought over – in the area of the Ancre around Albert and in the Santerre around Villers-Bretonneux – were officially described as a *Zone Rouge* (red zone). It was considered uninhabitable and uncultivatable for evermore as, indeed, were great tracts of land around the Verdun battlefield. These latter were designated as national parks, afforested and then left for nature to perform her own slow healing process. Villages completely disappeared.

Not so in Picardy. Although it was said of Albert after the war that *'Il ne reste que le nom et la Gloire* '[Only the name and Glory remain], the townspeople insisted (as did the citizens of Ypres in Flanders) on returning to thir sad ruins and recreating their town. The Picard, so deeply tied to his land, returned to till the impossible mess that had been made of his smallholding. It hardly seemed possible that normal life could ever resume. Even before the war ended, John Masefield walked *'The Old Front Line'* and described it in vivid terms. 'It is as though the place had been smitten by the plague', he wrote.

The *Berliner Tageblatt* described the region as a 'desert incapable for a long time of producing the things necessary to life'. The precious upper covering of fertile soil, from which the agricultural economy drew its living, had almost completely disappeared and the limestone substratum was laid bare. The huge mine craters gaped. The great one at la Boisselle was 200ft in diameter and 81ft deep in 1919. Wooden crosses marked the mound of British graves in its depths, a skull guarding them for years. Even as long after the war as 1928 it was thought that Serre could never be rebuilt. Thiépval, whose economy depended on its wealthy château (which was not rebuilt) was also slow in its rebirth, and never attained its former size.

The gradual rebuilding of the villages and towns took place in the Twenties, when the style known as *Art Deco* (from the name of the exhibition, *Arts Décoratifs et Industriels Modernes* in Paris of 1925) was at its short-lived apogée, leaving an extraordinary architectural legacy. Its trade marks of geometric shapes, sunbursts and zig-zags can be glimpsed in the wrought iron gates of farms and cottages, the designs of windows, the proud new station at Albert, and the incongruous church spires, like the somewhat bizarre concrete fretwork of Lamotte Warfusée.

The rebuilding was done using the reparation money voted to the ruined villages by the Treaty of Versailles. This was augmented by funds raised by subscription in many British cities and towns. The British League of Help inaugurated an 'adoption' scheme (see Biaches above), and, for instance, Birmingham adopted Albert (hence the street name 'Rue de Birmingham'); Sheffield – Bapaume, Puisieux and Serre (where so many of her 'Pals' fell); Maidstone – Montauban; Wolverhampton – Gommecourt; Derby – Foncquevillers; Llandudno – Mametz (where the Welsh fought so gallantly); Stourbridge – Grandcourt; Ipswich – Fricourt; Tonbridge – Thiépval; Canterbury – Lesboeufs and Morval; Hornsey – Guillemont; Brighouse – Courcelette; Gloucester – la Boisselle and Ovillers; Portsmouth – Combles and Flers; Folkestone – Morlancourt and Leamington-Spa – Biaches (qv).

Imported Polish labourers helped to clear the battlefields, and the scrap-metal merchants prospered. The 'iron harvest', however, seems to be eternal, and Picard ploughs turn up tons of it each year (qv).

The Picard

That the Somme presents today a peaceful, prosperous, bucolic face, with the Santerre's fertile fields that once were the granary of the Roman army, producing their habitual record harvests; that the Somme flows through tranquil, verdant banks; that the pastures of the little farmsteads around la Boisselle and Beaumont Hamel are calmly grazed by fat, sleek stock – are all due to the character and personality of the Picard.

They descend from the Belgae – a mixed race of Celtic and Teutonic stock. Their traits are a fierce pride in, and loyalty to, their land; resistance to change; quickness to defend liberty and rights; inherent honesty and courtesy. They are hard-working and independent of spirit, and they were determined to coax their battered land back to life.

One can imagine what torments the war must have caused to such people. Until ordered to leave by the military authorities, they would cling to their shell-torn homes and farms. They also had the humiliation of peremptory requisitioning to bear. Yet most of the personal accounts one reads by Allied soldiers' talk of comfortable billets, much fraternising behind the lines, and families who kept their promise to look after the tragic crosses which marked pals' graves. There are far fewer reports of profiteering from the captive market of the soldier here than on other areas along the front. After the war, a number of Tommies came back to Picardy, married their wartime sweethearts and settled down on their old battlefield. The daughter of one of them, Marie Baudet, née Salter, served her father's country with the ATS in World War II.

The ancient language of Picardy, a dialect with 'Romano' origins, is unfortunately dying out with the older generation. But the pilgrim will still hear its mysterious tones in isolated villages along the Somme and in folk songs and recipes.

DISTRICTS OF PICARDY FOUGHT OVER IN THE SOMME BATTLES

The Amiénois
The real heart of the province includes its capital city, Amiens, which was known by the Romans as Samarobriva (Bridge over the Somme). Its strategic position as the gateway to Paris and its situation on the great river made it an important distribution centre for local products. These include linen (woven from local flax) and woad (the blue dye used by the ancient Britons). Amiens was much damaged in the two World Wars, but some typical Picard houses remain in the picturesque and well-restored Old Quarter of St Leu. The city boasts an interesting stone Circus (opened by its famous citizen Jules Verne, who is buried in la Madeleine Cemetery and whose house at the corner of Bvd Jules Verne and rue Charles Dubois has been preserved), the Museums of Picardy and of Local Art and History, and a Costume Exhibition.

The castle-like Town Hall, Corbie

The Amiénois is a region of great natural beauty: of water and woods, hills and valleys, and heavy morning mists. It includes: Doullens (qv) with its Citadelle, planned by François I in 1525 and completed under Louis XIV, in the north; Bertangles (qv) with its imposing eighteenth-century château; Corbie (qv); Bray (qv) and the whole Valley of the Ancre, from Albert to Hamel. It therefore encompasses the greatest section of the British Front Line of 1 July 1916 and was part of the post-war *Zone Rouge* (qv).

In the Amiénois the traditional farm, with its courtyard and distinctly rural odours (what Bairnsfather called 'a rectangular smell') still exists – and many of them were rebuilt to the old format after the war. You will hear the skylarks singing over the scores of beautifully kept cemeteries and memorials, and Roses of Picardy bloom everywhere – as does the 'Flanders' poppy. Farm cottages have become exceedingly popular with British expatriates, fascinated by researching the battles of 1916 and 1918, who often buy them and convert them to B & B establishments.

In this region one sees evidence of a phenomenon which was widespread, but is now dwindling. It is the strange terraced formation of steep slopes, known locally as *rideaux* (literally 'curtains') or *remblais* ('lynchets'). Contrary to popular belief they have nothing to do with viniculture. Wine has not been produced in Picardy since the Middle Ages, soon after Henry V's invading troops got drunk at Boves on local wine. It was with their backs to a three-tiered slope of *rideaux* that Edward III ranged his batailles at Crécy – with devastating results for the French. Masefield, on his wanderings along '*The Old Front Line*' in 1917, noted them (he always referred to them as *remblais*) near Hébuterne, near Matthew, Mark, Luke and John Copses at Serre, in the outskirts of the village of Beaumont Hamel, near 'Y' Ravine. You will see them on the right of the road from Amiens to Querrieu. Masefield speculates that 'they are made … by the ploughing away from the top and the bottom of any difficult slope', and this is a theory subscribed to by some local historians. The manifestation is also seen in Kent.

Throughout the region restaurants, from the simplest to the most sophisticated, serve delicious local dishes: *Poissons de Picardie* (Picardy fish – normally eels, river trout or turbot, in sorrel sauce, or with leeks and cream), duck, veal and pork, *e.g. Le Caghuse* (pork cooked in onions, butter and white wine) or flavoursome and tender *Pintadeau* (young guinea fowl). Perhaps the most popular dish is the *Ficelle Picarde* (a savoury pancake with ham, cheese and cream). Follow any of these with the famous macaroons or *Tuiles* (made of chocolate and almond) from Amiens or the rich *Gâteau Battu* (made with a large quantity of egg yolks and butter) or *Galuchon* (a sweet currant bread) – delicious!

The River Somme

The Somme is a river which meanders, changing its aspect at every bend, from a wide expanse of fast moving water to a myriad of secret pools (étangs), branches and canals, shaded and secluded by lush foliage. These pools are the delight of the weekend fishermen and hunters, whose cabins throng the banks. The river yields a variety of fish, the greatest delicacy being the eels, which are caught in *Anguillières*. From them is made *Pâté d'Anguilles, or Anguilles à l'Oseille* (eels in sorrel sauce), *Anguilles du Hourdel* (eels in a sauce of onions, parsley, egg yolks and vinegar), *Anguilles au Vert* (eels with spinach, sorrel, mint, sage, etc). In these tranquil pools, duck, snipe and other game birds are stalked by the hunters, often with colourful decoys. Duck pâté, therefore, is another local speciality, as is *Canard Sauvage* (wild duck) with a variety of sauces. Boat trips may be made along the Somme, which, with no great stretch of the imagination, will conjure up pictures of the hospital barges which plied from the battle area to Amiens after the 1 July 1916 battles. Apply to the local **tourist office** (qv).

Fishing on the Somme from at Chipilly

The Hortillonages

The name for these small gardens, made in the rich mud and silt of the marshy banks of the fragmented rivulets of the Somme above Amiens, comes from the Latin *Hortus* – garden. They have long been a picturesque tradition, now sadly dwindling. They are tended from the flat-bottomed black boats, *Bateaux à Cornet* that, until 1976, transported the crops to the market at the Quai Parmentier in Amiens. Leeks, onions, carrots, radish, cauliflower, crisp lettuce and many other varieties of vegetables and salad stuff grow to perfection in the dark soil. They are the ingredients for *Soupe des Hortillons* (mixed vegetable soup with chunks of bread) and other soups, and an array of savoury flans and quiches, known as *Flamiches*, for example, aux Poireaux (with leeks and cream), *des Hortillons* (vegetables and ham) and many more variations. Guided visits by boat may be made to the Hortillonages – apply to the local **tourist office** (qv)

The Santerre

As the origins of its name implies (from the Latin *sana terra* – good earth) this is an extremely fertile plain, broadly bounded by the Somme in the north and the Avre in the south. It encompasses Villers-Bretonneux, the site of bitter fighting in 1918, but otherwise mostly covers the French sector of the 1 July battle. Because of the carnage and destruction which took place on the rich soil, it too became part of the proposed *Zone Rouge* after the war. But the land was recultivated, and now sugar beet, wheat, salsify, spinach, potatoes (brought to France by Parmentier, citizen of Montdidier), sweet corn, tender little peas and flageolets, flourish in the expansive fields of the Santerre. It is the centre of the vegetable canning industry, producing the perfect accompaniment to the rich game dishes of the region, or as the basis of soups, such as *Potage Crécy* (carrot soup) or *Soupe aux Endives* (chicory soup). During the hunting season, local farmers and 'weekenders' from Paris and other regions beat the fields and woods, shooting hare, rabbit and game birds. Be vigilant when walking across fields in the autumn. The sound of shots can often be too realistic and close for comfort. *Lapin Farci à la Picarde* (stuffed rabbit with beer, cider etc) and *Lapin aux Pruneaux* (rabbit with prunes) are among the tasty results.

The Somme is a region to be enjoyed, not only for its history, but for the many delights of its picturesque landscape – but beware, it can be very muddy!

WHERE TO STAY/WHERE TO EAT/ LOCAL TOURIST OFFICES/GUIDES

SOMME BATTLEFIELDS' PARTNERS

The Departemental Tourist Committee, the Péronne Chamber of Commerce, the Historial and the Somme 1916 Museum have created a quality brand for owners of accommodation (hotels and b+b), restaurants, transport businesses, shops, tourist guides and offices who serve the visitor to the Somme battlefields. Applicants are vetted by the Committee and attend a short course at the Historial.

If successful they must display the brand logo which will indicate their quality and status. The authors are proud to be Partners. Contact: Somme Departmental Tourist Committee, see below, also http://www.sbpartner.org'.

Towns which provide a convenient base for your stay and/or which offer restaurants for lunch/dinner breaks are listed below with details of their **Tourist Offices** where further lists may be obtained. You can contact them for more detailed information on hotels, restaurants, general local tourist information, holidays and calendar of events – the serious student of the battlefields may well wish to avoid the latter as local hostelries will be full and roads congested.

Hotels and restaurants that are conveniently on the routes are mentioned as they occur in the Itineraries and are printed in **a distinctive typeface**. Any comments about particular establishments, as ever, depend upon the patron and chef of the day.

ALBERT. Tourist Office: 9 rue Gambetta, BP 82, Albert 80300, Tel: +(0)3 22 75 16 42. Now known as 'Le Pays du Coquelicot' (Poppy Country). E-mail: ot.albert.ancre@wanadoo.fr. Website: www.ville-albert.fr. **Open:** Oct-March Mon-Fri: 0900-1230 and 1330-1700. Sat: 0900-2000 and 1500-1700. April-Sept Mon-Fri: 0900-1230 and 1330-1830. Sat: 0900-1200 and 1400-1830. Sun and holidays: 1000-1230.

Le Royal Picardie, 3 star Best Western. Reported as more expensive but perhaps more sophisticated than other hotels in the region. No lunch-time restaurant service. Avénue du Gen Leclerc. **Tel :** +(0) 3 22 75 37 00. E-mail: royalpicardie@wanadoo.fr

Hotel de la Paix, 2 star. A favourite with battlefield tourers (especially the 'Friends of Lochnagar' (qv)). 10 refurbished rooms, excellent restaurant. No lift. 43 rue Victor Hugo. **Tel:** +(0)3 22 75 01 64 E-mail: This appears when you google the hotel.

Hotel de la Basilique, 2 star. Opposite the Basilique as its name implies. Popular restaurant. Tel : +(0)3 22 75 04 71. E-mail: hotel-de-la-basilique@wanadoo.fr

Hotel Ibis, 2 star, by the second roundabout on the D929. Bistro (evening only)/bar. 57 rooms, secure parking. Ideal location for battlefield touring. Tel: +(0)3 22 75 52 52. E-mail: h6234@accor.com

Camping du Vélodrome, Allée Charles Queret. **Tel:** +(0)3 22 75 22 53. E-mail: campingalbert@lapost.net

Auberge de la Vallée, Authuille, within easy reach of Albert. Delightful location on banks of the Ancre. Gourmet food (2 Michelin 'forks') but reasonable menus. Closed Mon and Wed & Sun evenings. Tel: (essential to book) (0)3 22 75 15 18. www.auberge-ancre.fr

Hotel de la Paix, Albert

AMIENS. Departmental Committee for Tourism in the Somme [CDT] (Director François Bergez), 21 rue Ernest Cauvin, 80000 Amiens, **Tel:** +(0)3 22 71 22 71. E-mail: acceuil@somme-tourisme.com

Tourist Office Métropole: 40 Place Notre-Dame, BP 1018 Amiens cedex 1, Tel: +(0)3 22 71 60 50
E-mail: ot@amiens-metropole.com
There are **hotel/restaurants** to suit all budgets and tastes in Amiens including:
Hotel le Carlton of WW1 fame (qv), 3-star 42 rue de Noyon, **Tel:** +(0)3 22 97 72 22 E-mail : reservation@lecarlton.fr
Le Saint Louis, 2-star, 24 rue des Otages. **Tel:** +(0)3 22 91 76 03 E-mail:info@amiens-hotel.fr
Express by Holiday Inn, 3-star, 10 Bvd Alsace Lorraine (near the station), **Tel:** +(0)3 22 22 38 50 E-mail: express@hieamiens.com
Hotel Ibis, 2-star, 4 rue du Lattre de Tassigny. **Tel:** +(0)3 22 92 57 33 E-mail : h0480@accor-hotels.com
Without restaurant but establishments with character:

One of the enticing buffets, Flunch, Albert-Méaulte

Hotel Marotte, 5-star, 3 rue Marotte. Lounge Bar and Coffee Shop. **Tel:** +(0)3 60 12 50 00 E-mail: admin@hotelmarotte.com

Grand Hotel de l'Univers, 3-star, Best Western, 2 rue de Noyon. **Tel:** +(0)3 22 91 52 51 E-mail: hotelunivers.amiens@wanadoo.fr

Mercure Amiens Cathédrale, 4-star, 17-19 Place au Feurre. **Tel:** +(0)3 22 22 00 20 E-mail: h7076@accor.com

Le Prieuré, 3-star, 6-17 rue Porion. Tel: +(0)3 22 71 16 71. E-mail: hotel-le-prieure@ornage.fr

There is a variety of restaurants around the station area and, for charm, in the St Leu district, known as 'The Little Venice of the North' where picturesque umbrella-shielded tables line the bank of the Somme. Notable is **Les Marissons**, Pont de la Dodane, St Leu. **Tel:** +(0)3 22 92 96 66. http://www.les-marissons.fr/

At 593 route de Rouen is **Le Vivier**, specialising in fish and sea food. **Tel:** +(0) 22 89 12 21. E-mail: contact@restaurantlevivier-amiens.com

Longueau. Within reach of Amiens and easier of access is the group of hotels near the commercial centre here where there is also a supermarket where you can buy picnic items and fill up with petrol.

3-star **Novotel Amiens-Est**, **Tel:** +(0)3 22 50 42 42. E-mail: HO396@accor-hotels.com. **Restaurant** with attractive décor overlooking the outdoor pool.

2-star **Campanile Amiens**, excellent **Buffet. Tel:** +(0)3 22 53 89 89. E-mail: amiens@campanile.fr **Hotel Formule 1**, Tel : +(0) 08 91 70 51 59. E-mail: H2310@accor.com

En route **to Amiens off the A16.** Take exit 21 and follow signs through Flixécourt to Hangest-sur-Somme. By the station is The **Restaurant du Canard**, an attractive restaurant with gourmet cuisine and a very reasonably priced menu du jour. **Tel:** +(0)3 22 51 18 95. www.restaurantducanard.com An ideal lunch break on the way to Amiens on the Western Approach.

ARRAS. Tourist Office: Hôtel de Ville, Place des Héros, Arras, **Tel:** +(0)3 21 51 26 95. Fax: +(0)3 21 51 26 95. E-mail: arras.tourisme@wanadoo.fr This makes a convenient base for Vimy and for the Somme battlefields if you don't mind a bit of daily motoring. It is also an ideal lunch break. All around the station square is a variety of restaurants and cafés from 'quick snack' (and what better for lunch than a *Croque Monsieur* or half a *baguette* with *jambon de Paris* or *Camembert*) to gourmet. **The Astoria**, 10-12 Place Maréchal Foch, is a good compromise. Highly recommended is **La Coupole**, 26 Boulevard de Strasbourg, **Tel:** +(0)3 21 71 88 44, with a great Parisian *brasserie* atmosphere and décor and fine seafood specialities. The only 4-star hotel in Arras is the **Hotel de l'Angleterre**, Place Maréchal Foch, **Tel:** +(0)3 21 51 51 16. A Conference Centre has been built in the square with a 3-star **Mercure Hotel**, **Tel:** +(0)3 21 23 88 88. E-mail: H1560@accor.com

The 3-star **Hotel Moderne**, Bvd Faidherbe, **Tel:** +(0)3 21 23 39 57. E-mail: contact@hotel-moderne-arras.com, is opposite the station. At 3-5 Place de la Croix Rouge is the 3-star Best Western **Hotel de l'Univers**, with fine restaurant. **Tel:** +(0)3 21 71 34 01. E-mail: univers.hotel@najeti.com

There is a 2-star **Ibis**, 11 rue de la Justice, **Tel:** +(0)3 21 23 61 61. E-mail: H1567@accor.com and on the outskirts there is a **Campanile, ZA les Alouettes**, good buffet. **Tel:** +(0)3 21 55 56 30. E-mail: arras.stnicolas@campanile.fr

Les Places (Squares) with their picturesque Flemish baroque arcades also offer a variety of eating possibilities. Beneath the Grand' Place is a huge car park. Under the Gothic Town Hall and Belfry Tower are the Boves (qv) – underground tunnels and chambers much utilised in the First World War and now visited from the Town Hall.

AUCHONVILLERS
Avril Williams Guest House & Ocean Villas Tea Rooms, Conference/Meetings Facilities (see pages 116 and 117). Tel : +(0)3 22 76 23 66. E-mail: avwilliams@orange.fr Web site www.avrilwilliams.eu

BAPAUME. Tourist Office: Hôtel de Ville, Place Faidherbe. **Tel:** +(0)3 21 59 89 84.
Leaflets on the history of the town and lists of restaurants/hotels are available here. This can make a convenient base or lunchbreak for the Somme. There are two hotels: the 2-star **La Paix** (a Logis de France), Avénue Abel Guidet, with an excellent restaurant, **Tel:** +(0)3 21 07 11 03. Fax: +(0)3 21 07 43 66, and the 1-star **Le Gourmet**, rue de la Gare, **Tel :** +(0)3 21 07 20 00. There are several restaurants, including the **Stromboli Pizzeria Tel:** +(0)3 21 59 88 51.

CORBIE. Tourist Office of the Bocage and Les Trois Vallées: 30 Place de la République. **Tel:** +(0)3 22 96 95 76. E-mail: officetourismecorbie.80@wanadoo.fr Very helpful staff. Lists of local *Chambres d'hôte*, gîtes and camping sites (many in delightful rural settings) and local restaurants. Here the key to the Church is kept. Market day Friday, when parking is unavailable in the main square. This picturesque town on the banks of the Somme has a spectacular Benedict Abbey St Pierre founded in 657 and 16th Century Church (qv) and a fairy tale castle for its *Hotel de Ville*. Corbie makes a perfect base for a lunch or overnight stay.
    It now boasts the fantastic **'Maison d'Hôte' Le Macassar** hidden behind an unprepossessing white façade at 8 Place de la République. Macassar is the hard wood much used in the 20s and 30s when this large private house was refurbished in the 'modern' styles of *Art Nouveau* and *Art Deco*. Many of these ornamental features remain and hosts Miguel De Lemos and Ian Nelmes have added much authentic period décor and furnishings. There are five superb themed suites with luxurious modern bathrooms (some with whirlpool baths) and four elegant salons and a courtyard for guests to enjoy [naturally no young children please]. Breakfast and evening cocktails included in room price. Evening meal on prior request (especially on Sunday when local restaurants tend to close). Tel: +(0)3 22 48 40 04. E-mail: info@lemacassar.com Website: www.lemacassar.com

La Table d'Agathe, with good regional dishes. Closed Mon and midweek evenings in winter. 6 rue J & M Truquin (off the main square towars the Hotel de Ville). **Tel:** +(0)3 22 96 96 27.

Brasserie Le Fauquets (closed Sun and Mon evening). Good choice of menus, fast service if required. 8 rue Charles de Gaulle (near the Church). **Tel:** + (0)3 22 48 41 17.

DOULLENS. Tourist Office: le Beffroi, rue du Bourg. Tel: +(0)3 22 32 54 52. E-mail: office-de-tourisme-doullens@wanadoo.fr Lists of restaurants, hotels and tourist attractions and events available. This is an attractive town with its 13th Century Belfry and 16th/17th Century Citadel – the largest in France – with guided visits during the summer. It is the capital city of the area known as *le Doullennais*. There is a handful of small hotels and a variety of *chambres d'hôtes, gîtes*, camping sites and restaurants in and around the town.

ETAPLES. Tourist Office: La Corderie – Bvd Bigot Descelers. **Tel:** +(0)3 21 09 56 94. E-mail: contact@etaples-tourisme.com
    This delightful fishing port on the Bay of the Canche is a seafood lover's paradise. Markets every Tuesday and Friday. It makes a perfect lunch stop on the way to the Somme – but make sure you get there well before the prompt kitchen closing hour of

1400. A variety of restaurants along river front offer freshly caught fish and shellfish, notably **Aux Pêcheurs d'Etaples**, Quai de la Canche, Tel: +(0)3 21 94 06 90,

There are several small, individual hotels in the town itself (list from the **Tourist Office**) and the conveniently situated (next to the CWGC Cemetery) 2 star Interhotel de la Baie, Tel: +(0)3 21 89 99 99. E-mail: 166208@inte3rhotel.com. Terrace overlooking the Bay. Restaurant closed lunchtime. Otherwise you will be spoilt for choice at nearby Le Touquet.

MONTDIDIER. Tourist Office: Place Général de Gaulle. **Tel:** +(0)3 22 78 92 00. Worth a visit is the impressive War Memorial by Albert Roze in the Place de la République inaugurated on 12 July 1925, the day the town was awarded the *Légion d'Honneur,* and the **French Military Cemetery**, rue de Roye, which contains 7,406 French WW1 burials (of which 1,617 lie in two ossuaries), 24 French WW2, 1 Belgian, 1 Italian and 13 RAF, 1 RAAF, 10 RCAF from WW2.

Information is given here on the history of the town and some of its famous citizens, lists of restaurants (a variety of cafés, pizzerias, crêperies and traditional hostelleries), of b & bs and gîtes and its three hotels:

Le Condé, 2-star, 1 Place de la République. **Tel:** +(0)3 22 98 08 62.

Le Dijon, 2-star, 1 Place du 10 août 1918. **Tel:** +(0)3 22 78 01 35.

Le Mouton d'Or, 10 Boulevard du Général Debeney. **Tel:** +(0)3 22 78 03 43.

MOREUIL. *Mairie:* Place Norbert Malterre. **Tel:** +(0)3 22 35 33 33. Details of restaurants and accommodation in the locality, local events.

PERONNE. Tourist Office: 1 Place André Audinot, 80200 Péronne, **Tel :** +(0)3 22 84 42 38. Website: www.hautesomme-tourisme.com. This historic town is the recommended base for those approaching the battlefields by the Eastern Route (qv), principally because of the Museum, the Historial de la Grande Guerre, built behind the façade of the 12th Century Château. Also of note is the Town Hall whose 18th Century façade survived the Great War and whose bell tower plays the soldiers' song *Le Madelon.* The Best Western 3-star Hotel Saint Claude, is in the central 42 Place du Commandant Louis Daudré, with two restaurants. **Tel:** +(0)3 22 79 49 49. E-mail: hotel.saintclaude@wanadoo.fr Also in Place Louis Daudré is the pizzeria/restaurant **Le Central, Tel:** +(0)3 22 84 60 75.

Opposite the entrance to the *Historial* is the attractive **Bistrot d'Antoine, Tel:** +(0)3 22 85 84 46.

On the outskirts the **Campanile Hotel** has now become the 2 star **Fasthotel Relais** and is completely renovated, **Tel:** +(0)3 22 84 22 22. E-mail: peronne@directfasthotel.com

At Exit 13 of the A1 motorway, next to a motorway services petrol, information station and cafeteria, at Assevillers is the 3-star **Ibis Styles Hotel**, Spacious bedrooms, **Tel:** +(0)3 22 85 78 30. E-mail: HO50@accor.com Adjacent to it is a **Formule 1 Hotel**, **Tel:** +(0)3 22 85 90 38.

ACKNOWLEDGEMENTS

In addition to all those who gave us assistance and information in previous editions of this we would like to thank those who have been generous with their help in this new edition. They include: Richard Dunning, owner of the Lochnagar Crater; François Bergez, Director of Somme Tourisme; Hervé François, Director the Historial; Teddy and Phoebe Colligan, Curators of the Ulster Tower and their daughter, Carol Walker of the Somme Association; Thapedi Masanabo, Curator, Delville Wood Museum and Information Centre; Philippe Drouin, Chairman of the Somme Remembrance Association; Avril Williams, Auchonvillers; Bernard Delattre, *Maire* of Pozières; Bruno Etévé re Polish

Memorial, Lihons; Ross Bastiaan creator and designer of the Australian Bronze Memorial Plaques , J-P. le Palec re Aviateur Aubry and Jessica Wise re Sqn Cdr Petre *et al*. Finally - throughout - David Hemingway and all of the supportive team at P & S.

PICTURE CREDITS

In addition to all those who provided photographs in previous editions, we would like to thank those who have been generous with their help in this edition: Jessica Wise (Lochnagar at sunset); Somme Association (for Wooden Cross) and Teddy Colligan (for the trenches, Thiepval Wood); Ian Johnson (16th (Newcastle) Bn, Northumberland Fusiliers Plaque, Authuille); Philippe Drouin (McIver VC Memorial); Appeva (Le P'tit Train); 'Pierre Grande Guerre' (51st Highlander, Newfoundland Park); Terry Heard & Brent Whittam [ww1cemeteries.com] (Heumann, Mills & Torrance); Jackie Hayes, (American Somme Cemetery, Bony) ....
All other photos were taken by the authors.

'Men who march away...' Great War Society, 1 July, Lochnagar

INDEX

Forces, and their Memorials, are listed in descending order of size, i.e. Armies, Corps, Divisions, Brigades, Regiments, Battalions, followed by Private/Individual Memorials in alphabetical order... Many other units are mentioned in Cemetery descriptions throughout the book. Victoria Cross holders are listed alphabetically under the heading 'Victoria Cross' in the General Index. Some are also to be found in the main General listing, indicated VC.

FORCES

MEMORIALS

Museum/Exhibition/Visitor's Centres

War Cemeteries

GENERAL INDEX

Abbey Wood, 205
Achiet-le-Petit, 261
'Adoptions', 31, 147, 215, 228, 251, 264, 270, 306, 341, 129,
Agincourt, 54, 340
Aiken, Alex, 185
Albert, King of Belgium, 9
Albert Medal, 229
Albert, town, 29, 47, 68-70, 72-5, 82, 140-1, 224, 266, 340
Alexander, Ian, 338, 334
Alice, Princess, 105
Allenby, Gen Sir Edward, 130,
Allex, Cpl Jake, MoH, 225
Allward, Walter, 45
Amade, Gen D, 198,
American Battle Monuments Commission, 323
American War Memorials Overseas, 324
Amiens, 25-6, 29, 48, 196-202, 204-6, 213, 304, 340, 343
 Cathedral, 188, 198-9, 234, 340
 Nearest Point to, 205, 304, 317
Ancre, River and Valley, 12, 69, 104-5, 108, 110, 123, 340, 343
ANZAC Day, 26, 211-12, 286
Apollinaire, Guillaume, Poet, Playwright, 272
Arras, 23-5, 68-9, 130, 132-5, 278-80, 284, 286, 330
Art Deco, 33, 70-1, 132, 218, 234, 263, 296, 302, 306, 341, 348
Art Nouveau, 218, 348
Ashwell, Lena, Concert Party, 53
Asquith, Herbert Henry, British Prime Minister 1908-16, 186
Asquith, Lt Raymond, 200
Assevillers, 29, 197, 244-6, 265, 278
Association Internationale des Sites et Musées de la Guerre de 1914-1918, 334
Auchonvillers (Ocean Villas), 68-9, 114--17, 123, 320
Austin, Ron, 236
Australian Battlefield Tour stops (ABT), 207
Australian Unknown Soldier, 207-9
Australian War Memorial, 207, 221
Authuille, 22, 68-9, 96-100, 104, 278, 319
Ayette, 69, 132
Ayre family, 113

Bairnsfather, Capt Bruce, 93, 118, 221
Baker, Sir Herbert, CWGC Architect, 59, 100, 103, 153, 180
Balfour, Arthur, 65
Ball, Albert, VC, DSO + Bars, MC, 61,
Bapaume, 196-7, 254, 258, 260, 263-6, 272, 278, 280-2, 337
Barbot, Gen, 34-6
Barbusse, Henri, 39
Baring, Maurice, 61, 240
Barnett-Barker, Brig Gen R., DSO, 141
Bastiaan, Ross, (*see also* Aust Mems), 30, 88, 191, 209, 212, 217, 238, 272, 286, 337
Battle of Britain Museum, Hawkinge, 222
Baudet, Marie, 342
Bayley Hardy, Rev Theodore, VC, DSO, MC, DCM, 131
Bazentin-le-Grand, 186
Bazentin-le-Petit, 20
Beaucourt, 105, 278
Beaumont Hamel, 16, 21, 42, 79, 82, 93, 100-101, 108-9, 111-114, 120-124, 278, 320, 327, 334-5, 340-1, 343
Bean, C.E.W., 41
Beaurains, 117
Beaurepaire, Château de, 54
Bell, 2nd Lt Donald Simpson, VC, 150
Belloy, 57, 265, 267-8
Bergez, François, Director Somme Tourism, 86
Bernafay Wood, 158-9, 169, 171
Bertangles, 26
Biaches, 270
Birmingham, 75
Blackburn, 31, 192
Black Day (for German Army), 26, 215
Bliss, Arthur, 97, 200
Bliss, 2nd Lt Francis Kennard, 97, 200
Blockhouses/Bunkers, 88-9, 115, 131, 187, 261,
Blomfield, Sir Reginald, CWGC Architect, 59, 63-5, 102, 117, 137, 235, 253
Blunden, Edmund, Poet, 104-5, 116
Bois Allemand, 163
Bois d'Hollande, 68

Bois Français, 163
Bois de Wallieux trenches, 242-3
Booth, Lt M.W., cricketer, 63
Botha, Gen Louis, 180
Bottom Wood, 150
Bouchavesnes, 227, 257, 274-5
Boulogne, 27, 48-50, 84
Boves, Arras, 133-4
Braithwaite, Lt V. A. L., 125
Braque, Georges, 246
Bray, 141, 196, 221-2, 227-8, 231-2, 278, 314, 333
Brie, 314-15, 317
Briquet, Olivier, 72
British Expeditionary Force (BEF), 9, 11, 16, 23, 204
British League of Help, 270-1, 341
Brittain, Vera, 52, 59, 135
Brown, Capt A. Roy, 221
Brown, William, 116
Buchan, John, 144, 172
Bull, Private A. E., 125, 129
Bull Ring, the, 51-3
Bullard, Gen R., 299
Bullecourt, 10, 23, 286, 337
Burke, Lt Col C.J., 138
Bus-les-Artois, 62
Butte de Warlencourt, 196, 209, 258-260
Butterworth, Lt George, MC, 74, 94-5, , 154-5, 192-3
Butterworth Trench, 140, 192-3
Byng, Gen Sir Julian, 28, 41, 47, 70, 259

Cachy, 197, 205-6
Caesar, Julius, 339
Cambrai, 227
Cameron Wilson, Capt T. P., 11
Cantigny, 299-300, 324
Cappy, 221, 334
Carey, Maj Gen C. G. S., 234
 Carey's Force, 27, 199, 234-5, 317
Carisella, P.J., 62, 221
Carlton-Belfort Hotel, 200
Carnoy, 162
Cart de Lafontaine, Lt-Col H.P., 181, 198,
Carton de Wiart, Lt-Gen, VC, 68, 83, 90
Casualties, passim, 9, 76, 88-9, 99-100, 105, 108, 113-14, 157, 160, 184, 326-7
Caterpillar Valley, 20, 155-8, 160, 162, 186